GEOFFREY CHAPMAN THEOLOGY LIBRARY

The Sacraments of Initiation

GEOFFREY CHAPMAN THEOLOGY LIBRARY

THE SACRAMENTS OF INITIATION
Baptism
Confirmation
Eucharist

Liam G. Walsh

GEOFFREY CHAPMAN
LONDON

#/7951678

A Geoffrey Chapman book published by
Cassell Publishers Limited
Artillery House, Artillery Row
London SW1P 1RT

First published 1988

ISBN 0 225 66499 2

Nihil obstat: Father Anton Cowan, *Censor*
Imprimatur: Monsignor Ralph Brown, *V.G.*
Westminster, 17 May 1988

The *Nihil obstat* and *Imprimatur* are a declaration that a book or pamphlet is considered to be free from doctrinal or moral error. It is not implied that those who have granted the *Nihil obstat* and *Imprimatur* agree with the contents, opinions or statements expressed.

British Library Cataloguing in Publication Data
Walsh, Liam G.
    The sacraments of initiation
    1. Catholic church. Baptism.
    I. Title
    265′.1

Typeset at the Alden Press Oxford London and Northampton

Printed in The U.K. by Biddles Ltd., Guildford

Contents

    9.1   The New Testament   201
    9.1.1 Accounts of institution   201
    9.1.2 St Paul   203
    9.1.3 St John   206
    9.1.4 The letter to the Hebrews   210
    9.2   The tradition of the Fathers   211
    9.2.1 The Apostolic Fathers   212
    9.2.2 The Eastern Fathers   216
    9.2.3 The Latin Fathers   222
    9.3   Mediaeval theology   228
    9.3.1 Ninth to twelfth centuries   229
    9.3.2 St Thomas Aquinas   233
    9.4   The Reformers and the Council of Trent   243
    9.4.1 The Reformers   244
    9.4.2 The Council of Trent   248
    9.5   From Trent to Vatican II   255
    9.6   Second Vatican Council   260
    9.7   Ecumenical convergence   262
    9.8   Systematic essay   265
    9.8.1 A sacramental meal   265
    9.8.2 Sacrament of the gift of eternal life   266
    9.8.3 For the forgiveness of sins   268
    9.8.4 Presence of Christ in the sacrament   269
    9.8.5 Presence of the body and blood of Christ   271
    9.8.6 Theologies of the real presence   273
    9.8.7 Sacrament of the Church   277
    9.8.8 Through the ministry of priests   278
    9.8.9 Sacrifice of the Church   279
    9.8.10 Effects of the Eucharist   283
    Study questions   291
    Further reading   292

10   **Epilogue**   **294**
    10.1   The theologian and the catechist   294
    10.2   The unity of initiation in theology and catechesis 296
    10.3   From life to fullness of life   297
    10.4   Life choices   301
    10.5   The story of salvation   302
    10.6   The last word   302

    Bibliography   **304**

    Index   **311**

Foreword

The welcome given to this series by reviewers and readers has confirmed those who planned it in their conviction that they are meeting a real need of the present generation in the Church. The appraisal and revision of Catholic life that was undertaken and set in motion by the Second Vatican Council called for a fresh approach to the study of Christian doctrine: one which would continue to observe the classical norms and scope of the systematic teaching of the Gospel as practised from the beginning, while benefiting from the new methods and instruments of study that are now available.

The *Geoffrey Chapman Theology Library* sets out to communicate the essentials of each chosen area of study through the personal reflection of an experienced scholar and teacher who has made his mark in his own particular field. Each volume attempts to survey the documentary materials needed in the investigation of its theme, the special problems and topics of interest that centuries of study have thrown up, and the questions asked in the controversies of the present. As far as possible, Catholic beliefs are expounded and discussed in relation to the established and contemporary teaching of other Christian bodies and of other religious faiths, so that some indication at least is given of the doctrinal dialogue necessary for the understanding and reconciliation in faith which is the purpose of the Christian mission.

The changes made by the Second Vatican Council in the celebration of the sacraments of the Church have been the most obvious way in which the Council has affected Christian practice. If they are to produce their desired results, systematic explanation is required, relating these changes to the needs of human life and showing how they contribute to the shared understanding of our personal and communal aim and tasks. Liam Walsh's book discusses both the anthropology and the theology of the sacraments by which new members of the Church are introduced to life in Christ and enabled to share in the loving obedience he offers to our Father in heaven.

Catechists and parish priests will find this volume in the series particularly useful as a unifying study of the various adaptations of pastoral practice that have recently been made. Christian initiation receives here a commentary that goes beyond the provision of historical and practical detail to show its profound psychological and spiritual significance, so that theological study relates to pastoral practice in this quietly phrased but intellectually powerful guide.

Michael Richards

For Sheila, Ann and Donal,
with Alison and Dick

My thanks to Father Michael Richards for prompting the book and nudging it along in a good direction, while letting me have my own say about most things. Paul O'Leary, OP read the text with the kind of critical care that makes one feel blessed to have such brothers; he put me right on a number of things, but still thinks my ecclesiology is a bit too hierarchical! The generosity of Helen and Mac McGoldrick from Boston greatly eased my typing chores. Margaret Ormond, OP was a more than perceptive proof reader. The students of the Angelicum whom I enjoyed teaching about sacraments 1984–88 would be surprised to know how much their looks of enthusiasm but sometimes bewilderment, of insight but sometimes boredom, no less than their questions and answers, have written themselves into the book.

San Clemente
Rome
14 September 1987

Abbreviations

AAS	*Acta Apostolicae Sedis*
ACW	Ancient Christian Writers
BEM	*Baptism, Eucharist and Ministry* (World Council of Churches, Faith and Order Paper 111)
CCSL	Corpus Christianorum, series latina
DACL	*Dictionnaire d'archéologie chrétienne et de liturgie*
DS	H. Denzinger and A. Schönmetzer (eds), *Enchiridion Symbolorum* (32nd ed.)
DTC	*Dictionnaire de théologie catholique*
ICEL	International Commission on English in the Liturgy
LG	*Lumen Gentium* (Vatican II, Dogmatic Constitution on the Church)
LNPF	Library of Nicene and Post-Nicene Fathers
ND	J. Neuner and J. Dupuis (eds), *The Christian Faith in the Doctrinal Documents of the Catholic Church* (rev. ed.)
PG	J.-P. Migne (ed.), *Patrologiae cursus completus, series graeca*
PL	J.-P. Migne (ed.), *Patrologiae cursus completus, series latina*
RCIA	*Rite of Christian Initiation of Adults* (Note: in the interest of pastoral utility and convenience, the definitive ICEL edition somewhat rearranges the contents of the *Praenotanda* of the Latin *editio typica*. Hereafter, references to paragraphs in *RCIA* give the number from the English definitive edition; followed in some instances by the number from the *editio typica*, in square brackets.)
SC	*Sacrosanctum Concilium* (Vatican II, Constitution on the Sacred Liturgy)

Introduction

RITE, WORD AND LIFE: METHODOLOGICAL CONSIDERATIONS FOR A THEOLOGY OF SACRAMENTS

To become a Christian is to join a community of people who believe that Jesus Christ brought eternal life into this world and who celebrate together their sharing in that life while they are waiting for it to be fully realized when Jesus comes again. Believing in *life* and celebrating the wonder of it is a good description of what it is to be a Christian and a member of the Christian Church. Belief is brought about and expressed in *word*. Celebration is invited and expressed by *rite*. Christians are known as people of words: they have a story to tell about how God has given eternal life to humans and a doctrine about the meaning of the story. They are also known as people of rites; as people who come together for Mass or the Lord's Supper (or whatever synonym is used for their ritual meal of bread and wine) and who initiate new members ritually by baptizing and confirming them. But they would like to be known most of all as people of *life*. The word in which they believe is the word of life. The rites they practise are for the giving and celebrating of life.

The rites of initiation into the Christian community (Baptism, Confirmation and Eucharist) are specially concerned with life because they mark the first giving of the fullness of life in Christ which is proclaimed and made available in the Christian community. They cannot be life-giving in this way unless they are accompanied by the word of life: the story of the giving of eternal life has to be told to the initiates and the essential meaning of it explained. The story and the explanation must deal with the form and meaning of the rites, and with how they serve to insert human life into eternal life. It is the business of the theology of sacraments to provide such an explanation, so that the story can be told in relation to the rites in a way that makes them life-giving.

All theology is a word. It draws from the words of faith — from the story of the giving of eternal life that is told in the Scriptures and from the continuous telling and explanation of it in the tradition of the Church. It draws from the words of human wisdom about the reality and meaning of human life. A theology of sacraments, however, has the peculiarity of being a word about rites. It directs the word of faith towards the human experience inherent in rites, so that when the sacramental rites of the Christian Church are celebrated a word will be available that can make them be truly life-giving.

The interaction of rite, word and life is a common subject of study by the anthropological sciences. Human life in all its spheres is full of ritual, and of words and stories and myths that go with the rites. The theology of sacraments can learn much from the sciences that study human ritual. Indeed, it has to learn from them and take account of their methods in its own methodology. Without calling into question in any way their divine origin as sacraments it has to respect their anthropological status as rites. It has to see them as instances of that irrepressible human instinct to imitate and dramatize things or events or persons that are important for human life, to remember and re-create them symbolically at certain times and in certain places. It has to allow for all that is known about how rites affect critical moments of human life like birth and death, puberty and marriage, initiations into and affirmations of belonging to a social group — critical moments that are captured and held in a manageable way by rites, so that the life-experience and tension in them can be adequately dealt with.

Rites have their own peculiar intelligibility, which can never be fully expressed in words. Although there is a story behind most of them, there is something more in them than any story can tell. They can continue to be performed even when the story that gave rise to them has been forgotten. But rites do seem to call out for a story, and a story may be invented for them when the original one has been lost or is no longer relevant. The story is really an explanation of how the rite has a bearing on human life. The explanation may be a simple narrative but it may also develop into a quite sophisticated philosophical analysis of the rite and its story. The Greeks created myths to explain their rites but they also turned these myths into a kind of theology. A Christian theology of Baptism, Confirmation and Eucharist will want to gather all the words that have been spoken about these rites within the Christian tradition and all the speculation that has been done about them, in order to understand them in the bearing they can have on human life. Classical theology may be more comfortable with words than with the particularity and concreteness of rites. It is itself, indeed, a form of word. But if it is to be a theology of sacraments like Baptism, Confirmation and Eucharist it has to be a word not about ideas but *about rites*, and about their bearing on life.

The anthropological sciences explain how it is within the life of particular communities and their culture that rites develop and have meaning. They, and the words about them, are carried by a tradition, and the community lives by the tradition. People find in their words and their rites a way of dealing with the more critical issues of life that confront them regularly and test their ability to survive and prosper. Birth and death, entry into adulthood, marrying, illness, buying and selling, political decision-making, the recurrence of the seasons and the fertility of the earth are the kind of moments in the cycle of life that are solemnized by ritual. Unique events like the conquest of what has become the homeland, decisive battles won, the birth of great leaders are also commemorated ritually, because they have meant the difference between life and death to the community. To the extent that they are human rites Baptism, Confirmation and Eucharist will be touching some such crucial moments in the life of the Christian community, and of the persons who make it up. A theology of these rites will have to identify these moments and explain how the rite with its story allows people to deal with them.

The crucial moments that are dealt with by rites are, even in anthropological terms, sacred moments. Anthropology uses words like mysterious, numinous, fearsome, beyond-the-rational to define this sacredness. In stories that go with rites it is often described in a language that speaks of God, the gods, good and evil spirits and their interventions in human life. Anthropology can be quite neutral about the truth of this language, because it is not concerned with the existence or otherwise of God or the gods, but only with how belief in God affects human behaviour. Obviously theology cannot be neutral about the issue and will claim some competence to judge between the true and the false in the rites and religious stories of humanity. But it can do that without discounting the deep insights into human nature and God's way of dealing with it that are revealed in the anthropological analysis of all human rites, even of those that invoke a god who may be a purely mythical creation, unsubstantiated by any kind of critical verification.

The theology of sacraments has to be about the rites that are celebrated within the Christian community of the Church. The word that it listens to about the rites and how they bear on life has to be the word that is spoken in that Church. There is an anthropological basis for this, even before one considers the imperatives of theology itself in relation to the Word of God and its transmission in the Church. Rites and stories hold communities together and point them towards their future. As a group of people becomes self-conscious and protective about its identity, its stories and rites become official. Not any story will do and not any rite will do to express and give direction to the life the group wants to live and the future it wants for its children. Those who come to hold authority in the community take responsibility for the stories and the rites. The men and women of the word — the story-tellers and the thinkers — become themselves authorities about the word; and those who lead the rites come to lay down the law about them. They become the 'prophets' and the 'priests' that are found in some form in every community. Those who hold general authority over the life of the community (the 'kings') also find ways of having a say in what stories and what rites prevail. One can find these authority patterns at work in all kinds of human communities, ranging from primitive societies, with their sages, their priests and priestesses, and their chiefs, to the developed societies of today in which a well-structured establishment controls what is accepted as the national tradition, what ceremonies and holidays appropriately celebrate it, and how traditions and rituals are to be used as factors of political unity and stability.

There is another authority factor that has to be taken into account in studying rites. The record of rites and of the stories that go with them can itself become sacred. Religious texts are not the only ones that develop this kind of sacredness but they do have it with particular explicitness. When the history of a people is thought to be in the hands of God it is not difficult to see how the telling of that history should also be believed to be cared for by God and somehow inspired by him. The sacred books of religions become a source and a standard for rites and their explanation. They often tell of the origin of rites and of the effect they have on human life, attributing them to God himself. Thus the Christian Scriptures are the normative source for any study of Baptism, Confirmation and Eucharist, because it is in them that the story of the origins of the community and of its rites is authoritatively set down.

Once a community like the Christian Church commits itself to a certain account of its origins, to a set of fundamental rites and to an authorized word about them, it faces the problem of keeping rites and words in contact with a life-process that is subject to many forces of change. Ritual is uneasy with change. An important part of its function is to ensure stability and the homogeneity of a group. However, when stability is conceived in an immobile and purely conservative way the rites can lose contact with real life. Both they and the society which they supported can become fossilized. The highly ritualized civilizations of Central and South America, for example, coped no better with the cultural and religious challenges of the Conquistadores than they did with their military assaults, and whole cultures disappeared or went underground. Coping with change is a challenge that faces particularly those who hold authority in the community — whether it be of the prophetic, priestly or kingly kind. If those who control the rites and their story lack the will or the imagination to see that life is never an exact repetition of the past but a continuity in change they will cut the rites off from real life and thus destroy their value. It is especially in the word that is spoken with and about the rite that the challenge of change is met. New generations with new life-experiences have to be told in a new way how the rite can have a bearing on their lives. Otherwise they will not find in the rite a way of dealing with crucial moments of their life and a way of making appropriate choices about them. When rites and the words that go with them are not affecting choices about the serious issues of life they gradually lose their status, first for individuals and eventually perhaps for a whole people. They drift towards being fable and folklore, while life begins to look elsewhere for ways of dealing with its crucial moments and expressing its goals. The rites and stories of ancient Egypt, for example, no longer have much effect on the contemporary Egyptian nation, which lives by a different story and by different rites. A new story and new rites may grow up just because the old ones have been found wanting. It may also be imported or imposed from outside. If a new power group wants to change the life of a people it can do this by introducing a new story and new rites or by distorting if not suppressing the old. Since the Bolshevik revolution the Russian people has a whole new story about itself and Red Square has become the place of assembly for a new set of rituals. The classics of Russian history may still be read, its art enjoyed and its rituals remembered but, officially at least, this has nothing much to do with the real life of the people. Those who think it does run the risk of being considered subversives.

These general anthropological observations about the effect of change on the understanding of rites suggest a further methodological requirement for a theological study of Baptism, Confirmation and Eucharist. One must obviously start with the Scriptures. But one must then follow the story of how the community of the Church coped with the changes in life-experience and perception among its members over the centuries in which it has claimed to have remained faithful to the identity given to it in the apostolic age recorded in Scripture. The rites themselves have evolved. More significantly, as the Christian community gathered new people to itself and lived through new ages, the story has grown and the explanations have multiplied. Besides those of the Scriptures the community has a multitude of other words to speak with its rites. This is the liturgical and theological tradition. Some of it was a successful adaptation of rite and word to new life-situations. More of it is the checking by Church authorities of adaptations that were considered to be destructive of the original, constitutive tradition that is recorded in Scripture. Parts of it represent dangerous periods of decadence when the rites drifted away from life, or when they were being misinterpreted and misused in the interest of goals and values that were not really those of the Christian community. It is only from a study of this entire tradition that one can discover how the rites have come to be what they are today, why they are thought about and spoken about as they are, and how they can still contribute to the survival of the Christian Church. It is this present understanding of the rites, coming out of the tradition but looking to the here and now of life, that a theology of Baptism, Confirmation and Eucharist will want to provide. It will want to offer a consistent, intelligible and satisfying word that can make the celebration of the rites profoundly influential in the lives of men and women today.

OUTLINE OF THIS BOOK

The indications about methodology that are suggested by looking at Baptism, Confirmation and Eucharist in the anthropological framework of rite, word and life are important for a theology of these sacraments. Theology has to respect the human reality of things no less than God himself does. It is in the human reality of these rites that God gathers his People together, saves them from sin and brings them to eternal life. They are divine realities, but they function in the way rites function in any human community. Theology has, however, its own methodological imperatives. It must start its study of Baptism, Confirmation and Eucharist by examining what the Scriptures have to say about them. This material is accepted as the word of God, of the true God, who reveals himself and saves the world in the history and teaching that is recorded in the Scriptures. The anthropological reasons for beginning a study of Baptism, Confirmation and Eucharist with the Scriptures are thus confirmed while being given a new status. The issue now is not how and why the rites function but how and why they function as actions of God, of the true God, in which he saves his People. The anthropologist can study rites and their story without judging what is true or false in them. The theologian believes that the story is true and he trusts the rites; indeed, he speaks in and for a community that stakes its life on these words and rites.

The theological meaning of Baptism, Confirmation and Eucharist will emerge more clearly from the Word of God if one explores what is said there about the general question of rite and its place in the life and story of God's People before going on to discuss the individual rites. There are important things that can be said about Baptism, Confirmation and Eucharist together as rites and sacraments, and as sacraments of initiation, before going on to discuss each of them singly. Chapters 1–3 will deal with them on this general level. Chapter 1 covers the scriptural material. It pays special attention to the relationship between rite, word and life in biblical religion. This is a critical question in anthropological terms, but even more so in theological analysis. Compared with other religions of humanity the Old Testament already shows some unique features in its working-out of this relationship. In the New Testament the relationship is altogether unique. Jesus, who is way, truth and life, brings about a total identification of rite, word and life in his own person. He is at once Word made flesh, Priest and Victim in a temple that is his own body, Eternal Life in his risen body. The understanding of Christian rites is dominated by this truth, because their whole purpose is to realize throughout time and space what God does once for all in Jesus. Rites which are not at one with his word and his life have no place in the New Testament.

Theology has its own reasons for studying the tradition in which the word of God has been handed on and preserved in the Church, and in which the rites have been developed and maintained. It makes its own, while going beyond them, the anthropological reasons for doing such a study. The Christian community has had to work hard to maintain for itself the unique relationship which Jesus set up between rite, word and life. In its thinking and in its practice it has continually had to find ways of realizing it anew, to keep pace with its own growth and with changes in the life-experience and perceptions of its members. It has had to deal with all the deviations that any human system of ritual is prone to. It has had to save the rites from superstition as well as incredulity, and from being distorted by a careless or un-Christian word that might put them at the service of a life that was not truly Christian. The struggle, carried on in both theory and practice, is bound up with the fortunes of the word 'sacrament'. This became the technical Christian word for the rites of the Church. It serves to state the unique relationship that exists in them between rite, word and life, along with the ground for that, which is Christ's presence in them. The tradition about this word is the key to understanding the theological and liturgical tradition about any of the individual sacraments. It will be examined in Chapter 2.

The Scriptures and the tradition between them make it possible to understand theologically what the Christian community thinks today about its sacraments and why it celebrates them the way it does. The community remembers its origins and its past, not just for anthropological reasons connected with survival but because it is in such a tradition that God has given it his word and the rites that are made life-giving by fidelity to that word. Each generation, however, has to do its own re-working of the tradition, putting it together in a critical, systematic way in view of the questions that are being raised in the community by new generations of people. It is such a present understanding of the rites, coming out of the tradition but looking to the here and now of life, that a theology of Baptism, Confirmation and Eucharist will want to provide. It will want to be a word that can make the contemporary celebration of the rites profoundly life-giving. The testing of such a theology will have to be done not only in the lecture hall but also in the baptistery and around the altar and, above all, in the lives of those whose participation in the sacraments has been informed by it.

The questions that are put about Baptism, Confirmation and Eucharist today have in them the more general questions about the whole sacramental system and about how these three sacraments relate to everything else in the sacramental order. The three sacraments form, in fact, the initiation phase of a ritual system that has four other structural sacraments and a multitude of secondary rites called sacramentals. It is by this sacramental system and by the word of faith that accompanies it that the Christian community is constituted as Church, as Body of Christ and as People of God. This is the perspective in which Baptism, Confirmation and Eucharist are set in Chapter 3. What is presented there is, in summary form, a general theology of the sacramental economy. It shows the profound ramifications and inter-connectedness of the question that will come up about the individual sacraments. Even though it is put in rather classical terms it is still offered as a theology for today. There can be alternative theologies of sacrament that meet special ecclesial and cultural situations more immediately. But they, too, need to face eventually the issues that the great theses of classical sacramental theology deal with. A position on these issues is present, at least in the form of presupposition, in every theology of sacraments. Sooner or later they have to be discussed, even at the price of seeming a little less than relevant to immediate contemporary needs.

When one begins to look at an individual sacrament against such a theological and anthropological background one will want to see it as a rite, accompanied by an appropriate word, that gives life. The discussion on each of the three sacraments being dealt with here begins with a chapter on its rite (Chapters 4, 6, 8). A fairly detailed description of the rite is given as the starting-point for theological reflection. The description is taken from the official texts in which the Church prescribes how the rite should be performed. It will read so much more realistically if it is accompanied by direct experience and observation of actual celebrations of the sacrament. To describe the rite of a sacrament is already to begin to understand it. Although there is an inherent mysteriousness in all rites there is no deliberate cult of obscurity in the Christian sacraments. The rites are made as clear as they can be, and it is believed that the less explanation they require the better. Yet they do gain from some explanation. It comes in a first phase from a growth in sensitivity to the richness of the actions and words that make up the rite. Ritual actions are always heavy with tradition, with memories and precedents. These can be brought to the surface by developing an awareness of the origin and history of the rite. They can be intensified by a discovery of how the rite addresses certain deep human experiences and needs in a way that has clear parallels in other cultural and religious expressions of the human psyche. Here one will be appealing to the findings of the historical and psychological sciences, especially in their studies on religion. On a more specifically theological plane the ritual actions can gain meaning from a comparison between them and the recurring patterns of divine action that are recorded in the Scriptures. The words that form part of the rite are an even richer vehicle of meaning than the ritual actions. Although they are somehow ritualized they are not mere incantations. They give a ritual action, which by itself may be open to any number of interpretations, its specifically Christian meaning. In the rite they register along the whole range of human perception, stirring the depths of the unconscious, prodding memory, nourishing the poetical instinct and formulating judgements of intelligence. To bring out these values of the ritual words (not just those at the core of the rite — the sacramental 'form' — but all the words used throughout the rite) is to develop a deep theological understanding of the rite in its relationship to human life. One could call this way of understanding the rite a liturgical theology of the sacrament. It remains within the language of the rite itself. It has a certain self-sufficiency and may be quite adequate for certain situations in the life of the Church. Certainly it is the only sure ground for further theological reflection on the sacrament.

There are, however, many words besides those of the rite itself that affect the celebration of a Christian rite and give it its influence on life. There are scriptural passages, there are patristic catecheses, there are technical analyses of systematic theology, there are the words of preaching, and there are the catecheses that are spoken in the church, in the classroom and in the nursery. There are also dogmatic pronouncements which were made to settle disagreements among Christians about the meaning and value of the rites. And because dogmatic definitions did not always resolve differences, and Christians went their separate ways with contrasting views on the rite, there are now agreed or convergence statements in which they try to restore unity to the sacramental belief and practice of the Church. All of these words are about the rite. Their value comes from how well they give life and light and authenticity to the faith of those who actually practise the sacrament. Although they are always grounded on the words that form part of the rite they go beyond them into explanations and ideas and a vocabulary that suits their particular purpose. This kind of explanatory text is found already in the Scriptures, side by side with the descriptive texts that are the source of the actual rites. Paul has theological explanations of Baptism that suppose knowledge of what the rite is. John has his discourse on the bread of life that supposes the accounts of the Last Supper but does not repeat them. Later texts speak of the sacraments in the pedagogical language of catechetics, or use the technical terms of systematic theology, like sign and cause, instrument, character, encounter, visibility, *ex opere operato* and so on. The tradition has found such words necessary for the good celebration of the rite. It has taken texts which use them as readings to go with the celebration of the rite and as nourishment for the preaching that is done at it. A theology of any Christian rite has to listen to these words and let its own thinking be formed by them. They are the subject of the chapters on the word devoted here to each of the three sacraments (Chapters 5, 7, 9). Each of these chapters concludes with an essay in the systematic theology of each sacrament. This is an attempt to set the particular sacrament within a comprehensive, critical vision of how God — the true God — is at work in the world, drawing all the things that he has made back to himself in love. It is an identifying of the principles and presuppositions that one inevitably employs in even the most superficial discourse about sacraments and, assuming that they are critically tested and organized in the systematic theology one is using, a way of giving one's theology of the sacrament its deepest rational verification. One should not claim too much for any systematic theology. But without some attempt at it one cannot claim to have dealt with the questions that can be asked about a sacrament at the deepest level.

There are other questions that remain to be asked about Baptism, Confirmation and Eucharist. All theological questions are about how these rites relate to life. Eventually these questions become so particular and individual that they cannot be answered outside the particular life-situation in which they arise. They enter the province of catechetics and preaching. They cannot be covered directly in a work of theology. The best one can offer are some suggestions for dealing with them in a way that will respect the theological word about the rite and its special relationship to life that characterizes Christian sacraments. This is what will be attempted in the Epilogue.

FURTHER READING

On rites and their place in human life:

A. van Gennep, *The Rites of Passage* (originally written 1908; repub. by University of Chicago Press, 1960).

G. van der Leeuw, *Religion in Essence and Manifestation* (London, 1938).

F. W. Dillistone, *Christianity and Symbolism* (London, 1955).

R. C. Zaehner, *At Sundry Times* (London, 1958).

M. Eliade, *Patterns in Comparative Religion* (London, 1958); and *The Sacred and the Profane* (London, 1959).

E. O. James, *Sacrifice and Sacrament* (London, 1962).

L. Bouyer, *Rite and Man* (Notre Dame, 1963).

V. W. Turner, *The Ritual Process* (London, 1969).

R. Bocock, *Ritual in Industrial Society* (London, 1973).

L. Mitchell, *The Meaning of Ritual* (New York, 1977).

F. Isambert, *Rite et efficacité symbolique. Essai d'anthropologie symbolique* (Paris, 1979).

G. Fourez, SJ, *Sacraments and Passages* (Notre Dame, 1983).

On word in relation to rite:

L. Bouyer, *Rite and Man* (Notre Dame, 1963).

K. Rahner, 'The Word and the Eucharist' in *Theological Investigations* 4 (London, 1966), pp. 253–286.

D. Tracy, *The Analogical Imagination* (London, 1981), especially in his treatment of 'manifestation' and 'proclamation'.

On the use of story in communities of faith:

J. Shea, *Stories of God: An Unauthorized Biography* (Chicago, 1978); and *Stories of Faith* (Chicago, 1980).
T. Tilley, *Story Theology* (Wilmington, 1985).
J. Navone, SJ, *Gospel Love. A Narrative Theology* (Wilmington, 1985).

Most writers on sacraments do some general theology of the sacramental economy before treating the individual sacraments. However, the boundaries that Scholastic theology set between 'sacraments in general' and 'sacraments in particular' are no longer so clearly marked. Some theologians pay special attention to the rites and do a theology of liturgy. For an illustration of different theological methods of putting together the biblical, liturgical, patristic, historical, dogmatic and pastoral material that needs to be dealt with in a general theology of sacraments, compare the following standard works:

A. M. Roguet, OP, *Christ Acts Through the Sacraments* (Collegeville, 1954).
B. Leeming, SJ, *Principles of Sacramental Theology* (London, 1956).
L. Bouyer, *Liturgical Piety/Life and Liturgy* (Notre Dame/London, 1956).
A. G. Martimort, *The Signs of the New Covenant* (Collegeville, 1959).
C. Vagaggini, OSB, *Theological Dimensions of the Liturgy* (Collegeville, 1959).
K. Rahner, *The Church and the Sacraments* (London, 1963).
E. Schillebeeckx, *Christ, the Sacrament of Encounter with God* (London, 1963).
J. L. Segundo, *The Sacraments Today* (New York, 1973).
J. Martos, *Doors to the Sacred* (London, 1981).
C. E. O'Neill, OP, *Sacramental Realism* (Dublin, 1983).

1

Biblical orientations

Baptism, Confirmation and Eucharist, as rites of the Christian Church, come out of and receive the first authoritative statement of their meaning in the Scriptures of the New Testament. Each of them has roots in the Old Testament, without which its emergence in the New Testament cannot be fully understood. But more importantly each of them builds on a general experience and understanding of rite that is presented with considerable anthropological and theological richness in the books of the Old Testament. The Bible tells the life-story of God's chosen People. It includes descriptions of their rites and accounts of the part they play in life. The Old Testament presents a pattern of interaction between rite, word and life that has its own historical consistency but that also reaches out to a future transformation. Knowing that pattern and these expectations, one can better appreciate the radical newness, and yet the continuity in contrast of what the books of the New Testament have to say about rite and word in the life of the new People of God, of which they are now the story. The New Testament teaching about individual rites such as Baptism and Eucharist can best be understood against this background.

1.1 RITE, WORD AND LIFE IN THE OLD TESTAMENT

In anthropological terms the Old Testament tells the story of a tribe of nomadic origin that, after a period of settled development and eventual oppression in Egypt of the Pharaohs, found freedom in escape and in a momentous journey across the desert, at the end of which they came to the land between the river Jordan and the Mediterranean, which they conquered and settled as their own. It is the story of their social, economic, religious and cultural development in that land, of their struggles to survive in difficult times and to grow in all the areas of human enrichment when circumstances were favourable. Religion, in its beliefs and its rites, plays a central part in this story. It touches every facet of life and is itself filled with the stuff of life.

But the Old Testament is a theological, not just an anthropological telling of the story of Israel. It is the story of what God was doing for his People and of how they responded to him. It is about the rites in which they found assurance of God's continuing care for them and in which they addressed themselves to him in crucial moments of their life. It is a covenant story, about the working-out of an agreement between God and his People. God is the one who initiated and repeatedly renewed the covenant. He promised blessings to his People — blessings of the most real-life kind: they would have children, many of them, so that they would not only survive but would become a great nation; they would have a land of their own, with food and drink from it; they would conquer their enemies and live in peace; they would know how to dance and sing, and in old age each would sit comfortably under the shade of his or her own vine or fig tree.

God did things for his People. And to make sure they knew it he told them the true story of what he was doing with them by inspiring their prophets, their story-tellers and the writers of their holy books. He gave them a book of the covenant. As well as telling them what God was doing for them, this book also told them what he expected of them. It spelled out in the form of law and exhortation their side of the covenant. It gave them very detailed moral laws about how they should live in the main areas of individual and social choice. It also told them the religious rites they should practise. In the rites they were expected to experience what it was to be God's People and to express their acceptance of that. The rite of circumcision marked the initiation of individuals into the covenant and into membership of God's People. It evoked the original call of Abraham and somehow repeated it for individual Israelites. Other rites recalled what God had done for them at the Exodus. His action of bringing them out of Egypt, through the Red Sea, across the desert and into the land he had given to their fathers had become a prototype of his saving actions and of the response his love generated in his People. The rites of the Passover recalled and somehow repeated the pattern of this saving act of God, and gave Israelites an opportunity to renew their fidelity to the covenant of Sinai. To gather at table with their family and friends, to have the kind of table-talk of memory and hope that unleavened bread and bitter herbs and the slaughtered lamb evoked, to eat this food and to drink wine in the cups of blessing — all this was to live the Exodus experience again and to feel it being realized in their own life. It was to make a memorial (*zikkaron* in Hebrew; cf. 8.2.1 and 9.1.1 below) of God's saving act. There was a host of other rites that were to mark the life of an Israelite. Like circumcision and the Passover celebrations they took their meaning from the story of Israel and from the belief of those who cherished the story that they truly were God's people. The story was told again and again in folk tradition and eventually from books. It began as the story of this particular people but as time went on it gathered into itself the story of all humankind and of the very cosmos. It became a creation story within a salvation story. The rites did not always reflect this wider perspective and there is not a little exasperation in the words of the prophet Malachi when he says 'I have no pleasure in you, says the Lord of hosts, and I will not accept an offering from your hand. For from the rising of the sun to its setting my name is great among the nations, and in every place incense is offered to my name, and a pure offering; for my name is great among the nations, says the Lord of hosts' (Mal 1:10b-11).

As words and rites established themselves, the authority that emerged in Israel began to take responsibility for them. The men and women of the word always carried authority. They are the *prophets*. The most famous among them were the great preachers and interpreters of the fortunes of the People. Many of the sacred books came to be attributed to them, from Moses who was supposed to have written the five books that stand at the head of the Bible to Malachi, which was the name given to the last of the prophets to have a book ascribed to him in the Hebrew Bible. Responsibility for the word, especially in its written form, was also vested in people called scribes, who emerged at the time of the exile in Babylon (cf. Ezra the scribe in Nehemiah 8:1; note that in the following verse Ezra is called a priest). *Priests* were responsible for the rites, and a priestly class exercised considerable power in Israel. Once stable political structures developed in Israel overall responsibility for the life and times of the people was given to the *king*. As life, word and rite were interdependent so were the offices of prophet, priest and king. Those who held one would regularly be concerned about the affairs of the others. They would blame each other when things went wrong in the life of the People. For a long time most of the blame was put on the king (cf. the books of Samuel, Kings and Chronicles). But the hope of better times was also bound up with the coming of an ideal king, a new David. In the course of time this figure of hope gathered to himself, in an ideal balance, the offices of priest and prophet.

If the historical kings of Israel were often far from the ideal, so also was the balance between rite, word and life in the behaviour of God's People. Much of the Old Testament is a complaint about it and a hope that things would get better. It was in the crises of life that the problem was most immediately felt: crops failed and there was hunger, leaders quarrelled and there was internal strife, enemies broke in and destroyed, there was death and deportation, there seemed to be no sign of a happy end to the story. That tested faith in God and his covenant: it was not what he promised his People. There was a temptation to blame God for the catastrophes. When those responsible for the faith of Israel, be they prophets, priests or the king, dealt with the problem, they had to nail that lie by proclaiming the absolute fidelity of God to his covenant. A certain amount of grumbling and taunting of God does remain as a kind of literary form in the Scriptures, but the basic thesis is that the fault has to be on the side of the People. The analysis that is recorded in the Bible is mostly that of the prophets. The reforms attributed to kings and priests do give an indication of their thinking, but there was almost always a prophet around to put the thinking into words of preaching and eventually of writing. A favourite technique of the prophets is to re-tell the story of Israel, but in a way that points up its relevance to the contemporary life-situation. The message is that the People has forgotten its own story, or not understood it properly, that the Israelites have not been faithful to their own tradition. This new telling of the story ends up by being itself part of the story (as in Deuteronomy, Chronicles and parts of the Wisdom literature) and a recognized projection of it towards the future (as in the strictly prophetic books).

Another part of the analysis of the problems of life in Israel centres on rites. Things are going wrong with life because the rites given by God to his People are being neglected, or have been contaminated with pagan forms of ritual, or are being performed in a purely legalistic way without much relation to the real-life choices of private and public morality. The prophets can give any of these three reasons, although the last is the most characteristic of their analysis. The prophets are not against rites. But they want them to be in accordance with the tradition and to be an honest expression of moral choices. If the Israelites are proclaiming themselves to be God's People in their rites they must behave like God's People in their lives. The prophets often blame the priests and the king for letting the rites deteriorate, but when the king and priests undertake a serious reform they have the support of the prophets. (See, for example, the covenant renewal under King Josiah described in 2 Kings 22 – 23.)

And yet the prophets do keep alive a certain dissatisfaction with the rites of the Old Testament. They seem to want something less prone to formalism and less liable to become an excuse for avoiding the real choices of life according to the covenant. The book of Jeremiah has a powerful page (chapter 31) that looks forward to a time when life will be full and abundant again because God will have made a new covenant that will be written on people's hearts. People will act from inner conviction and personal wisdom rather than because somebody else tells them what the law says. There does not seem to be any special place for Temple rites in Jeremiah's city of this new covenant. The whole city, not just a temple area, will be sacred (vv. 38-40). Perhaps Jeremiah is saying that, as the sacred words will have become identified with life through being written on the hearts of people, so will the sacred actions. Isaiah was certainly moving in that direction in his prophecies about the Suffering Servant (42:1-9; 49:1-6; 50:4-11; 52:13 – 53:12) whose own life and death would do all that rites of sacrifices were being expected to do in the old covenant, to the point that he himself can be described as the covenant given to the people (42:6; 49:8).

I.2   RITE, WORD AND LIFE IN THE NEW TESTAMENT

The first Christians believed that in Jesus God made the definitive covenant promised by the prophets of Israel. They believed themselves to be the People of the New Covenant. No sooner had they come to this certainty, on the day of Pentecost, than they began to tell their story and to celebrate it in rites. What they told about themselves centred on the event that brought them into existence as a community of believers — the death and resurrection of Jesus and his glorification in power at the right hand of his Father. Their story, written in the books of the New Testament, is the story of him; the rites they began to practise are memorials of him (Shorter, chs 4–5).

The new covenant, like the old, is made with words. There is a story in it and there is a promise; there are explanations and there is a new law. But the story is all about a living person, Jesus, who was born, who died, who rose from the dead, who is with the Father from whom he sends the life-giving Spirit on the whole of creation; the promise is of the second coming of Jesus; the explanations are mostly about the unique way that God is at work in Jesus because of who Jesus is in the deepest level of his person; the law is all about behaving in the way Jesus behaved. Jesus put much of this into words himself: he exercised, although in a special way, the rôle of a prophet. He commissioned his disciples to go on speaking about him. They are people of the word, a word that they believe to be the word of life. The first letter of John opens with a powerful statement of how the Christian word is identified with the living reality of Jesus. The teaching of the Prologue of the gospel of John that Jesus is the Word of God made flesh establishes the most profound continuity between words about Jesus and the reality of God's personal life that is in him, because he is the Word of God in person. The words are realistic because they are of the Word.

The new covenant is also made with actions. These are seen to be in continuity with the rites of the old covenant and are often described in terms of them: there is a new Passover, there is a new circumcision, there is a new anointing. But they are not ritual actions. There is no risk that they could be ever separated from life, because they are, in fact, the personal life-actions of Jesus. The new covenant is made not only by Jesus but in him; he is the one promised in Isaiah 42:6: 'I have given you as a covenant to the people, a light to the nations'. His acceptance of his call and his total dedication to the work of his Father is his real circumcision; the choice he made that led to the shedding of his own blood, his acceptance of death and his being raised to life from the dead was the Passover in which his Father made the new covenant of life; his sitting at the right hand of the Father in an eschatological triumph that is marked by the outpouring of the Spirit sets up the new community of God's People through whom the world is transformed and the cosmos recreated. It is not through rites that Christ acts but through his own body; his body makes all previous rites obsolete. If people are going to have their lives brought in touch with the work of God, they must now do it by getting in touch with the body of Christ. Indeed the community of those in whom the work of God is now identifiable is itself called the body of Christ; to be a member of it is to be one of his members. If one is a member of a living body one is oneself alive. If there are to be rites in the community of the new covenant they must somehow be filled with the life that is in the body of Christ.

The letter to the Hebrews is a proclamation of the coincidence of word, rite and life in Jesus. It begins by identifying him as the one in whom the word of God reaches its fullness, the one who is uniquely beyond the earlier prophets and the angels, because he is the Son whereas they were only ministers of the word. The theme of the word brought to its fullness in Jesus is intertwined in Hebrews with the more dominant theme of his priesthood. He is both 'apostle and high priest of our confession' (Heb 3:1). His priesthood consists first of all in a real-life identification with his brothers and sisters (2:10). He exercises it by offering himself in death and by entering the heavenly sanctuary where he lives to make intercession for us. His priestly action is described in reference to the rites of the old covenant, especially to those practised in the Temple. In accomplishing these rites in a new way he has made them obsolete. He now lives forever in a heaven that, while it may be described in the imagery of the Temple, is clearly no place for rites.

So overwhelming is Hebrews about the passing of ritual priesthood that one might suppose it leaves no place for rite in the work that God is now doing in the world through Christ and his Spirit. The hard things Paul has to say about the law of the Old Testament and its ritual prescriptions and his polemic against circumcision in Galatians suggest something similar. Jesus himself, according to the Gospels, did not seem to see much future for the Temple and therefore for ritual religion. The age of the Spirit, with its worship in spirit and in truth proclaimed in the writings of John, seems the very antithesis of sacred places and sacred actions and sacred personages. Prophets in the new covenant could make an even stronger case against ritualism than did their predecessors in the old.

Yet rites there were from the beginning, and their introduction is attributed to Jesus himself. Chapter 2 of the Acts of the Apostles relates that when the new covenant was first announced in Jerusalem on the day of Pentecost and the people who accepted the preaching of Peter asked 'what shall we do?' they were told, among other things, to 'be baptized' (v. 38). When they were baptized they were gathered together into a community that met regularly for, among other things, 'the breaking of bread' (v. 42). The two actions are mentioned regularly enough in the New Testament, and are so related to critical moments of the life of Christians that one is already justified in calling them rites. Other actions like anointing with oil and laying-on of hands are already beginning to take on ritual shape. And the making of a marriage can, of course, hardly but be a rite. The New Testament suggests some continuity between these ritual actions and the rites of the Old Testament. Baptism is a new kind of circumcision according to Colossians 2:11–13; Luke's account of the Last Supper presents it as a new Passover meal; marriage, representing the union between Christ and the Church, realizes the dream of oneness between Jahweh and his People that was evoked by marriage in the Old Testament (Eph 5:21–33).

However, the differences between the rites of the new covenant and those of the old are profound. The originality is in the way the new rites relate to the life that is in Jesus and in his members. It can be perceived by reflecting (a) on the kind of rites they are, (b) on the way they are related to the word that is preached about Jesus, and (c) on their being authoritatively controlled by the tradition that comes from the apostles. The priestly, the prophetic and the kingly in them is all centred in Christ.

(a) The rites of the new covenant are drawn from 'ordinary' life rather than from the typically religious sphere. Sacrifice of animals, offerings of first-fruits, physical marks of initiation, sacred places, incense, reverential gestures are all left aside, and there is no provision for a ritual priesthood to tend any such rites. Instead there is a bathing in water, an eating at table, anointings with oil, hand touches of nearness, comfort and blessing. The religion of Jesus is of the prophetic sort. It is not forcing things too much to say that, in giving his followers rites drawn more from ordinary life than from the religious patrimony of his people,

Jesus was making a prophetic statement about the need to make rites an expression of real life. Such rites could more easily be from the heart, suited to a covenant that was to be written on the heart. They are appropriate to the life that is given within, in the end times when the Spirit is poured out.

There is something still deeper about these rites that relates them uniquely to the life that is in Jesus. They are actions that Jesus performed during his own life, the life that he shared in such obviously human ways with his disciples on earth before he shared it with them in the resurrection. Jesus was baptized in the Jordan, he sat down to eat and drink with his friends, he touched people for healing and comfort, he shared in a wedding feast. When the disciples did these things together after the resurrection, did them repeatedly and ritually, they were, no doubt, expressing many things that were on their minds about the present and the future. But they could never forget that, in the past, they had done these same actions with Jesus. His 'in memory of me' dominated everything and brought the rites into the heart of the life-experience they were having in Jesus.

(b) The life that the disciples were receiving from Jesus was being proclaimed in their words. These words of the apostolic preaching provided a setting for the rites. According to the command of Jesus, Baptism was to be done within a process of teaching that would call forth faith in Father, Son and Holy Spirit: 'Go therefore and *make disciples* of all nations, baptizing them in the name of the Father and of the Son and of the Holy Spirit, *teaching them to observe* all that I have commanded you . . .' (Matt 28:19–20). The first baptisms on the day of Pentecost were of 'those who *received his word*' (Acts 2:41). The table is a place of conversation and the rite inaugurated at the Last Supper was set in the midst of many words. The breaking of bread that is introduced in Acts 2:42 is accompanied by '*the apostles' teaching* . . . and *the prayers*'. All these words and teachings and prayers proclaimed the reality that was present in the rites. They are words of and about Jesus. People who had come to believe in them — and by that very fact had made them their own story, their way of understanding, their law of life — could not but centre the rites on Jesus and on their life in him.

(c) The rites, like the words, are already becoming official in the New Testament, and therefore subject to the authority of the leaders of the community. The title that Jesus gave to the leaders of the community of his disciples says much about the kind of life he wanted the community to have and about the rôle that rites would play in it. He called them neither prophets nor priests, nor kings, nor any derivatives of these, but apostles. Although they are men of the word, the apostles are not prophets. There was a category of leaders in the community called prophets, but they are distinguished from the apostles. Nor are the apostles presented as priests. Paul, who is an apostle by a special title, does claim to be 'in the priestly service of the Gospel of God, so that the offering of the Gentiles may be acceptable, sanctified by the Holy Spirit' (Rom 15, 16), but there is nothing in this text to link 'priestly service' with a priestly performance of rites. Paul did baptize some people, but says he was not sent to baptize (1 Cor 1:14–17), and neither he nor any of the other apostles is presented as presiding at the Eucharist. Nor did the apostles give priestly titles to those to whom they gave authority in the communities, but the more neutral, almost secular titles of presbyters and bishops (*episkopoi*). Least of all are the apostles kings. The contrast Jesus made between their authority and that of 'the kings of the Gentiles' (Luke 22:24–27) should have made that clear once and for all. If it took two centuries before the Church felt ready to give its leaders priestly titles, it took even longer for it to dare to give them titles or modes of address drawn from the usages of royalty (Lords, Excellencies, Reverend Sirs!).

The title 'apostle' presents the leaders of the community of disciples as, above all else, representatives, envoys, messengers of Jesus. Their status and mission is entirely relative to him. Because the fullness of the Kingdom has come in Jesus, nothing that is not from him and about him can lay claim to be of God. The apostles are authorized witnesses to Jesus. They lived with him during his days on earth and they recognized him in his resurrection. They authorize the words that are spoken in the community about him. They must also authorize the rites that are done in memory of him. Through this apostolic authorization the community is able to be in touch with the life of Jesus in its words and in its rites. Whatever other authority figures emerge later in the Church, whether they be of the prophetic, priestly or kingly kind, can only claim to have control over rites and words to the extent that they are faithful to the tradition that comes from the apostles. That is the guarantee that the community is living the life of Jesus.

Through the tradition that comes from the apostles, then, and particularly through the words of the tradition that surrounds them, the rites of the new covenant remember and embody the reality of Jesus — the reality of his life that he now lives at the right hand of his Father and communicates through the Spirit to those who live in his body which is the Church. For the believing community the rites of the new covenant have a realism in relation to life that no other rites have ever claimed. They are revelations of the Word made flesh, in whom all prophecy is fulfilled; they are actions of the Eternal High Priest, in whom all worship is centred; they bring about the universal reign of God that is established in Christ and pervades all things through the Spirit. The community that celebrates these rites is alive with his life. Its story is about the working-out of his Lordship and its rites are a remembering of his saving action until he comes again.

The dream of the prophets about rites that are all of a piece with life has come true in the community of those who believe in Christ. And yet not entirely. On the one hand, there is the euphoric description of the first community in Acts 2:42–47, in which life is gloriously at one with word and rite. On the other hand, there is soon an outbreak of 'murmuring' in that same community about the distribution of food, which did not seem to match the table fellowship of the 'breaking of bread' (Acts 6:1). Paul, on the one hand, can deduce, in Romans 6, seemingly as a matter of inevitable fact, a whole pattern of living from the meaning and reality of Baptism; he can solve problems of conscience about eating meat that might have been offered to idols by appealing to the 'cup of blessing which we bless . . . the bread which we break' (1 Cor 10:16). On the other hand, he finds that same Corinthian community living in a way that makes nonsense of the rite of 'the Lord's Supper' (1 Cor 11:17–34).

Paul's way of dealing with the inconsistency between rite and life in Corinth shows, however, that the problem is quite different from what it was under the old covenant. An Old Testament prophet would have told the Corinthians that, because of the way they were living, their rite was vain and unacceptable to God. Paul deals with the question differently. He tells them patiently what the tradition has to say about the rite. It is, he says, the proclaiming, in the bread and in the cup, of the death of the Lord in the reality of his flesh and blood. The fault of the Corinthians is that they have not discerned this reality — which is there whether they discern it or not (and it does not matter much to the argument whether by 'body' in v. 29 Paul means eucharistic body or ecclesial body or both). The incongruity he is pointing out is not between the life of the Corinthians and the symbolism of the rite they are performing but between their life and the reality of Christ proclaimed in the rite. The value of the rite comes from the reality of the body and blood of Christ before it comes from the behaviour of the community. If they really knew and accepted the reality of the body of Christ that is proclaimed and present, their lives would soon be changed and they would be blessed by God accordingly: they would behave differently towards one another and they would be freed from illness and death (vv. 30–32). The rite would then have meaning for them because the reality of their own lives would be in continuity with the reality of Christ.

Paul does not deal any differently with Baptism. In Romans 6 (vv. 1–14) he explains how Christians have died to sin through being baptized into Christ Jesus. And yet they still sin! When Paul talks about the sins of Christians he never suggests that there is anything wrong with their Baptism. The rite does not become empty because of their sinful lives. He never makes a contrast between baptism of the heart and baptism of the flesh that would be comparable to what he does when discussing circumcision. To question the value of Baptism would be to question the reality of Christ. Because it makes one a member of the body of Christ, and because Christ is alive never to die anymore, Baptism is always life-giving.

The scandal of lives that are not in accord with words and rites should be greater among Christians than among other people because of the uniqueness they claim for the new covenant. Christian theology will always have to wrestle with this problem. Why is it that Christian rites sometimes do not seem to work? It will use the analogies of human ritual and the precedents of the Old Testament to try to understand the inconsistency. But in fidelity to the New Testament it will always have to press these explanations to a point that respects the unique relationship of the rites of the new covenant to the word of the Gospel and to the life that is in Christ. To a very large extent it was to do this that the word 'sacrament' came to be employed in Christian theology as a general name for the principal rites practised by the community of believers.

STUDY QUESTIONS

1   Analyse the interaction of word and rite in any one of the covenant making or covenant renewing assemblies of Israel, and consider how this affected the life of God's People.
2   Study in the life of one of the prophets of Israel the kind of relationship he or she had with priests and kings, and how this affected the prophetic message.
3   Reflect on the revolt of the Maccabees against Greek culture in terms of word, rite and life.
4   Gather texts from the letter to the Hebrews that have a bearing on the relationship between life, word and rite in God's dealing with his People.
5   Reflect on the Christology that underlies what Paul says about Baptism in Romans 6:3–11.
6   If Jesus was hesitant about accepting the titles Prophet and King during his ministry, what might he have said to someone who wanted to call him Priest?
7   In New Testament terms, what does it mean to say that Jesus instituted the rites of Baptism and Eucharist?
8   What are the texts in the New Testament that might give the impression that the apostles were more concerned with the word than with rites? What is the significance of these texts for an understanding of Christian sacraments?
9   Reflect on the biblical experience of 'memorial' (*zikkaron, anamnēsis*) as an interaction between word, rite and life.

FURTHER READING

Biblical dictionaries have articles on the key words referred to in this chapter: covenant, circumcision, memorial, sacrifice, passover, word, people, prophet, priest, king, temple, body of Christ, apostle, church, baptism, breaking of bread etc.

The rites of the Old Testament are dealt with in:

R. de Vaux, OP, *Ancient Israel. Its Life and Institutions* (London, 1961).

There is a good presentation of biblical patterns of worship in:

L. Bouyer, *Liturgical Piety/Life and Liturgy* (Notre Dame/London, 1956).

For the New Testament:

O. Cullmann, *La foi et le culte dans l'église primitive* (Neuchâtel, 1963), part of which had already appeared in English in his *Early Christian Worship* (London, 1953).

On the word of God in Old and New Testaments:

A. Shorter, WF, *Revelation and its Interpretation* (London, 1983).

2

Rites called sacraments

'Rite' is a useful generic word that allows one to speak of Baptism, Confirmation and Eucharist together and to state some important truths about their place in human and religious experience. Although it is not a biblical word it could denote the biblical realities examined in the preceding chapter. It is, in fact, used in the language of the Church to describe what Baptism, Confirmation and Eucharist, and other such activities, are in their external shape and form. The books which prescribe how they are to be celebrated are entitled *The Rite of*. . . . But it is not the word that the tradition of faith has selected to describe what is most profoundly distinctive about these activities. The word that has come to do that is 'sacrament'. It has come to be the Church's generic word for Baptism, Confirmation, Eucharist, as well as for Penance, Anointing of the Sick, Marriage, and Ordination to Ministry. It is a biblical word originally but in the course of a long history of application to the rites of the Church it has gathered to itself refinements of meaning that it did not have in its biblical origins. There has been an ebb and flow in that history, as new shades of meaning were added to the word or old ones lost. At times the Church has used the word with a technical precision that allowed it to say things that badly needed to be said about the rites at that particular moment (for example during the Middle Ages). At other times the word became a bone of contention between churches and they each defined it in their own way to make the point about their differences (for example, during the controversies of the Reformation). Still again it has been used to bring back to the consciousness of faith aspects of the rites that had been somewhat forgotten (as at Vatican II). It is necessary to tell the story of this word and what it said at different times about the rites of the Church before one can sense what it might mean today. The word carries resonances of all the phases of its story and these must affect how we use it to talk about Christian initiation and its rites.

2.1   *SACRAMENTUM* AND *MUSTĒRION*

The English 'sacrament' comes from the Latin *sacramentum*. When Christians first began to describe something as *sacramentum* (Tertullian is the earliest Latin writer in whom there is a record of the usage) they were identifying it as related to the sacred; they were also saying that it stood for secret things, that it marked out people as having been initiated into some area of privilege and responsibility, that it expressed a commitment to some form of service (for different shades of meaning of *sacramentum* in Tertullian see the index to CCSL edition of his works, vol. 2, p. 1604; for early history of the word see Mohrmann and de Ghellinck, *Pour l'histoire . . .*). The oath that soldiers took on entering the service of the emperor was called a *sacramentum* (details in Navickas, pp. 7–11). That particular use of the word evoked many of the qualities that Christians wanted to attribute to their rites, especially to the rites of initiation. Tertullian used the analogy, and it was certainly one of the reasons why he called the rites *sacramenta*. Because the emperor was thought to be divine a commitment to fight in his service was sacred. One was marked forever by it (quite literally, sometimes, by having some image of the emperor tattooed on one's person). One gained access to all sorts of privileges, as well as to responsibilities, and to the inside information that went with that. To call a Christian rite a *sacramentum* in that sense was to say that it was a commitment to the service of the true God, an entry into the company of other Christians and an initiation into the secret, sacred truth they shared about life and death and eternity. In likening Christian initiation to an oath, *sacramentum* said it was a word, a ritualized word, a binding word about what one wanted to do with one's life.

That was a lot to say about Christian rites. If *sacramentum* could say it, that would probably have been enough to justify its place in the Christian vocabulary. But if that was all it said it would hardly have become the distinctive, technical word that it has become in the language of Christian faith. In fact, *sacramentum* acquired another function in Christian language which really made its fortune, and which ultimately made it an even more appropriate term for Baptism, Eucharist and the other major Christian rites. It came to be used as a translation of the Greek word *mustērion*.

In Greek, *mustērion* has a general meaning of 'secret', with a sense of the sacredness of all secrets. The Greek Bible used it in that sense. It is the word that the RSV translates by 'secret' in Tobit 12:7: 'It is good to guard the secret of a king, but gloriously to reveal the works of God'. If kings have their secret plans ('mysteries' in Judith 2:2) and can reveal them to their intimates, the secret of the destiny of all kingdoms is known only to God and can only be revealed by him. *Mustērion* is used in the expression of this idea in Daniel 2 (vv. 18, 27, 47). When Daniel has interpreted the strange dream of Nebuchadnezzar the king says: 'Truly your God is God of gods and Lord of kings, and a revealer of mysteries, for you have been able to reveal this mystery' (v. 47). The later Wisdom literature of the Old Testament connects Wisdom with the making and the revelation of this secret plan of God for all human history and uses *mustērion* for what RSV translates 'the secret purposes of God' (Wisdom 2:22; cf. 6:22).

St Paul takes up this language of mystery, and its Old Testament field of thought, to describe the Christian Gospel (1 Cor 2:6–16; Col 1:9–20; 2:2–4; Eph 1:9–23; 3:1–6; Rom 16:25–27; the word is also used in Matt 13:11; Mark 4:11; Luke 8:10; Rev 1:20; 10:7; 17:5). The mystery, which is God's plan for the reconciliation of all things, is finally realized, and shown to be realized, in the cross of Jesus, in his resurrection and sending of the Spirit. The mystery is put into words and proclaimed in the preaching of the Apostles. Those who believe in their word and enter the Church have the mystery revealed to them.

For all that he has to say about the mystery the only time Paul comes close to calling a rite of the Christian community a mystery is when he is presenting the Christian meaning of marriage (Eph 5:22–33). The marriage of Christians represents and realizes the work of Christ for his Church and the response of the Church to Christ. 'This mystery is a profound one', says Paul, 'and I am saying that it refers to Christ and the Church' (v. 32). In this text Paul seems to be thinking more of the day-to-day living-out of marriage than of the ritual solemnizing of it, so one is not yet at the point of having a Christian rite called a mystery — although rite and life are so close in marriage that the distinction is almost academic. Much of what Paul has to say about Baptism and Eucharist, and of the bearing they have on life, is strikingly similar to what he has to say about marriage, but he does not call them mysteries. However, he would surely see the mystery proclaimed in them, since they are an integral part of that Gospel which makes the life of the Church be a revelation of the mystery of God.

When Christians came to translate their Greek Scriptures into Latin they sometimes rendered *mustērion* by *mysterium*, somewhat as English would later develop the word 'mystery' to translate it. But they also translated it by *sacramentum* — and there is no obvious reason why they chose one translation rather than the other. Scholars are not quite sure why they used *sacramentum* as the equivalent of *mustērion*. There is no particular precedent for doing so in classical Latin. But it is a fact that they did so, and the fact says a lot about what they thought of *sacramentum* and of anything they called *sacramentum*. When the Greek Fathers came to use the word *mustērion* for the rites of the Christian faith the Latins were ready with *sacramentum* to say everything the Greek word wanted to say about the rites. Their word, in its turn, became enriched with the biblical teaching about the mystery of God and the mystery of Christ, and could consequently bring these fundamental ideas to bear on the understanding of Christian rites.

2.2   CLEMENT AND ORIGEN

In the writings of Clement of Alexandria and Origen one can see some of the important lines of thought that led the Greek patristic tradition to call the rites of the Church *mustēria*. The Alexandrians made extensive use of *mustērion* and its derivatives. They were interested in the special knowledge (*gnōsis*) enjoyed by Christians. In broad terms one can say that they thought in Platonic categories, according to which the world of the senses is a world of images and symbols behind which, or above which, lies the true world of divine ideas and ultimate spiritual reality. To get at the reality represented by the images was to enter their mystery (their mystical sense). In the Christian world, texts of Scripture, formulations of faith such as the Creeds, and the rites of the Church were special images and symbols that needed this kind of interpretation. In imaging and symbolizing the mystery of God they too were somehow mysteries. They allowed one to get in touch with the divine reality when they were suitably, that is mystically, interpreted (Neunheuser, chs 3–4).

There is little doubt that in the thinking of Clement and Origen the primary bearer of mystery is the word. But they see how the word is ritualized in the celebrations of the Church, especially in Baptism: the rite concretizes the biblical types proclaimed in the texts and brings them to bear on the life of Christians. For example, the biblical stories of deliverance by water are made concrete in the water-ritual of Baptism. Baptism is a mystery because it shows forth the reality of salvation that was already realized, although in a shadowy form, in the events of the Old Testament and was fully realized in the death and resurrection of Christ. The Word is at the heart of the mystery that is in Baptism. The 'bath of water' is likened by Origen to the physical cures worked on people's bodies by Jesus. Like them it is a symbol of the spiritual healing which the Word works on those who have faith (*Comm. in John*, VI, 23). It is the Word that calls forth faith and in that faith heals. Rite is never separated from word, and both yield up their hidden meaning together by being related to the mystery that is in Christ. It is the task of interpretation and catechesis to reveal this meaning. There is also the task of spelling out the implications of word and rite for life in a moral kind of exegesis.

2.3   THE MYSTERY RELIGIONS

Another linguistic usage had to be absorbed before Christians were entirely at home with calling their rites *mustēria*. The word was used to describe ritual cults that were being practised in the Graeco-Roman world side by side with Christianity. There was nothing very mysterious about the official cult of the emperor: it was civic and civil but not much more. The religion of the household gods was more intimate, but not very exciting. Out of the eastern parts of the Empire, however, had come a variety of cults which claimed to give a deeper encounter with the reality of nature and the cosmos, and promised an experience of liberation from the drabness of existence into some kind of fuller life. The devotees of Demeter went to her shrine at Eleusis in Greece, while the devotees of Isis and Osiris, and particularly of Mithras, set up their centres of cult throughout the Empire. Each cult had its mysteries. It had a story, which was usually a myth about how the god or gods made the world, gave it fertility and overcame the various death-dealing forces that trouble it. The story was kept secret and revealed only to initiates. Initiation was by a series of ritual actions (Mithraism had seven) during which the initiates were given a progressively fuller knowledge of the story (which would be at the same time an explanation of the successive ritual stages) until they were finally admitted into the full secret of the cult. The process of initiation, and the story which was revealed in it, was supposed to make a profound difference to the life of people and to admit them to a higher form of existence. The whole process, including rite and story, had to be kept secret. The cult was a mystery.

The parallels with Christianity were too close for comfort, especially when it became known, as it inevitably did, that the story was sometimes about the death of a god, about the shedding of blood that brought life, about descents from and ascents to heaven, and that the rites included sacred meals and various libations and washings. Already about the year 150, Justin Martyr found it necessary to explain away the parallels. Having described the Christian Eucharist in his *First Apology* (n. 66) he adds: 'The evil demons, in imitation of this [what Jesus did at the Last Supper] ordered the same thing to be performed in the Mithraic mysteries. For, as you know, or may easily learn, bread and a cup of water, together with certain incantations, are used in their mystic initiation rites'. Justin does not call the Christian Eucharist a mystery here. Even if he had seen reasons for doing so, the risks of reducing the Eucharist to the level of a Mithraic or any other cultic ritual were too great at this stage of the development of Christian language. Tertullian saw the parallels, too, and vigorously rejects any real similarity between the *sacra* of the mystery cults and the *sacramentum* of Christian Baptism. His only use of *mysterium* is in reference to pagan rites.

In a development of which historians are still trying to give a coherent account, the reserve about calling the rites of the Christian faith *mustēria* was eventually overcome. A beginning had been made by Origen and by the time of Athanasius the statements are explicit (*Oratio II contra Arianos* 42; *Oratio III contra Arianos* 33: *PG* 26, 236 and 393). The self-confidence which Christians gained during the fourth century and the decline or suppression of the pagan mystery cults made it easier to call the rites of Christian cult *mustēria*, and even to allow the word to carry with it some discreet analogies with the pagan cults. Certainly, these cults, with their combination of story and rite, and their offer of a life-changing experience, were better models for showing how Christian rites were rooted in human experience than were the official cults of the state religion. The Greek mystagogical catecheses of the fourth century are quite at home with *mustērion* as a word for the Christian rites. The two Latin sets of catecheses that come from St Ambrose are called *De Mysteriis* and *De Sacramentis*.

2.4 THE MYSTAGOGICAL CATECHESES

The ongoing history of *mustērion* and of its application to the rites of the Church by the Greek Fathers from Origen onwards would, no doubt, be instructive, as would that of *sacramentum* in Latin, but for the purposes of the present chapter it is sufficient to draw attention to what *mustērion* and *sacramentum* had come to stand for around the end of the fourth century when Cyril of Jerusalem, Ambrose of Milan, John Chrysostom and Theodore of Mopsuestia spoke their great catecheses to those who were experiencing the rites of Christian initiation. Nor is it necessary to work out whatever interdependence there might have been between these four great preachers. It seems reasonable to say that they are four witnesses to a way of thinking and speaking that had become so widespread as to be universal in the fourth century.

While there can be no substitute for actually reading the text of the catecheses (conveniently edited in Yarnold), attention can be drawn to some general features of them that bear on the use of *mustērion* and *sacramentum*. They are about *rites*, and it is these they call mysteries/sacraments. The rites are the full liturgy of Christian initiation of adults (Baptism, Confirmation and Eucharist) solemnly celebrated in the Church at Easter. The word, spoken and read, is an integral part of the rite to be explained. The preparatory rites of the catechumenate are also explained within the ambit of mystery, but there is a preferential use of 'mystery' to refer to the central core of the rite (e.g. Theodore, II, 1). It is the sermons on these central rites of Baptism, Confirmation and Eucharist that are properly called 'mystagogical' (the *mustagōgos* was the one who explained the rites of initiation to candidates in the mystery religions). Mystery and sacrament are not so much definable theological terms from which conclusions could be drawn about the rites as mood-words that convey an atmosphere. They express the sacredness, the awesomeness, the hiddenness and need to keep secret, the symbolic character of the rites and hence correspondingly the need for them to be explained. There is not much explicit appeal to the Pauline *mustērion*, but the explanation of the rites of Baptism and Eucharist is deeply Pauline. There is constant reference to the Scriptures — to texts being read in the course of the celebration but to others as well. Clearly the mystery is in the rite only in the setting of the *word*. The types and figures of the Old Testament give the rites their symbolic resonance; the proclamations of the New Testament about the salvation that is in Christ reveal the grace that is given in the rites. The reality that lies beneath the rites is discovered in the word. The reality is the salvation that comes from God, the climax of the mystery accomplished in Christ. The word draws forth faith. It is only in faith that the real meaning of the rites can be accepted (cf. for example Chrysostom, II, 9–11; Theodore, II, 13–16).

The change of *life* brought about by the rites and required by them is also explained in the catecheses. It is a gift given in the rite but it is also a personal decision called for by the rite. There is an element of contract or covenant in the rite. It is referred to in the explanations of the rite of renouncing Satan. A new contract is being made with Christ, in place of the one that bound people to Satan. The language of sacrament is used about it (Cyril, I, 1–11; Ambrose, I, 5–8; Chrysostom, II, 17–21; Theodore, II, 1–12), which means the word still carries something of the sense of commitment and oath that it had in the original Latin usage that has been noted in Tertullian.

2.5 THE LATIN TRADITION AND ST AUGUSTINE

In the catecheses of Ambrose, with the easy interchange of *mysterium* and *sacramentum*, and with the use of both words for things such as texts of Scripture, other doctrinal expressions of the faith, realities of the life of Christ such as the Incarnation and Passion, as well as for the rites of the Church, one is still in a world of thought and language that can be shared comfortably by pastors and theologians from the Greek and other Oriental Churches. Generally speaking, the Churches of the East have remained with that kind of thinking (Ware, ch. 14). However, whereas the Greeks had only one word (*mustērion*) to deal with, the Latins had two. Almost inevitably one of them came to be favoured when it became necessary to talk specifically about the rites, and this was the word that was made to carry the kind of sharpened thinking required by the doctrinal controversies about the rites that bothered the Western Church in the fourth and fifth centuries. That was *sacramentum*. *Mysterium* came to be used more particularly for the doctrinal expressions of the realities of salvation and for the realities themselves in so far as they were thought about in faith (as in 'mystery of the Trinity' or 'mysteries of Christ'). The distinction came about quite gradually. Indeed the equivalence and interchangeability of the two words was never quite lost in Latin theology. It is periodically re-employed (as in the theology associated with Vatican II), and with great profit for the life of the Church.

The controversies that led to the technical development of *sacramentum* occurred mainly in the Church of North Africa, which, in Tertullian, provided the first evidence of its use. By the end of the fourth century the Church of North Africa had been divided for more than a hundred years by disagreements about the nature of the Church and contrasting views about the ecclesial value of baptisms, ordinations and eucharists celebrated by sinners (for the different phases of the dispute see Kelly, pp. 200–211, 409–417; for Cyprian's use of *sacramentum* see Navickas).

The origins of the debate can be seen already in Tertullian. He adopted the Montanist position that only the saints (*pneumatici*) formed the true Church and so only they could truly baptize. This touched issues of pastoral decision as well as of teaching. What should be done about people who came to the Church from heretical or schismatic churches in which they had already been baptized, ordained, admitted to the Eucharist? What if they had been admitted to these rites but had never renounced a sinful life? Or what if they had betrayed the faith under persecution? Should they be baptized again, ordained again? And if so why? It was a question of whether the Church could recognize as sacraments rites performed by sinners. St Cyprian thought the negative position was more reasonable, and claimed to have the support of seventy-one of his brother bishops from North Africa. But his reasoning went against the tradition of the Church, which, as his contemporary Pope St Stephen reminded him, was the decisive argument in such matters (relevant texts in Palmer, pp. 112–113; ND 1401).

One can recognize in Cyprian's reasoning something of the protest of the prophets that rites that were not all of a piece with life made nonsense of the covenant of God. But his logic owes more to the old than to the new covenant. Paul saw the incongruity between the behaviour of the Corinthians and their celebration of the Lord's Supper. But because he believed that the Eucharist celebrated a covenant made in the body and blood of Christ he could not conclude that the rites of the Corinthians were empty. The body of Christ was there, and they were it, if they would but discern the reality. Fortunately Cyprian did not push his logic to the limits that Tertullian did. His ecclesiological instinct, if not his theory, was sound enough to keep him from the puritan hypothesis of the Church as a community of saints. But others who took up the same issue later were not so discreet. Out of a controversy about the ordination of a certain Caecilian as Bishop of Carthage in 311 came a new, Montanist-type teaching about the Church and its rites, and a schism that deeply divided the Church in North Africa. The schismatic groups, who were named Donatists after Donatus, one of their principal exponents, based their teaching on the view that the Church was a community of saints which had no place for sinners. Hence rites performed by sinners were not really of the Church and could not be sanctifying. Converted sinners should be baptized into the Church of the saints, i.e. the Donatist Church, whether or not they had already been baptized by and into another Church. The scandal of lives that were not in accordance with Christian rites and words, and the scandal of rites and words that did not seem to produce effects of holiness in the lives of people, were thus eliminated, at least theoretically. The sinners who came from another Church had simply never been baptized or ordained and their Eucharist was not of Christ.

The Donatist theory must have been attractive for people who were serious about their Christianity, serious about Christian rites, serious about the demands of being in the Church. Yet it went against something that lay deep in the Christian tradition of practice and teaching. Optatus of Milevis did much to expound orthodox teaching on the subject (Kelly, pp. 411–412; texts of Optatus in Palmer, pp. 115–119). But it was Augustine who brought the full catholic tradition to light and, in doing so, gave *sacramentum* technical refinements that have remained with it ever since.

Augustine does not yet reserve the word 'sacrament' for the rites of the Church. Scripture, the Creed, the sign of the cross, the Lord's Prayer and many other sacred things are still sacraments in his language. But he does begin to look more carefully at what the word means when applied to the major rites of the Christian faith. He uses the anthropological idea of sign (*signum*) to explain what these things called sacraments are, and shows how that fits them into the normal psychological and pedagogical procedures of human life (his idea of sign can be gleaned from, among other places, *Letters* 54 and 55 *Ad Januarium*, 98 *Ad Bonifatium*, 138 *Ad Marcellinum* [PL 33]; *De Doctrina Christiana* 3, 13 [PL 34]; *Contra Faustum* tom. 19, nn. 12–14, 17 [PL 42]; *De Civitate Dei* 1.10, c. 6, 20 [PL 41]). A sign is always a sign of some 'thing' (*res* in Latin). The Platonic strain in Augustine's thinking comes into play here. Behind the visible, tangible world of human experience lies the world of invisible reality, the world that is truly real. Our world of the senses is full of signs and images of 'the real thing'. Christian rites are part of this arrangement. One has to look behind them to discover the thing they signify. This was, of course, something that the tradition had been wanting to say about them by calling them mysteries and sacraments. Augustine has many ways of describing the reality that is signified by the Christian rites, but ultimately they all come to saying that the reality is Christ. If he says it is the Passion and resurrection it is because these are actions (mysteries) of Christ; if he says it is the Church it is because the Church is the whole Christ, head and members; if he says it is grace it is because grace is the life of Christ, the head, given to his members.

That the reality (*res*) signified by a sacrament is Christ is the heart of Augustine's understanding of what it means to call the rites of the Church by that name. It is also the heart of his answer to the Donatists. The rites are what they are, are what the word 'sacrament' says they are, because Christ is in them, because the Church is in them, because grace is in them. This is what is given by ministers of the sacraments and what is received by members of the Church. Augustine explains how ministers and believers give and are given life by being caught up in the sanctifying, Christ-forming, Spirit-filling power of the sacraments. But because of the Donatist controversies he has to think about sacramental celebrations in which this does not happen. Ministers of churches that are in heresy or schism are sinners, cut off themselves from the life of grace. People who receive sacraments in these churches are sinners and do not receive the sanctification of grace. Not alone are they sinners but they sin in celebrating the sacraments unworthily. And there are other sins of which ministers and participants can be guilty besides heresy and schism. But whatever it is, the sin of ministers or participants does not destroy the reality of Christ that is in the rite. Provided it is properly celebrated the rite remains a sign of the reality of salvation. It remains a sacrament. (Relevant texts of Augustine in Palmer, pp. 119–129.)

Obviously, it would be easier to believe that a rite is a real sacrament if one could explain that even people who are not sanctified are still somehow affected by it. Augustine works out a theory on this point which explains the effects of Baptism in a way that justifies the practice of not rebaptizing converts from other churches, which the Catholics were defending against the Donatists. It is a theory that has had a lasting effect on the theological understanding of sacrament. He takes up the biblical image of 'seal' that the Fathers of East and West had been using to talk about Christian initiation. Paul had said that Christians were sealed by the Holy Spirit (2 Cor 1:22; Eph 1.13–14; 4:30). They were marked, set apart for the life that was in them through the gift of the Spirit. To be sealed in this way was to be made like Christ, because the Father had also set his seal on him (John 6:27). A seal is an identifying mark, a sign of ownership, a setting-apart or consecration for special purposes. The original Latin meaning of *sacramentum* conveyed much the same idea. In describing Baptism as a sacrament the Christian tradition was saying that it marked people out, consecrated them as Christians, and did so as a kind of visible sign. It was this Christian marking that Augustine seized on to explain how the baptism of a sinner could have some real effect. Once the minister made the appropriate sign and the participant entered freely and intentionally into it, he or she was 'signed, sealed and delivered' for Christ, whether or not they were repenting and having their sins forgiven. They had really received a sacrament of Christ, even if they had not begun to live like Christ. That sign of belonging to Christ would remain with them. If they did later repent of their sins and begin to live in Christ it would be the effect of the sacrament they had already received. They would not need to be baptized again. (See Galot, pp. 36–41.)

The way of thinking about the effects of a sacrament that Augustine developed in his controversy with the Donatists about Baptism is also applied by him to Ordination and Confirmation (texts in Palmer, pp. 125–126). It becomes, with some adjustments for the other sacraments, an integral part of the sacramental theory that the Western Church inherited from him. Enlightening and necessary as are the distinctions he made about the effects of a sacrament, they carry a risk. If a sacrament can stand even when its life-giving effects are not being received by the participant, the possibility is opened up of justifying the making of a sacrament for reasons other than its life-giving effect on the participant. Or, at least in the case of a sacrament that cannot be repeated, one may be tempted to take a chance: if it does not sanctify the participant now it may do so later. There is in the theory a risk of detaching the sacraments from life and of countenancing a certain formalism in ritual. It is a risk that was not always avoided by those who took over Augustine's teaching in the Middle Ages and subsequently.

There is, however, another essential element in the sacramental theory of Augustine that greatly minimizes the risk of separating rite and life. It is the attention he gives to *word* in relation to the sacramental rite. Augustine lived in a Church that still celebrated many adult baptisms (including his own!) and prepared people for them with an elaborate catechumenate. The word of preaching and instruction enfolded the rite. It is also at the core of the sacramental sign. In a famous passage from his *Treatise on the Gospel of John* (80, 3: text in Palmer, p. 127) he explains how it is the word that gives an element such as water its power to cleanse in Baptism. This joining of word and element, in a single sign, makes the sacrament to be a kind of visible word (which, in the context of this passage, relates it for Augustine to the joining of Word and flesh in the incarnation). The spoken word makes a sacrament, not because of its sound or its obvious meaning, but because it expresses faith, the faith of the Church and of the one receiving the sacrament. The word expressed in the Scriptures, the Creed, the preaching and catechesis of the Church is all of a piece with the prayers and formulas that are spoken in the rites. All these words breathe life into the rites and relate the rites to the real life of Christians. They do it, ultimately, because in them is the Word of God in person. He is the reality that gives all these words of faith, and particularly the sacramental words that go along with the element, their life-giving power.

2.6   THE SCHOLASTICS AND ST THOMAS AQUINAS

By the end of the twelfth century a need for pastoral discernment, backed by a growing theological consensus, brought the Latin Church to recognize that seven of its rites had a special status, and that what was believed about that status could be expressed by saying that they, and they only, were sacraments. The theological consensus about seven sacraments was given authoritative expression during the twelfth century in the *Sentences* of Peter Lombard. The doctrine was included in the 'Profession of Faith of Michael Palaeologus' formulated by the Second Council of Lyons in 1274 (ND 28). Such a development supposed that the word 'sacrament' had a special meaning when applied to these seven rites. Mediaeval theologians set about synthesizing and refining the Augustinian definitions of the word so that it would express what was peculiar to these rites, and to nothing else in the same way. That produced more precise thinking and language about the rites as sacraments. It also, of course, carried the risk of separating these seven rites from the wider context of symbolic activity and proclamation of the word that was always in the mind of Augustine when he used the word 'sacrament'.

Thomas Aquinas had a determining influence on how the Middle Ages dealt with the Augustinian tradition and handed it on in the Church. In his treatment of the sacraments in the *Summa Theologiae* (IIIa, qq. 60–90) he holds fast to Augustine's idea that sacraments are signs. Some of his contemporaries were afraid that sign was too thin an idea to convey the full realism and power that the tradition saw in the sacraments, and were looking to the ideas of cause (of grace) for a more reliable definition. Thomas, however, chooses sign as the defining feature of sacraments (q. 60). His understanding of sign, although basically Augustinian, has more Aristotelianism than Platonism in it. It is a little more intellectualist than mystical: the word that is part of the rite is a word of meaning more than of shadowy symbolism, and the whole rite offers and calls for instruction. For Thomas the reality signified in the sacrament is sacred and mysterious, but the sign itself should make sense.

Thomas does a careful analysis of how the life of grace comes from sacraments (q. 62). He takes the fact that it does so as a given of the tradition and tries to understand how it does so. He uses the technical categories of causality, particularly of principal and instrumental causality, to explain how God could use something like a sacrament to give divine life to humans. He does not lose sight of his definition of sacrament as sign in this analysis. It is in signifying that the rite causes grace (*Sacramenta significando causant: De Veritate*, 27, 4 ad 13). God reveals his grace in the sacrament as he gives it. Thus the sacrament gives form and finality to grace as well as giving it existence (q. 62, a. 2). This means he cannot lose sight of the Christ-centredness of sacraments. Christ is the principal embodiment of grace (IIIa, qq. 7–8). He gives it its primary form. Sacraments are signs of Christ — of the paschal mystery of his death, of the grace that comes from him into our life on earth, and of the glory he promises when he comes again (q. 60, 3). It is the Passion of Christ that gives the sacraments their meaning as well as their life-giving power (IIIa, 60, 5). The identification of these causalities, operating in a sign, allows Thomas to explain the personal factors that come into play in the making of a sacrament (q. 64). A sacrament is an act of God (a. 1 and 2), an act of Christ (a. 3 and 4), an act of the Church acting through its ministers (a. 5–10), and none the less for all that (indeed, because of it) it is a grace-act of the participant. This co-ordination of causalities can be described as Thomas's attempt to put some reasonable order into the many different things that the tradition had been wanting to say about the rites of the Church by calling them mysteries and sacraments. (He connects the *mysteries* of the Incarnate Word with the *sacraments* of the Church in IIIa, 60, prol.)

One of the most creative parts of Thomas's theology of sacrament is what he has to say about character (q. 63). Under pressure from the Donatists, Augustine had come to the conclusion that sacraments can have an effect even when they do not give grace, and had used the idea of seal to express his thinking. Thomas is able to develop Augustine's thinking about the seal without the pressure of any polemic and to use it to clarify important ecclesiological and Christological features of the rites called sacraments. Three of the sacraments, Baptism, Confirmation, Ordination, give a spiritual mark or seal, which he calls character. The Latin *character* transliterates a Greek word which the patristic tradition had already associated with the seal. It means something like 'exact reproduction of' — which is what a seal often was. The Fathers noted that in Hebrews 1:3 Christ is said to be the 'character of the Father's substance' (RSV: 'the very stamp of his nature'). As Christ is the likeness of the Father, so Christians are stamped, sealed with the likeness of Christ by the Holy Spirit: they bear his character.

The character given by sacraments is itself, in the mind of Thomas, a qualification for giving and receiving sacraments. The idea of qualification, or power, has to be seen in the sphere of sign-making activity, since to make a sacrament is to make a sign. It takes qualified people to make effective signs (it takes a policeman to stop traffic with the wave of a hand!). Since the principal cause of the effectiveness of sacraments is God, the power given in the character is instrumental. It enables people to act as God's instruments, either for their own benefit (qualifying them to receive the grace of the sacrament) or for the benefit of others (qualifying them to give grace to others). This giving and receiving of grace is for our justification and the taking-away of our sins. But as it occurs in a sacramental rite, it is also, says Thomas, an act of worship (*cultus*). The signs in which grace is given and received are cultic signs. The character, as a power to make these signs in the Church, is a power to set up and partake of sacramental worship. At this point Thomas is bringing to light something of what the tradition of faith meant by calling the rites of the Church mysteries/sacraments. The rites are, in a term made famous by Odo Casel, 'cult-mysteries'. The death and resurrection of Christ that they embody is simultaneously the source of life for the whole of creation and the worship of God from the whole creation. Because the rites are of Christ they are grace-filled and worship-filled, and they could not be one without the other. In presenting the character as a power to make signs of Christian worship Thomas takes theological reflection beyond any kind of merely *ad hoc* answer to Donatism and makes it carry a profound truth about a full Christian sacrament. This worship side of sacrament is as much a point of identification with Christ for the Christian as is its grace-giving side. Since the only worship now acceptable to God is that of Christ the Priest, Thomas presents the character as a sharing in the priestly power of Christ (IIIa, 63, 3).

The character thus understood is also a point of identification with the Church as Body of Christ. The Church is a communion of those who live in the grace that Christ, the Head, gives to his Body. At the same time it is the community of those who live institutionally together on earth in the profession of faith and the celebration of sacraments. In presenting the character as a qualification to make those signs of faith that are sacraments Thomas is saying that they make people to be members of the sacramental, institutional Church. Ecclesiology was not a distinctive theological issue for Thomas. But clearly his idea of the character is his way of expressing at one and the same time a deeply ecclesiological view of sacraments and a deeply sacramental view of the Church. He does not lose sight of what Augustine had to assert against the Donatists. The Church continues to be the visible Body of Christ even when some of her members are not living in the grace of Christ. The characters are given, and work, even when the persons who have them are not in grace. They work because they are sacramental sharings in the power of Christ, who is always present in and for his Church. What Augustine defended about particular sacraments against the Donatists is true of the whole character-built Church. This is Thomas's way of accounting for what the tradition meant when it called the whole Church a sacrament.

Word continues to be inseparable from *rite* in Thomas's thinking about sacrament. His somewhat intellectualist conception of sign already inclines him to see the sacramental rite as a word, and he regularly refers to the instructive value of sacraments. But he also notes that sacraments require instruction (e.g. q. 71, a. 1 on Baptism). He has a strong sense of the biblical typology inherent in sacraments and gives explicit attention to it in studying individual sacraments (Baptism in q. 70 *passim*; Confirmation in q. 72, 2; Eucharist in q. 73, 6). But his most formal attention is given to the sacramental words spoken at the core of the rite. He sees them as a spiritual (i.e. intelligible) factor that gives precision to the significance of the material element or action. It is in this sense, on the level of signification, that he adopts the terminology 'matter' and 'form' for the element and word that come together to make a sacrament. The element or action has a soft, open, human signification that would work in any number of ways: in this it has something like the openness that is characteristic of prime matter. The words draw out of this openness a precise Christian signification: in this they have something like the existentially determining rôle that form has in relation to matter. Like Augustine, Thomas insists that the sacramental word is a word of faith. Faith recognizes in it the personal Word of God, and it is this Word who gives power to the sacramental words (IIIa, q. 66, 5 and 3). The faith in the Word that the Church professes in its sacramental word is the same faith that it professes in its Scriptures and its Creeds, and that is communicated in its preaching and teaching. In the rite the believer is carried by all these words to the reality of the life of God that is given in the Word made flesh. (For a critique of Thomas's teaching on word and sacrament see Rahner, 'Introductory Observations . . .', p. 152.)

The *life* that Thomas sees coming from the Word in sacraments is the life of grace, virtues and gifts. Thomas puts his treatment of sacraments at the very end of his theology (only the general resurrection remains to be dealt with after sacraments). Methodologically, this means that he wants to see the sacraments as the ultimate, historical realization of the whole process of God's work of creation and self-giving and the moral response in which humans receive that gift. The *Summa* is an exploration of the mystery of God as he is the origin of all things and as he brings all things back to himself in love. Thomas's concern to maintain the sense of this two-fold theological movement, from God and to God, can be seen in his analysis of sacraments as simultaneously sanctification (from God) and worship (to God). It is in this sense, too, that his theology of grace, as sovereignly efficacious gift of God which is at the same time free moral choice of humans, finds its existential verification in sacraments: they are, at one and the same time, life-giving acts of God for humans and moral decisions of humans to live for God. As such they bring into play the whole earthly striving towards happiness of men and women, as humans and as Christians — all that is involved in the life of grace, virtues and gifts. But sacraments add something essential to that life (q. 62, a. 2). Life for God has certain critical moments in its continuous development which are specially graced by God by being sacramentalized. By that very fact the whole life of grace, virtues and gifts — the whole return of the creature to God — is inserted into Christ and into his Body which is the Church. In the theology of St Thomas, when one has fully understood what the sacraments are there is nothing more that needs to be thought about except the resurrection!

2.7   REFORMATION AND THE COUNCIL OF TRENT

The tradition of faith carried by the word 'sacrament' is alive and well in the theology of St Thomas. It is presented in a new analytical way, and with some new technical concepts, as part of a systematic theology. The other great original Scholastic theologians did the same kind of thing. Their views are not always those of Thomas, but one recognizes in them the same basic tradition of faith. However, the very technicality of the Scholastic theology of the sacraments and the new elements in its vocabulary can hide its continuity with the tradition. And it has shorthand phrases that can easily become jargon, pithy principles that can easily become clichés. Movements to renew sacramental theology have been tempted to think that they have to shake off the whole Scholastic analysis of sacrament if they are to recover the tradition.

The Reformers of the sixteenth century certainly believed they had to rescue the faith of the Church about sacraments from Scholasticism. But it is well to know what kind of theology of sacraments the Reformers were hearing from Scholasticism. It was, in fact, a quite decadent version of what had been worked out by Thomas and others in the creative period of mediaeval theology. In one sense the seeds of decadence were already there at the time of Thomas. They were in the sacramental practice of the time, which was already becoming ritualistic and losing touch with the language and symbols and feelings of real life (Jung-mann, pp. 77–100). New devotional and even sociological concerns were having their effect on sacramental practice. By the late Middle Ages liturgical decadence had become even more pronounced. The better Scholastic theory was used by Church authorities to try to correct abuses and to give direction to practice. But at the same time the theory was being pushed along certain eccentric lines in an attempt to make some sense of the practice. It was still accepted that the sacramental rites should have a bearing on life, and that sacramental doctrine and preaching should be a word that would explain the connection with life and promote it. But the life that the rites were being related to was an increasingly strange mixture of traditional Christian values, new devotional forms, superstitions, and socio-religious concerns of a world that was going through major convulsions like the Black Death, the discovery of the New World and a cultural Renaissance. A new word came to be spoken, in order to provide some explanation of how Christian rites might be connected with this life. It used jargon and clichés abstracted from Scholasticism, without the sensitivity of the early Scholastics to the balance of the tradition. For example, if people were baptized indiscriminately, and Jews forcibly so, the practice was justified on the grounds that sacraments were necessary for salvation and produced their effects *ex opere operato* (see below): a splash of water administered simultaneously with the appropriate form of words was guaranteed to get anyone into heaven, and indeed was the only such guarantee that existed. Baptism on those terms was certainly connected with life. It was believed to give the life of Christ that is proclaimed in the Gospel. But it was also thought to be effective for promoting a particular form of society. It was easier to manage citizens when they were all baptized into the same Church and subject to its discipline. The way the necessity of Baptism for salvation was understood gave a religious reason for treating those who were not baptized (particularly Jews) as dangerous dissidents; and it added a religious motivation to the ambitions of colonial conquest. The theory about Baptism came to reflect these social concerns, and the sermons of the time have their stories about the wonderful *ex opere operato* effects of Baptism on converts from Judaism and paganism. The controlling word from the Scriptures and the patristic tradition was not always able to make itself heard among these stories from contemporary life.

Something similar was happening with the Eucharist. For example, men were being ordained to the priesthood in numbers that had little relationship to the traditional ministerial needs and structures of ecclesial communities but very much relationship to the contemporary desire of people to have as many Masses as possible said for the living and the dead. Elements of the general Scholastic theory of sacrament and of its theology of the Eucharist were used to justify this practice. The Eucharist thus understood played a major part in the life of people and of society. But it was not quite the place the scriptural and patristic tradition had given the rite. For example, the theory was much less persuasive about the need for actually eating the bread and drinking the cup in the Eucharist than it was about the value of looking at the consecrated host at the elevation (Jung-mann, pp. 90–92). Stories were told about how looking at the host affected one's life, and a theory was ready to explain how that could be so. The economic consequences of this way of practising and thinking about the Eucharist were considerable: the Mass stipend and the giving and receiving of indulgences were a much more important part of life than the paying and collecting of taxes in a society in which religious faith and the afterlife were taken so seriously.

Nobody is very surprised nowadays that when the Reformers, like the prophets of old, began to speak up against all that they found decadent in the Church they vented a lot of their wrath on everything that the word 'sacrament' seemed to stand for in mediaeval theology. They castigated the way sacraments were practised and ridiculed the theory that patronized the practice. They wanted to liberate the Church from an understanding of sacrament that they found incompatible with the life of grace that God is giving to his people in the new covenant. This life is a gift of God, given in his word of promise, realized in Christ who takes away our sins, and experienced in faith by those who accept the word of promise that is fulfilled in Christ. It is the word, accepted in faith, that justifies and gives life. No human works can take away sin and give life. As the Reformers understood it, the Scholastic theory seemed to be purveying sacraments as works that contain and give grace literally 'by the work worked' (*ex opere operato*). This was to claim for them something that only the word of promise, received in faith, can do. It would seem to make them a kind of alternative to the word. The distinction between word and rite, which was an obvious fact of life, was being turned into a distinction between word and sacrament (whereas in the tradition the sacramentality of the rite was guaranteed by the word). Catholics, it could be thought, were for sacraments while Protestants were for the word.

Protestants, of course, retained some rites, and continued to call them sacraments. Baptism and the Lord's Supper were so clearly required by the Scriptures that the Reformers could not but find a place and a meaning for them in Christian life. The word 'sacrament' was so well established among the early Fathers that only the most radical among the Reformers were prepared to abandon it. So the task was to rethink the meaning of the word as a term for those Christian rites that were given in the Scriptures. With some appeal to Augustine and other Fathers, sacrament was taken to mean sign. But what the rites are signs of is not something contained within themselves but the promise contained in the word of God: they are pledges added to the word of God, as a kind of visible guarantee that God is faithful to his promise. They can also be made useful to the believer as a sign of his or her faith in the promise. So the sacraments accompany the grace of justification. But what justifies is the word of promise received in faith, not the sacrament. On this understanding, sacraments of the New Law function no differently from those of the Old. All the difference is in the word that they guarantee, which in the new covenant is a word already fulfilled in Christ.

In putting word right at the centre of sacrament, the Reformers made a powerful bid to make the rites authentic acts of Christian life. The biblical word dominated the rite in the liturgical practice of the Reformers: it was read, it was preached about, it was inculcated as the moral norm of living. Only those rites explicitly required by the Scriptures were to be taken as divinely instituted and deserving of the name 'sacrament'. The sacramental words of Baptism and Eucharist, because they were biblical words, were also taken as proclamations and were read aloud, in the language of the people. It was only to the extent that the rite served the word of promise and the word of faith that it had value. The rites were redesigned with this in mind and strenuous efforts were made to bring a living, biblical faith to bear on sacraments. The frequency of celebration was to be measured by the needs and possibilities of this faith. (Selected texts of the Reformers in Palmer, pp. 149–166; liturgies of the Reformers and sacramental thinking that underlies them in B. Thompson and Brilioth.) All this was certainly in line with a basic imperative of the Christian tradition about the necessary interaction of word, rite and life, which was something that the Church badly needed to be reminded about in that age of sacramental decadence. But the price paid for the remembering was the forgetting of, or at least a distraction from, a fundamental element of the tradition that had always been associated with the words 'sacrament' and 'mystery', namely, the guaranteed presence of God, giving life in Christ and the Spirit, in the rites of the Church, and the reality of that presence even when the people making the sacrament were not living in accordance with the rite.

And yet the forgetting was often more a polemical expedient in a debate whose terms had been set by Scholasticism than a real denial. Certain things had to be said, whatever the cost, in order to dislodge the Scholastic theory on the nature of sacrament. But the forgotten elements were remembered in other contexts. Luther took the scriptural words 'This is my body . . . this is the cup of my blood' as being literally true, and therefore saw the Eucharist as a mystery/sacrament that contained the living Christ and gave his life to those who received it. Calvin had a strong sense of the presence of Christ in the Eucharist, at least during the celebration of the sacrament. Baptism was still considered by most of the Reformers to be necessary for salvation and many of them continued to believe that it could save infants who were not yet ready for personal acts of faith. These and other elements of the traditional content of the word 'sacrament' survived the anti-Scholastic polemic and continued to be witnessed to in the sacramental theory and practice of the churches that grew out of the Reformation — even when they did not sit very easily with the idea that sacraments are merely signs of the faith that justifies.

The Council of Trent, in dealing with the challenge of the Reformers, gave the Catholic Church a dogmatic teaching and way of speaking about its rites that dominated subsequent centuries and will always have to be taken seriously when Christians talk about sacraments. The objective of Trent was to reform the Church, and that included reforming its practice of the sacraments. On sacraments the Council believed it had to dissociate itself from many of the reforms initiated by the Protestants and from the thinking that inspired and claimed to justify those reforms. Trent's most-remembered teaching comes in the form of canons that condemn Protestant errors. Since what the Protestants denied was most often a Scholastic formulation of the tradition, the condemnations of Trent are phrased in Scholastic language and draw special attention to those elements of the tradition that were being forgotten by Protestants. There is not much attempt to find common ground with the Protestants — such, for example, as might have been provided by the Augustinian idea of sign. Rather, the differences are accentuated. It is assumed that Catholics affirm what Protestants deny. Catholic doctrine on sacraments comes from Trent, then, with a heavy concentration on what needed to be reaffirmed against Protestant denials, and with little attention to what Catholics and Protestants might have together retained of the tradition. It comes in Scholastic formulations that are careful enough to avoid the banalities of late mediaeval theology (and thus the more obvious Protestant objections), and yet firm enough to draw a line between Catholic and Protestant positions. (Texts of Trent in Palmer, pp. 166–176; good analysis of them throughout Leeming; canons on sacraments in general in ND 1311–1323.)

At the heart of what Trent has to say about sacraments is that they are truly acts of God and of Christ, and that the life that comes from God through Christ and the Spirit is truly in them and is truly given by them — which is something that the words 'mystery' and 'sacrament' had surely meant throughout the Christian tradition. That is expressed in the canons on sacraments in general by saying that they are profoundly different from the sacraments of the Old Law (can. 2), and that they are objectively different from one another (can. 3) because of the particular gift of divine life they contain. This is the basic reason for the statement about the sacraments being necessary for salvation (can. 4), about their containing grace and conferring it *ex opere operato* on those who do not place an obstacle (can. 6 and 8), about conferring it always (can. 7), about imprinting a character (can. 9), about requiring an ecclesially competent minister (can. 10 and 11), even if he is a sinner (can. 12), and about the need to follow approved rites (can. 13). It is the reason why the identification and numbering of sacraments, and the institution by Christ of each of the seven so identified (can. 1), becomes a dogmatic issue (one can only be sure Christ is in them if he has instituted them himself).

2.8   FROM TRENT TO VATICAN II

The teaching of the Council of Trent about sacraments — about the general meaning of sacrament and about each of the seven sacraments — provided the Catholic Church with a word about its rites in the centuries that followed the Council. It marked the word that was spoken in preaching, in catechetical instruction, in theological discourse. It helped very much to make the rites sources and expressions of that renewed life in Christ that the Church could boast of in the Counter-Reformation period. It was a word that echoed the stresses and passions of the Reformation and continued to irritate and probably mislead Protestants. It was a controlled word that tended to limit readings from the Scriptures and the Fathers about the sacraments to what was of apologetical interest. Apart from the rather formal Epistle and Gospel at Mass there was not much reading of the Scriptures in association with the liturgy, nor much biblical preaching. And yet for all its Scholastic dress, one can argue that the Catholic word of Trent preserved the mainstream scriptural and patristic tradition about the rites that the word 'sacrament' stood for, and kept it reasonably close to life. As time went on, the Baroque and the Romantic ages had no great difficulty with the Tridentine word. They moulded it, and they moulded the celebration of the rites to their own peculiar conception of life, and the Catholic tradition more than held its own. Neo-Scholasticism explored the mediaeval theories of sacramentality once again, sometimes with originality, but generally within the Tridentine framework (Leeming is a good representative).

The contemporary Roman Catholic word about sacraments is, however, somewhat different from the Tridentine word. 'Sacrament' today says many things about the rites that were said differently, or not said at all, in Trent and Counter-Reformation theology. The pastoral strategy of Vatican II to promote the relationship of rite to life is rather different from that envisaged by the stern, standardizing discipline of Trent and the papal legislation that implemented the Council. To understand historically how this new word has come to be spoken one would need to look at the evolution of human life, and of Christian thinking about it, over the last century or so. One would need to have some sense of how the experience of being human, and the way of reflecting on it, has changed under the influence of people like Darwin and Freud and Marx. One would need to bear in mind how different internal currents affected the way the Christian churches interpreted modern life in the light of the Gospel word. There was the biblical movement which allowed the Church to recover the original freshness of the inspired word of God in telling the human story as God's story. There was the patristic movement that restored contact with the classical literature and art of the faith that was created during the centuries when cultured Greek and Latin minds had their earliest encounters with the Gospel message. There was the liturgical movement that restored a sense of the richness and diversity of forms of celebration that lay behind the rigid rubrics of current Roman and other liturgies, and gave hope that it was possible once again to adapt liturgy to life. There was the ecumenical movement that opened up the traditions of the different churches to each other, with a readiness to discover what they shared, and what each could say about the fullness and balance of the tradition of faith and liturgical practice. There was the pastoral and missionary movement which took advantage of each of these other movements to explore how the faith and sacraments of the Church could become life-giving for people of the twentieth century.

Each of the movements that marked the Church in the twentieth century had its word to say about sacraments. A theology of sacrament began to emerge which put those words together and analysed them technically with the help of ideas drawn from the great theological and magisterial tradition, as well as new ideas drawn from current philosophy and other areas of theology. What 'sacrament' had come to mean in progressive Catholic theology when Vatican II set about renewing the life of the Church could be fairly described in terms of the work of four major theologians. It could be said to be the product of the restoration of the patristic sense of 'mystery' that will always be associated with Odo Casel, OSB; of the integration of the theology of sacraments in a theology of the entire liturgy, such as one gets from Cipriano Vagaggini, OSB in *Il senso teologico della liturgia* (1957, trans. as *Theological Dimensions of the Liturgy*, 1959); of the powerful demonstration by Karl Rahner, SJ, in his *The Church and the Sacraments* (1963), that underlying the sacramentality of the seven rites, there is a sacramentality of the Church, which allows one to call the Church itself a sacrament (the *Ursakrament*, which is translated 'fundamental sacrament'); of the closely-reasoned synthesis put together by Edward Schillebeeckx, OP in *Christ the Sacrament of Encounter with God* (1963), in which the full richness of the tradition (which Schillebeeckx had studied in detail in an earlier work called *De Sacramentele Heilseconomie*, 1952) is ordered systematically in terms dictated predominantly by the theological method of St Thomas, but also by current personalist thinking.

The word that Vatican II comes to say about the rites of the Church reflects the life-giving movements that had been at work in Christian experience for half a century or more, and the theology that had grown out of and at the same time monitored those movements. It is a word that tries to show how the rites are filled with life: the mysterious life of Christ and the Spirit, on the one hand; the real life and concerns of present-day people, lived in the faith of Christ, on the other. It is a word that states its own continuity with what was said at Trent, and with the Scholastic theology that gave Trent its ideas and language. But, in the style of the theology of the day, it gives body to the geometric jargon of Scholasticism and Trent with the original apostolic freshness of scriptural statements, the classical roundedness of the Fathers and the images and reminiscences of the pre-mediaeval liturgical tradition of East and West. It keeps 'sacrament' as a generic word for the seven rites recognized as such by the Catholic Church, and reaffirms the Tridentine definitions about it. But 'sacrament' is a much richer word in Vatican II than in Trent. As well as being used of the rites, it is also used to describe the rôle of the Church as sign of salvation set up among the nations and instrument by which Christ brings his saving life to the whole universe. This sacramentality attributed to the Church affects, of course, the sacramentality seen in the rites, and their relationship to the Church. The Council also restores scriptural and patristic richness to the word 'mystery', and transmits that to 'sacrament' both by the equivalence it assumes between the two words and by the way it sees the paschal mystery of the death and resurrection of Christ at the heart of all liturgical celebration of Christian sacraments.

2.9   LIFE, WORD AND RITE IN THE TEXTS OF VATICAN II

Vatican II deals most directly with the rites of the Church in its Constitution on the Liturgy, *Sacrosanctum Concilium* (Flannery, pp. 1–36). At the heart of the liturgy it sees the seven rites called sacraments, and among these it singles out the Eucharist for special attention with a separate chapter (ch. 2) entitled *De Sacrosancto Eucharistiae Mysterio*. The other six sacraments are dealt with in the following chapter under the title *De Ceteris Sacramentis et de Sacramentalibus* ('The Other Sacraments and the Sacramentals'). While the term sacrament is applied only to the seven rites recognized as such by the Catholic Church, the idea of sacramentality pervades the whole treatment of the liturgy. Right from the start the liturgy is put in series with 'the mystery of Christ and the real nature of the true Church' (n. 2), and the nature of the Church that the text goes on to expound would be described by contemporary theology as sacramental. If the sacraments are put in series inwardly with the Church and with Christ, they are put in series outwardly with that multitude of ritual practices that are called sacramentals, which brings sacramentality into almost any imaginable area of human life. The conception of sacramentality being employed in the Constitution is one that puts together life, word and rite in a careful balance. The pastoral concern to develop in the Church a liturgy that is filled with life and a Christian life that is nourished by the liturgy is stated in the introductory paragraphs (nn. 1, 2). The theological explanation of how the gift of God is unfolded progressively by word and rite in the Old Testament, in Christ, in the Church ('from the side of Christ came forth the wondrous sacrament of the whole Church') and in the liturgy is given in nn. 5–8; and particularly in n. 7 which explains how the living Christ is present and active with the Church in its liturgy. The life that Christians are expected to live, responding to and participating in the word and rites celebrated in the Church, is described in nn. 9–13. These theoretical statements are followed by an outline and justification of the practical steps that need to be taken in the Church so that Christians can more effectively put their lives into the liturgy and draw life from it (nn. 14–46). If there was ever a suspicion that the Catholic tradition stood for a ritualism that was formal and somehow removed from the real-life situations of God's people, the word of Vatican II in this first chapter of *Sacrosanctum Concilium* should set it to rest.

The belief that word is inseparable from rite in sacramental liturgy is put in various ways in the first chapter of the Constitution. There is an interesting preliminary statement of it in n. 2 that reflects the Council's dominant missionary, but also sacramental, view of what people are in the Church: '. . . it [the liturgy] marvellously increases their power to preach Christ and thus show forth the Church, a sign lifted up among the nations, to those who are outside, a sign under which the scattered children of God may be gathered together until there is one fold and one shepherd'. References to the prophetic word, to the ministry of preaching and teaching, to the reading of Scripture go hand in hand with references to the work accomplished in the flesh of Christ and the rites of the Church in nn. 7–13 (n. 9 is particularly significant on preaching and instruction), while the need to instruct the faithful, and the study required of those who have that responsibility, are highlighted in the statements about liturgical participation in nn. 14–20. The norms for the reform of the liturgy that complete this first chapter, especially those 'Based on the Educative and Pastoral Nature of the Liturgy' (nn. 33–36, but especially n. 35) are full of concern for the word and for its part in making the rites to be life-giving. There is a reference in n. 33 to what Trent has to say about the need for instruction on and within the Eucharist. But the place that Vatican II gives the word in the making of sacraments is much more profound and pervasive than Trent was able to recognize. Vatican II is able to reach out to that part of the tradition about sacrament that was specially patronized by the Reformers, whereas Trent had to be cool about it because the Protestants seemed to make it the only thing that mattered.

With such a conception of the interaction of word and rite the Constitution is able to make this quite sweeping claim about how all human life can be interpenetrated by the sacramental order: 'Thus, for well-disposed members of the faithful the liturgy of the sacraments and sacramentals sanctifies almost every event of their lives with the divine grace which flows from the paschal mystery of the Passion, Death and Resurrection of Christ. From this source all sacraments and sacramentals draw their power. There is scarcely any proper use of material things which cannot thus be directed towards the sanctification of men and the praise of God' (n. 61).

Among other documents of Vatican II that speak of sacraments the Constitution on the Church, *Lumen Gentium* is particularly important (Flannery, pp. 350–426). It develops the sacramental view of the Church noted in *Sacrosanctum Concilium* and explicitly calls the Church the sacrament of salvation (nn. 1, 9, 48). It is 'in Christ' that the Church is a sacrament (n. 1) and it is his life that is manifested and communicated in it. When the Constitution comes to explain how Christ's priestly work is continued among God's People, it does so by an analysis of Christian life that weaves together sacraments and virtues (nn. 10 and 11). The life that people draw from the sacraments is lived out in different areas of moral choice by the appropriate virtues. The life of virtue, in turn, gives human realism to the sacraments, and makes the priestly People to be a witnessing and transforming force in the world — makes them be that very Church that the Constitution calls a sacrament.

The Constitution of Vatican II that speaks most directly about human life, *Gaudium et Spes* (The Church in the Modern World), has quite a lot to say about the Word, but almost nothing about sacraments. There is one striking reference to the Eucharist in a paragraph (n. 38) dedicated to 'Human activity: its fulfilment in the Paschal Mystery'. It reads: 'Christ left to his followers a pledge of this hope and food for the journey in the sacrament of faith, in which natural elements, the fruits of man's cultivation, are changed into His glorified Body and Blood, as a supper of brotherly fellowship and a foretaste of the heavenly banquet'. But a kind of studied reticence seems to be observed in other places where the significance of Christ and the Church in relation to human life is being expounded and one might have expected an explicit reference to the sacraments as well (e.g. nn. 22, 32, 45). Perhaps it is that the theological word on how particular rites of the Church are related to specific experiences of the contemporary world, whose agenda is no longer being set by the Church or even by Christian culture, has yet to be worked out. Certainly, the Vatican Council nowhere offers sacraments as a kind of easy and 'pious' solution to the complex issues of contemporary human life, or encourages any exaggerated confidence in sacraments without evangelization and catechesis. Paul VI stated this more positively after the Council in a passage (n. 47) of *Evangelii Nuntiandi* (1975) that is a fine statement on the relationship between word, rite and life:

> Evangelization exercises its full capacity when it achieves the most intimate relationship, or better still a permanent and unbroken inter-communication, between the Word and the Sacraments. In a certain sense it is a mistake to build a contrast between evangelization and sacramentalization, as is sometimes done. It is indeed true that a certain way of administering the Sacraments, without the solid support of catechesis regarding these same Sacraments and a global catechesis, could end up by depriving them of their effectiveness to a great extent. The role of evangelization is precisely to educate people in the faith in such a way as to lead each individual Christian to live the Sacraments as true Sacraments of faith — and not to receive them passively or to undergo them (ND 1336).

2.10   ECUMENICAL CONVERGENCE ON SACRAMENTS

While the Roman Catholic Church has been filling out its dogmatic word about sacraments with biblical and patristic material, and letting this enriched word become more operative in the celebration of sacraments, the major churches issued from the Reformation have been losing some of their inhibitions about the sacramentality of rites. Along with increased sacramental practice they are developing a teaching that converges with what Catholics are saying about the rites. There are points of doctrine about individual rites that still divide churches, and there is still disagreement about how many rites should be called sacraments, and in what precise sense. But there is a broad area of agreement about sacraments between Catholics, Protestants and Orthodox, and it seems to be growing. An important stage in the convergence is represented by the Lima Document of The World Council of Churches (Faith and Order Paper no. 111) on *Baptism, Eucharist and Ministry* (commonly referred to by the acronym BEM). This document, product of several decades of study and consultation by theologians of the different traditions, has already been received very positively by many churches (see Thurian (ed.), *Responses . . .*). In its official response (sent by the Secretariat for Promoting Christian Unity to the Faith and Order Secretariat in August 1987) the Roman Catholic Church recognizes in BEM much of its own faith about Baptism, Eucharist and Ministry, and much of what it teaches when it calls these rites sacraments. It is to be noted that the word 'sacrament' itself is used rather sparingly in BEM (of Baptism only in n. 23; of Eucharist in nn. 1, 2, 13; of Ministry in nn. 41 and 43). The Catholic response accepts the reticence about the word which 'because of its complex history needs a great deal of explanation in inter-church conversations'. However, it does suggest rather firmly that BEM would have profited from a deeper study of the concept of sacrament and a more well-defined use of the term. Some of the ambiguities found in the text might have been avoided, and the way the rites work and what they do might have been stated more plainly if the thinking about sacrament had been clearer, especially as regards its grounding in ecclesiology.

2.11   THE SACRAMENTS OF BAPTISM, CONFIRMATION AND EUCHARIST

When a theologian sets out to talk about Baptism, Confirmation and Eucharist, he or she will be carrying the weight and the wisdom of the tradition about Christian rites that has been sketched in this chapter. It is a tradition that is bound up with the fortunes of the word 'sacrament'. Most theologians will want to say that Baptism, Eucharist and Ministry are sacraments, and will hope that this can be a useful thing to say about them. Unfortunately the word is no longer useful in the way Tertullian found it useful. For him *sacramentum* was a conventional word, and to use it about a rite of the Church was to use the known to explain the unknown. But by now 'sacrament' has gathered such a richness of meaning to itself that it needs to be explained itself before it can be useful for understanding the rites of the Church. The explanation requires one to look at the tradition that has affected the meaning of the word and to take a stand on what is most consistent and central in it. For Catholic theology, and probably for ecumenically-minded theologians of all the churches, Vatican II may claim to have done a discernment of the tradition that has proved remarkably useful. It has put together the biblical revelation, the patristic tradition, a judicious measure of Scholasticism, the dogmatic teaching of Trent (without its polemical toughness) and ideas developed in contemporary theology by people like Rahner and Schillebeeckx, in a way that has provided a platform for understanding the sacramental economy and the place of individual sacraments within it. Certainly what the Church of Vatican II has done and thought about individual sacraments — the restored rites and the general instructions about them that are presented in the new liturgical books — is hardly intelligible without a general study of the tradition of sacramentality adopted by the Council.

STUDY QUESTIONS

1   Do an exegetical study of the texts in which St Paul uses the word *mustērion*.
2   Select some passages from Origen in which *mustērion* or its derivatives appear; examine the kind of exegesis of biblical texts that may be associated with his use of the word.
3   Study Augustine's teaching on *signum* in his *De Doctrina Christiana*, book 3 (*PL* 34).
4   Read and comment on *Summa Theologiae*, Part IIIa, q. 64, a. 1–2 in the context of a discussion on the institution of sacraments.
5   Study the teaching of Martin Luther on word and sacrament in his *Pagan Servitude of the Church* (*De Captivitate Babylonica*; see Bibliography).
6   Do a comparison between the ordering of questions about sacraments in B. Leeming, *Principles . . .* and E. Schillebeeckx, *Christ the Sacrament . . .* , noting the continuity as well as the differences in treatment.
7   Study the use of 'sacrament' in the Lima Document on *Baptism, Eucharist and Ministry*; compare it with the understanding of *sacramentum* that is expressed in the canons *De Sacramentis in Genere* of the Council of Trent.

FURTHER READING

References to specialized studies on *mustērion* and *sacramentum* in the Fathers can be found in dictionaries and manuals of patrology; patristic and magisterial texts on 'sacrament' in:

P. Palmer, SJ, *Sacraments of Worship. Liturgy and Doctrinal Development of Baptism, Confirmation, and the Eucharist* (London, 1957).

On *mustērion/sacramentum* in writers of the first three centuries (Clement, Origen, Tertullian):

B. Neunheuser, OSB, *Baptism and Confirmation* (New York, 1964), chs 1–4.

On the mystery religions:

H. Rahner, *Greek Myth and Christian Mystery* (trans. from German; London, 1963).

For the mystagogical catecheses:

E. Yarnold, SJ, *The Awe-Inspiring Rites of Christian Initiation. Baptismal Homilies of the Fourth Century* (Slough, 1972).

On the sense of sacramentality in patristic exegesis:

J. Daniélou, SJ, *The Bible and the Liturgy* (trans. from French; Notre Dame, 1965).

On *sacramentum* in St Augustine:

Neunheuser, ch. 5.

Historical material, with distinctive theological interpretation, in:

O. Casel, OSB, *The Mystery of Christian Worship* (trans. from German; London, 1962).

For critique of Casel's position on 'mystery':

L. Bouyer, *Liturgical Piety/Life and Liturgy* (Notre Dame/London, 1956), ch. 7.
I. Dalmais, OP, in A. G. Martimort (ed.), *The Church at Prayer* I: *Principles of the Liturgy* (trans. from French; new ed., Collegeville/London, 1987), pp. 266–271.

On *sacramentum* in the Latin tradition:

J. de Ghellinck, *Pour l'histoire du mot 'Sacramentum'* (Louvain, 1924).
C. Mohrmann, *Latin vulgaire, latin des chrétiens* (Paris, 1952).

On sacraments in Orthodoxy:

T. Ware, *The Orthodox Church* (Harmondsworth, Middx, 1963).

On the Middle Ages and St Thomas:

P. Garland, *The Definition of Sacrament according to St Thomas Aquinas* (Ottawa, 1959).
T. Marsh, 'The Sacramental Character' in *Sacraments*, ed. D. O'Callaghan (Dublin, 1964).
J. Gallagher, *Significando Causant. A Study of Sacramental Causality* (Fribourg, 1965).
L. Walsh, OP, 'Liturgy in the Theology of St Thomas', *The Thomist* 38 (1974), 557–583.

On sacramental theory and practice during the later Middle Ages, read general histories of the liturgy on the period; particularly useful is:

J. A. Jungmann, SJ, *Missarum Sollemnia. The Mass of the Roman Rite* (trans. from German; 2 vols, New York, 1951/55; abridged 1-vol. ed., New York/London, 1959).

On the Reformers' understanding of 'sacrament', particularly with reference to the Eucharist:

Y. Brilioth, *Eucharistic Faith and Practice, Evangelical and Catholic* (trans. from Swedish; London, 1930).
B. Thompson, *Liturgies of the Western Church* (New York, 1962).

The decrees of the Council of Trent on sacraments can be found in:

J. Neuner, SJ and J. Dupuis, SJ (eds), *The Christian Faith in the Doctrinal Documents of the Catholic Church* (= ND; rev. ed., Bangalore, 1982/London, 1983).

The decrees of Trent on sacraments are analysed in relation to Protestant positions, and post-Tridentine developments in Catholic theology are noted in:

B. Leeming, SJ, *Principles of Sacramental Theology* (London, 1956).

On the sacramental theology associated with Vatican II:

D. O'Callaghan (ed.), *Sacraments* (Dublin, 1964).

For an ecumenical sacramental theology:

F. J. van Beeck, *Grounded in Love: Sacramental Theology in an Ecumenical Perspective* (Washington, 1981).

3

A theology of sacrament

Within the tradition of faith detailed in the preceding chapter theology continues to do its systematic thinking about sacraments, listening to and also challenging the workings of the contemporary Christian mind. It must do that within the framework of a general systematic theology. When one talks theologically about sacraments one is bringing into play everything that one knows about God and his plan for the universe, and about the meaning of human life and history. Sacraments are, in fact, the final events in the historical working-out of the relationship between God and humans — the economy of salvation — which is the overall subject of systematic theology. The only thing that remains to happen between God and his People after sacraments is the resurrection. There is a theology of sacraments current in the Church today which has the great merit of situating itself within a deep analysis of the mystery of God and his relationship with the entire creation and its history, which uses a trinitarian Christology that is at the same time deeply sensitive to the humanness of Jesus, and which employs an ecclesiology which sees the community of believers both as gathered together by the grace of Christ and the Spirit and at the same time as mediating that grace to all those who are being saved. It uses the word sacrament on each of these three levels of analysis — theological, Christological, ecclesiological — taking advantage of its analogical elasticity to show how they interpenetrate without confusing them: Christ is the Sacrament of God, the Church is the Sacrament of Christ, and the seven sacraments are different actualizations of the basic sacramentality of the Church. Such a systematic understanding of sacramentality uncovers the deep roots of the unity of the sacramental economy and lets one see each individual sacrament in relation to all the others and to the entire economy.

3.1   CHRIST, THE SACRAMENT OF GOD

In very general terms sacramentality refers to any manifestation in a sign of the mystery of God's life — the giving of it by God and the receiving of it by humans. It denotes the simultaneous manifestation and realization of the gift of God, the telling of it that is also the doing of it, the invitation to divine life that has already within it the response. It occurs most perfectly in Christ. He is the Word of God made flesh, who does not just speak for God but is God; he is and does what he says. He is also the perfect human response to God, his Father: he accepts the design of God in obedience and does what he is told to do. He preached the message of salvation from God and gave his life for it on the cross. When God approved him by raising him from the dead he became in his body the full human manifestation of divine life and the perfect possessor of it. He lives to make intercession for us, expressing and making his own our need and desire for salvation. At the same time he is the giver of the gift of God because he is established in power with the Father as the sender of the Spirit. He is, for all these reasons, the primordial Sacrament of God.

As soon as one says that Christ is *the* Sacrament of God one is already bound to say that all other sacramentality is derived from him and draws its power from him. During his life on earth he gathered around him people who would always remember him, and in that remembering carry his salvation throughout time and place. He gave his disciples words and rituals for remembering. When he made his death on the cross to be the expression of his total dedication to the Father he also made the ritual memorials of his death, which would be celebrated by his disciples, to be expressions of his dedication. He adopted them as expressions of his wish to make his death salvific for all those who would remember him in faith. Christ carried this human decision about his death and about every ritual remembering of it into the timelessness of his glorification. It is what allows him to be personally present to every ritual celebration that those who believe in him do in memory of him. In that personal presence his humanness is the instrument of the divine act that gives salvation.

3.2   THE CHURCH, SACRAMENT OF CHRIST

The memory of the risen Christ is kept alive, by word and rite, in the community of believers founded on his apostles. In telling the story of Christ as vouched for by the apostles and in performing the rites given by the apostles in memory of him, the members of the Church make him present throughout time and space somewhat as his personal body made him present to those who saw and heard and touched him during his days on earth and in the event of the resurrection. In Paul's terms, they become his body. The Church itself is very much a matter of 'bodies'. It is not some kind of impersonal administrative institution but real people of flesh and blood who tell the story and do the rites. They each have their own personal story which they work into the story of salvation; it is the crucial moments of their lives that give point to the rites that are celebrated. In the rites they identify their own story with the story of Christ and their own life-experience with his. Those who look at such a community can hear and see Christ in the lives of its members, and specifically in their words that speak about him and their rites that celebrate him; and they can feel the power of his person. The prophetic, priestly and kingly rôles that Christ fulfils in his own person for the salvation of the world are shared by this community. That is why it can be called the Sacrament of Christ.

In this community Christ is both received and given in a visible way, as befits a sacrament. The Church is both the gathered community of the saved and the gathering community of those who bring salvation ('the Church . . . in its entirety is at the same time both community of the redeemed and the redeeming institution': Schillebeeckx, *Christ the Sacrament* . . . , p. 58; see Congar, *The Mystery of the Church*, pp. 110ff.). The receiving is the most important and lasting reality of the Church as sacrament, but the giving has a certain logical priority. The community goes out to seek its members. The giving of Christ in the Church is made possible by a series of ministries, both of the prophetic and of the priestly kind, which carry an authority that comes from the kingly power of Christ. All members of the Church are authorized to do the giving in some form or other. Through Baptism and Confirmation they have a special relationship with Christ that qualifies them to act and be seen to act in his name. Some ministries are reserved to the ordained and the community can only be recognized as the body of Christ when it enjoys the special conformity to Christ that the ordained bring to it. But ultimately it is the receiving of grace that builds up the community in the likeness of Christ. Without the receiving the Church would not be the body of Christ. It would not be his Sacrament. The giving will end when he comes again, but the receiving will last forever. The ministerial Church, with its equipment of sacramental characters and prophetic gifts and pastoral powers, is for the time of waiting; the grace-filled Church, united by and in love, is forever.

Nevertheless, the sacramentality of the Church is consistent with a certain independence of the giving of grace from its receiving. While the objective containing and showing-forth of the grace of Christ that is really being lived by people is the full sacramentality of the Church, the ability to go on doing that even when the lives of individual members of the Church, and particularly those called to be ministers of word and rite, are not fully Christian is an indispensable feature of it. During the time of waiting for the final coming of Christ members of the Church may be unfaithful to his grace. But because Christ has brought them into a special relationship with himself when he called them to be prophets, priests and kings in his Church, and to some specific ministries in it, they can go on acting in his name even when they are not living in his grace. His fidelity to his choice is stronger than the vacillations of those he has chosen. Contemporary theology uses some ideas taken from the traditional theology of the sacramental character, and its distinction from sacramental grace, to express this feature of the Church in sacramental terms. It is not just in the performance of its rites but in its entire prophetic, priestly and kingly life that the Church is recognized as having a power to make Christ present and visible that can function even when those who are exercising it are not fully living in Christ. In such a theology the objective reliability of individual sacraments and their independence of the holiness of the minister can be seen as a particular instance of something that is part of the very nature of the Church.

3.3   SACRAMENT AND WORD

Sacramentality pervades the entire life of the Church. It is not helpful to restrict it to the area of Church rites, although it is realized in a special way in them. Everything about the Church, including its preaching and teaching, is sacramental in the sense already explained. The distinction that came to be made in theology between word and sacrament has sometimes given the impression that these are separate, almost alternative ways of access to grace. Contemporary theology insists on their complementarity. What needs to be remembered is that the distinction sacrament/word does not correspond exactly to the distinction rites/words. The distinction between rite and word is descriptive: there are rites in the life of the Church and there are also words. The distinction between sacrament and word, on the other hand, is a theological analysis that invites separate consideration of two essential aspects of the reality of the Church, which are present together wherever the Church exists. The sacramentality of the Church is realized through the interaction of words and rites. It is realized in the rites and it is realized in the words as well. The rites of the Church would not be sacraments without the words that are part of them and that surround them as preaching, teaching and celebration. The words are sacramental because they are directed towards the rites, are made concrete and tangible in them, are confessed and celebrated in them. The rites take on the character of word because they embody the Word and the words that he speaks through and with them — as the actions of his flesh gave concreteness to the word of life that he was and spoke. They combine with the words to make the whole Church be word — that embodied word that originally took flesh in the concrete historical reality of Christ. Word, then, is not an alternative to sacrament, because it is itself sacramental through its association with the rites of the Church. Sacrament is not a refuge from word because rites are only sacraments by embodying the word. Sacrament and word, then, express two aspects of the life of the Church. The first is affirmed particularly, but not exclusively, by the concreteness of its rituals, the second by the fluency of its words.

3.4   BAPTISM AND EUCHARIST

From Christ, who is the Sacrament of God, through the Church, which is the Sacrament of Christ, are derived the ritual actions and words that are called sacraments in the Church. From a systematic point of view they are sacraments because they are particular realizations of the sacramentality of the Church, and therefore of Christ. Because of that rootedness in Christ and the Church they are intimately connected with one another. Reasons can be given for the connections. They form part of the theology of each individual sacrament.

Logically and historically the first two sacraments of the Church are Baptism and Eucharist. They are the two rites in which, from the very beginning, the Church has expressed itself and drawn people into membership of itself and thus into Christ. There is no Church without them. The Eucharist is the fullest expression of the sacramentality of the Church. As a festive taking of food it is, from the human point of view, the ultimate ritual celebration of life — of having it and growing in it and anticipating its consummation in the eternal now of God. It has Christ, the source of life, present in it in the fullest possible way — in the community of those gathered in his name by and under those to whom he has entrusted the apostolic ministry, in the word about him which is read from beginning to end (whereas in other rites only special passages are read) and comprehensively preached, in the bread and wine which are proclaimed to be the body and blood in which he consummates his sacrifice and gives life to the world, and in the Spirit who gathers all who share the one bread and wine into the one body of Christ.

Yet the Church cannot have the sacrament of the Eucharist without the sacrament of Baptism. Life has a beginning, and the Eucharist does not ritualize that beginning. To be in the Church one has to leave the world of sin and escape from the power of the devil, and the Eucharist does not ritualize that original deliverance. Being in Christ means passing with him from death to life, and the Eucharist does not ritualize that passage. It is Baptism that ritualizes these different aspects of the crucial moment of life's beginning. It gives people their original Christian existence and identity and inaugurates their membership of the Church. It does so, however, not as an end in itself but in view of the Eucharist. Baptism is a once-for-all beginning. The life that it inaugurates is for growing and for ever. Baptism expresses that, not in itself but in its movement towards the Eucharist. The Eucharist is a rite of the continual nourishment and growth and consummation of life: it brings together the community in which life is fostered; it tells the complete story of the community in an authoritative word of God which gives life meaning and direction; it contains the body and blood of Christ which is the food of life; and it anticipates the banquet of heaven which is the possession of eternal life. Without its relationship to the Eucharist Baptism would not measure up to the full sacramentality of the Church. Thus, the liturgical and doctrinal tradition sees the Eucharist as completing the process of Christian initiation begun in Baptism. One is not fully a Christian until one has taken part in it for the first time. It is only after First Communion that one is ready to live Christian life to the full and to take one's ongoing part in making the Church be the body of Christ.

3.5 CONFIRMATION

In the Catholic and Orthodox traditions the process of Christian initiation has another rite besides Baptism and Eucharist that is recognized as a sacrament. This is what is called Chrismation in the East and Confirmation in the West. Something like it is also found in the Protestant tradition; but it is not thought helpful to call it a sacrament. The complexities of the story of Confirmation will be dealt with in Chapters 6 and 7. Here it is enough to make some remarks of a systematic sort about Confirmation in relation to Christian initiation and the sacramental system, based on well-established practices of the Church and some constants of the theological tradition.

As a sacrament Confirmation must ritualize some aspect of the sacramentality of the Church in relation to Christ and his rôle in sacramentalizing the gifts of God. The scriptural passages read with the rite and the theological tradition about it have linked the rite of Confirmation to the Pentecostal outpouring of the Spirit. Baptism already ritualizes Christ's gift of the Spirit in the Church, because there is no beginning of life without the Spirit. But there is an aspect of the gift of the Spirit that is not clearly ritualized in Baptism. The Pentecostal outpouring of the Spirit marks the coming of the 'last days'. God has now done everything he is going to do by way of public salvation event. This means that the proclamation of salvation is now the responsibility of men and women in a way that it never was before. The Church is a missionary community of men and women who know that they, and only they, can save the world before the Lord comes again. They do not expect any new salvation acts of God. But they do not need them because they have received within themselves the Spirit of power and the tongues of fire, with which they can preach the Gospel to the ends of the earth. To be a member of the Church is to be caught up in this mission and in the unique sense of responsibility it entails; it is to have a sense of maturity about life and behaviour that corresponds to the mature age of salvation that was inaugurated at Pentecost and to the maturing inner resources then given to the Church. Confirmation can be seen as a way of ritualizing this eschatological, missionary aspect of the mystery of salvation that is unfolded in Christ and his Spirit in the Church, and of its acceptance by those who become Christians.

There is an explanation here of why the Church would want to confirm everybody. People are not fully Christians until they have experienced ritually this aspect of the gift of God. The Greek churches confirm, as a matter of course, everyone whom they baptize. The Latin churches often separate Confirmation from Baptism, but they too want eventually to confirm all those they baptize. They do it immediately in danger of death. More significantly, they do it before granting the baptized access to any kind of public and evangelizing rôles in the Church, and notably to Marriage and Orders (it is required for licitness, though not validity, of these two sacraments). They do admit the baptized to the Eucharist before Confirmation. From the perspective of the sacramental system and the centrality of the Eucharist in it there is an incongruity here. The Eucharist is the sacrament of the full Church, not just the Church of the saints already gathered but the Church that is still in a state of mission, calling out to those who are yet to be saved to come and eat at the table of the Lord. To enter fully into this sacramental aspect of the Eucharist one needs to be confirmed as well as baptized.

3.6   CHRISTIAN INITIATION AND THE OTHER SACRAMENTS

Baptism, Confirmation and Eucharist are initiation into Christian life. For all its eschatological fullness that life has to be lived out in time in the midst of the world. The last chapter of the story has, indeed, been written, but in the enigma of the Apocalypse. In the meantime it is still being written in another, more realistic language, in the daily lives of Christians. The rites of initiation reflect this sense of the completeness and yet incompleteness of the Christian story — what some exegetes call the 'already' and the 'not yet' of biblical eschatology. The Eucharist is both heavenly banquet and food of the pilgrim people. It is at once celebration of praise and thanks for what is already realized and intercession for what has yet to be accomplished in the mission of the Church. What has to be accomplished is directed by the moral imperatives of Christian living that are the consequences of Christian initiation. But there are also rites that mark this earthly phase of Christian life and enter into its story, four of which are believed to have the same sacramental status as the rites of initiation. The initiation into Christian life accomplished in Baptism, Confirmation and Eucharist is also initiation into Orders, Marriage, Penance and Anointing of the Sick. One cannot understand the sacraments of initiation without at least some general reflection on how they are related to these other four sacraments that sustain Christian life during its time of waiting in the world.

3.6.1   Orders

When people are initiated sacramentally into Christian life they find themselves in a Church that is ministered to and presided over by persons who continue in different ways the office given by Jesus to the apostles as the foundation of the Church and the guarantee of its unity. Their ministry takes the form of overseeing the words and rites by which the community lives. To accept initiation is to accept their authority over the words and rites that one has made one's own, especially as these are celebrated in the Eucharist. It is to accept them as symbols and guarantors of that unity of word and rite and life, without which the Church would not be body of Christ and Sacrament of his grace. One can do this with security because the giving of this ministry has itself the status of sacrament. The Church commits a distinctive part of its own sacramentality to those whom it ordains as its ministers. By the sacrament of Orders it proclaims that its words and rites make it the Sacrament of Christ only when they are duly presided over by the ordained. The ordained, for their part, have an essentially sacramental rôle that has to be consonant with the general sacramentality of the Church. They represent Christ in his action of gathering and pastoring and being head of God's people for the Kingdom. That action was priestly, because it was consummated in Christ's giving of himself to his Father and to his brothers and sisters in a sacrificial death. Hence the ordained are, sacramentally, priests. This sacramental priesthood has to respect all that makes the Church a Sacrament of Christ, and all that Christian initiation conveys. Those ordained to the priesthood cannot just be persons who tend the sacred rites. They also have a particular responsibility for the prophetic word spoken in the Church, without which the Church would not be the Sacrament of Christ. Although ordination gives real power in the Church, its exercise must be seen as a sacramental service, that allows the baptized, who are already prophets and priests by their Baptism, to be the Body of Christ. Although ordination gives leadership and authority within the mission of the Church, its sacramentality requires it to operate in a way that respects the gifts and missionary responsibilities of the confirmed, by which they represent the presence of the eschatological Spirit within the Church. Although ordination gives a consecration to make the eucharistic offering in the person of Christ, it must be seen to acknowledge the right of the initiated to eat at the table of the Lord and to be seen to be his Body.

3.6.2 Marriage

For Christians the time of waiting in the world is a time of loving. Love has to take account of the sexual factor in human relations. Because they live with a sense that the time is short Christians have thought that there might be more freedom to love in these latter times by not marrying. They listened to what Jesus said about those who make themselves eunuchs for the sake of the Kingdom (Matt 19:11–12) and about there being no marrying and giving in marriage in the resurrection (Matt 22:30), and to Paul's advice to the Corinthians (1 Cor 7:25–40) about it being better not to be married because 'the form of this world is passing away', and came to recognize that the state of celibacy chosen for the sake of the Kingdom is a living proclamation of the eschatological values already inherent in the life begun by Christian initiation. Likewise, the human experience of sacrifice and of the kind of dying that celibacy brings has helped them to understand the eschatological choices inherent in Baptism, Confirmation and Eucharist. But Christians, following the gospels and Paul, also recognized in marriage the values of the life they have been initiated into by these three sacraments, particularly the pilgrim and missionary side of it. The stable bonds of marriage, and the opening of human love in it to the future, in the persons of children and children's children, is what makes the world continue and creates its time and its history. Marriage is a commitment of human love to the *saeculum*, to the world. Christians recognize that, as a pilgrim people with a mission of giving life to the world in its time of waiting, their marriages give visibility and effectiveness to the special quality of human love that they have learned in Christ. One of the favourite images for that love in the Christian story has always been the love of husband and wife. The image becomes a reality in the marriages of Christians. The way that married Christians express human love in dealing with sexuality, with nurture and responsibility for children, with community-build-ing, with social structures and politics, with their entire worldly involvement makes the Kingdom of God come. To say that Christian Marriage is the sacrament of human love in time is to say that it retells the story of the world in terms of Christ's love for his People and makes that love a force in shaping human history, until he comes again and there will no longer be marrying and giving in marriage but only the marriage feast of heaven.

The sacraments of initiation prepare people for the sacrament of Marriage and so get some of their own meaning from it. Baptism has consequences for the living-out of human love in the area of sexuality. It enables those who are called to celibacy to make that way of life an expression of the eschatological meaning of the Christian life, entering already through the element of death inherent in the voluntary renunciation of sexually fulfilled love into the resurrection where there is no marrying or giving in marriage. It enables those who marry to give themselves in human love to their partner with a completeness that matches the baptismal way Christ gave himself to his Church (Eph 5:25–30). This is the only kind of marriage the baptized are capable of — not because Canon Law says so but because they have entered a new life and begun a new story about human love that can only be expressed in a Christian rite. Since through Baptism their personal story has become the story of God, told in Christ and the Spirit, their contribution to the story of the world as husband and wife, as parents establishing a family tree in and through their children, as citizens caught up by their marriage in the social and economic realities of their own place and time must be something specifically Christian. Their lives must be an unfolding of the Gospel and a making of the Kingdom in all the concreteness of human love in the world of time.

Confirmation reinforces the witnessing and missionary status of the sacrament of Marriage and its own meaning is made concrete by its relationship with marriage. Marriage can build up a nuclear family, a tribe, a social class, a nation, and can cement loyalties within these groups. By that very fact it can also become a factor of inward-looking particularism and self-centredness in any one of these groups and fuel hostilities between them and other such groups. Confirmation will not allow Christian marriage to be of this sort. The men and women who received the Spirit at Pentecost became people for whom human love sealed in marriage could never again lock them into any kind of tribal or linguistic particularism, because they were now committed to living and preaching a Gospel story that breaks down all such barriers and hostilities. Those confirmed in this Pentecostal Spirit have the same responsibilities. Their marriages do, indeed, build families, and may occur within tribal loyalties, social classes, cultural and national identities. But they can never let their marriages be caught up in the self-centred, predatory interests of such groups. They will rather stand for a human love that reaches across such barriers, that keeps open house and hospitality from which no one is excluded simply because he or she is not of the family, and that works for a social order in which class is not discriminatory. Nothing less is consonant with the sacramentality of the Church, especially as it is expressed in the sacramentality of Confirmation.

The Eucharist provides initiation into Christian marriage in a still more intimate way. It unites the body of a Christian to the body of Christ. It is that same body that becomes one with the body of a marriage partner. It is because the bodies of Christians are seen to be made one with Christ in the Eucharist that their becoming one with one another in the sexual bond of marriage becomes Christ-bearing and Christ-revealing, and can be a sacrament of the human love of Christ for his brothers and sisters who form his Church.

3.6.3   Reconciliation

The life to which people are initiated by Baptism, Confirmation and Eucharist is meant to grow towards that fullness that is already celebrated in the Eucharist. During the time of waiting for the coming of the Lord, however, it can stop growing, and thereby be threatened with extinction. Or it can be deliberately renounced, as it has been deliberately chosen. The Eucharist ceases in these cases to be an expression of life and a nourishment of life. The person is once again a sinner and no longer part of the eucharistic community which is the Church. But because the eucharistic community is there for giving life it reaches out to those who have ceased to live with it no less than to those who have not yet begun to live with it. When its call to reconversion and its offer of pardon are accepted by those who have sinned, it has a rite for reconciliation and readmission to sacramental life, which is one of its sacraments. To be initiated into Christian life is to be initiated into the possibility of needing and availing of this sacrament of Reconciliation. The essential requirements of the sacrament are changeless (repentance, confession of sin within the Church, works of penance, absolution by a minister of the Church), but the form they have taken and the way they have been put together has varied strikingly over the centuries (variations in the number of times the sacrament could be availed of, in the kind of detail required in the confession of sin, in the type and severity of works of penance, in the form of absolution). Christian initiation has been affected by the different ways the sacrament of Reconciliation has been celebrated in the Church. When the penitential discipline was very severe people sometimes thought it might be a good idea to postpone their initiation until late in life, so that they might be less likely to sin after their Baptism and thus avoid the rigorous demands of sacramental penance. When the discipline of Penance has been relatively easy, people may have seen it as a convenient way of remedying sinful ways not completely renounced in Baptism and so been tempted to go into Baptism with something less than the radical conversion the sacrament requires. But whatever view of Penance prevails it is clear that Christian initiation has to take account of the possibility of subsequent sin, and of the sacrament by which sinners can be reconciled again to the Church and restored to Christian life and growth in the Eucharist.

3.6.4   Anointing of the Sick

Christian initiation carries with it the guarantee and the anticipation of bodily resurrection. Baptism begins it and the Eucharist is the daily promise of it. Illness and death might seem to be a blight on the hope embodied in the eucharistic community. Paul has an enigmatic remark in 1 Corinthians 11:30 ('that is why many of you are weak and ill, and some have died') that seems to suggest that a Christian community that celebrated the Eucharist properly would be free of illness and death. He is more sober in his expectations later in the epistle when he talks about the resurrection (chapter 15). Some Christians will have died before the Lord's coming and will be raised from the dead at the last trumpet (v. 52). All others will be changed 'for this perishable nature must put on the imperishable' (v. 53). Baptism is not far from the mind of Paul in this discussion (cf. v. 29) and the body of Christ is at the heart of his argument. It is in this perspective of the resurrection, proclaimed in word and sacrament, that one can best understand how the Christian community cares for its members who are sick and in danger of death. It has a ritual of anointing and prayer done by the heads of the community that calls the sick back to health and back to the eucharistic assembly in which they are nourished for life and resurrection. This ritual healing is recognized as a sacrament. If bodily health is restored the rite is a sign and anticipation of the resurrection, as the healing miracles of Jesus were signs and anticipations of the Kingdom. If the person anointed does not recover and dies, the sacrament is seen as entry into that final healing which is the resurrection, and believed to be effective in removing the final vestiges of sin that would block the full fruits of resurrection and entry into the banquet of heaven. In this case anointing is joined with a final participation in eucharistic communion.

Christian initiation, then, includes being given access to a sacramental way of dealing with illness and death during the time of waiting for the coming of the Lord. By this sacrament the Church is able to ensure that its eucharistic assembly is not distressed unduly by the wear and tear of age and the disruptive effects of illness. It has a guarantee that it will be graced by healthy people, whether health takes the form of physical well-being, or of peaceful, sin-free coping with illness, old age and death, or of the ultimate life-ensuring passage to resurrection.

3.7   TECHNICAL QUESTIONS ABOUT SACRAMENTS

The life of the Christian community is affected by many rites besides the seven called sacraments. Some of these are called sacramentals. They can have much in common with sacraments and form an integrated ritual pattern with them. Civil rituals, too, like those that express patriotic sentiments and civic duty, can be integrated in the sacramental life of Christians. But the theological claims made for the seven sacraments and for the way they incorporate the sacramentality of the Church and of Christ are quite distinctive and separate them from all other rites. There are some standard technical questions that have been devised by sacramental theology to identify sacraments and define what distinguishes them from all other rites. The origin and drift of these questions have been seen in the preceding chapter. It is useful to outline here how they are put and answered in general terms by contemporary theology, and to take a position on them which will serve for dealing with the individual sacraments of Baptism, Confirmation and Eucharist.

3.7.1 Divine institution

The fundamental question for distinguishing a sacrament from any other human rite is a question about its origin. If it is to be all that it is claimed to be it must somehow come from God. It must express a verifiable divine initiative rather than be a merely human invention. But exactly what about a sacrament must have come from God? The meaning of the question, and therefore the answer to it, supposes an analysis of the make-up of a sacrament. Anthropologically a sacrament is a rite made up of actions and words; actions and words involve people, who do and say things and have things done and said to them; and their actions and words may involve the use of objects. This complex of actions, words, objects and people makes up a sign or symbol. A sacrament is a sign, and it is precisely as a sign that it is believed to give God an opportunity to enter human life with his grace in a way that is congenial to humans and allows them to respond appropriately. It is about a sign that one wants assurances of divine origin, not about the material elements of the rite, which can come from a variety of human sources. It is what is signified by the way they are put together that one would want to trace to God, because that is what indicates that he is acting and what he is doing.

The way this question is dealt with is further affected by another piece of analysis that is needed in sacramental theology. One can identify a central core of symbolism in each sacrament which stays constant under a variety of ritual forms. It is found in some central words and actions/objects of the rite. These were called the matter and form of the sacrament from the Middle Ages until quite recently. Even if the terminology has been dropped the idea that gave rise to it (but which it did not always subsequently convey) remains in the thinking of the Church. It is thought necessary to define for every sacrament what are the words and action without which one cannot have its essential symbolism, and therefore the sacrament itself; and with which, in extreme situations, one can have it even if all the rest of the rite cannot be performed. All sorts of practical judgements about the celebration of sacraments depend on the definition of how this core symbolism is assured, and the law and teaching of the Church state it as clearly as the needs of the time demand. It is theologically tempting to make the question about the divine origin of a sacrament be a question about these essential words and actions that the Church identifies. There have been periods in the history of theology when the question was so understood, and valiant efforts were made to prove that each of the seven sacraments was divinely instituted in this sense. However, contemporary theology sees the question of divine origin as bearing on the signification of the rite before it bears on the ritual words and elements. It is the meaning of the rite which is the unchanging substance of the sacrament. And this is what is divinely given and unchangeable. The Church may have some discretion about the ritual elements but it has absolutely none about the meaning to be signified by the rite. Apart from side-stepping many of the difficulties that exegesis and historical investigation have raised against attempts to establish a divine origin for central words and elements of all seven sacraments, this way of putting the question of the divine origin of sacraments seems to be more in keeping with the Church's belief that sacraments are signs. What is looked for, then, to establish the divine origin of a sacrament is evidence of the divine intention to be present in grace at a particular moment of human life in a significant rite, rather than evidence of the choice of the rite itself. The rite, however, is not indifferent to the divine choice. All the sacramental rites come out of the story and images and historical experiences in which the intentions of God have been revealed. The Church has never felt free to go outside that tradition in any choices it has had to make about rites. Some of the rites are attributed to the personal choice of Jesus by the Scriptures (Baptism and Eucharist); the others can be all traced to the Church of the apostles, although a precise determination of some of them has been made by the later Church (Confirmation, Orders). But what is of more importance for the divine origin of a sacrament is to be able to find something in the life, if not in the commands, of Christ that establishes a divine intention to communicate a gift of salvation in a particular human life-situation, a gift to be ritualized in memory of him. Christ is seen to institute a sacrament as much by what he was and did, and by the imagery and historical tradition in which his life was expressed, as by commands he gave to perform certain rites.

3.7.2   Participants and ministers

Questions about divine origin or institution consider sacraments on the properly theological level — the level on which they are identified as acts of God in Christ on behalf of human salvation. Their divine origin distinguishes them from all other human rites. There is another series of questions that explores the ecclesiological level of sacraments. A sacrament has to be recognizably an act of the Church, calling into play its status as Sacrament of Christ. The Church itself already affirms this about seven rites when it lists them as its sacraments, defines their meaning, provides for their celebration in its official liturgical books and gives them priority in its pastoral care. They are also singled out by the stipulations that the Church makes about the people who participate in them and about those who minister in them. It takes people to make a sacramental sign, people who receive and people who give. The theological questions that are asked about them reveal something of how the Church is expressing itself in sacraments.

Because the Church is the community of believers it requires that the participants (those for whose benefit the sacrament is being celebrated, those who receive it) have faith. The Church will only celebrate one of its sacraments with and for those who share its faith. Because the Church is the community of those who save and are being saved, the participant is also expected to have some intention of making the rite a step on the way to his or her salvation. Even if the theological analysis of this intention shows that a minimal degree of explicitness is adequate to meet the needs of the Church, it also shows that it can never be dispensed with entirely. To receive a sacrament is to join in an ecclesial act; it is to contribute to the making of the Church. The Church will only recognize itself in those who join it by choice, and therefore by some kind of intention. Along with faith and intention the Church requires that the recipient of a sacrament should respect the interconnectedness of the sacraments, and particularly the priority of the sacraments of initiation. One has, for example, to be at least baptized before receiving the Eucharist, and to be confirmed before being ordained or married. The Church is constructed by this interlocking pattern of sacraments and without respecting it one cannot properly take advantage of the Church. Finally, the Church requires of the one who receives a sacrament an openness to the gift of grace, at least to the extent of not putting any moral obstacle in its way. The Church is the community of people who make holy and are being made holy. It wants no sacramental commerce with those who refuse holiness. Sometimes it happens that the Church is deceived into celebrating a sacrament with those who refuse holiness, or even with those who do not believe or have no intention of seeing the rite as a sacrament of salvation. Sometimes these deceptions will destroy all sacramentality and what is done will be only an empty rite. At other times there may still be a real sacrament because the Church finds in some others among its members a response to the gift of God that takes the place of the contribution to the sacrament refused by the one for whom it was originally celebrated. But this does not diminish in any way the insistence of the Church that those who participate in sacraments must have faith, intention and openness to grace. It cannot do otherwise if it believes that these people have an essential part to play in making sacraments be an expression of the Church's own sacramentality.

In sacraments the Church is both giver and receiver. The giving is examined in the theological questions that are asked about the minister. He gives as representative of Christ, acting in and through his Church. He acts by human choice and therefore must have some intention of doing what the Church does. He is obviously expected to believe in what he is doing and to act out of the kind of love that makes the Church want to give the grace of God to its members. If he does not believe, or if though believing he does not care much for those to whom he ministers sacraments, the Church community will nevertheless let its own faith and love take hold of the rite and make it a sacrament. Anything else would not be consonant with the missionary urge of the Church to save all humankind, and would be rather unfair to the participant. But there is one ministerial requirement that the Church does not believe it can supply for, because it is rooted in the sacramental system which makes the Church be itself. The interconnectedness of the sacraments can sometimes require a competence in the minister that is given by a prior sacrament. This arises when the significa-tion of the sacramental words and actions depends on the significance of the person who says and does them, and he gets that signification from another sacrament. The Church will not be able to express itself in the rite without such a sacramentally qualified minister. A Eucharist celebrated by a community that is not presided over by an ordained priest cannot sacramentalize the Church in the way the Eucharist is designed to, nor can a rite of Reconciliation or an Anointing of the Sick. Without an appropriately ordained minister they are not sacraments. The phase of initiation represented by the rite of Confirmation likewise requires that the minister be an ordained head of an ecclesial community. Orders can only be given on behalf of the Church by those who already have them. These, and all the other ministerial requirements, are an obedience by the Church to its own sacramentality and to the way it is realized in the different rites that it calls sacraments.

The qualification to be a participant and a minister in sacraments is associated theologically with the sacramental characters. The characters of Baptism, Confirmation and Orders are variously required for action and reception in sacraments. Contemporary theology handles questions about the character, and its relationship to grace, in a way that also probes the ecclesiological level of sacraments. Grace and character have traditionally been presented as two distinct, separable effects of sacraments. This has sometimes been done in a way that gave the impression that they are two end-products of sacraments, with the character being a kind of second-best gift of God that one can hold on to even when one does not accept grace. Contemporary theology draws attention to the tradition that the character is not just an effect of a sacrament but is itself a contributing factor to the making of sacraments. In the language derived from Augustine it is a *res et sacramentum*. The character is seen as giving one a capacity to function as a member of Christ and of his Church in the process of one's own sanctification and that of others. The accent is less on how it marks the soul than on how it gives an ecclesiological and Christological qualification to human action which allows a person to make ritual signs that are, and are recognized to be, acts of the Church and of Christ, and therefore grace-bearing. Characters are required of participants and ministers in sacraments because the Church of Christ is required in them.

3.7.3 Sacramental causality

There is a further set of theological questions that probe the distinctive reality of sacraments even more profoundly than do questions about institution and ministerial requirements. They are questions about how sacraments produce their effects, and about the kind of divine and human causality that is at work in them. It is here that theology explores the ultimate meaning of divine institution and the reason why ministerial and participation requirements of sacraments are sharply distinguished from those of sacramentals in the law of the Church. The law stipulates that certain things are necessary for the validity of a sacrament. But it is not its validity that makes a sacrament work. It works because it is the action of God taking place within a significant human action.

A contemporary re-reading of the tradition about how God causes grace in and through sacraments cannot avoid the metaphysical question of how God acts in and on his creatures. If one excludes or is agnostic about such action one will hardly get beyond an anthropological understanding of sacraments. Assuming a realistic metaphysics of divine action on creatures (such as one finds, for example, throughout Part Ia of the *Summa* of St Thomas, especially in Ia, q. 6, q. 8, q. 15, q. 20, q. 43, q. 44, q. 105), one will want to give due attention to the peculiar way in which God acts on free, responsible creatures. It can be established as a general law of the divine ordering of things that when God acts (as 'efficient cause') on creatures who are responsible for their own destiny, he makes them aware of the kind of action he is moving them to (thus giving it its 'formal/exemplar cause') and makes them desire the goal of the action (thus giving it its 'final cause'): this allows the person being moved to make the action and its finality their own (on the interdependence of efficient, formal and final cause see St Thomas, Ia, q. 5, a. 4). When the action and its goal are movements of saving grace that lead to God, the formal and final causes are a type of revelation, in terms of human ideas and desires, of God as the exemplar and final cause of grace, no less than its efficient cause. They are signs of how (form) and why (finality) God is acting to grace a human person, and also signs and expressions of the personal decisions of the one receiving grace. This analysis of God's action underlies and is illustrated in the mystery of Christ. Christ embodies and exercises the saving action of God (exercising 'efficient causality'); at the same time he reveals the God towards whom all those being saved are drawn (as embodying the 'final cause'); and simultaneously he models the kind of action in which the saved respond to God's action and reach out towards him (serving as 'formal/exemplar cause'). The same pattern of divine causality underlies the sacraments, in which the mystery of Christ is brought to bear on people in the Church. God gives life to his people in sacraments. His life-giving action takes the form of words that reveal him to them as origin and goal of the life they are receiving, and of rites that make that revelation suitably concrete and tangible for creatures who live in the body. These words and rites simultaneously give form to and concretize the activity of those who come to life in response to his grace. In this pattern of causality words and rites act as signs not as things. They express the reciprocal action of God and of his People, and in expressing it make it possible for it to occur. But they are signs of salvific human action only because they are first signs of God who is causing that action.

The technical term 'instrument' has served throughout much of the Christian tradition to state the subordinate status, and yet the dignity and indispensability, of human action in relation to the divine (which is the principal cause) in sacraments. Something like it will always be needed to keep the anthropological in line with the theological in the analysis of sacraments. The Thomistic tradition has paid special attention to the physical realism of this instrumentality of human action in the making of sacraments. It would argue that an explanation of sacramental action in terms of moral causality (the view that a sacrament causes grace because it has an intrinsic value or worth that establishes a claim in God's grace) does not by itself do justice to the mysterious power and presence of God that the tradition has generally recognized to be at work in sacraments. Modern studies about the 'mystery' inherent in acts of Christian worship seem to confirm the theological preference for a physical rather than a merely moral instrumentality. However, these same studies, and the general development of sacramental theology, make it clear that to reduce the instrumental causality of sacraments to the merely physical is to fail to do justice to another aspect of the tradition about sacramentality. Sacraments are not simply a point of contact between God and his People, in which something invisible happens. They are moments of communication, through the medium of signs. All the intentional elements — the way the sacrament notifies the intentions of God to cause grace here and now to designated recipients, as well as the kind of grace he intends to give and the particular response he expects to it — are included in the instrumentality of the sacrament. A theory of sacramental causality along these lines rejoins, from what it would claim to be a deeper metaphysical perspective, contemporary personalist theologies of sacraments, and fits well into the categories of invitation/response and the phenomenology of sign which they use to analyse the interaction of the divine and human in terms of personal relations. Because it offers a metaphysical ground for the application of personalist categories to God, it probably sits more comfortably than merely personalist theologies with the dogmatic tradition about the ontological reality of sacraments, which the Council of Trent defined in terms of 'containing grace' and causing it *ex opere operato*. It locates the ultimate basis for the objective reality of sacraments and of their reliability in the face of human fallibility in the guaranteed action of God. When humans carry out their proper ministerial and participatory tasks in making a sacramental sign in and for the Church, Christ is truly present as both gift of God and perfect human response, and the work of God is unfailingly being done, even if it is finally obstructed by some obstacles to grace placed by individual recipients.

The theological analysis of the unique causality of grace that occurs in sacraments sets them apart from all other rites and activities of the Church. It shows how profoundly they are linked with God's saving action through Christ and the Church. It is also the basis for the statements that are made about sacraments being necessary for salvation. If God causes grace in the way a theology of sacraments explains, it would seem impossible to be saved without sacraments. Theology has various questions to ask which lead to refinements of this claim: sacramental experience is, indeed, necessary for human salvation but God can and does act to save outside the Christian sacraments; some sacraments are necessary for all believers, others only in particular circumstances; the grace of sacraments can be given in certain cases without the actual sacrament. What emerges from these considerations is that sacraments are for the benefit of humans and their salvation. When they serve that purpose God wants them to be used. When they do not he gives people another way. And yet the sacramental way has a kind of normative value in the history of salvation and the other ways of salvation that God uses will always show traces of it.

The theological discussions that have been outlined in this chapter are part of the Christian story within which the rites of the Church are celebrated day by day. It is the part of the story that deals with the rites themselves — where they come from, why they have the form they do, how they work, how important they are for the life of God's People. When theology explores these questions, when it relates each one of the sacraments to the others within the sacramental system, when it relates them to the sacramentality of the Church, and that in turn to the sacramentality of Christ, and when it situates that whole pattern of sacramentality within a general theology, it is building up a critical and systematic account of the place of rites in the story of God's People. This is the story that has to be told if the rites are to remain really in touch with life. There are many ways of telling it. The way of systematic theology is not always the best, especially in an actual celebration of a sacrament. But it does provide a critical basis for the biblical and liturgical telling of it, and for the preaching and catechesis, and the praying and the singing that are needed if the sacramental rites of the Christian people are to be life-giving and life-expressing.

STUDY QUESTIONS

1   How does the theology of the Trinity influence the theology of sacraments?
2   How does a theological understanding of the priesthood of Christ influence the way one thinks about sacraments?
3   Examine the relationship between 'People of God' and sacraments in the teaching of *Lumen Gentium*.
4   There are other ways of understanding the connection between the seven sacraments, and of explaining why they should number seven, besides that given in this chapter. Find and evaluate some of them.
5   Study and compare the way the word 'institution' is understood by any three contemporary theologians who discuss the divine institution of sacraments.
6   How does the minister of a sacrament discover and make his or her own 'the intention of the Church' in celebrating that sacrament?
7   Examine the philosophical category of causality with a view to its use in a theology of how sacraments produce their effects.

FURTHER READING

Modern works that offer a systematic general theology of sacraments are listed in the Introduction (p. 9) under *Further Reading*.

The general sacramental theology of St Thomas, found in *Summa Theologiae*, IIIa, qq. 60–65 (Blackfriars ed., vol. 56, *The Sacraments*, ed. D. Bourke, London/New York, 1975), still merits careful reading.

4

Baptism: the rite

4.1   DESCRIPTION

It is well to begin the study of Baptism with a summary description of the rite. It is in the rite that the sacramental event which theology sets out to understand is experienced. It is best to have primarily in mind the rite for adults. It is in this that the Church expresses all that it means by Baptism, without qualification. Other forms of the rite, such as that for children, are no less Baptisms. But because they are adapting the sacrament to particular circumstances they are best understood by comparing their special features with the unqualified rite, which is that for adults (*RCIA*, nn. 48–224; *Rites*, Initiation, pp. 40–102).

The essential core of the rite of Baptism is a bathing in water, with an invoking of the names of Father, Son and Holy Spirit. This is the universal belief and practice of Christians (apart from a few rare groups who have a 'baptism of the Spirit' without the use of a water-rite). They do the bathing in different ways. Almost all agree that the most appropriate way of doing it is to immerse the person being baptized wholly or in part in water. The churches of the Eastern tradition, both Orthodox and Catholic, do this as a matter of course (although allowing exceptions in emergency situations). Some of the evangelical churches of the Latin and Western traditions will only baptize in this way. But most churches of the West settle in practice for a pouring of water on the head of the one being baptized. There is also a practice, which has always been problematical, of sprinkling water over those to be baptized. The immersion or pouring is usually done three times, corresponding to the three names that are invoked.

A person is baptized in a particular Christian community — normally a parish — which takes responsibility for the sacrament and registers it. The rite is celebrated by that community, gathered under the presidency of its ordained ministers, one of whom (bishop, priest or deacon) does the actual baptizing. One or more members of the church sponsor the person to be baptized and take special responsibility for him or her. The rite is celebrated in a part of the church building set aside for Baptism which in its location and design expresses that Baptism is the way of entry into the community, and in its decoration evokes the meaning of the sacrament. The time for celebrating Baptism is set by the general rhythm of the Church's liturgical life. The Vigil of Easter, when the death and resurrection of Christ is being celebrated with special solemnity, is considered the most appropriate time. The feast of Pentecost is also favoured. Within the weekly rhythm, Sunday, the day of the Lord's resurrection, is the preferred day.

Preceding the essential core of the baptismal rite, suitably distributed in time and place, there are secondary rites that accompany the transition that the one to be baptized is making from one way of life (dominated by sin and the devil) to another (in Christ and his Church). They are rites of welcome and introduction to a period of training and trial in Church membership, called the catechumenate; they are rites of renouncing the way of sin; they are rites of conversion to and instruction in Christian beliefs and Christian ways of living. They touch the person through the body in a series of blessings, signings and anointings; they address the mind in words and teachings; they monitor and approve the progressive commitment being made. Viewed in the theological framework of rite/word/life they are rites that mark the gradual introduction of a person to the full Christian story (they include, for example, the giving of the sacred books and learning the words of the Creed and the Our Father) and the gradual transition to the way of life of the community that lives by that story. With this kind of preparation the central rite of Baptism — the bathing in water — is more likely to be a real acceptance of the climax of the Christian story — the death and resurrection of Jesus — and a real entry into new life through the ritual re-enactment of it.

The central rite is followed by ceremonies that express the new life that the baptized enjoy in Christ and the Church. They are anointed with perfumed oil called chrism. When a continuous rite of initiation is being celebrated this anointing is the sacrament of Confirmation. When, however, the baptized person is not to be confirmed at that time there is still an anointing with chrism, but with a prayer that refers it to the consecration of the baptized as prophet, priest and king in the body of Christ, rather than to the special gift of the Holy Spirit that Confirmation gives (RCIA, n. 222 [224]). After anointing the initiated are dressed in white and given a candle that has been lighted from the Easter candle; they are then admitted to the Eucharist. In the weeks following their Baptism new Christians are meant to receive special attention from the Church, especially in liturgical assemblies. They are meant to be told in the fullest possible terms the meaning of their first experiences of Christian rites and the effects this should be having in their lives. It is ultimately in life that rite and word have their mettle tested.

4.2　HISTORY

Because ritual needs to be stable it is important to be able to state that Baptism today is substantially the same as it has been from the beginning. However, there have been some developments in the rite, and the way it is done today can be better understood with the help of some remembering. One can go right back to the Jewish roots of Christianity (Delorme in George, pp. 25ff.). Ritual bathings were practised in Judaism. They usually had to do with the procedures of cultic purification. In the period of Christian origins it seems that ritual washings were also used in the initiation of pagans into Judaism. And they were also used in those movements and sects, like that associated with Qumran, that dedicated themselves to righteousness and expected the coming of the Kingdom. Baptism was so prominently associated with the preaching of righteousness and the coming of the Kingdom in the message of John that he was called John the Baptizer. He drew people out into the desert and baptized those who accepted his call to conversion in the river Jordan, presumably by immersion. This is how Jesus was baptized. It must have set something of a pattern for the way the apostles subsequently baptized in the name of Jesus. The New Testament, however, does not give any information about their rite of Baptism beyond the essential statement that it was to be done in water and 'in the name of the Father and of the Son and of the Holy Spirit' (Matt 28:19). When Acts speaks of Baptism or baptizing 'in the name of Jesus' (2:38; 8:16; 10:48; 19:5; 22:16) it does not seem to be giving an alternative liturgical formula (although confession of faith in the name of Jesus would, in New Testament terms, imply a confession of faith in Father, Son and Holy Spirit) but rather describing Christian Baptism by way of what sets it apart from the baptism of John or any other type of baptism (Neunheuser, chs 1, 4; on a possible primitive baptismal formula in Acts 8:37 see Cullmann, *Baptism*, pp. 71ff.).

There are two important texts about the rite of Baptism from the second century. The *Didachē*, generally dated about AD 100, already allows a triple pouring of water on the head in place of immersion in running water. It recommends that Baptism be preceded by some days of fasting, by the baptizer as well as the baptized and by others who can do so (*Didachē* 7: text in Palmer, pp. 1–2 and Whitaker, p. 1). St Justin gives a more detailed description of the process of Baptism, with special attention to how the community takes an active part in it. There is a phase of preparation during which the community prays and fasts with those who 'are persuaded and believe that those things which we teach and describe are true, and undertake to live accordingly'. The candidates are then 'led by us to a place where there is water' and are 'washed in the water in the Name of the Father and Lord God of all things, and of our Saviour Jesus Christ, and of the Holy Spirit . . .'. Afterwards they join the community ('those who are called brethren') in common prayer 'for ourselves, for him that has been enlightened, and for all men everywhere . . .'. They then take part in the Eucharist (*First Apology*, 61: text in Palmer, pp. 3–4 and Whitaker, pp. 1–2).

Justin's account of Christian Baptism, being addressed to pagans, is marked by a certain discretion. The next important document on the rite of Baptism is an internal document of the Christian Church and has no such reticences or circumlocutions. St Hippolytus of Rome, writing about AD 215, gives a very full description of Christian initiation in his Treatise on the Apostolic Tradition, XVI–XXIII. It includes almost all the elements of our present-day Roman rite of Baptism. There is a catechumenate, which may go on for two or three years, during which there are regular assemblies for teaching, examination of conduct, prayer, blessings and exorcisms; the candidates are assisted by sponsors. During the period immediately preceding the Baptism there are daily assemblies for prayer and exorcism. On Friday and Saturday there is fasting and on Saturday night there is a vigil during which there is reading from Scripture and instruction. Here is how the central part of the rite is described:

XXI. 1. And at the hour when the cock crows they shall first [of all] pray over the water.

2. When they come to the water, let the water be pure and flowing.

3. And they shall put off their clothes.

4. And they shall baptize the little children first. And if they can answer for themselves, let them answer. But if they cannot, let their parents answer or someone from their family.

5. And next they shall baptize the grown men; and last the women who shall have loosed their hair and laid aside their gold ornaments. Let no one go down to the water having any alien object with them.

6. And at the time determined for baptizing, the bishop shall give thanks over the oil and put it into a vessel and it is called the Oil of Thanksgiving.

7. And he shall take other oil and exorcize over it, and it is called the Oil of Exorcism.

8. And let a deacon carry the Oil of Exorcism and stand on the left hand. And another deacon shall take the Oil of Thanksgiving and stand on the right hand.

9. And when the presbyter takes hold of each one of those who are to be baptized, let him bid him renounce saying:
   I renounce thee, Satan, and all thy service and all thy works.

10. And when he has said this let him anoint with the Oil of Exorcism, saying:
   Let all evil spirits depart far from thee.

11. Then after these things let him give him over to the presbyter who stands at the water. And let them stand in the water naked. And let a deacon likewise go down with him into the water.

12. And when he goes down to the water, let him who baptizes lay hand on him saying thus:
   Dost thou believe in God the Father Almighty?

13. And he who is being baptized shall say:
   I believe.

14. Let him forthwith baptize [*baptizet: probably*, let him dip. So also 16 and 18] him once, having his hand laid upon his head.

15. And after [this] let him say:
   Dost thou believe in Christ Jesus, the Son of God,
   Who was born of the Holy Spirit and the Virgin Mary,
   Who was crucified in the days of Pontius Pilate,
   And died,
   And rose the third day living from the dead,
   And ascended into the heavens,
   And sat down at the right hand of the Father,
   And will come to judge the living and the dead?

16. And when he says: I believe, let him baptize him the second time.

17. And again let him say:
   Dost thou believe in the Holy Spirit in the Holy Church,
   And the resurrection of the flesh?

18. And he who is being baptized shall say: I believe. And so let him baptize him the third time.

19. And afterwards when he comes up he shall be anointed with the Oil of Thanksgiving saying:
   I anoint thee with holy oil in the Name of Jesus Christ.

20. And so each one drying himself they shall now put on their clothes, and after this let them be together in the assembly.

XXII. 1. And the bishop shall lay his hand upon them invoking and saying:
   O Lord God, who didst count these worthy of deserving the forgiveness of sins by

the laver of regeneration, make them worthy to be filled with thy Holy Spirit and send upon them thy grace, that they may serve thee according to thy will; to thee is the glory, to the Father and to the Son with the Holy Ghost in the Holy Church, both now and ever and world without end. Amen.

2. After this pouring the consecrated oil and laying his hand on his head, he shall say: I anoint thee with holy oil in God the Father Almighty and Christ Jesus and the Holy Ghost.

3. And sealing him on the forehead, he shall give him the kiss of peace and say: The Lord be with you.
And he who has been sealed shall say:
    And with thy spirit.

4. And so shall he do to each one severally.

5. Thenceforward they shall pray together with all the people. But they shall not previously pray with the faithful before they have undergone all these things.

6. And after the prayers, let them give the kiss of peace.

[There follows a description of the Eucharist.] (Palmer, pp. 8–12; Whitaker, pp. 4–7.)

Whether or not the rite described by Hippolytus had much historical influence, it certainly has most of the elements that form the classical shape of the rite of Baptism. Some of these elements are not yet found in the early records of other liturgical traditions, or are found in a different order. There are differences about the anointings, especially those done immediately after the bathing in water. The Syrian tradition has the trinitarian words said in the form of a statement or prayer rather than in the form of questions as in Hippolytus (texts in Whitaker, pp. 21ff.). This eventually became common practice. Some rites, like the Roman, retain the questions immediately before the bathing, which is then done 'in the name of Father, Son and Holy Spirit'.

The development of the Roman rite of Baptism from those early centuries to the present day can be followed in the liturgical books (texts in Whitaker, pp. 153ff.). One may note some of the factors that help to explain how the rite reached its present state. The liturgical season of Lent, set up as a time of conversion, fasting, prayer and instruction in preparation for Easter, and therefore also for Baptism, took to itself many of the tasks of the catechumenate. This enriched the liturgy of Baptism, even if it did carry the risk of formalizing it. It was particularly useful for those who had been baptized as infants, helping them to work out the full sacramentality of their Baptism; it also prepared Christians to exercise their responsibilities for the newly baptized, particularly if these were their own children. However, as the centuries went by, the practice of celebrating Baptism outside the preferred seasons of Easter and Pentecost became more common. Away from Lent the catechumenate was less easy to manage. When Europe became almost entirely Christian the great majority of those to be baptized were infants. A rite was developed for baptizing them which was a rather ill-disguised adaptation of the rite for adults. It provided the dominant experience of Baptism in the established churches. Of necessity it gave more prominence to the passive ritual elements that suited an infant than to the elements of the rite that called forth personal prayer and decision. The participation of the community in infant baptism became quite limited from the Middle

Ages onwards. In the course of time a rather passive ritualism came to be accepted as normal, even in the Baptism of adults. Adults were, indeed, prepared for Baptism by instruction and prayer, but these were not often ritualized — although it was provided for in the Latin liturgical books. That situation lasted in the Catholic Church until the reforms associated with Vatican II.

The reforms called for by the Council (*SC*, nn. 64–70) were meant to restore values of the tradition that had become obscured. The post-conciliar rites are a call to recover the truth and realism of the ritual that one senses in the early tradition. This is particularly evident in the full rite for adults that has already been described. The rite for children is realistically designed to meet their situation. It draws the community and the parents of the child into the rite in a way that expresses their acceptance of responsibility for the Christian nurture of the child, without which the Baptism cannot normally be celebrated.

4.3   RITE OF INITIATION

One can get a feel for the rite of Baptism not only from its own history but also from the way it matches the general patterns of human behaviour that are revealed by anthropological studies, especially in the domain of religion. Baptism can be classed as an initiation rite. One does not need to be a professional anthropologist to have a sense of what initiation is and how it is ritualized. Life is full of beginnings and of passages from one stage of life to another. There are the passages of age, from childhood to teenage, to young adulthood, to middle age, to old age. The way one dresses, the company one keeps, the language one uses change from one of these ages to another; and there are significant moments when one feels the change and gives it expression in some decisive, socially-recognized gesture. These are the rites of passage, of initiation to a new stage of life. There is another experience of initiation when people join something. They commit themselves to an ideal (like Scouting), or to a social task (in a political party), or to an enthusiasm (a fan club). Something changes in their life and they develop new relationships. The rites of joining may be little more than giving one's name and paying a subscription, accepting a card or badge, making some promises, but in their own way these are rites of passage that mark a new beginning.

Christian Baptism is such a rite of passage or initiation. One is joining something, starting to keep new company, thinking and feeling differently about certain things, Even if the rite is simple the issues are serious. They are matters of life and death. Anthropology and other social and psychological sciences can help one to understand something of what is going on. They can explain how deep psychic and social life-forces are at work and issues of life and death are being worked out in rites of passage that may on the surface be banal and even slightly ridiculous to outsiders. Initiation rites in primitive cultures are a fruitful area of study and comparison here, because they show the human life-process in unspoiled and un-self-conscious simplicity. An analysis of them, especially on the psychological level, can help one to understand how the rites of Christian Baptism can be touching the human spirit on the deep level where it wrestles with issues of life and death.

The Jewish initiation rite of circumcision is of particular interest for understanding Baptism (see de Vaux, pp. 46–48; Cullmann, *Baptism*, pp. 56–70). While it was, and still is in a variety of cultures, a rite of tribal initiation, it became for Israel a divinely given sign of their being God's People, bound to him by covenant. It was the way of entry into the covenant community and the mark of belonging to it. The physical intimacy of it ensured that it had a deep impact on the sense of identity, life and destiny of a whole race of people. The Christian tradition has found many features of it that typify Baptism as the initiation rite of the New Covenant (Col 2:11–12; for the Fathers see Daniélou, pp. 63–67; St Thomas, *Summa*, IIIa, q. 70).

And yet Baptism is as different from circumcision as the new covenant is from the old. Christianity has, in fact, distanced itself from the kind of rites that are an inevitable part of being born and growing up within a particular racial or cultural tradition. Baptism is not a rite of tribal or cultural initiation. It is a rite of freely chosen entry into a community in which the only basis of belonging is the choice of God, and in which there is no longer Jew or Greek, slave or free, male or female. From this point of view, rites of free choice and personal conversion offer a better anthropological model for Baptism than do rites of growing up and growing old within a particular culture. The study of the mystery religions of the Graeco-Roman world is helpful here (see 2.3 above). On a more secular and contemporary plane, one could examine the rites by which people enter various political movements, especially of the radical sort — even if they are no more than the growing of a Che Guevara beard! In these, as in the initiation rites of the mystery religions, there is a preoccupation with salvation or liberation, with escape from all that leads to slavery and death, with patterns of change that have once proved themselves and may be repeated again, with joining and helping to create a new people who will enjoy life and freedom in a new world to come.

4.4 A WATER-RITE WITH WORDS

Baptism is initiation into a salvation process that is believed to have been going on for a long time. The one who gives salvation is the God who made the world and brings it to its consummation. The bathing in water that forms its core is a remembering of past salvation events that are believed to be significant in the present. To know what is going on in the rite one needs to be aware of what those events were and why they can be evoked by water. One needs some help from history. One can also be helped by psychology. The salvation process into which the rite is believed to initiate people is something that happens at the deepest possible level of human life. To understand how a bathing in water can play a part in it one needs to have a sense of how such a rite can touch deep levels of the human psyche. These two areas of science — the historical and the psychological — have in recent times thrown a great deal of light on the symbolism of water in Baptism by unfolding its general significance in relation to human experiences of salvation (Eliade, *Patterns* . . . , pp. 188ff.).

There is in the Bible a record of salvation events in which water played a memorable part, either as a physical element or as a dominant image. History has to weigh up that record. Some of it is heavily mythological. And yet it is about real people who had real experiences and survived as a nation to tell about them. And it is about a real God. The Bible is not just a story invented to explain certain peculiarities of the human condition, as are many religious myths. There are real events underlying the biblical stories about how God made and saved the world through water. They tell in their own way how it was from a watery chaos that the world was originally formed, how water destroyed sinners but saved Noah and his family in the Flood, how water destroyed the Egyptians and saved the Israelites at the crossing of the Red Sea, how water was given in the desert and how the waters of the Jordan stood back to let God's People enter the promised land, how the mystique of water was used by the prophets of Israel, how Jesus was baptized in the waters of the Jordan, how he used bathing and the water image in his preaching.

The psychological sciences can probe the impact, conscious and unconscious, of stories, images and dreams about water. There are well-established patterns linking water to the human way of dealing with life and death, birth and re-birth, creation and renewal, salvation and destruction. It can be shown how these patterns are being worked out in the biblical stories about water and in the remembering of these stories that is done in the rite of Baptism.

One can understand, then, how the prayer of blessing that is said over the water before it is used in Baptism (*RCIA*, n. 215 [215, 216, 389]), with its historical allusions and mystical depth, is such a powerful reinforcement of the act of baptizing. So are the selected Scripture readings provided with the rite and the kind of preaching that is expected. These words of telling and evoking are the kind of words that belong within the baptismal rite. There are other words about Baptism in the language of the Church that are explanatory rather than proclamatory, that resolve theological problems rather than reinforce fundamental faith, that systematize thinking for the benefit of the mind rather than affirm a moment of decision. These are necessary words for the life of the Church and will be dealt with in the next chapter. But they do not belong within the rite itself. What belongs there are words that give direct and immediate reinforcement, by way of historical reminding and psychological evocation, to the ritual elements, particularly to the core rite of bathing in water.

4.5   IN THE NAME OF . . .

The words that are spoken with the central rite of Baptism definitively fix its Christian meaning and call forth a definitive act of faith on the part of the one being baptized. They are words that personalize the action. The one being baptized is named; the one who is baptizing says 'I' (in the Roman rite; in the Eastern rites the passive voice is used); and the God for whom the baptizer acts and from whom the one being baptized believes salvation is coming is personally named as Father, Son and Holy Spirit.

Words commonly have a personalizing function in religious ritual (see Bouyer, *Rite and Man*, ch. IV). They say what one person is doing to and for another in the rite. They can, of course, become mere incantations, and then the rite becomes a thing rather than a personal action. But when they are speech, and not just sound, they put the 'I' and the 'Thou' into ritual. When there is speech there is a person speaking and a person being spoken to. The baptizer is an 'I'. However, he is a minister, acting in the name of someone else. He baptizes in the name of God, Father, Son and Holy Spirit. He knows that name because God has revealed himself, through all the events and words of the history of salvation, to be Father, Son and Holy Spirit. The saving events that are being remembered in the water-rite belong to this self-revelation of God. The Baptism of Jesus, at which the Father identified him as his Son, and the Holy Spirit came upon him, is a climactic moment in that personal revelation of God. Christian Baptism is such a moment when it is done in the name of Father, Son and Holy Spirit. These words distil the whole history of salvation, and its summarization in the Creeds of the Church, in the personal names of the God who acts and shows his face in that history. In making his name known to people God gave them a certain power over him — not a magical power but a power that comes from a freely given familiarity. It is this power that a baptizer calls on when he acts in the name of Father, Son and Holy Spirit. His baptizing is recognized as being the saving action of God, Father, Son and Holy Spirit, that is, the personal heart of the history of salvation.

The person being baptized becomes the 'Thou' in face of the 'I'. The ritual is his or her personal response to the trinitarian God who is present and active in it. This is a response of faith. Even if the words of Baptism no longer take the form of a profession of faith, as they did in the rite of Hippolytus, they are still an act of faith in the whole history of salvation, and in the credal formulations of it, because they are an acceptance of the personal God who reveals himself in these saving actions.

That the sacramental words are words of faith marks a critical difference between Christian Baptism and all rites that rely on myth. A myth is a good story, which can have its beneficent effect whether what it tells happened or not. Writing a letter to Santa Claus or visiting him has had a profound effect on countless children, even though they eventually discovered that there was no such person in reality. The nature rites of all ages have been founded on cosmic myths; they 'worked' even though the stories were fantasies. Christianity says that God exists, and believes that he is Father, Son and Holy Spirit. What the Son did for our salvation really happened and will happen when he comes again. The Spirit is a real person, who is transforming us and our world. To believe is to affirm the reality of things. The Gospel is a story. There are mythical elements in its telling, and it is all the better for that. But it is a true story and a dream come true. The words that accompany the water rite of Baptism mean just that. They mean that what is being done is not merely an imaginative working-out of some human urge or need for a salvation experience, but that it is an objective gift of a God who is really there, and who is revealing himself in this gift as Father, Son and Holy Spirit. It is in these words of faith that the sacramentality of Baptism is ultimately affirmed.

STUDY QUESTIONS

1   Do a critical liturgical assessment of a celebration of Baptism in which you have taken part.
2   Study the layout and decoration of some famous baptisteries.
3   Study the influence which preparation for Baptism has had on the choice of liturgical readings during the season of Lent.
4   What influence had the celebration of Baptism on the formulation of the Christian Creeds?
5   Analyse some secular rites of initiation in your culture and compare them with Baptism.
6   Prepare an explanation of the principal parts of the rite of Baptism for use in baptismal homilies.

FURTHER READING

The rite of Baptism:

Ordo baptismi parvulorum promulgated 15 May 1969. Published in ICEL English translation as *Rite of Baptism for Children* (1969).
Ordo initiationis christianae adultorum promulgated 6 January 1972; emended second printing containing *Praenotanda de initiatione christiana*, 1974. Published in ICEL English as *Rite of Christian Initiation of Adults* (interim version, 1974; definitive edition, 1985).
Both available in official editions, but also in *The Rites of the Catholic Church* (Pueblo, New York, 1976); new translation of the introductions in *Documents on the Liturgy 1963–1979* (Liturgical Press, Collegeville, 1982).

Presentation of the rite in:

J. D. Crichton, *Christian Celebration: The Sacraments* (London, 1973; repub. London, 1981), esp. ch. 4.
A. Kavanagh, *The Shape of Baptism: The Rite of Christian Initiation* (New York, 1978).

On Jewish antecedents:

F. Gavin, *The Jewish Antecedents of the Christian Sacraments* (London, 1928).
J. Delorme, 'The Practice of Baptism in Judaism at the Beginning of the Christian Era' in A. George, SM, and others, *Baptism in the New Testament* (trans. from French of 1956; London, 1964).

History of the rite of Baptism in standard histories of the Liturgy; texts in:

E. C. Whitaker, *Documents of the Baptismal Liturgy* (2nd ed., London, 1970).

On baptisteries:

H. Leclercq, 'Baptistère' in *DACL* 2.I:382–469.
W. M. Bedard, *Symbolism of the Baptismal Font* (Washington, 1951).
J. G. Davies, *The Architectural Setting of Baptism* (London, 1962).

On the general anthropology of rites of initiation:

A. van Gennep, *The Rites of Passage* (repub. Chicago, 1960).
M. Eliade, *Birth and Rebirth* (New York, 1958) and *Patterns in Comparative Religion* (New York/London, 1958).

5

Baptism: the word

5.1 VARIETY OF WORDS

The story that goes with a rite can be told in a number of different ways: there is a straight telling of things that happened; there is an idealizing of events in poetry and song; there is a moralizing version of it; it can be told in prayer; there is a polemical comparison of the true story with falsified versions of it; there is a reflective, even critical telling of it in the light of various philosophical-type questions that may arise about it. One can find all these different ways of telling the story of salvation in the Old Testament. The historical books do it in one way, the Psalms in another; the legal codes moralize about it and the prophets can be polemical about distortions of it; the Wisdom literature is reflective and philosophical. One can find the same variety of literary forms in the New Testament. They are continued throughout Christian literature.

It is from this story of salvation in its variety of forms that the words that accompany Baptism are drawn. The rite gets its fundamental existence and meaning from the facts that are told about Jesus in the gospels and Acts, and summarized in the Creeds: he is the Son of God, born of the Virgin Mary, who was baptized, preached and did good, died and rose again, sent his apostles to preach and baptize, founded his Church on them and filled it with the Holy Spirit, until he comes again to bring resurrection and eternal life. This is the story that is told in every catechesis of Baptism. It is evoked in another way in the tradition of prayers and hymns and poetry (and also in music and painting) about Baptism. On it is based a moralizing literature about Baptism that emphasizes the preparation and dispositions needed for it and the obligations that follow from it. There is also a polemical literature about Baptism, which defends its true relationship to the work of salvation against distortions. And there is a reflective literature that reasons in a systematic way about the questions that thinking people have wanted to ask about how this rite could be all that Christians claim it to be.

Baptism uses these different kinds of words in accordance with its own needs. It incorporates some of them directly into the rite. The trinitarian words that are spoken at the core of the rite are the quintessential statement of the Christian story, because they are a naming of the God who is its constant subject. The Creed that is used fills out this 'biography' of God. The prayers used in the rite are part of the poetry of belief, expressing human response to what is happening in the rite. The scriptural passages that are read are the first, normative statements of why Christians baptize and of how they understand the rite. These texts, however, are already less central to the rite itself than are the sacramental words and the prayers. They find their place in the scene-setting for the rite, during the catechumenate, during the Liturgy of the Word that precedes the sacrament proper, and in the explanatory instructions that follow the sacrament. Still farther away from the centre are the words that have been deposited in the tradition by the moralizing, polemics and systematic reflection that has accompanied the celebration of Baptism in the post-scriptural era. There is no casuistical moral theologizing within the rite of Baptism; the technical word 'original sin' is used only once in the Roman rite, and then in a very secondary prayer; the word 'character' never appears; there is hardly an echo of the polemics of the Reformation.

Yet the words of the tradition that remain unspoken in the rite itself have a profound influence on Baptism. They are an essential part of the story that Christian believers bring to bear on their celebration of the rite. If they are not remembered, or are remembered badly, the rite will deteriorate into formalism, magic or nonsense. It is the task of Christian theology to keep them always present and influential, even when the rite itself does not directly use them. And to the extent that new words become necessary to keep the story truthful and effective it is the task of theology to coin these words. The rite is for life, and life keeps on throwing up new questions about it. They can only be answered by an old story if the story is properly interpreted. Theology tries to do that constant critical interpretation of the rite of Baptism and its story for the sake of life. The magisterial authorities of the Church monitor the interpretation for continuity and genuineness. Preachers, especially in the actual celebration of the rite, and catechists in preparing people for the rite, play an indispensable part in this theological relating of rite and story to life. It is with these words of catechists, preachers, theologians and *magisterium* that this chapter is concerned.

5.2   THE NEW TESTAMENT

Along with descriptive texts that say what Baptism is, and prescriptive texts that command that it be done, there are in the New Testament explanatory texts about Baptism that say what it means in the design of God for the salvation of his people (the texts are catalogued in George, pp. 13–22). This meaning already begins to show through in the descriptive texts, especially when they are read against their Old Testament background. In Acts 2:37–42 Baptism is presented as the way in which those who 'receive the word' about Jesus (that by his death and resurrection he has been established by God his Father as Lord and Christ: vv. 14–36) and who repent, are granted forgiveness of their sins and receive the gift of the Holy Spirit; by Baptism they are gathered into the community of those who 'devote themselves to the apostles' teaching and fellowship, to the breaking of bread and the prayers'. All the essential ideas about Baptism are in that text.

Some of them are found again in the description of the baptism of the eunuch from Ethiopia by Philip in Acts 8:26–40. They are present, although in a more condensed way, in the command of Jesus to the apostles in Matthew 28:16–20, made in virtue of the power that has been given to him, to go and teach all nations, gathering people together as disciples who believe in their preaching, baptizing them in the name of Father, Son and Holy Spirit, teaching them to live in the way Jesus commands; all this to be done in the assurance that Jesus himself remains with them until the work of salvation is completed.

The accounts of the baptism of Jesus in the Synoptics include, in their own way, a theology of Christian Baptism. They present Baptism as a beginning by placing it at the beginning of the ministry of Jesus. They relate it to divine sonship by making the baptism of Jesus be the occasion when he is proclaimed by the Father to be his beloved Son. They relate it to the outpouring of the eschatological Spirit ('baptism in water and the Holy Spirit') by telling how the Spirit came upon Jesus. These texts give Baptism its Christological and trinitarian ground. They also give it a soteriological basis by relating it to the death and resurrection of Christ. When John would have refused to baptize Jesus he was persuaded to change his mind by the words '. . . for thus it is fitting for us to fulfil all righteousness' (Matt 3:15). 'Righteousness' here means the demands that God makes on sinful humanity. Jesus would meet those demands, not as a sinner but for sinners, by going to his death. In accepting baptism for the sake of righteousness he is already giving himself, in a symbolical anticipation, to death. He did, in fact, speak later of his death as a baptism (Luke 12:49–50), and invited the sons of Zebedee to 'be baptized with the baptism with which I am baptized' (Mark 10:38).

St Paul makes frequent reference to Baptism and has a well-developed theology of it (Duplacy, Giblet, Tremel in George; Cullmann, Baptism; Schnackenburg). He places the rite within the working-out of the gift of faith, by which those who are called to justification take hold of the grace of Christ. Although Baptism is done by the Church and its ministers, it is above all an action of Christ taking hold of those who are being saved, and a way in which sinners lay hold of the salvation which he brings. It is this Christ-centredness that gives Baptism its power to draw people together into one, regardless of who baptized them (1 Cor 1:12–17), or whether they are Jew or Greek, slave or free, male or female (1 Cor 12:13; Gal 3:27–29). It is in the Church that this gathering of people in Christ takes place: or rather, the Church is this gathering of people in Christ. Paul tells those who are gathered together in the Church that they are the body of Christ (1 Cor 12:27; Rom 12:5). The community is the body of Christ in the sociological sense of the term, because it is an organized group of people who, having different gifts and tasks, hold together and co-operate in the name of and for the sake of Christ. But for Paul the Church is body of Christ in a much deeper sense. The Semitic realism of his thinking makes him envisage contact between persons as something that occurs in a concrete, bodily fashion. To contact Christ is somehow to contact him bodily. The realism of the contact is experienced when the Church gathers to break a bread which is 'a participation in the body of Christ' as a result of which 'we who are many are one body' (1 Cor 10:16–17).

Paul's language about Baptism has to be given the same kind of realistic interpretation: 'as many of you as were baptized into Christ have put on Christ' (Gal 3:27) describes a relationship with Christ that is a flesh-and-blood sharing with him which makes people sons of God as he is Son. To believe in Christ and to be baptized into him is to be joined to his body; to draw life from him is to be a member of his body (see 1 Cor 6:12–20). Because the baptized are members of Christ they are members of one another (Rom 12:3–8). Together in him they build up the body of Christ, which is the Church.

In Romans 6 Paul explains the level at which Baptism effects this identification with Christ that grafts people into his body and makes them form the Church as his body. He explains how Baptism is a life-giving contact because it takes away sin and death and gives new life through resurrection. The underlying principle is that Christ took away sin by his dying and rising: he died to sin once for all, and he rose to new life in God (vv. 9–10). The application to Baptism is by way of a symbolical interpretation of the rite: going down into the water provides an experience of dying, and coming up, revived and refreshed, provides an experience of resurrection. The death and resurrection is with and in the death and resurrection of Christ, in which victory over sin is believed to be achieved. Hence, those who are baptized into Christ Jesus die to sin and rise to newness of life. Their sins are taken away: they are free of them; they no longer live in them but in God. All this is the grace of God, justifying those who believe, making them slaves of righteousness, where they had once been slaves of sin, and assuring them of the return that is 'sanctification and its end, eternal life' (v. 22).

To be baptized into Christ in the sense expounded in Romans 6 is to belong to Christ and to somehow share his status and his destiny. It is on this basis that Paul links Baptism with the theme of 'sonship' in Galatians and explains how it makes the baptized to be children of the Father along with Christ: 'For as many of you as were baptized into Christ have put on Christ . . . . And if you are Christ's, then you are Abraham's offspring, heirs according to promise . . . . when we were children we were slaves to the elemental spirits of the universe. But when the time had fully come, God sent forth his Son, born of woman, born under the law, to redeem those who were under the law, so that we might receive adoption as sons. And because you are sons, God has sent the Spirit of his Son into our hearts, crying, "Abba! Father!" So through God you are no longer a slave but a son, and if a son then an heir' (Gal 3:27 – 4:7). By introducing the 'Spirit of his Son' into his line of thought Paul is opening the way for the prominent place given to the Spirit in the understanding of Baptism, particularly in the Synoptic accounts of the baptism of Jesus, and in the gospel of John. Paul expounds the idea of sonship in connection with the work of the Spirit in chapter 8 of Romans. He does not mention Baptism there, but it is arguable that the movement of his thought is still being influenced by what he had said about Baptism in chapter 6.

The theology of Baptism in the Johannine writings is done more by way of allusion than by direct reference to the rite (on the 'sacramentalism' of John see Brown, *Gospel*, I, pp. cxiff.). Symbols and images drawn from the Exodus story and the preaching of the prophets about the latter days are used to deepen the understanding which Christian communities should have of their by now familiar rite of water-baptism. They come in the statements of John the Baptist about Jesus (John 1:19–36), in the discussion with the Samaritan woman (4:7–15), in the discourse at the feast of Tabernacles (7:37–39), in the account of the healing of the man born blind (John 9), in describing the washing of the feet (13:1–11), and in the Passion narrative, especially in 19:31–37). These texts convey the paschal meaning of the rite of Baptism (Jesus the lamb . . . blood and water . . .) and its connection with the eschatological outpouring of the Spirit. In the discourse with Nicodemus (John 3) there is a direct reference to Baptism. It is presented as a re-birth 'of water and the Spirit' (using, among other things, the womb symbolism of water), without which one cannot enter the Kingdom of God (v. 5). The source of this baptismal re-birth is indicated by references to the Spirit (v. 8), to the cross (v. 14), to the saving will of God (the Father who sends his Son, vv. 16–18), and its acceptance is by faith (vv. 15, 18) and living according to the light (vv. 19–21).

Although it does not have explicit references to Baptism, the first letter of Peter does refer to some important baptismal themes. It has, indeed, sometimes been suggested that the first part of it is a kind of baptismal catechesis. In chapter 1 there are references to being 'born anew' (1 Pet 1:3; 1:23; cf. 2:2), through the resurrection of Jesus Christ from the dead (1:3), through 'the living and abiding word of God' (1:23). The themes of the 'spiritual house' and the 'holy priesthood' introduced in chapter 2 subsequently became closely associated with the theology of Baptism.

5.3   THE THEOLOGICAL TRADITION: THE FATHERS

Baptism is so central in Christian life that there are very few Christian writers of consequence who have not contributed something to the theological tradition about it. There have also been doctrinal deviations and heresies about it, and these have given rise to definitions and directives from the *magisterium* of the Church. The tradition has been documented and analysed by historians of doctrine (Neunheuser; patristic texts in Palmer and Yarnold). An important strand of it is associated with the development of the theological concept of sacrament, much of which occurred by way of reflection on Baptism. This has been dealt with in Chapter 2. Some other technical issues that have arisen will come up in the systematic theology of Baptism to be presented below. Here it is enough to introduce some major theological works from different periods of the tradition, and the principal magisterial texts that deal explicitly with Baptism. These are texts that serious students of the theology of Baptism will want to look at in their entirety and not just in occasional quotations.

The oldest theological monograph about Baptism is the *De Baptismo* of Tertullian, written in North Africa about 200, while Tertullian was still a Catholic (CCSL I, pp. 275–295; trans. Souter). His subject in these twenty brief chapters is the rite of Baptism, which he describes in some detail. To explain it he employs most of the themes and images that are provided in the New

Testament; and he adds some ideas of his own associated with the word 'sacrament' (cf. Chapter 2 above). He sets out to explain, against some heretics who were already beginning to question it, how such ordinary things as are used in the Christian rite could produce such divine effects as were claimed for it: in other words, he opens up the fundamental problem of sacramentality. In his explanations he uses some analogies from pagan cults, but at the same time strenuously denies that Baptism is on their level. He deals with practical issues that were arising in the Church of his day — the necessity of Baptism for salvation, the Baptism of infants (he thinks it better to delay their Baptism until they can choose Christ for themselves), the forgiveness of sins committed after Baptism, the relationship between martyrdom and Baptism, the Baptism of heretics (which he considers valueless) and the relationship of Baptism to the Eucharist. In short, he does what a theologian of Baptism will always have to do: he thinks critically and coherently about the rite practised in the Church in the light of what the Word of God has to say about it, in a way that relates it to contemporary human experience (pagan religions, military service . . .), that answers the misunderstandings and objections of heretics and non-believers and that gives direction on various pastoral issues that were arising in the Church.

The mystagogical catecheses already introduced above (2.4) contain classical theological teaching on Baptism. Their subject is again the rite, as it has been experienced by the newly-baptized. They deal with the fundamental theological issue of the sacramentality of the rite, and with its effects. They do so in a language and set of ideas that are predominantly biblical. Because of the catechetical setting in which they were given they do not give much attention to the kind of theological question that might be divisive in the Church or to philosophical explanations of how Baptism works. And yet there is firm reasoning and logic in them. They give the Church a thoughtful account of its own rites of initiation that is a product of cultured classical minds, retelling the primitive scriptural story in an appropriate way to people formed in that Hellenistic culture.

Even though the Greek Fathers of the fourth century did not produce systematic treatises on Baptism they thought deeply about it. One can get the flavour of their thinking from reading *Sermon 40: On Baptism*, from St Gregory of Nazianzus (*PG* 36, 361–396; trans. Browne and Swallow). Two ideas about Baptism that were specially important for the Greek Fathers can be found well expressed in this sermon: Baptism is an illumination (*phōtismos* in Greek); Baptism is a seal (*sphragis*). The idea of illumination or light coming from Christ goes back to the Scriptures, especially to St John. St Justin uses it about Baptism in his *First Apology*, 61: 'This washing is called enlightenment (*phōtismos*), because those that are experiencing these things have their minds enlightened'. The idea is also important in the general sacramental theology of Clement and Origen. In them and in the Greek Fathers generally it is connected theologically with the word and instruction that goes with Baptism, and with the insight that baptismal faith gives into the mystery of God and his ways. It means more than intellectual knowledge: the light that illumines is also a fire that burns with the intensity of love and the penetration of mystical insight. The idea of seal is used by the Greek

Fathers especially in connection with the work of the Holy Spirit in Baptism. It says that Baptism definitively transforms, marks, anoints, consecrates as God's possession the one who gives himself to Christ. Whereas in the Latin tradition the idea of seal becomes concentrated in the idea of baptismal character, it remains a much more comprehensive idea in the Greek Fathers, which can draw to itself almost everything that needs to be said about Baptism.

St Augustine develops much of his theology of sacrament in connection with Baptism, as indicated in Chapter 2. His *De Baptismo contra Donatistas* is a classical statement of the theology of Baptism as sacrament (*PL* 43, 107–244). It sets an important part of the agenda for subsequent theology of Baptism in the Latin Church. The technical development he gives to the idea of seal is particularly important for the theology of the baptismal character. Another major contribution of Augustine to the theology of Baptism comes out of his dogmatic controversies with the Pelagians. One of the flaws that Augustine identified in their theology of grace showed in their claim that infants did not need to be baptized. Augustine argued that infants need the grace that comes in Baptism because they are sinners, involved in that original sin that affects all those born of Adam. In Baptism they are joined to the New Adam and receive from him the grace that takes away the original sin and establishes them in holiness. Since Augustine could not imagine a Baptism that would be without faith, he appeals to the faith of parents or sponsors to explain how the Baptism of an infant is a true Baptism. Without this Baptism infants remain in original sin. If they die they cannot see the face of God. Augustine was not able to find a way out of the awful theoretical consequences of this position, which would be that unbaptized infants who die are condemned to hell. Putting them on the fringe (*limbus*) of hell was the best he could do (*Sermon* 244: *PL* 38, 1337). Later theologians would wrestle with this Augustinian problem about the fate of unbaptized infants and some would propose less drastic solutions than he did. But what they rarely called into question was the link that Augustine established between Baptism and original sin. The doctrine of original sin has its biblical roots in the Pauline teaching about how the sin of Adam brought death into the world, and in the Genesis story of the Fall. It drew strength from the tradition of baptizing infants and from Augustine's reasoning about that (see his *De peccatorum meritis et remissione et de baptismo parvulorum ad Marcellinum* [*PL* 44, 109–200], esp. Lib. I). Belief in original sin eventually became an indispensable dogmatic constituent of the theology of Baptism in the Western Church.

5.4   ST THOMAS AQUINAS

From Scholastic theology one can profitably read the questions that St Thomas devotes to Baptism in the *Summa* (IIIa, qq. 66–71; Blackfriars ed., vol. 57). By now Baptism is clearly separated, both ritually and theologically, from Confirmation. Thomas studies it according to the technical framework for the analysis of sacrament that was becoming standard in his day: the rite itself in terms of sign, institution, essential matter and form, ceremonial, alternatives (Baptism of desire and of blood); the minister; who should be baptized and what is required of them; the many-sided effects of Baptism; circumcision as the principal Old Testament type; the rôle of catechesis and exorcism. Thomas's theology of Baptism is still a theology of the whole rite of the sacrament. It is a theology that is still patently biblical, even while it employs the technical categories of sacramentality. It also reflects the pastoral, liturgical and even sociological (e.g. the discussion about baptizing children of Jewish parents) situation of the Church of his day. If he does set apart the essential matter and form for special analysis he does not consider his theological reflection complete until he situates this core sign within the full rite of the Church (q. 66, 10). In his justification of the rite and his explanation of why it includes catechesis and exorcism (q. 71) he shows a traditional appreciation of the rôle of the word in Baptism. This appears also in what he has to say about the relationship between Baptism and faith — although it is somewhat obscured by his insistence on the sacramental principle that a Baptism can be a true sacrament even if the recipient or the minister does not have explicit faith. The faith of the Church is always present and active in Baptism (cf. q. 68, 9), as it must be in any sacrament.

5.5   THE REFORMATION AND TRENT

The relationship between Baptism and faith became a major point of controversy at the Reformation. Later generations of Scholastics had paid relatively little attention to the place of faith in Baptism and, in a general way, to the subjective side of the sacraments. It is significant that the Decree for the Armenians issued by the Council of Florence in 1439 (ND 1412), although it presents the faith of the Church about Baptism in a definitely Scholastic schema, omits anything that would correspond to St Thomas's question 68 about the recipient of the sacrament. The views of the Reformers on Baptism were in keeping with their view on justification and sacraments. Justification of the sinner is by faith alone; sacraments are of value to the extent that they are signs of subjectively experienced saving faith. The sacraments of the New Covenant are not really different in this from the rites and ceremonies of the Old Law. Of themselves they are merely works. Some Reformers (the 'Anabaptists') carried this principle to the point of defying the tradition of baptizing infants and of never repeating a Baptism for them or anyone else: they baptized only adults; and they rebaptized those who might have been baptized as infants when they came to experience justifying faith and conversion later in life. The majority of Protestants, however, respected the traditional belief that infants could and should be baptized. Nevertheless, in their theology they saw Baptism as a sign of the personal faith that justified rather than as an act of God who justifies in and through the sacramental sign of faith. The dogmatic definitions of the Council of Trent on Baptism have to be read in this light. There are important texts that situate Baptism within the process of justification in the Decree on Justification (ND 1928–1934); and the

Canons on the Sacrament of Baptism (ND 1420–1433) express Catholic teaching by way of condemnation of the errors that the Protestants seemed to be making. There is also important teaching about Baptism in the Decree on Original Sin (ND 507–513). The Reformers had no doubt that Baptism had to do with the removal of original sin. But their explanations of how Baptism dealt with sin were in line with their general theory of justification. To Catholics they seemed to be saying that the taking-away of sin was a kind of covering-over or non-imputation rather than a radical removal. In dealing with these issues Trent gave dogmatic status to a realistic doctrine of original sin, and to a realistic rôle for Baptism in taking it away.

5.6   MODERN THEOLOGY

Catholic Counter-Reformation theology of Baptism was solidly Tridentine. It used mainly Scholastic categories to expound and defend the doctrine of the Church. It was interested in doctrine more than in rites. When it did deal with the rite it was mainly to examine what was necessary for canonical validity, rather than to reflect on how the rite could be a humanly satisfying, word-enlightened experience of the work of salvation. But towards the end of the nineteenth century the theology of Baptism began to be affected by studies on the history and psychology of religion, and on the history of Christian liturgy and its interpretation in doctrine. Baptism lent itself particularly well to the general liberal interpretation of religious phenomena that was being developed around the turn of the century. Established theology reacted strongly against what it saw as the reductionist tendencies of this new kind of theology. The condemnation of Modernism by Pope Pius X included, in the Decree *Lamentabili* of 1907, a reference to errors about Baptism (ND 1437–1444). However, orthodox theology eventually found ways of reconciling the dogmatic tradition about Baptism with the new sciences. It did for Baptism what it was doing generally for sacramental theology (see Chapter 2 above). This is the kind of theology of Baptism that one finds in the Constitution on the Church (*Lumen Gentium*, nn. 7, 10, 11, 14) and the Decree on Ecumenism (*Unitatis Redintegratio*, n. 22) of the Second Vatican Council, and it is well respected by the canonical prescription about Baptism in the 1983 Code of Canon Law (cans 849–878). One finds it in the standard manuals of Catholic theology, like that of M. Schmaus (*Dogma* 5).

A major discussion on the relationship between Baptism and faith was opened up by a lecture of Karl Barth, published in English as *The Teaching of the Church regarding Baptism* (SCM, London, 1948). Basically, Barth argued that, because justification was by faith in God's word of promise, Baptism only made sense as an expression of personal faith and conversion. He did not, then, see a place for infant baptism in the Church. Barth argued his case on an exegesis of the New Testament texts about justification and Baptism. He claimed that the reasons why infant Baptism had been introduced and maintained in the Church, even by the major leaders of the Reformation, were extraneous to scriptural teaching and

often of a political nature. Not all admirers of Barth followed his views on
Baptism. His exegetical arguments were countered by Cullmann and Jeremias.
Catholic theologians contributed to the debate on exegetical grounds (see Duplacy in George, pp. 118–158). They also noted that there were dogmatic issues
about justification and the nature of sacrament at stake. As well as appealing to
the teaching of Trent in these issues they were able to document the tradition that,
while always seeing Baptism as a sacrament of faith, saw too that the faith of the
baptizing community allowed the sacrament to be effective in those who, while
not yet capable of personal faith, would be brought to it by Christian nurture
within the community.

5.7   ECUMENICAL CONVERGENCE

Catholic theology has been able to convince many Protestants, and to remind
Catholics, that its dogmatic tradition about Baptism includes a profound appreciation of the necessity of faith for the justification that God works sacramentally in Baptism. It has welcomed the recovery of a traditional sense of sacramentality among many Protestants. There are still, however, Protestants who are
unable to accept infant Baptism and who will rebaptize those whom they
consider to have come to personal faith for the first time. Some fundamentalist
sects take this line. But so do Baptist churches. And Karl Barth has defended the
position with high theological seriousness (see above). Ecumenical dialogue has
gone some way towards resolving these differences. BEM (see 2.10 above), and
the positive responses of so many churches to it, show how far Christians have
come together in their theological understanding of Baptism. The responses do,
however, show up some problem areas that remain for discussion between the
churches. In the official Catholic response there is a request for greater clarity in
the notion of sacrament being used to describe Baptism, for more attention to
the ecclesiological significance of Baptism, for explicit attention to the doctrine
of original sin in defining the range and kind of sinfulness that is overcome by
Baptism, for a clearer exposition of the necessity of Baptism for human salvation,
for a treatment of the 'seal of the Spirit' that might explain why Baptism is not
repeated, and for more clarity in stating the relationship between Baptism and
Confirmation.

5.8   A SYSTEMATIC ESSAY

To do a systematic theology of Baptism is to try to see with some clarity how
God is at work in the rite, gracing a crucial moment of human life, in a way that
brings people towards their fulfilment in himself. To do this one has inevitably
to use a whole structured set of ideas, worked out in other areas of systematic
theology, about God and the world, about God's grace and human response to
it, about the sending and mediatorial work of Christ, about the Holy Spirit and

the Church, about the general pattern of sacramentality that marks the gracing of human life and its return to God in the Church, through Christ and the Spirit. For a Christian theology of Baptism one has to use ideas that are the fruit of reflection on the Christian tradition of faith. For systematic theology these ideas have to be made intellectually coherent. And they have to be made to reflect real, contemporary human experience if they are to provide a word that will help Christians to relate whatever is being thought about theologically — in this case the rite of Baptism — to their real life.

5.8.1   Summary statement

Here is a summary statement of a systematic theology of Baptism, which will then be commented on phrase by phrase. (The commentary will be using material from the tradition of faith about Baptism that has already been presented in this chapter. The ideas will not be documented again. The value of a systematic essay should lie in the clarity it brings to an already known tradition of faith. It should be an *intellectus fidei* that reviews an *auditus fidei*):

Baptism is a work of God, in which he realizes his intention of giving salvation and the forgiveness of sin to all humankind, by incorporating into Christ, through regeneration in the grace of the Holy Spirit, and adoption to divine sonship those who believe in the Gospel and are converted from sin; this work is realized in and through the Church which is the community of those who proclaim Christ's death and resurrection and re-enact it in a water-rite that, as a sacrament, signifies and effects regeneration, incorporation and adoption by Father, Son and Holy Spirit.

5.8.2   . . . a work of God

If systematic theology is presenting things from God's point of view, the first thing it must say about Baptism is that God is acting in it. This is to say what the tradition has been wanting to say about Baptism from the beginning by calling it a mystery and later a sacrament. It is to call into play for the understanding of Baptism the whole theological analysis of God's being and action, which carries the mind beyond myth to metaphysics. It is to affirm the ontological ground and reality of Baptism. It is also to require that the celebration of Baptism be in some way a mystical, contemplative experience, without being for that any less a human experience.

5.8.3   . . . salvation . . . to all

Systematic theology analyses the history of salvation from God's point of view. A fundamental principle of the analysis is that God wishes all to be saved. In this present phase of the history of salvation Baptism embodies that divine intention.

It is offered to all — Jew and Greek, slave and free, man and woman. It is a simple rite using an element that is universally available and a symbolism that is universally appealing. It is carried throughout the world by believers with a missionary urgency that sometimes borders on the reckless, and is administered with a generosity that is always prepared to give the benefit of the doubt. For it is believed to be the gift of a God who wishes all to be saved by it. If it is claimed to be necessary for salvation this is thought to be a blessing, not a constraint. God's saving action will never be restricted to its actual use. There are other theological principles, to be considered in a moment, that require a certain moderating of the passion to baptize everyone. But they will not deaden the missionary urgency to baptize because they do not negate the principle that Baptism embodies the universal salvific will of God.

5.8.4 . . . the forgiveness of sin

The history of salvation that is analysed in systematic theology is the revelation of a loving, merciful God. The full depth of this loving mercy is seen in a salvation that is not just the divinization of creatures but is also the justification of sinners. In theology sin is more than ethical failure and deviation from moral norms. It is also, and primarily, a paradoxical reflex of the mercy of God. It is only in the light of the mercy of God that one recognizes sin for what it is — a human refusal to respond to the love of God. Correspondingly, the mercy of God is the assurance that, as far as God is concerned, sin is there to be forgiven. The universal salvation that gives divine meaning to Baptism includes the forgiveness of sin. Indeed, the salvation given by Baptism is sometimes described in the Scriptures simply as the forgiveness of sin (e.g. Acts 2:38). This is also how the Church's faith in Baptism came to be formulated in the Creed of Nicaea-Constantinople: 'We acknowledge one Baptism for the forgiveness of sins' (ND 12).

When the Scriptures and the Creeds say Baptism is 'for the remission of sins' they are referring to the full range of sins that adult humans commit, and that they repent of when they are baptized. Baptism is for the remission of personal sins. But there is in the theological tradition another facet of sin that has had a profound influence on the theological understanding of Baptism. It is expressed in the doctrine of original sin. One has to be careful about the way this doctrine is used in the theology of Baptism. While belief in universal human sinfulness, stemming from Adam and Eve, is taught clearly in Scripture, the distinctive doctrine of original sin, as it emerged notably in Augustine, is very much bound up with reflection on the Baptism of infants in the context of the controversy with Pelagianism. To make the forgiveness of original sin in this sense the distinctive purpose of Baptism is to make infant rather than adult Baptism the model for understanding the sacrament. This carries the risk of obscuring the personal response that God requires of sinners when he forgives them in Baptism. It could make the personal sins of an adult seem some kind of secondary condition that has to be remedied incidentally in the sacrament. It could encourage the tendency, which always has to be resisted by Catholic sacramental theology, to think of Baptism as having some kind of automatic, quasi-magical effectiveness in relation to original sin. Such a view does justice neither to Baptism nor to original sin. Infants are given the grace of God in Baptism: it is a grace for 'the forgiveness of sins' because they have inherited sinfulness from Adam and can only be sanctified by having that link with Adam broken. The inheritance of Adam takes a different existential form in adults. They make a decision about it in their personal moral life. They either choose God, and by that very fact are freed from all their sin; or they refuse God, and to that extent 'convert' original sin into personal sins. It is this personalized sin of theirs that is forgiven in Baptism. That is why the sacrament is designed to call forth personal faith and conversion. One can go on from there to provide a theological explanation of how this principle is verified in infant Baptism. It is much more difficult if one starts with infants and their original sin to give personal faith and conversion their due place in the theology of Baptism.

On this issue of Baptism and sin it is important to keep firmly in mind the connection between sin and death that is central in Paul's reflection on what came to be called original sin. While later theology found the key to the universality of sin in our being born from Adam, Paul finds it rather in the death we inherit from Adam. Death is the manifestation of our sinfulness in all its forms. And everyone dies. Salvation and the forgiveness of sin will somehow have to make sense of universal death and in doing so overcome it. This is the perspective that will allow one to understand Baptism as a rite of death and life, in which sin is overcome. It will also allow one to understand why all humans are called to Baptism.

With deliverance from sin and death comes liberation from all the forces that promote death and evil throughout the universe. These powers of death are variously imagined and conceived in the Christian tradition. The liturgy of Baptism uses the biblical images of the Devil and of the worldly institutions that seem to represent his dark power and pressure on humans to refuse the reign of God and the saving Spirit of Christ. Baptism is an act of faith in the victory of Christ over these powers of darkness. The baptized renounce them and are made aware that, in the power of the sacrament, they are delivered from them.

5.8.5 . . . incorporating into Christ

The most distinctive component of Christian systematic theology is the analysis of how God's will to save humankind is realized in the sending of his Son to be human in solidarity with all other humans, to live with them, to die for them, to rise from the dead as the firstborn of a new creation, to send the Spirit into the world for completing the work of salvation, and to come again at the end to restore all things to his Father. Christ is recognized as the only Saviour. He was that in anticipation for those who lived before his coming. He is so for all those who are now alive and for those yet to be born. The issue of salvation is now somehow or other a choice for or against Christ. This is the Christological presupposition of Baptism. To be baptized is to choose Christ as the only Saviour.

To choose Christ is to choose a very specific way of salvation. In choosing one who saved by dying and rising from the dead, one is accepting that life comes out of death. One is accepting that the overcoming of sin is done by the overcoming of death. Jesus is one of us who went through death without sin, crowning with his death a life of loving obedience to God his Father which had never been marred by any sin. His passage to resurrection is the definitive human victory over death and over sin. This is the soteriological ground of Baptism. Christ invited those who would be saved from their sins to die with him in order to rise again. He described his own death as a baptism and was actually baptized in a sort of ritual anticipation of the death he would die 'to fulfil all righteousness' (Matt 3:15). It is because of this, confirmed by an explicit command attributed to himself in the gospels, that to choose Christ as Saviour is, in practice, to choose Baptism. The choice for Christ is, indeed, made by faith. But faith is a decision to identify with this concrete historical person, whose Gospel says that he is available for this kind of contact in the rite of Baptism. The words are categorical. One cannot have Christ without Baptism. The qualifications made in 5.8.4 have to be made again here. As God has ways of saving those who do not explicitly choose him, so he has ways of saving those who do not explicitly choose Christ. He has ways of saving those who are not actually baptized. However, the necessity of Baptism as the way of contacting Christ remains a central affirmation of Christian faith, and a central motivation of Christian missionary effort.

The contact with Christ that is made in Baptism is called incorporation. The word is derived from the Latin word for body (corpus). Human contacts occur in and through the body. Life on all its levels is transmitted through bodily contact. Systematic theology has an analysis of how Christ in his body is the 'instrument' of God's saving action, and of how the life of grace is communicated to us by bodily contact with Christ. Baptism is the first moment of contact, and it is a contact that holds. The other sacraments, and particularly the Eucharist, develop the contact. Because it is the first and basic contact with the body of Christ, Baptism is said to incorporate us into him. This theology is, of course, derived from Paul's teaching about the body of Christ. His ideas will have to be discussed more fully in a moment when the ecclesiological principles engaged in Baptism are being looked at. For the present it is enough to note the bodily realism that is inherent in Paul's Christology and soteriology, and in his understanding of how humans lay hold of salvation in Christ. In statements like 'Do you not know that your bodies are members of Christ. . . ?' (1 Cor 6:15) he is inviting theology to give a strongly realistic interpretation to that first life-giving contact with Christ that occurs in Baptism and that is called incorporation.

5.8.6 . . . regeneration in the grace of the Holy Spirit

Systematic theology can analyse the reality of the Holy Spirit on different levels.

On the trinitarian level it studies the person of the Spirit and the mission of the Spirit in relation to the Father and the Son. The concrete realization of the mission of the Spirit is studied in the theology of creation and of human grace. It is on this level that the biblical story of the Spirit, starting at creation and culminating in Pentecost, and the theological reflection of the New Testament authors on this gift can be analysed. The Spirit is the ultimate gift of God's love, who creates and re-creates the universe, peopling it with children of God by giving a new life of grace to those who were dead in sin. The Spirit, sent by Christ from the Father, is the immediate divine agent of the justification of sinners, and his grace (habitual or sanctifying) is the created transformation that makes saints of sinners.

The action of the Spirit in Baptism, and the corresponding effect of it in the person being baptized, is well described by the word regeneration. It is one of the classical words in the tradition about Baptism. Taken literally, it simply means re-birth but imaginatively it draws its colour from the rite that it describes, which is a passage through the waters of death and burial to a new birth from the womb of those same waters. It suits the creating and life-giving rôle attributed to the Spirit in Scripture and the Creed. It is the pneumatological counterpart of incorporation: it says that Baptism makes one be alive in the Body of Christ by giving one rebirth in the Spirit.

Christian Baptism is in water and the Holy Spirit. The Spirit is active in Baptism and is given in it. Scriptural and patristic statements about the gift of the Spirit in Baptism are frequent and clear. What has led to some uncertainty in the tradition is the attempt of theology, begun perhaps already in the New Testament, to relate the different phases of the work of salvation to different phases of the rites of Christian initiation. Acts 8:14–17 seems to associate the gift of the Spirit with a laying-on of hands by the apostles that could be separated from the water-rite of Baptism in the name of Jesus. In some of the patristic theologies of initiation the gift of the Spirit is associated with an anointing and 'sealing' that follows the baptismal bathing. As long as Christian initiation was a single, continuous rite, all of which could be called Baptism, there was little danger that this line of thought would separate the gift of the Spirit from the water-rite of Baptism. However, when the rite called Confirmation came to be recognized as a sacrament distinct from Baptism, having a certain independence of it, some theologies thought they could define its distinct theological meaning by reserving the gift of the Holy Spirit to it, leaving Baptism to be defined Christologically: Baptism would be entry into the death and resurrection of Christ, Confirmation would be the acceptance of the Pentecostal gift of the Spirit. This question will be dealt with later, when the ritual and theological tradition about Confirmation has been examined. For the present it is enough to say that it is theologically inconceivable that Baptism could be incorporation into Christ, the forgiveness of sins and the laying-hold of God's salvation without conveying the grace of the Holy Spirit.

5.8.7   . . . adoption to divine sonship

Those who are regenerated in the Spirit and incorporated in the Son of necessity
become children of the Father: they become 'sons in the Son'. The theme of
adoptive sonship is constant in the tradition about Baptism. Along with regeneration and incorporation it reflects the trinitarian pattern of the sacrament. It is the
distinctive action of the Father in Baptism and expresses the distinctive relationship which the baptized have to him.

5.8.8   . . . believe. . . are converted

The mystery of grace is that the Holy Spirit causes the very human response in
which grace is received, and that the response remains fully human and fully free.
Systematic theology does the best it can to understand this mystery of how grace
is simultaneously gift and free moral choice. It is such a theology of grace that
one needs in order to understand how the gift of God in Baptism requires human
acts of moral choice. This is a theology of justification. It is affected by the
controversies of the Reformation and, for Catholics, guided by the dogmatic
decrees of the Council of Trent. All Christians agree that Baptism requires faith
and conversion on the part of the one being baptized. The catechumenate that
prepares for Baptism is a school of faith and conversion. The water-rite with its
words is a decisive act of faith and conversion. A ritual washing even with the
appropriate words that is not being met somehow by faith and conversion is not
Christian Baptism. Faith here is an assent to and choice of Christ as Saviour, not
just for the generality of humans but specifically in one's own personal regard.
It is an assent to his person as witnessed to and catechized by the word of teaching
that is spoken in the apostolic Church. It is an assent to Christ through assent to
credal statements of the Church and such dogmatic teachings as have been found
necessary for their elucidation and defence. Conversion is a turning-away from
sin in a turning towards God: it is a life-changing decision to put an end to sin
in one's life and to make a beginning of life in the new creation inaugurated by
Christ and the Spirit. In this sense faith and conversion belong to the most radical
level of moral choice. They have to if they are to correspond to the radicalness
of Baptism. Baptism is about a decision for or against the God who saves the
world in Christ. It brings one to the crucial moment of choice between life and
death. To call it a crucial moment is to evoke the cross ('crucial' comes from the
Latin word for 'cross') where the issue of life and death was played out to its
ultimate, prototypical conclusion. To accept Baptism is to choose life over death.
It is to pass from death to life. Only a choice as radical as that made in faith and
conversion could give human reality to that passage.
  Catholic no less than Protestant theology sees faith and conversion as gifts of
God. But there are theological differences between the Catholic and Protestant
view of how the human effort that goes into them is evaluated morally and
anthropologically. The Catholic tradition sees no threat to the gift of God in

crediting human choices with moral and meritorious value. It sees grace as a transformation of the ontological roots of human behaviour more than as a subjective stirring of the spirit. It has an approach to Baptism that is cool and pedagogical by comparison with the appeal to strong subjective faith-experiences of sinfulness and of being forgiven that seems more typically Protestant. The Catholic tradition can claim, too, that its ontological view of grace can offer a better explanation of how the requirement of faith and conversion are met in the Baptism of infants (see below, 5.9.2). The Protestant theology of grace is more likely to find the practice problematical.

5.8.9 . . . in and through the Church

A systematic theology will include an ecclesiology, in which it will explain how the grace of Christ and the Spirit is mediated through the community of believers, and how it builds those who are being saved into the body of Christ and the temple of the Spirit, until Christ comes again to restore all things to the Father. The Church 'is at the same time both community of the redeemed and redeeming institution' (see above, 3.2). This two-sided reality of the Church is, in one sense, the fruit of reflection on the sacraments. Once it has been established, however, it becomes an important key for understanding Baptism, and particularly why it is said to have the twofold effect of grace and character.

The Church is 'redeeming institution', or instrument of salvation, in that it is a community equipped to preach the Gospel and celebrate rites in which people take the Gospel into their lives and make it their own personal story. In its preaching and its rites the Church makes Christ present to people in a tangible way and gives the Spirit in an experiential way. It is in the community of the Church that Christ is contacted in the body and people are incorporated into him. Here one must take up again Paul's idea of the Church as body of Christ. The Church is the body of Christ in the sense that any organized group of people can be called a body. But Paul transforms the banal, metaphorical use of the term with the physical realism that he sees in the contact there is between Christ and those who are joined to him by grace. To say that the Church is the body of Christ is to say that it is a socially organized group of people who, in the diversity of their gifts and services, do bodily things like speaking and caring and ritualizing, by which they bring those who are to be saved (including themselves) into bodily contact with Christ. Baptism is the first full contact that is offered. In it the Church joins people to the body of Christ, incorporating them into him. In that very process it incorporates them into itself. Being made members of Christ, they simultaneously are made members of the Church. They begin to act as Church people, joining in the task of building up the community as body of Christ. Their action brings the gift of the Holy Spirit, from which flow new life, spiritual gifts and lively participation in the communion and mission of the Church, to themselves and to others. To be baptized is to make oneself part of the Church as community of the redeemed. It is to be ready to take full part in the Eucharist as the banquet of those who are saved in Christ. It is to contribute one's gifts to making the Church the instrument of salvation for others as well as for oneself.

Here one has the ecclesiological correlative of the two levels of effectiveness that are claimed for Baptism: it is said to give a character and to give grace. It is grace that makes the Church be the community of saints. But the Church itself co-operates in the receiving and giving of that grace. The co-operation takes bodily form: it is done by acts of speaking, caring, ritualizing, in each of which there is giving and receiving. As ecclesial actions these are Christ-actions. They are recognized to be his actions because they are done by people who are baptized. Baptism qualifies and equips them to represent him. It is this ability that is technically called the baptismal character. In Scholastic language the character is said to be the *res et sacramentum* of Baptism. It is a *res* (reality) in that it is signified and give by the rite of Baptism (which is the *sacramentum tantum*). It is simultaneously a *sacramentum* (sign) because it marks a person out as someone who can make the symbolic actions of the Church be actions of Christ, and therefore grace-giving (grace being the ultimate *res tantum* of every sacrament). If it is by the grace of Baptism that Christians are built into the body of Christ, which is the Church, it is by the baptismal character that they themselves participate in the making of the sacrament that gives this grace.

The baptismal character is said to be a sharing in the priesthood of Christ. The Church is able to mediate salvation only because it contains within itself the priestly mediation of Christ. This priestly quality of its mediation is realized in its celebration of sacraments. It sets up a system of ritual worship that is grace-giving because it is the visible realization of the priestly worship of Christ: it is so because the members of the Church share in different ways in the priesthood of Christ. This sharing has been identified since St Thomas with the sacramental characters. When the baptismal character is said to be a sharing in Christ's priesthood it is being defined as a qualification to perform ritual acts of worhip in the Church that Christ will make to be individual instances of his priestly work of salvation.

Because there is giving and receiving of grace in the Church the priesthood of Christ is shared in different ways by those who minister and by those who receive. The way of the recipient has a real priority. Christ can only be expected to make his priestly action available when someone calls out for it and is open to it. It is only in the face of a recipient that a minister acts in the Church. A person who is being baptized makes a gesture of appeal and openness to grace in undergoing the rite. The minister of the rite makes a gesture of giving. Their interaction makes it possible for Christ to realize his priestly action in the sacrament. If a person being baptized can make this priestly contribution to his own Baptism it must be because Baptism itself gives a sharing in Christ's priesthood that then becomes operative in the sacrament. That is precisely what the character (as *res et sacramentum*) is claimed to be. It is an effect of Baptism that allows a person to participate in his/her own sanctification. It is a sharing in Christ's priesthood that makes the sacrament be an act of Christ on the recipient's own behalf. Because it is for receiving, the baptismal character has been described as a passive power. This does not mean the rôle of the participant in Baptism is merely passive. He/she has to do something — all participation in sacraments is active. But what is done symbolizes receiving rather than giving. It is the minister who represents the giving side of the sacrament and shows forth that side of the Church. This is true even when the one who ministers is not an ordained person, as in a Baptism done by a layperson or even by a non-believer. They represent the Church as the giver of salvation. It is even more obvious when the minister is ordained. The character of Orders is said to be active. But the active characters build on the passive ones and depend on them. Without baptismal sharing in Christ's priesthood the sacraments would not be what they are supposed to be and the Church would not be what it is believed to be.

There is another truth about the Church that is reflected in the distinction made between grace and character in Baptism. There are sinners as well as saints in the Church. There are baptized people who fall back into sin. There may even be people who were baptized but never received the grace of the Holy Spirit. There is the possibility of rejecting the Spirit even in the very act of Baptism. Something can go wrong with the faith and conversion that is the personal moral reality of Baptism. The very communion of grace that binds people together in the body of Christ can be refused. If all faith and conversion were refused there would simply be no Baptism, because there would be a deliberate refusal to give the rite any Christian or ecclesial significance. There would be no intention of being baptized. But it is possible for a person to refuse conversion and the normal consequences of faith, and yet maintain some kind of assent to and vague yearning for the salvation that is offered in Baptism. To do that would be to go along with what the Church thinks it is doing in Baptism (to 'have the intention of doing what the Church does'). In that case the Church truly baptizes. Even when it is done in a church that is isolated from the great catholic communion of the Church, Baptism, provided it is properly celebrated, is an act of the Church of Christ and joins one to it. The baptized person takes hold of something of Christ, even if not accepting full incorporation into him. He or she becomes a member of the Church. The possibility is kept open that at some future date the baptized person might be able to take advantage of being in the Church to accept the gift of the Spirit by full faith and conversion. The Latin tradition spoke in this sense of a 'revival' (*revivificentia*) of sacraments (see Schillebeeckx, *Christ the Sacrament* . . . , pp. 181ff.). There is a theological explanation of this possibility in the baptismal character. It is seen as a real belonging to Christ. The one who has it can never be totally rejected by the Church (there may, of course, be various disciplinary degrees of exclusion) but must be ministered to for his or her salvation. Such people may also themselves minister to the salvation of others. When they are eventually brought to faith and conversion their decision will be referred back to their original Baptism. They will never need to be baptized again. The character thus understood is a power that abides, because one never ceases to be baptized and one can always claim to act in virtue of one's baptismal status. It marks one on a very deep level of one's personality (in a body/soul anthropology it is said to be a quality or mark of the soul), because it is concerned with that most profound of personal choices, which is to believe or not to believe in the salvation offered by Christ.

The ecumenical force of Baptism can also be articulated by the distinction between grace and character. When the communion of love is broken in the Church and the ministries of grace of one ecclesial community are refused by or to another, people find themselves being baptized into different churches. When ecumenical efforts begin to be made to restore unity the motive force is surely grace. It is a grace that, like the 'revived' grace of Baptism in those who received the sacrament without repentance, comes from their Baptism. The oneness of Baptism remains a constant bond, unspoiled by the sins that brought about the original divisions, or by those that hardened them in time and that weigh today on those who have inherited them. It is a designation and a call in every Christian to restore the unity of Christ's Church. It is more basic than grace because it keeps prompting Christians even when they are yet far from that full baptismal grace that will unite the churches in love. Ecumenical Christians see in one another's Baptism a permanent reality — and Catholics can call it the character — that is a shared belonging to Christ and to his one Church, and an openness to grace and to the ecclesial ministries of grace once they can be identified and agreed upon. Just as the fact of being baptized remains a life-line for sinners within the Church and can eventually bring them to the ministries of grace, so it is a bond for separated Christians that points them ontologically towards a common search for communion in grace and for shared access to the ministries of grace. It is a powerful bond, because it entitles Christians to call on the unfailing priesthood of Christ that is drawing all things into grace and communion.

If Baptism builds up the Church in both the giving and the receiving of grace, it is important for the understanding of the sacrament to remember that the Church is the instrument of salvation (giver of grace) only in order that it may become the communion of saints (receiver of grace). The instrumentality of the Church, and all that the sacramental characters stand for, will end with the coming of the Lord at the Parousia and only the communion of grace will remain. The baptismal character is functional and is at the service of baptismal holiness. Incorporation into Christ in the Church is meant to be a growth towards the full maturity of being in Christ, through a progressive transformation by the Holy Spirit. It is meant to be part of a collective growth of the body of Christ in which faith and conversion grow into love and communion. This is the full ecclesial effect of Baptism. It is where Baptism reaches into the Eucharist.

5.8.10 . . . proclaims . . . death and resurrection . . . rite

Since it is by his death and resurrection that Christ is the universal Saviour, it is as dying and rising that the Church must present him to those who are to be saved. It does so by telling the story of those events and proclaiming their meaning for human life in its preaching. Within that preaching it celebrates Baptism as a rite in which humans act out a dying and rising that they believe to be the dying and rising of Christ: they go down to be buried with him in the waters of death and come forth cleansed, refreshed, reborn to resurrection. Baptism is the first point of contact and identification with the body of Christ. It is incorporation into Christ by identifying with what he did — living and dying and rising — in his own body.

5.8.11   . . . sacrament, signifies and effects . . .

At this point a general theology of sacraments (see above, Chapter 3) can make its contribution to the understanding of Baptism. The water-rite and words are a sign, in the sense that term has in sacramental theology. They provide people with a congenial human experience through which God's action is mediated to them and their own response is simultaneously expressed. The experience is congenial for all the reasons that sacramental theology gives for the use of signs in human sanctification. In practice, a considerable pedagogy may be needed to make it so, using the kind of images and ideas dealt with earlier in this chapter and in Chapter 4.

The rite and words of Baptism, when properly performed, cause what they signify. The technical analysis of sacramental causality (see above, 3.6.3) can help to put order and a certain philosophical toughness into one's understanding of the process that has been described in the preceding commentary. The action of God, of Christ in his humanness, of the Church in its community and ministers, and of the participant can, in a Scholastic-type theology, be co-ordinated in terms of principal and secondary as well as instrumental causality — provided that is done in a way that respects the proper causality of signs. A theology working with phenomenological tools of analysis will do the same thing in the categories of personal encounter. There will also be technical explanations of how an obstacle can be put in the way of the grace of Baptism so that no effect is produced even though there is a real sacrament.

The effect of Baptism is described as 'regeneration, incorporation and adoption'. The fact that it takes three ideas to describe it is a reflection of the trinitarian God who works in it. God has revealed himself to be Father, Son and Spirit in the events of the history of human salvation. Each divine Person has been revealed in a distinctive personal rôle and relationship. Baptism brings that total work of salvation to bear on the individual being saved by invoking the divine Persons by name and calling forth a trinitarian profession of faith; it signifies and causes the distinctive effect of each and relates the person being baptized to each of them in a distinctive way.

5.9   ADDITIONAL THEOLOGICAL QUESTIONS

There are other questions that a sacramental theology may want to ask in its own particular terms about Baptism. Among them are: what are the precise elements and words that make up the essential sign (the matter and form); how was it instituted; who is its minister; what are its effects? They can be answered readily enough on the basis of the ideas and information about Baptism already presented. The essential sign is made up of a bathing in water and the trinitarian words. The institution (see above, 3.7.1) is attributed explicitly to Christ in the New Testament. The normal minister of it is bishop, priest or deacon, but 'in imminent danger of death and especially at the moment of death, when no priest or deacon is available, any member of the faithful, indeed anyone with the right intention, may and sometimes must administer baptism' (*General Introduction to the Rite of Christian Initiation*, n. 16); what is required of the minister is the intention of doing what the Church does, which is normally verified by the correct and respectful carrying-out of the rite of the Church. The effects of Baptism are the grace of incorporation into Christ, regeneration in the Holy Spirit and adoption by the Father, as well as the baptismal character. In the history of theology one can find elaborate discussion about each of these points. Some of it came out of meticulous philosophical enquiry. Much of it, however, originated in a rather ritualistic and legalistic approach to sacraments, and in the need to solve corresponding problems of pastoral casuistry. The recovery of a more traditional sense of sacramentality has made many of the details of those debates rather irrelevant. One admires the calm and simple statements about Baptism and its requirements in the *General Introduction to the Rite of Christian Initiation* of 1972. They provide a sensible perspective for dealing with most of the practical questions and intellectual curiosities that are likely to arise about Baptism.

There are, however, some theological questions about the necessity of Baptism for salvation that still need a somewhat extended discussion. There is little difficulty about the application of the principle of necessity for salvation (see above, 3.7.3) to Baptism in the case of those who know about it and can actually be baptized. They quite simply cannot be saved if they culpably refuse Baptism. It is pointed out in this context that the necessity in question is not just something that arises from a command (*necessitas precepti*) but that it arises from the very nature of things (*necessitas medii*). There is an ontological, not just a legal connection between Baptism and salvation. A consequence of this is that those who do not know about Baptism, or who cannot be baptized, are not simply dispensed from it. A distinction is made between the reality of Baptism (*res*) and the rite (*sacramentum*). One can be had without the other. Those who through no fault of their own cannot receive the rite of Baptism must receive the reality of it, whether they know it or not, if they are to be saved. How they do it has been thought about theologically in the Church in connection with three questions: (1) the salvation of those who, although not baptized in water, make a personal choice for salvation in what are called Baptism of blood and Baptism of desire; (2) the Baptism of children; (3) the fate of children who die without Baptism.

5.9.1 Baptism of blood and of desire

The scriptural texts that require Baptism for salvation (Matt 28:19; Mark 16:16; John 3:5) seem categorical. No alternatives are offered to those who want to be saved after the resurrection. The assumption seems to be that there could be no neutrality about the God of the Lord Jesus Christ. If one did not accept him one was rejecting him, either by clinging to the God of the Law or by worshipping the gods of Greece and Rome. Though the principle enunciated in 1 Timothy 2:3–4 ('God our Saviour, who desires all men to be saved and to come to the knowledge of the truth') is maintained, the earliest known Christian admissions that people are actually saved without the rite of Baptism come from the third and fourth centuries (Hippolytus, *Apostolic Tradition*, XIX, 2; Irenaeus, *Adversus Haereses*, III, 16, 4; Cyprian, *Letter* 73, *ad Jubaianum*; Ambrose, *De Obitu Valentiniani*, 51: *PL* 16, 1374–1375). They are about catechumens who die before they can be baptized, especially when they die as martyrs. They are, therefore, about people who already believe in Jesus Christ as Saviour and accept his Church. If they are martyred for his name they do realistically what Baptism is designed to do ritually. Their death, indeed, expresses their faith in a better and more decisive way than ritual Baptism: they actually die with Christ, with a view to sharing in his resurrection; they become members of the heavenly Church even though they have never been full members of the earthly Church. In these early texts and in the subsequent tradition martyrdom is called a Baptism of blood. That terminology says something about martyrdom and it says something about Baptism. About Baptism it says that the reality of the sacrament is brought about essentially by faith in Christ and sharing in his death: any significant human action that manifests these choices unequivocally is entitled to be called a Baptism. About martyrdom the term 'Baptism of blood' says that shedding one's blood gives salvation only to the extent that it is an act of faith in and imitation of the death of Christ: only when dying stands for what the rite of Baptism stands for does it guarantee salvation and resurrection. The martyr can do without ritual Baptism because he or she achieves the reality that the rite is designed to express, and eventually to cause, in another, more immediate way. Catholic theology considers Baptism of blood to be an even better way of salvation than ritual Baptism (St Thomas, IIIa, q. 66, 12). In this it is also saying that what should be aimed at in ritual Baptism is the kind of faith and identification with Christ unto death that the martyrs show.

Reflection on martyrdom let theology see that what goes on in the mind and heart of a person can have a baptismal effect whether it is expressed in the rite of Baptism or in some other significant way. That modified the seeming intransigence of the biblical texts about the necessity of Baptism, and made it easier to recognize that anybody who lived and died well could be said to be baptized and therefore saved. The earliest texts on this envisage only the case of catechumens who died before there was time to baptize them. They had faith and conversion and the intention to be baptized. This intention found expression in their acceptance of the catechumenate. But it also found expression in their death which, presumably, they experienced in faith as a dying in Christ. Such a readiness to die in Christ was inherent in their intention to be baptized. The term that eventually emerged to describe this way of salvation is 'Baptism of desire'. Like the term 'Baptism of blood' it says that the reality of salvation is gained essentially by faith and conversion which are somehow related to dying in Christ. Actual death takes the place of ritual dying also in this case. But natural death does not have the inherent challenge to the Christian that death by martyrdom does. To refuse ritual Baptism on the grounds that one would eventually be baptized in one's own death would be to refuse the very guarantee given in the Gospel that one's death would be Christian. Catholic theology has accompanied its teaching about Baptism of desire with a warning that anyone who, knowing what the Gospel says about the necessity of Baptism for salvation, does not take reasonable steps to be baptized in water cannot claim to be saved through Baptism of desire. (The magisterial statements on the necessity of Baptism, at least of desire, for salvation are in ND 510, 1405, 1408, 1419, 1424, 1437/42, 1928.)

The concept of Baptism of desire can be sustained easily enough when it is postulated for catechumens who die before being baptized. Baptism of desire, in this case, includes an actual desire of Baptism. It is more difficult to see why it should be postulated for explaining the salvation of the far greater number of people who know nothing whatever about Baptism and have no explicit faith in Christ. A case could be made for doing a theological turnabout on the question: one might first work out a general theology of salvation without any reference to Baptism, and then introduce Baptism as a particular, privileged way of salvation for those who are called to the Christian faith; there would then be no need to postulate a Baptism of desire for those who know nothing about Christ or Baptism. (Note that Vatican II does not use the term 'Baptism of desire' when explaining in *Lumen Gentium*, n. 16 how non-believers are saved and belong to the People of God.) While such a theology would have some advantages it would have some difficulty about accounting for the centrality of Christ in God's plan of salvation and about the place of the Church in it, and about the claims of Christian eschatology. The necessity of some form of Baptism for salvation is an expression of these great truths of Christian faith. To dispense with Baptism of desire would also deprive Christian theology of a valuable image for stating an important truth about all human salvation and for suggesting what it is in any human religion or ethical system that might be salvific. Christian faith affirms that anyone who lives well, in accordance with conscience, is being saved. The notion of conscience supposes some form of belief in an ultimate good to which one gives oneself in a decisive act of choice, and for which one is ready to renounce anything in one's life that is incompatible. To do this is to choose life. But one can only choose life when one has made some sense of the enigma of death. The choice of good and the renunciation of evil must be strong enough to hold in the face of death, which puts a question-mark before every hope of life. To choose to live well is somehow to take the sting out of death. It is to be ready to die well. This profound truth about the human condition is given theological colour by the claim that Baptism of desire is required by all for salvation. What Baptism stands for in any of its forms is an act of faith that life has conquered death, that there is a way of experiencing death that gives life. To talk about Baptism of desire for all who are saved is to say that, however they express it, all must make a choice for life that overcomes death, that they must leave aside all that is not life-giving, that they must identify with people and institutions that care for life and oppose all who are hostile to it. That is to say something profoundly helpful about human life. It is to provide an insight into what it is in the great religions of humankind and in all forms of religious experience as well as of secular humanism that makes them salvific. That is also to say something important about Baptism, because it shows how the rite of it touches the most profound needs and desires that are shared by all humans.

The theology of Baptism of desire remains a way of expressing the Christian faith that all salvation comes through Christ and the Church. Anyone who chooses the victory of life over death implicitly accepts all that gives life, whether he can identify it or not. Implicit in what is called Baptism of desire is the choice of Christ and the Church. Implicit in it, too, is the acceptance of the eschatology that sees the ultimate choice facing the whole of creation as a choice for or against Christ; and that he is believed to be the one who will eventually judge all human choices; and that — although it will come as a surprise to many — he will judge them in reference to himself (Matt 25:34–46). Because it believes it has a mission to bring about this final consummation of things in Christ the Church will never let its teaching about Baptism of desire become an excuse for not proclaiming the Gospel way of salvation to all, calling them to join Christ and his Church already in time through the water-rite of Baptism.

5.9.2   The Baptism of children

There is nothing in the early records of the Christian tradition to suggest that there was a time when the Church did not baptize children. While some statements of the Scriptures about the place of faith in Baptism can raise theoretical difficulties about the practice (cf. K. Barth) there is no factual evidence that it was not done. There is no reason to believe, for example, that when whole households are said to have been baptized (Acts 10:44–48; 16:15; 16:33; 1 Cor 1:16) the children, even of tender years, were excluded. It is known that, at the time the Scriptures were being written, children of Jewish proselytes were baptized into the Jewish faith along with their parents. There is no evidence that Christians did otherwise (Cullmann, *Baptism*, pp. 25, 51–53; Jeremias, *Infant Baptism*, ch. 1; Duplacy in George, pp. 127–133). Although there are some indications in the second century that children were baptized, the positive evidence does not appear until about AD 200. Tertullian in Africa, Hippolytus in Rome and Origen in Egypt (references in Duplacy, p. 129) say it is the common practice of the Church and has been from the beginning. Tertullian did not think it was a very good idea and would have preferred that children were not baptized 'until they could know Christ', but his position is reckoned to have been eccentric. When a significant number of potential Christians began, especially in the fourth century, to postpone Baptism it was often for less worthy motives. The reaction of pastoral leaders of the Church to these delays re-states and gives reasons for the tradition of baptizing people as soon as possible, and even in infancy. Pelagian thinking challenged some of these reasons, especially those which saw infants as being subject to sin and therefore in real need of Baptism. But their denials were concerned more with the meaning of infant Baptism than with the fact of it.

St Augustine in taking up the challenge of Pelagianism did some influential thinking about how Baptism worked in children and why they needed it. The part of his teaching that became notorious is the connection he made between the Baptism of children and original sin: children are born in original sin, and the only way they can be freed from it is by Baptism in water. It followed from this, Augustine had to reluctantly admit, that if they died without Baptism they could not be saved. The acceptance of the teaching of Augustine on this point in the Western Church confirmed and intensified the sense of urgency about baptizing infants, especially if they were in danger of death. This becomes the dominant concern in magisterial pronouncement up to the Reformation (ND 1405, 1407, 1419). Of course, there is more than this to the teaching of Augustine, and of the tradition generally, about the Baptism of children. There are explanations of how Baptism incorporates children into Christ and into the Church, and of how the faith of parents and other members of the Church enfolds them and gives significance to their Baptism (St Thomas, III, q. 68, 9; q. 69, 6). Protestants had difficulty about this doctrine because of the way they understood justification by faith. But only some of them refused to continue the practice of baptizing children or practised re-baptism of those who had been baptized as infants. The Council of Trent condemned these Protestant positions (ND 1430–1433). Its justification of infant Baptism is entirely in terms of original sin (ND 511). One has to wait for the post-Vatican II Rite of Baptism for Children (1969) and an Instruction on Infant Baptism, *Pastoralis Actio* (1980) from the Congregation for the Doctrine of Faith (ND 1443–1446) for a fuller magisterial teaching on the subject. Both these documents give careful attention to the assumption that has always been in the tradition — even if it has not always been reflected in practice — that infant Baptism only makes sense to the Church when the parents of the child want it and are ready, with the help of the Church, to ensure that the child will be formed in accordance with the life that has been given to it in Baptism. It is forbidden to baptize a child without these assurances. The prohibition does not hold when the child is in danger of death. For many centuries the practice has been to baptize all infants in danger of death, unless their parents positively oppose it. It is believed that the sacrament makes them children of God, frees them from original sin and makes their death a passage to resurrection.

A theological understanding of the Christian tradition about infant Baptism is best gained by looking first at the gift of God that is in it and then, in the light of that, at the human need that it meets. As a general rule one only gets a good theological understanding of human need when one has first thought about what God has done for human fulfilment. God offers salvation to all through Christ and the Church gathered in the Holy Spirit. He gives that salvation to everyone who does not actually refuse it. His gift (grace) produces within them the appropriate response that accepts it. They are brought to life and freedom and human realization by the gift of God. What God does for them is not something they can afford to be indifferent to: to refuse it is to refuse their own human fulfilment from the God who made them be what they are. Baptism embodies the offer and action of grace from God, as well as the human response to it. It embodies it as given and received in the Church. For this reason it has within it not just the ministry of the Church that gives grace but also the Church's response of faith and love that receives grace. The response of the individual to the grace of Baptism is always cultivated and carried within this response of the community. The cultivating and carrying takes the form of a comprehensive solidarity with the human situation of the person to be baptized, which makes it possible for him or her to take hold of the grace of God being given in the sacrament. A Christian community that would, for example, disregard the fact that one of its catechumens was hungry or suffering some other human degradation, on the grounds that Baptism was only concerned with the 'good of souls', would hardly have much success in encouraging an appropriate response in that person to the saving grace of God. A Baptism offered in that spirit would be a poor sign of the saving love of God. The human situation of a child is one of promise and dependence. What it can become depends on its parents. In identifying with the care and responsibility felt by the parents, the Christian community shows that it wants the gift of God for the child in Baptism. It is in this wanting of the Church (its faith in God's will to save this child) that the gift of God is actually given. What is wanted is everything that the parents want for nurturing their child towards health and happiness. The Church community may have to help to feed the child if the family is poor; it may want to provide suitable schooling if that is not otherwise available. The Church makes its own the concern of the parents to provide everything that can make the child capable of growing towards good personal decisions about life and love.

Central among the choices for which parents want to prepare their children is the one to be made about God and his offer of salvation. It is this, and not the choice about what church they will belong to or what religion they will practise, that is at stake in the Baptism of children. However, if parents do believe that it is in Christ and his Church that God offers the fullness of life to humans they will want their child to have the opportunity of belonging to the Church, as they will want it to have all other opportunities of growing towards life-fulfilling choices. They will want this belonging to be as complete as possible, to the point of being a real belonging to Christ. Such a being in Christ, in the Church, is the most secure, objective guarantee that the nurture the child receives from its earliest days will bring it to a personal choice for God when it becomes capable of such a choice. For parents to deprive their children of such a rooted nurturing in grace would be like, even if on a different plane, letting them face their first sexual encounter without giving them any prior experience of the tenderness of human love, or any instruction about sexuality, or without showing any care for their proper physical development.

There is nothing in this explanation of the Baptism of children that requires a distorting or truncating of the sacrament itself. Baptism as already defined for adults can also work for children. It is an act of God being met by an appropriate human response of faith. The faith as always is a gift of God. It is being professed by parents, sponsors and other Church members in the rite of Baptism. They ask, in faith, for the baptismal grace that leads to faith for one for whom they are responsible and who is dependent on them for his or her very being. A child is vulnerable to and therefore receives every act of care or carelessness that enfolds it, beginning from the womb of its mother. The fact that it reaches adult life is the result of what others do for it; and the direction that its life takes is affected by everything that happens to it. The Christian community provides a mothering, beginning it with the womb-experience of Baptism, that makes it possible for the child to receive the gift of grace in the way it receives all other gifts. There are charming analyses in psychological literature of how all the care that a baby is given — cuddling, bathing, talking to — and the reactions that these call forth, affect its growth into personhood (Schillebeeckx, *Christ the Sacrament*, pp. 133–137). The grace of God is in all these forms of care, especially when they begin to take explicitly Christian forms like praying with the child and telling it the Christian story. This is how the grace of Baptism is able to produce its effects until it is eventually appropriated personally in faith by the child who becomes an adult. As Baptism has been a physically experienced symbolic event with psychological and educational consequences, so it gives a grace that is an ontological reality that has moral consequences. This is sanctifying grace, given in a habitual state and subsequently activated as the child awakens to moral responsibility and the demands of the life of virtue (St Thomas, IIIa, q. 69, 6).

The grace of God given in Baptism is a redeeming and remedial gift. It justifies in taking away sin. It is a passage from belonging to the old Adam to being under the headship of Christ, the new Adam. It takes away original sin. In adults this sin has become the object of personal decision, which has either removed it (Baptism of desire) or affirmed it by personal sins (see above, 5.8.4). By the mere fact of being born, a child shares the ungraced state of the race, which is what is meant by being under the headship of Adam. It has made no moral choice about its situation and therefore the most that original sin can be for it is the absence of justifying grace. This grace is given to it when it is baptized into Christ, the new Adam. It is given for growth towards its own acceptance in faith. By that very fact it is given for the taking-away of everything that would prevent or distort growth. The negative influences that an adult has to struggle against in order to persevere and grow in grace also affect a child. Although rooted in its own being, they are brought to bear on it by the people and institutions that surround it. The Church community that brings it to growth will also be working to overcome these influences wherever they are found, and to protect children from them. The overcoming of sin in the child by the action of the community belongs to the grace of Baptism. It is an integral part of the taking-away of original sin. It is theologically feasible that this taking-away of sin should begin without a conscious personal act of conversion, because the sin in question is an inherited, not a freely chosen state in the child. The conscious rejection of sin will come when the child becomes an adult, and will be the fruit of the grace into which the child has grown. If that rejection is not made in due course the person once baptized will become a sinner again. His or her sin will be affected by, but not attributable to, the sinful state of the human race because it will have been the result of a personal choice. In the Catholic tradition it is dealt with in the Church by the sacrament of Reconciliation, not by any repetition of Baptism.

If it is considered to be more profitable theologically to think about the Baptism of children as growth in grace before thinking of it as the removal of original sin, one will take the requirements that the Church sets for such Baptism very seriously. One will simply not baptize until one has very clear guarantees of the intentions and ability of parents to form the child towards a full adult life of grace, and until one can count on the kind of support from an ecclesial community without which this cannot be realized. But a certain theological and pastoral unease can be generated by such a theology and practice, and some parents can find it oppressive. Appeal is made to another theological principle: Baptism is necessary for salvation; for adults it may take the form of Baptism of desire or of blood if they cannot be baptized in water; but for children there is no alternative to Baptism of water; if they die without it they die in original sin. From the fourth century onwards this way of reasoning has loomed large in much Christian thinking about infant Baptism. One must baptize them, and quickly, because one must not put their salvation at risk. Every possible measure, including baptizing unborn or aborted foetuses, is to be taken to ensure Baptism in danger of death. Children of parents who are not Christian are also to be baptized in danger of death, even surreptitiously when it is thought the parents might object. The theological and even magisterial weight behind this view has to be given due respect. However, its application depends on how one understands the risk of damnation that unbaptized children are exposed to. The greater the risk the more strenuously one will work to eliminate it. If, on the other hand, there are alternative ways of salvation for unbaptized infants one will be under less pressure to baptize at all costs.

5.9.3   Children who die without Baptism

Augustine could see no way of salvation for children who die without Baptism. He first thought they might have enjoyed some sort of middle way between beatitude and damnation (*De Libero Arbitrio*, III, 66: *PL* 32, 1302) but under pressure from his polemic against Pelagianism he eventually concluded that salvation was all or nothing: infants who did not receive it through Baptism went to hell; their punishment was as mild as could be, but they were deprived of the vision of God. Other Latin Fathers and the Greeks who dealt with the issue were less absolute. Still it is Augustine's anti-Pelagian position that has always haunted Western theology. Because many of his premises, and especially his concern to maintain the dogmatic truth of the necessity of Baptism for salvation, were shared, it was hard to refuse his conclusions about unbaptized infants. Much of the effort was to soften it rather than to challenge it. Of course, theologians often made the point that God has ways of saving people that we know nothing about, and that he works miracles. But now and again some daring ones tried to work out a theory of how it might be done. The question was not very much discussed during the Middle Ages. When it was, use was made of a standard theoretical distinction between the punishment for personal sins, which was hell, and the punishment of original sin, which was exclusion from the vision of God, without any further afflictions. It could be said, by way of modification of the Augustinian position, that infants dying without Baptism would at least not suffer the pains of hell, although they would be deprived of the vision of God because they had never been reborn in grace. There was some attention given to the place where those being punished for original sin would be consigned. It was thought about by analogy with that *limbus Patrum* where the just of the Old Testament waited, on the fringe (*limbus*) of hell, for the coming of Christ, and from where he freed them when he 'descended into hell' after his death. The Fathers could be freed because they had had faith in Christ who was to come. There was no such hope for those in the *limbus puerorum*, where unbaptized infants were consigned. However, Limbo played a very insignificant part in the theology of the major Scholastics. St Thomas, for example, does not allude to it in his theology of Baptism in the *Summa*. The theological questions the hypothesis might have raised — its scriptural warrant, its coherence with theories of nature and grace, its implications for a theory of the general resurrection — were not dealt with to any extent.

In the sixteenth century Cardinal Cajetan questioned the Augustinian assumptions of Scholasticism about the salvation of unbaptized infants. He reasoned that at least the children of Christian parents could be saved without actual Baptism because of the desire of their parents to have them baptized. It seems that some questions were raised about his theory at the Council of Trent, but it was not censured. The *magisterium*, in fact, has had very little to say about the question over the centuries. The First Council of Lyons (1245) says nothing about it in its teaching *De sorte defunctorum* (DS 838) in which, among other things, it talks about Purgatory. The Council of Florence adopted, as part of general eschatology, the distinction between the punishment in store for those guilty of personal sins and those who die with only original sin, but it omits the words about the places in which these punishments are inflicted (*locis disparibus*) from an earlier papal text which it is citing (cf. DS 926). The Synod of Pistoia is censured for making light of the teaching about the place 'which the faithful commonly call Limbo of the Children' (DS 2626). Nothing more explicit or binding can be found in the teaching of the *magisterium*. Given that reticence, and the variety of views in the theological tradition, it is surprising to find Pius XII affirming in an address to Catholic midwives in 1951: 'In the present economy there is no other means than Baptism of communicating this [supernatural] life to the infant who has not yet got the use of reason. So that of all men it is true that "unless a man be born again of water and the Holy Spirit he cannot enter the kingdom of Heaven". Those who die in original sin go to Limbo' (*AAS* 1951, p. 841). The first two sentences of this statement have been affirmed constantly by the tradition of faith. But the final one has nothing like the same weight of authority or theological reasoning behind it. One can understand that the Pope, speaking to midwives, would want to make a strong case for baptizing infants in danger of death. Limbo was a familiar, if frightening, part of the Catholic cosmography, which could be counted on to move people to action. But many theologians are still prepared to search for an alternative to the theological postulate of Limbo and to look for a way of affirming the salvation of unbaptized infants that will not contradict the tradition on the universal necessity of Baptism, and the correlative universality of original sin (which are the doctrines that magisterial teaching has primarily wanted to defend).

The search for a solution has a properly theological motivation. True, it is even more deeply motivated by mercy, and by the desire to comfort families that have lost a baby before it could be baptized, and by a wish to make God look good — and theology is not indifferent to these reasons of the heart. But in a strictly theological sense it is motivated by the need to reconcile two indisputable theological principles. One of these is that Baptism is necessary for salvation. The other is that God wishes all to be saved. The second principle is at least as high in the hierarchy of truths as the first. No teaching about the necessity of Baptism that contradicts it can be acceptable. Of course, it can be argued that, even if God wishes all to be saved, he does not in fact save all, and therefore to say that unbaptized infants are not saved does not deny the principle. In reply it must be said that the reason some people are not saved is that they refuse the grace God gives them; or, as it is sometimes stated in the theology of justification, God does not refuse his grace to anyone who does what he or she can to accept salvation. Infants do not refuse the grace of God in any way; there seems no reason, then, why God's universal saving will should not be fulfilled in them. In truth, it is hard to believe that a God who so loved the world as to give his only-begotten Son for the salvation of all, and who is believed to take more delight in the saving of one lost soul that in the ninety-nine who are already safe, would set a baptismal requirement so rigid that it would exclude from salvation an infant who, through no fault of its own, does not fulfil it literally. Theology has managed to understand how God saves adults who do not fulfil literally the command to be baptized. It has been able to distinguish between the reality of Baptism (*res*) and the rite (*sacramentum*). If the reality can be given to adults without the rite, one cannot *a priori* exclude the possibility that the same thing can be done for infants. One cannot exclude it simply because one has not discovered how it could be done. One owes it to the God who wishes all to be saved to go on trying to find an explanation. (The subject was much discussed by Catholic theologians before Vatican II: see indications in *Further Reading*.)

The solution continues to be sought along various lines. One way is simply to reason from the universal saving will of God to the conclusion that unbaptized infants are saved, but in a way that we know nothing about because God has revealed nothing about it and there is no reason why he should. Another hypothesis is that infants are miraculously enlightened at the moment of death to the point of being able to make a personal decision about Christ. Such an enlightenment is not intrinsically impossible: if one who dies in infancy is capable in eternity of knowing God (or knowing what it is to be without God) it could very well be given the use of its spiritual faculties at such a level in the instant before passing into eternity. For some theologians the solution proposed by Cardinal Cajetan still seems worth following up, even if it has the limit of dealing only with the situation of children born of Christian parents. It can claim some support from the Scriptures. In 1 Corinthians 7:14 Paul seems to reason that the children of a Christian parent (he is talking about a 'mixed' marriage) are holy by that very fact, without any reference to Baptism. It is not possible to say with any assurance what is meant by the 'baptizing on behalf of the dead' that Paul refers to in 1 Corinthians 15:29. It could be a matter of pagans accepting Baptism in order to be able to rejoin deceased Christian relatives and friends (K. C. Thompson); or it could be a posthumous Baptism undertaken by the living on behalf of those who had become Christians but died without being baptized (Barrett, pp. 362–364). In any case, the practice was eccentric and did not survive in the Church.

The theories already mentioned are still rather closely bound up with the Augustinian and Scholastic statement of the problem. It is possible that a wider search of the Scriptures, that goes beyond questions of baptizing or not baptizing, would situate the question differently and perhaps open up other solutions. In a book called *From Limbo to Heaven. An Essay on the Economy of Redemption*, published posthumously in 1961, Fr V. Wilkin, SJ, did such a scriptural re-statement of the question, mainly in Pauline terms, and came up with a theological theory to explain the salvation of infants ('the blamelessly unbaptized') that has much to commend it. What follows is a summary, with some adaptation, of his ideas. Everyone born into this world is a child of Adam and comes under his headship. All are afflicted by his sin. This original sin is a sin of the race. People have it because, and as soon as, they are born into solidarity with the situation of the race. It is manifested in the death to which all are condemned. Christ overcame sin in overcoming death. In rising from death he made it possible for all who belong to the human race to overcome death and to rise with him. He became the new head of the human race, the new Adam, the new Lord of all creation and giver of the Spirit. He is bringing all things under his Lordship in the course of time, and will complete the transformation at the final resurrection, when he will deliver all to the Father. When that happens the human race will owe nothing any more to the headship of Adam because it will have come entirely under the headship of Christ. Infants who are not yet baptized are children of Adam. They represent the fallen, unredeemed state of the race. They represent it simply because they are human. They have contributed nothing personal to human sinfulness. Like all humans they are threatened with death and eternal exclusion from the kingdom of God unless they are somehow rescued from the headship of Adam and brought under the headship of Christ. Baptism is one way. But if they die without Baptism there is still another way. Since Christ conquered death for the human race, human death has a different significance from what it had under the headship of Adam. All who die now rise again and, by that very fact, come under the headship of Christ. Those who have died in personal sins will have put an obstacle to the full taking possession of them by Christ, to his full Lordship over them. But unbaptized infants will have put no such obstacle. Christ can see their death as an unimpeded sharing in his own death and their risen bodies as belonging entirely to himself. In the resurrection, for an infant just to be human is to belong fully to Christ, as at its first birth to be human was to belong to Adam. It represents the state of the race at its best as it once represented it at its worst. So, infants are saved by the very fact of the resurrection, without exercising any choice, as they were afflicted by original sin by the very fact of being born (about which they also exercised no choice). Fr Wilkin calls this a Baptism of the resurrection. The use of this term maintains the principle of no salvation without Baptism, as Baptism of desire and Baptism of blood do in the case of adults. Like these other terms it indicates that the reality of Baptism is given without the rite. Fr Wilkin was prepared to admit that unbaptized infants would have to wait until the general resurrection for their saving transformation in Christ, and would allow that their place of waiting could be Limbo. But at the resurrection Limbo becomes for them 'the baptistery of heaven'.

A theory along these lines certainly does justice to the principle that God wishes all to be saved. It follows Paul's teaching and imagery about how the divine will to save is actually worked out in the history of salvation. Within that vision it finds a significant event — resurrection — that has an obvious bearing on the issue of life and death for which Baptism is designed. It is a physical event (a new creation) that matches at the end of time the event at the beginning of time (creation) that is blighted by original sin. It respects the universality of original sin and the universal need to have it taken away by a reality of grace that comes in a form that can be called Baptism. Such a theory is not an invitation to become careless about baptizing infants, as if it would make no difference anymore whether they were baptized in water or not. It is not just caution but theological rigour that demands that no risks ever be taken with human salvation. Besides, there are many more reasons for baptizing children than the minimal one of taking away original sin. The prescriptions of the Church about baptizing infants in the first weeks of their life, and immediately if they are in danger of death (Code 867) are not undermined by a theological proposal that they may, as a last resort, be saved by a Baptism of the resurrection. However, a lot of the anxiety that the prescriptions may generate in parents and ministers of the Church, and the subsequent scruples and agony these may suffer if they have not succeeded in obeying these prescriptions, can be taken away by a credible explanation, grounded on God's own word, of how it is that God's will to save all is realized in unbaptized infants. It can also bring more serenity into people's obedience to the prescriptions of the Church (Code 868) that Baptism may only be given to infants whose parents request it, outside danger of death, when a Catholic upbringing can be guaranteed for them. Finally, such a theory accords well with, and can reinforce, a good general theology of Baptism. It sees Baptism, not as some sort of mechanical, magical rite but as a sacrament of God's love that respects the human condition, taking ritual form when this is what brings the best out of people but taking other forms when that is what is best for them. The word that makes the rite of Baptism to be life-giving rightly includes a word about when life is given without the rite.

STUDY QUESTIONS

1　Do an exegetical study of Romans 6, with a view to understanding the relationship between Baptism and justification in the thinking of St Paul.

2　Do an exegetical study of John 3, with a view to understanding John's theology of Baptism.

3　Study how St Cyril of Jerusalem presents the effects of Baptism in his mystagogical catecheses.

4　To what extent does St Thomas's doctrine of the baptismal character reflect the patristic doctrine of the 'seal' (*sphragis*)?

5　Examine how the relationship between faith and Baptism was understood by Martin Luther.

6　Evaluate critically the statement on Baptism in BEM.

7　Do a theological analysis of the article of the Nicene Creed, 'We acknowledge one baptism for the forgiveness of sins'.

8　Develop theologically the biblical teaching that by Baptism we become children of God.

9　In what sense is the Holy Spirit given in Baptism?

10　Reflect on the relationship between the necessity of baptism for salvation and the mission of the Church.

FURTHER READING

Scriptural teaching on Baptism in biblical dictionaries and in:

O. Cullmann, *Baptism in the New Testament* (trans. from German; London, 1950).
A. George and others, *Baptism in the New Testament* (trans. from French of 1956; London, 1964).
G. R. Beasley-Murray, *Baptism in the New Testament* (London, 1963).
R. Schnackenburg, *Baptism in the Thought of St Paul* (New York, 1964).
J. D. G. Dunn, *Baptism in the Holy Spirit* (London, 1970).

History of doctrine about Baptism in:

B. Neunheuser, *Baptism and Confirmation* (New York, 1964).

Patristic texts on Baptism in:

P. Palmer, SJ, *Sacraments and Worship* (London, 1957).
E. Yarnold, SJ (ed.), *The Awe-Inspiring Rites of Christian Initiation* (Slough, 1972).

On St Thomas:

J. J. Cunningham, OP, *Baptism and Confirmation* (*Summa Theologiae*, Blackfriars ed., vol. 57, London/New York, 1975).

On the issue of faith and Baptism, reflecting a Reformation debate:

K. Barth, *The Teaching of the Church Regarding Baptism* (1943; English trans. London, 1948).
O. Cullmann, *Baptism* (above).
J. Duplacy, 'Salvation by Faith and Baptism in the New Testament' in A. George and others, *Baptism*.

On ecumenical developments:

G. Wainwright, 'Christian Initiation in the Liturgical Movement', *Studia Liturgica* 12 (1977), 67–86.
M. Hurley, SJ, 'Baptism in Ecumenical Perspective', *One in Christ* 14 (1978), 106–123.
M. Fahey (ed.), *Catholic Perspectives on Baptism, Eucharist and Ministry: A Study Commissioned by the Catholic Theological Society of America* (Lanham, MD/New York/London, 1986).

General theology of Baptism in:

G. Wainwright, *Christian Initiation* (Richmond, VA/London, 1969).
T. A. Marsh, *Gift of Community. Baptism and Confirmation* (Wilmington, 1984).

On baptizing children:

J. Jeremias, *Infant Baptism in the First Four Centuries* (trans. from German; London, 1960) and *The Origins of Infant Baptism* (trans. from German; London, 1963).
J. C. Didier, *Faut-il baptiser les enfants?* (Paris, 1967).

On infants who die without Baptism:

P. Gumpel, 'Unbaptized Infants: Can They Be Saved?', *Downside Review* 72 (1954), 342–358; and bibliography on the subject in *Downside Review* 73 (1955), 317–346.
W. A. van Roo, SJ, 'Infants Dying Without Baptism', *Gregorianum* 35 (1954), 405–456.
L. Renwart, 'Le baptême des enfants et les limbes. A propos d'un document pontifical récent', *Nouvelle Revue Théologique* 80 (1958), 449–467.

6
Confirmation: the rite

6.1 DESCRIPTION

The primary form of the rite of Confirmation in the Latin Catholic Church is that given within the continuous rite of initiation for adults (*RCIA*, nn. 225–229; *Rites*, Initiation, nn. 227–231, pp. 102–104). A form is also provided for the celebration of Confirmation apart from Baptism. It is designed to take place within the Eucharist (*Rites*, Confirmation, nn. 20–31, pp. 306–311), or it may stand alone, as a separate sacramental celebration (*ibid.*, nn. 34–49, pp. 314–322). There is no special rite of Confirmation for children. However, the rite given for Confirmation in danger of death (*ibid.*, nn. 52–55, p. 324) is for use with children as well as adults. It states: 'It is of the greatest importance that the initiation of every baptized Christian be completed by the sacraments of confirmation and the eucharist . . . In the case of a child who has not yet reached the age of reason, confirmation is given in accord with the same principles and norms as for baptism' (n. 52).

The rite of Confirmation, whether as part of a continuous initiation or as a separate celebration, is meant to take place in a full assembly of the Christian community into which the person is being initiated. Ordinarily it is presided over by the bishop, who acts as minister of the rite. When, however, in the absence of the bishop, a presbyter is presiding at the ceremony of initiation of an adult he may confirm as well as baptize in one continuous rite. Those to be confirmed are accompanied by sponsors who present them and take responsibility for them before the community, as they or others will have already done for them at Baptism. The rite begins with instruction and prayer that evoke the Baptism that has preceded this moment and the gift of the Holy Spirit that is to be given in it. This phase is quite brief when Confirmation is part of a continuous initiation; it takes the more extended form of a liturgy of the word with a renewal of baptismal vows and profession of baptismal faith by the whole community when the Confirmation is being done as a separate rite. Then the presiding minister, and presbyters who may be authorized to assist him, stretch their hands over the candidates, while the minister prays the Father of Our Lord Jesus Christ to send the Holy Spirit and his messianic gifts on those who have been given new life already by water and the Holy Spirit (*Rites*, Initiation, n. 227, p. 103). Each candidate then comes forward, accompanied by a sponsor, who places a hand on his or her right shoulder, and is anointed with a perfumed oil called chrism, which will have been blessed by the local bishop during the liturgy of the previous Holy Week. The minister does the anointing by dipping his thumb in the chrism, placing the palm of his hand on the head of the candidate (although this detail is no longer prescribed) and tracing a sign of the cross with his thumb on the forehead; while doing this he addresses the person by name and says: 'N., be sealed with the Gift of the Holy Spirit' (ibid., n. 231, p. 104). The confirmed person answers 'Amen' and receives a greeting of peace from the minister. In the continuous rite of initiation, or when it is celebrated apart from Baptism but with Eucharist, Confirmation is followed by the Prayer of the Faithful and the Liturgy of the Eucharist. Otherwise the rite concludes with the General Intercessions and the Lord's Prayer.

6.2   HISTORY

The history of any rite can help one to enter into its present meaning. However, in the case of the rite of Confirmation, history is not an easy teacher. There is no mention of a rite called Confirmation in the records of Christian origins. When history does identify something from which such a rite is believed to have developed, it still leaves many gaps and puzzles in documenting an evolution to the point where Confirmation is recognized as a sacramental rite distinct from Baptism. The task is not made easier by the uncertainty that exists about the theological definition of Confirmation. Theological positions inevitably interact with the reading of historical sources: what one finds is affected by what one is looking for. Allowing for these limitations, and without pretending to give a complete history of the rite or to be altogether innocent of a particular theological point of view (see 3.5 above), one can still look at some well-established historical material and suggest how it throws light on the contemporary rite of Confirmation. The material about the rite will also be useful background for the study of the theological word about the sacrament that will be undertaken in Chapter 7.

There are two ritual actions, and a set of significant words to go with each, in the present rite of Confirmation. The actions are a laying-on of hands and an anointing with perfumed oil, called chrism. They come out of the biblical tradition. From the earliest times the hands were used to call down a blessing on specially chosen people (Gen 48:13–16), and to designate individuals for some status or rôle in the work of God (Num 8:10; 27:15–23; Deut 34:9). Jesus laid hands on children as a gesture of blessing (Mark 10:16) and on the sick for healing (Luke 13:13). As well as doing it for healing (Mark 16:18), the apostles laid hands on whole communities so that they would receive the gift of the Holy Spirit (Acts 8:17; 19:6). The gesture was also used for setting people apart for ministry in the Church (Acts 6:6; 13:3; 2 Tim 1:6). It is listed in the letter to the Hebrews as one of those topics that should be dealt with in the basic instruction of Christians (6:2). Anointing with oil, especially with perfumed oil, was one of the rituals of joy and festive celebration in the Old Testament (Amos 6:6; Prov 27:9); it was offered to guests as a mark of honour (Ps 23:5); to forgo or be deprived of it was a sign of trouble and mourning (Deut 28:40; Dan 10:3); to enjoy it would be part of the celebration of messianic times (Isa 61:3; Ps 45:7). Anointing was used to initiate kings into their reign (1 Sam 10:1; 16:13; 1 Kings 1:39), and in the consecration of priests (Exod 29:7; Lev 8:12; Num 3:3). There are texts that speak of the anointing of prophets (1 Kings 19:16–19; Isa 61:1) but it seems that this is a metaphorical way of describing their call rather than reference to an actual rite. Jesus was anointed by the woman who was a sinner, after she had bathed his feet with her tears (Luke 7:38 and 46), when his host had refused him these honours; and he is anointed by Mary the sister of Lazarus in spite of the indignation of Judas and the disciples (John 12:1–8; see Matt 26:6–13). In both these cases the gesture is given a messianic interpretation by the evangelists. The language of anointing is used in connection with the baptism of Jesus to describe how he was filled with the Holy Spirit (Acts 10:38) and also in a passage of Hebrews about his divine sonship (1:9). It is in a similar metaphorical sense that it is used in 2 Corinthians 1:21–22 and in 1 John 2:20 and 27 to describe how Christians share through Christ in the messianic gift of the Spirit and of truth. This text from 2 Corinthians brings together three words that are subsequently important in the language of Confirmation. The Greek word translated 'commissioned' in RSV is literally 'anointed', the word translated 'he has put his seal' is in the same participle form as 'anointed', which suggests that the act of anointing is the act of sealing; and the word that is translated 'establishes us' could be translated 'confirmed' (the Latin Vulgate has *confirmat*). For all this, it cannot be said that the language that Paul uses here evokes an actual Christian rite of anointing and sealing. The only ritual use of anointing attested by the New Testament is in the healing of the sick and the casting-out of demons (Mark 6:13). One might, of course, hazard a guess that if the bathing of Baptism was in any way realistic it would have been completed, like a normal bath, with some kind of anointing and perfuming, and that this would have been readily given a Christian significance.

Such evidence as there is for the rites of Christian initiation in the second century has no mention of laying-on of hands or anointing. But from around AD 200 onwards there is frequent mention of both rites. Tertullian seems to be following the sequence of rites in Christian initiation when he says:

> The flesh is washed that the soul may be made spotless: the flesh is anointed that the soul may be consecrated: the flesh is signed [with the cross] that the soul too may be. protected: the flesh is overshadowed by the imposition of the hand that the soul also may be illumined by the Spirit: the flesh feeds on the Body and Blood of Christ so that the soul as well may be replete with God (*De Resurrectione Carnis*, c. 8; other texts of Tertullian in Whitaker, pp. 7–10).

There are several mentions of both rites in the letters of St Cyprian, and indications that in danger of death and in reception into the Church of those baptized in heresy they could be separated from the other rites of Christian initiation (texts in Whitaker, pp. 10–12). Meanwhile, from the full description of the rites of initiation given by St Hippolytus in *The Apostolic Tradition* (text given in 4.2 above), one learns that, in Rome, there was an anointing before the rite of baptizing and two anointings after it, and a laying-on of hands in the act of baptizing as well as another afterwards. The pre-baptismal anointing is a rite of exorcism, and the oil used is called the oil of exorcism. The anointing immediately after the baptizing, with what is called the oil of thanksgiving, is accompanied by words that relate it to Christ. The second anointing, with consecrated oil, is done by the bishop. He lays his hand on the head as he anoints and seals the forehead, using a trinitarian form of words to describe what he is doing. This second post-baptismal anointing is preceded by a laying-on of hands by the bishop during which he prays that the Holy Spirit will come upon those who have been baptized.

The liturgical evidence from the fourth century shows the rites of anointing and laying-on of hands to be a regular part of Christian initiation in both East and West, in a pattern that broadly repeats that of Hippolytus. More prominence seems to be given in the East to the anointing than to the laying-on of hands in connection with the gift of the Holy Spirit. There is, however, one important liturgical tradition that differs from all others that are known about. The church of Antioch, and the many churches of the East that followed its discipline, had a signing with the cross and an anointing with perfumed oil, not just of the head but of the whole body, before the act of baptizing; and it had the laying-on of hands in the baptism itself. It is with this laying-on of hands that the gift of the Holy Spirit is associated (Milner, pp. 12–15; texts in Whitaker, pp. 12–20). Only in a few late accounts of this liturgy does an anointing or signing appear after baptism. This form of the rite of initiation lasted in the Antiochean tradition into the fifth century but then gradually gave way to the more general pattern. However, one cannot ignore the significance of the fact that, in this earliest documented phase of the tradition, there was such an important divergence, which did not cause any problems of discipline or communion in the Church, about the place and meaning of anointing and laying-on of hands in Christian initiation. It has to be taken along with the fact that even within the more generally accepted tradition there were different kinds of anointing, with different kinds of oil, and different ways of laying-on hands and signing with the cross; the words used with the rite also differ, as do the theological explanations of it (see below, Chapter 7). All this seems to bear out the view that the reality of Christian initiation is more fundamental to the faith of the Church than the ritual form in which it is expressed. There is, indeed, an inalienable core to that ritual, which is baptism in water; there are other rites that come out of the biblical and apostolic tradition, but without the binding force of baptism; they have a natural affinity with the rite of bathing and somehow suppose it; they have been used from earliest times to express aspects of initiation that it was thought good to ritualize more strikingly than the simple rite of baptizing did; what they express particularly is the messianic gift of the Holy Spirit, which is an essential component of any Christian initiation; in exceptional circumstances these rites can be separated from the rite of baptizing, but they are normally celebrated and thought about as part of a single process of initiation.

It was in the Western church, in the Roman liturgy, that a separate rite of laying-on of hands and anointing for the giving of the Holy Spirit was developed and came to be called Confirmation. These actions had been associated from the beginning, in all liturgical traditions, with the ministry of the bishop. It was he who normally presided at the ceremonies of initiation. Even though presbyters and deacons did many of the baptismal rites, the laying-on of hands and anointing for the giving of the Spirit would be done by the bishop. And it was he who presided at the Eucharist that completed initiation. It was obviously fitting that he, as head of the church into which people were being initiated, should be the one to complete the process. When the bishop was absent the rite would be presided over by a presbyter. In the Eastern churches, and in the churches of Africa and Spain, all the rites of initiation, including laying-on of hands and anointing, were done by the presbyter in that case. The unity of initiation was a paramount value. The reference to the bishop was always present, in the sense that the initiation was an act of the church of which he was the head. It was required also that the chrism used would be blessed by him. The Roman church, however, reserved the laying-on of hands and anointing to the bishop. When initiation was celebrated without his presence, these rites were postponed. An anointing with oil, similar to that prescribed by Hippolytus to be done by a presbyter immediately after the newly-baptized had come out of the water, was done and all were admitted to the Eucharist. But they had to wait until they could be brought to the bishop, or he could come to them, for the laying-on of hands and the anointing and signing with chrism for the gift of the Holy Spirit. This happened more and more frequently as the number of those to be initiated increased, the majority of them now being children of Christian parents, and as parishes were set up, many of them at some distance from the bishop's cathedral church. Outside Rome the practice first appears in the south of France during the fifth century and there are some decisions of local councils about whether the bishop both anoints and lays on hands or simply lays on hands in such a case (Milner, pp. 42–44). It is here for the first time that the bishop is said 'to confirm' what has been done in Baptism, and the rite he performs is called Confirmation. Other parts of Western Europe took longer to accept the need for a further episcopal rite of initiation if people had already been anointed by a presbyter after their Baptism, but eventually, by the tenth century, it had become standard practice in the Latin church (Milner, pp. 42–65). The rite, which eventually came to be written out in a separate book for the convenience of the bishop, consists of a laying of hands over all the candidates together, with a prayer that is a development of the basic text given by Hippolytus; this is followed by an anointing with chrism on the forehead and a signing with the cross, accompanied by a form of words that by the tenth century had come to be: 'N., I sign you with the sign of the cross and I confirm you with the chrism of salvation in the name of the Father, and of the Son, and of the Holy Ghost'. The Roman rite of Confirmation remained quite stable from then until the reforms of the Second Vatican Council. The gesture of anointing became more stylized: the palm of the hand was laid on the head and the thumb dipped in chrism was used to trace the sign of the cross on the forehead. It was a way of combining the laying-on of hands and the anointing. Another odd development occurred: the kiss of peace turned into a slap on the cheek! It is surmised that the kiss first became a caress on the cheek, which was easier to do when most of those confirmed were children, and that subsequently, under the influence of a somewhat militaristic theology of Confirmation that will be examined below in 7.3 the caress turned into a slap that symbolically tested the fortitude of the newly-confirmed in face of the hostilities of the world.

The Roman discipline of delaying Confirmation until it could be administered by the bishop came to interact with another peculiarity of the Roman rites of initiation. In the early centuries children were given the full rite of initiation (Baptism, Confirmation and Eucharist) in all the churches. This is still the practice in the Eastern churches. It lasted in the Roman church until the thirteenth century. When the bishop was present infants received all the stages of initiation at once. When he was not they had to wait for Confirmation like everybody else, but did receive the Eucharist. It was not always easy for parents to get young children to the bishop. They may also have lost some of the sense of urgency about the sacrament since Confirmation was not necessary for the salvation of their child in the way that Baptism was. In the early Middle Ages there are exhortations and ecclesiastical canons against the abuse of delaying the Confirmation of those who have been baptized as infants. It is variously required that it be done within a year of Baptism, or at the age of three, or at the age of seven. But then in the late thirteenth century a line of theological reasoning begins to appear which actually favours delaying Confirmation: it is argued that children would not understand the sacrament before they reached the age of seven and hence they should not receive it before then. This line of thinking eventually prevailed in the Latin church. The Catechism of the Council of Trent takes this rather cautious position: 'Here it is to be observed that, after baptism, the sacrament of confirmation may indeed be administered to all; but that until children have attained the age of reason its administration is inexpedient. If not, therefore, to be postponed to the age of twelve, it is most proper to defer this sacrament at least to that of seven years'. In parts of the post-Tridentine church Confirmation was given at an even later age than seven. The practice of giving First Communion to children when they were being initiated, even without Confirmation, had died out in the Latin church by the thirteenth century. The pattern of initiation for children had thus come to comprise three distinct and separate sacramental rites — Baptism, Confirmation and Eucharist. The order between Confirmation and Eucharist varied. But after the introduction by Pope Pius X of First Communion for children once they had reached the use of reason, it became standard practice for children to be admitted to the Eucharist before they were confirmed.

Significant features of the present Roman rite of Confirmation (described in 6.1) stand out more clearly against the historical background that has been traced here. In keeping with the general aims of Vatican II there is an attempt to recover the full richness of the tradition about Christian initiation in a viable, contemporary form. The rite restores the sense that Confirmation belongs within a larger process. It looks back to Baptism and forward to the Eucharist. This is obvious in the rites, whether for adults (*RCIA*, 208 [34]), or for children of catechetical age (*RCIA*, 281 [306], but especially 281 [344]). The possibility of maintaining this unity even when a bishop is not presiding is opened up by allowing a priest also to confirm in the continuous rite. However, the unified process of initiation is not restored for infants. In danger of death they are, indeed, confirmed after Baptism, but do not receive the Eucharist. A continuous rite is provided for children of catechetical age, so that their Confirmation precedes their First Communion. For children who have been baptized in infancy the Introduction to the Rite of Confirmation says: 'With regard to children, in the Latin Church the administration of confirmation is generally postponed until about the seventh year. For pastoral reasons, however, especially to strengthen the faithful in complete obedience to Christ the Lord and in loyal testimony to him, episcopal conferences may choose an age which seems more appropriate, so that the sacrament is given at a more mature age after appropriate formation. In this case the necessary precautions should be taken so that children will be confirmed at the proper time, even before the use of reason, where there is danger of death or other serious difficulty. They should not be deprived of the benefit of this sacrament' (*Rites*, Confirmation, n. 11). In the Code of Canon Law the 'age of discretion' is made normative for Confirmation. This makes it possible, if it does not actually demand, that all children can be confirmed before they receive their First Communion. Nevertheless, the Code does not seem to impose this order of initiation. It allows Episcopal Conferences to determine another age for Confirmation, which would presumably be later than the age of discretion. At the same time it also allows Confirmation at an earlier age, not only when the child is in danger of death, but when 'in the judgment of the minister a grave cause urges otherwise' (can. 891).

The decision to highlight the anointing with oil and to recognize it as the essential core of the rite can be appreciated better when one remembers how the tradition has associated the giving of the Holy Spirit in initiation with the laying-on of hands as well as with anointing, and with various combinations of these. The Catholic Church has now recognized that there is no single decisive tradition on the matter, that could claim the authority of Christ or the apostles. It has felt free to make a decision about what is best for the Church today. In assuming responsibility for fixing the essence of a sacramental rite, instead of claiming that it has been fixed from the beginning by the Apostles, the Church has done something which has an important bearing on how theology ought to understand the divine institution of sacraments (see above, 3.7.1). But the history of Confirmation shows that the decision is in no way arbitrary. It is an attempt to get the best out of the tradition, bearing in mind the criteria of sacramental theology and of the theologically informed pastoral strategy promoted by Vatican II. It also has the ecumenical value of adopting a form of the rite that is close to what is practised in the Orthodox churches. They have always centred the giving of the Holy Spirit on the rite of anointing with chrism, and actually call the rite corresponding to the Latin Confirmation by the name 'Chrismation'. The ecumenical factor is also to be noted in the decision to prefer the ancient form of words that has been maintained in the Eastern churches over the later Latin form, for expressing the meaning of the act of anointing. There are other good theological reasons for this preference, which will be examined in the next chapter. Merely from the ritual point of view it has the value of being a richer and more direct form that highlights, mysteriously but without ambiguity, the reality that Confirmation sacramentalizes — the sealing of Christians with the eschatological gift of the Holy Spirit.

6.3   RITES OF GOING PUBLIC

One can enter into the meaning of the rite of a Christian sacrament by developing a feeling for the symbols it employs and an awareness of the roots these have in human experience. There are difficulties about doing this with Confirmation. The symbols are ambivalent even in Christian terms. Oil is used in Baptism, in Ordinations, in Anointing of the Sick as well as in Confirmation. Hands are laid on in Baptism, Ordinations and Reconciliation. And the Holy Spirit is invoked and prayed for in every sacrament. The moment of human life to which the rite of Confirmation corresponds cannot be easily stated in reference to the stages of human growth, because there is no consistent tradition about the age at which people are confirmed. Nor does theology give decisive guidelines, because there is no single established theology of Confirmation. There is agreement that Confirmation ritualizes the giving of the Holy Spirit, but it is not quite so clear what particular aspect of the gift is being singled out, and how this differs from what is ritualized in Baptism and other sacraments. There is also the difficulty of finding credible equivalents to the Christian gift of the Holy Spirit in other religions or in secular social forms, and therefore of identifying parallel rites that might throw light on Confirmation. One has, therefore, to be tentative in proposing a reading of the symbols of Confirmation and admit that one's suggestions are affected by one's particular theology of the sacrament.

A beginning can be made by drawing attention to those moments in human life when one goes public. One has to take a stand sometime in relation not just to the people who form one's own family, with whom there are certain ready grooves and patterns of interaction, but to outsiders who are independent and unpredictable in their attitudes and reactions. One has to accept being part of a society in which relationships are established not by the intimacy of blood-ties but by the free and open exchange of ideas and choices. This is a moment when one takes oneself seriously and wants to be taken seriously by people from whom one has no claim to attention other than what one is by personal statement and behaviour. These moments are generally associated with entry into adult age. But they do not have to be so. Children can be caught up in the public stance of their parents. Jewish children, for example, have often had to suffer for what a particular society thought of their family; the children of politically important families have little choice about what society expects of them. On the other hand, the need to go public may come later than entry into adulthood. A person who develops intellectual or political convictions late in life often has to go through a process of taking a public stand about them. Nevertheless, the rites of entry into adulthood can serve as a convenient paradigm for how people go public. There are rites connected with going public as a sexual being — accepting oneself and having oneself accepted as a man or a woman. These are the rites of puberty, like debutante balls, or the more earthy forms of sexual initiation that may be practised in primitive societies; they are also the many informal rites that teenagers develop among themselves in Western society. There are rites connected with going public in the matter of eating and drinking, such as taking one's first drink in a pub. There are rites for assuming public responsibility, like getting a driver's licence or voting for the first time. And there are rites connected with one's career, like graduation or completing apprenticeship in a particular profession or trade. Rites like these provide a paradigm for Confirmation, not because they are generally rites of adulthood but because they are rites of going public. To use them in a way that dwells too much on the age at which they occur in human life would be to become locked into a position on the best age for Confirmation — making it a sacrament of transition to adult age — that cannot claim any more support from the tradition than that which favours Confirmation in infancy.

In any case, what one is trying to understand in Confirmation is a rite of anointing with perfumed oil. Perfumed oil has nothing distinctively to do with becoming an adult, but it can have a lot to do with going public. To be comfortable in one's body, to be well groomed and smell pleasantly does wonders for one's self-confidence and one's ability to face the world. Advertisers of lotions and deodorants play shamelessly on people's fears of not being appropriately 'sanitized', and promote the belief that the right-smelling cream or spray will make them an instant success in public. It is not without significance for the understanding of Confirmation that lotions and perfumes are often connected with bathing. They are more effective when the skin or hair has been washed clean. Indeed, bathing is somehow incomplete without these additional rites. There is also something significant in the fact that babies are oiled and powdered. It is not just for the comfort of the babies but also of their parents who want to show them off in public and to teach them gradually how to relate confidently to strangers. It is this rather earthy sense of the uses of oil and perfume that underlies the biblical symbolism already noted in the history of Confirmation (6.2). Anointing with oil had to do with public appearances: it prepared people for feasting with their friends, and was given as a mark of public honour to distinguished guests; it was used to designate people for public office (kings and priests) and become a symbol of the call to prophecy; it was employed in the New Testament as a symbol of the power of Christians to speak and act convincingly in the name of Christ, to be the 'good odour' of Christ.

There are other strains of symbolism in oil which reinforce its suitability for a rite of going public. It is used by athletes and people given to strenuous physical effort. So it becomes a symbol of strength and of the ability to deal with competition and conflict. This is a line of symbolism found congenial by a theology of Confirmation that sees it as the sacrament of Christian strength in the battle against the enemies of Christian life. The limits of such a theology will be discussed in Chapter 7. For the moment it is enough to note that, while it exploits a real symbolism of anointing with oil, it does not explain why the liturgy has always insisted that the oil used after Baptism should be *perfumed* (chrism) and by that fact different from the oil used during the catechumenate and in Anointing of the Sick. To make strength the dominant symbolism of oil in Confirmation could give the impression that to become a Christian is to take a belligerent or defensive stance towards the world, and to deprive the sacrament of something of that joyful, outgoing attitude of sharing and celebrating the good news of salvation that is communicated by the festive symbolism of perfumed oil. Oil gains further symbolism from the fact that it can be poured out: one can see and feel it flow; and yet it does not run off like water but stays on skin or hair; it penetrates the body, becomes part of it, keeps it moist and supple and, when it is perfumed, keeps it fragrant. Flowing, moistening oil that keeps hair from drying up and becoming tatty and dishevelled is taken as a symbol of conviviality and friendship in Psalm 133: 'How good and how pleasant it is, when brothers live in unity! It is like the precious oil upon the head, running down upon the beard, running down upon Aaron's beard, upon the collar of his robes'.

6.4   SEALED WITH THE GIFT OF THE HOLY SPIRIT

The words that accompany the anointing with perfumed oil in the rite of Confirmation are 'N., be sealed with the Gift of the Holy Spirit'. The oil is being used as a symbol of the gift of the Holy Spirit. The various symbolisms of anointing with perfumed oil mentioned already can be related readily enough to the way the Holy Spirit is imagined. The Spirit is 'poured out' on Christians (Acts 2:17 and 33; 10:44–48), as it was on Christ (Acts 10:38; Luke 3:21–22; 4:18 and 21), anointing him and making him be recognized as the Christ (a name which means 'the anointed one'). As oil would, the Spirit abides with and penetrates the life of Christians, consecrating them as a temple (1 Cor 3:16–17), making them 'the good odour of Christ' (2 Cor 2:14–17). The Spirit 'seals' and guarantees both the preaching of the Gospel (2 Cor 1:21–22) and the promised inheritance that is being waited for by those who believe (Eph 1:13–14). It makes them joyful (Acts 13:52). The Spirit gives them strength and confidence to be public witnesses to Jesus to the ends of the earth (Acts 1:8) and to speak in his name in difficult circumstances (Mark 13:11; Acts 4:8 and 31). The words 'sealed with the Gift of the Holy Spirit', then, identify and personalize the symbolism of the anointing. They say that it is the Spirit given at Pentecost that makes Christians be the special kind of public people that being bathed, anointed and perfumed signifies in a general way. It is the Spirit that gives them the inner resources and the gifts that make them ready to face the world, to give witness to the faith that is in them and, by doing so, to call others to share it, or at least to respect it. It is the Spirit that marks them publicly and definitively as belonging to Christ and to the

Father. The Spirit can be given at any age. So can the anointing of Confirmation. The gift of the Spirit is not connected with any particular stage of Christian life but with the very essence of that life. Pentecost says that, in the design of God, Christian life is a public life. The rite of Confirmation says the same thing. It says that to be a Christian one must be not just re-born in Christ but also be someone who goes public in his name with the self-confidence that comes from the gift of the Pentecostal Spirit. A confirmed infant is no less this kind of person for being dependent on its parents for its public status. An unconfirmed adult, although baptized, cannot yet be recognized as this kind of person.

6.5   LAYING–ON OF HANDS

There is another ritual action in Confirmation, which is the laying-on of hands. It is, like the anointing, done by the head of the community, who ordinarily is the bishop. It signifies the community character of the rite perhaps even better than the anointing. It is a gesture of authority. It is also a traditional gesture of commissioning. It is a way of saying that the person is being brought fully into the Church, represented by its local head, and being endowed with everything that the Church has to give. There is no holding back. Once a person is confirmed he or she cannot be an immature, pre-Pentecostal member of the Church, as the people of Samaria and Ephesus learned when the apostles, without any delay, laid hands on them for the gift of the Holy Spirit (Acts 8:4–18; 19:1–6). The laying-on of hands in Confirmation is accompanied by a prayer which expresses in more detail than do the words that go with the anointing what the Church gives in Confirmation. What it conveys is a personal sharing by one who is already baptized in Christ in the messianic gifts that the Spirit poured out on Christ himself for the preaching of the good news (Luke 4:18–21). What the consequences and responsibilities of these messianic gifts are is not spelled out in the rite. There is no dogmatizing or moralizing. That is left to the preachers and the theologians!

STUDY QUESTIONS

1   Compare the Catholic rite of Confirmation with Oriental rites of Chrismation.
2   Do an exegetical study of some texts from the Old Testament about anointing and its significance.
3   Compare the rite of Confirmation promulgated by Paul VI with what it replaced, and detail the historical and pastoral reasons for the changes made.
4   Describe some 'rites of going public' practised in a contemporary culture and suggest how they might help towards an understanding of the rite of Confirmation.

FURTHER READING

The rite of Confirmation:

Ordo confirmationis promulgated 22 August 1971 (includes the Apostolic Constitution *Divinae consortium naturae* promulgated 15 August 1971). Published in ICEL English translation as *Rite of Confirmation* (1975).

Ordo initiationis christianae adultorum promulgated 6 January 1972; emended second printing containing *Praenotanda de initiatione christiana*, 1974. Published in ICEL English as *Rite of Christian Initiation of Adults* (interim version, 1974; definitive edition, 1985).

Both available in official editions, but also in *The Rites of the Catholic Church* (Pueblo, New York, 1976); new translation of the introductions in *Documents on the Liturgy 1963–1979* (Liturgical Press, Collegeville, 1982).

The history and the significance of the rite are dealt with in standard works on the liturgy, and in:

M. Bohen, *The Mystery of Confirmation* (New York, 1963).
A. Milner, OP, *The Theology of Confirmation* (Cork, 1971).
J. D. C. Fisher, *Confirmation Then and Now* (London, 1978).
G. Austin, OP, *Anointing with the Spirit. The Rite of Confirmation. The Use of Oil and Chrism* (New York, 1985).

7

Confirmation: the word

The fact that the rite of Confirmation has shadowy beginnings and an uncertain early history raises a difficulty about setting down the words that have bound it to life in the Christian Church throughout its history. One cannot say with certainty that any given text from the Scriptures or the writers of the first few centuries is about Confirmation because one cannot identify any rite with certainty as being that of Confirmation. However, there are two constants of the tradition that can be used as guidelines in the search for texts. The first is that from the beginning a process of Christian initiation existed to which Confirmation, whatever ritual form it took, belongs. Secondly, Christian initiation includes the giving of the Holy Spirit and it is with that giving that Confirmation has to do. The word of the Church that can be taken to refer to Confirmation, then, is the word about the gift of the Holy Spirit, and about the way that gift occurs in Christian initiation. The issues one will be looking for a word on are: what is the rôle of the Holy Spirit in the making of a Christian; what is the justification for postulating that a rite beyond the water-rite of Baptism is needed to convey this gift of the Spirit; how does this further rite relate to the rite of Baptism in the giving of one and the same Spirit; what is the essential core of this other rite; what are the circumstances in which it is celebrated, who is its minister and in what conditions can it be separated from the other rites that make up full Christian initiation? Because of the complexity of the tradition about Confirmation the texts will need to be presented and analysed somewhat more thoroughly than those about Baptism in Chapter 5. (The analysis owes a great deal to the work of Milner; some translations used are his.)

7.1   THE NEW TESTAMENT

There are various currents of thought about the Holy Spirit in the New Testament, as there are about Christ. In broad terms they can be reduced to two (see Schweizer; Milner, pp. 81–96). One of these is found predominantly in St Luke (Acts and gospel) with support from Matthew and Mark. The other is in Paul and John. The first draws mainly on Jewish tradition for its ideas and images; the second seems to have absorbed some Hellenistic influences. Although chronologically the writings of Paul come before those of Luke it is convenient to take the texts from Luke first. They seem to represent a more primitive and simpler tradition. One can understand the Pauline and Johannine teaching better in relation to them rather than the other way around.

7.1.1　St Luke

The theology of the Holy Spirit in the writings of Luke owes much to Old Testament teaching about the spirit of God. The spirit, whether it is personified or not, is God's power in action, doing wonders in the history of his People for their salvation and selecting and inspiring the prophets and other leaders they need for the working-out of their destiny. In the Old Testament the spirit is transient and unpredictable in its manifestations. But the prophets do tell that it will be poured out in a definitive, abiding fullness at the end of time, as a force for the making of the messianic age. Luke sees this Spirit of God given and active in Jesus: in his birth (1:35); in his baptism (3:22); in the conflict with the Devil that marks the inauguration of his ministry (4:1); in identifying his preaching as messianic (4:18). Jesus is full of the Spirit. The messianic age has begun in him. Jesus, in turn, promises his disciples that the Spirit would be with them to teach them what to say when they were brought before synagogues and rulers and authorities because of the gospel they preached (Luke 12:11–12). After the resurrection, before he was carried up to heaven, he told the disciples (Luke 24:47–49) that 'repentance and forgiveness of sins should be preached in his name to all nations, beginning from Jerusalem', and that they were to be 'witnesses of these things', in view of which he would 'send the promise of my Father upon you; but stay in the city until you are clothed with power from on high'. Luke repeats this promise of Jesus in the opening chapter of Acts, in a form that is more explicit about the connection between the power they were to be given and the gift of the Holy Spirit: 'you shall receive power when the Holy Spirit has come upon you; and you shall be my witnesses in Jerusalem and in all Judea and Samaria and to the end of the earth' (Acts 1:8). The Spirit is given to them on the day of Pentecost (Acts 2:1–4). It is a dramatic coming of the power of God, in audible and visible manifestations: a sound like a mighty wind is heard and felt, and tongues as of fire are seen and felt. They are 'all filled with the Holy Spirit'. As Peter will soon explain (vv. 16–21) this fullness visibly manifested is the eschatological, messianic outpouring of the Spirit promised by the prophets. It has an immediate and spectacular effect. The disciples who had been gathered in the privacy of the upper room go out and about and begin to speak to everyone they meet in a language that their hearers understand: 'how is it that we hear, each of us in his own native language? . . . we hear them telling in our own tongues the mighty works of God' (vv. 8–11). The preaching of the Gospel to the end of the earth has begun. The disciples, filled with the Holy Spirit, are seen to be the ones who will carry it out. It may take time for this final work of salvation to be completed — there is a place for patience in the eschatology of Luke — but, however long it takes, it is the final work and those who announce it have the last word to say.

The Spirit continues to be with the first disciples and to manifest its presence in striking ways. It moves them to a new way of praying the psalms (4:25) and when their prayer ends the place where they are gathered is shaken (4:31); they speak in tongues (10:46 and 19:6); they prophesy (11:28); they are filled with joy (13:52); they stand heroically firm and are articulate in the face of persecution (7:55). Clearly they are people who have been transformed utterly and from within. Luke, however, is more interested in the external manifestations of the change than with analysing its inner reality. The ecstatic, spectacular expressions of what they have become are functional. They give the disciples a public impact and a boldness to speak the word about Jesus at each stage of that outward journey from Jerusalem to the ends of the earth. It is from the Spirit that their inspiration and courage come to take the initiatives required for the preaching of the Gospel (8:29; 10:19; 11:12; 13:4; 15:28; 16:6; 20:22).

On the day of Pentecost Peter promised that those who accepted his word, repented and were baptized would themselves receive the gift of the Holy Spirit (2:38). Three thousand people 'were added' that day (2:41). Luke says they were baptized, but says nothing about them receiving the Holy Spirit. However, the gift of the Spirit is prominent in other accounts that he gives of conversion and initiation. In Acts 8 he describes how a large group of people in Samaria were converted to Christ by the preaching of Philip and were baptized. When the apostles in Jerusalem heard about it they 'sent to them Peter and John, who came down and prayed for them that they might receive the Holy Spirit; for it had not yet fallen on any of them, but they had only been baptized in the name of the Lord Jesus. Then they laid their hands on them and they received the Holy Spirit' (vv. 14–17). What they had not received with their baptism and did receive with the laying-on of hands was some kind of visible manifestation of the Spirit. It must have been something quite impressive — like the speaking in tongues that accompanied the coming of the Spirit at Pentecost — because Simon, a man who had earned the reputation of being 'that power of God which is called Great' (v. 10) because of the magic he performed, wanted to buy the power of giving the Spirit from Peter, so that 'any one on whom I lay my hands may receive the Holy Spirit' (v. 19). Peter's indignation was not because Simon had associated the gift of the Holy Spirit with a laying-on of hands but that he had 'neither part nor lot in this matter, for your heart is not right before God' (v. 21). Simon had, indeed, been baptized with the other Samaritans, but he had not really repented. He did not belong in his heart to the community. Belonging is, in fact, a significant factor in the giving of the Spirit, according to Luke's account. The reason Peter and John were sent from Jerusalem was, it seems, to join this new community of Samaria in fellowship with the principal church, the church of the apostles in Jerusalem. The Spirit is given within this Church. It is the need for communion with the mother-church rather than any inadequacy in the power of the 'deacon' Philip that requires the presence of the apostles. Nor is there any suggestion that they alone had the power to give the Holy Spirit by the laying-on of hands. The phrase 'they had only been baptized in the name of the Lord Jesus' (v. 16) does not imply any shortcoming in such a baptism; but it does give the impression that baptism itself did not necessarily give the gift of the Spirit in a recognizable form.

Luke's description of the conversion of Paul and his initiation into the community of believers by Ananias (Acts 9:10–19) also gives a central place to the Holy Spirit. Ananias came to the house where Saul was: 'And laying his hands on him he said: "Brother Saul, the Lord Jesus who appeared to you on the road by which you came has sent me that you may regain your sight and be filled with the Holy Spirit." And immediately something like scales fell from his eyes and he regained his sight. Then he rose and was baptized, and took food and was strengthened. For several days he was with the disciples at Damascus. And in the synagogues immediately he proclaimed Jesus, saying "He is the Son of God." And all who heard him were amazed. . . . But Saul increased all the more in strength, and confounded the Jews . . . proving that Jesus was the Christ'. This is an account of Saul's acceptance into the community of believers at Damascus. It is the working-out of what Ananias had been sent to do by the Lord Jesus, so that Paul would regain his sight and 'be filled with the Holy Spirit'. The laying-on of hands is not directly referred to the giving of the Spirit here, but rather to the healing of Paul's blindness. The blindness and its healing are, however, closely woven into the process of Paul's conversion and initiation in Luke's account. (Later, a symbolical opening of the senses will find a place in Christian initiation, and illumination will be one of its more important images.) Paul is baptized. He then takes food. The reference to food could be a banal statement of fact: Paul needed strengthening because he had not eaten or drunk for three days (v. 9). But it could also be saying something about his initiation: taking food with people expresses fellowship with them, especially when it is done for the first time by one who had previously been an enemy; and Luke had earlier coupled 'partaking of food with glad and generous hearts' with 'the breaking of bread' in his capsule description of the first Christian community in Acts 2:46–47. What manifests Paul's being filled with the Holy Spirit which, according to the words of Ananias, should be the climax of the process, is not, however, any rite or gesture but his dramatic public appearance among his fellow-Jews as one who now believes and proves that Jesus is the Messiah. Like the charismatic manifestations on the day of Pentecost it provokes amazement among the Jews. Paul increases in 'strength' (the Greek word is the one Luke used in his accounts of Jesus's promise of the Spirit). He stands firm in the face of opposition. His behaviour surely confirmed his standing in the community. It was the disciples who arranged his escape over the wall of the city when he was threatened with death. Luke follows up his account of Paul's acceptance by the community at Damascus by telling how he came to be accepted by the Church in Jerusalem. The pattern is similar to that of the conversion of the Samaritans. Paul has some difficulty being accepted by the disciples at Jerusalem who found it hard to believe that he was a disciple (v. 26) until he is vouched for by Barnabas as one who had 'preached boldly in the name of Jesus' in Damascus (v. 27). Once he is accepted he again preaches boldly in the name of the Lord, disputing this time with the Hellenists (v. 29). When his life is in danger it is once again his newly-found brethren who rescue him. Paul is recognized as one of them, as being filled with the Spirit, by his bold and public preaching of the name of Jesus.

And this happens at the very beginning of his life as a disciple, quite some time before he, along with Barnabas, is set apart by the Holy Spirit and the laying-on of hands for his missionary journeys.

Luke's story of the conversion and initiation of Cornelius with his family and friends (Acts 10) is the story of how the Gospel was first preached to people who were not Jews. It is in obedience to the Spirit that Peter goes to Cornelius (v. 19). As he tells him and his assembled relatives and friends about Jesus 'the Holy Spirit fell on all who heard the word' (v. 44). The evidence offered for this outpouring of the Spirit is that those who had come with Peter 'heard them speaking in tongues and extolling God' (v. 46). Peter reasons from this phenomenon to the legitimacy of baptizing them, and he commands this to be done 'in the name of Jesus Christ' (v. 48). At their request Peter remains with the new converts for some days. The Spirit is here given without any action, ritual or otherwise, on the part of Peter, other than the preaching about Jesus. Its coming is visibly manifested by charismatic activity. The manifestation precedes the rite of baptizing. Later, when Peter is telling the Jerusalem community about the incident, he links the gift of the Holy Spirit with baptism: he recalls (11:16) a word of the Lord, 'John baptized with water, but you shall be baptized with the Holy Spirit'. Taken literally, 'baptism with the Holy Spirit' could here be a metaphor for the messianic outpouring of the Spirit, contrasted with the ritual baptism with water. Peter, however, saw the gift of the Spirit as an irresistible invitation to baptize Cornelius ritually. It is more likely then that 'baptism with the Holy Spirit' is being taken here as referring to the distinctively Christian way of manifesting repentance, which includes baptism and the giving of the Spirit. It is for this that the Jerusalem community 'glorified God, saying: "Then to the Gentiles also God has granted repentance unto life"' (v. 18). Luke does not see the gift of the Spirit given to Cornelius and his friends manifested in any missionary preaching. But the fact that they, who were not Jews, would be using the gift of tongues for 'extolling God' (10:46) was already a remarkable testimony which had a decisive influence on the missionary expansion of the Church.

There is another story of conversion and initiation in Acts 19, where Luke tells how Paul brought the gift of the Holy Spirit to some people in Ephesus who, although they believed in Jesus, had received only the baptism of John and knew nothing about the Holy Spirit. They had learned about Jesus but without any normal communion with the Church. It was a situation that even the great Apollos had been in, until he had been taken in hand by Priscilla and Aquila (18:24–28). Paul explains to the group at Ephesus that John baptized 'with the baptism of repentance' in view of the one who was to come after him (v. 4). To explain what he is going to do for them he does not use a contrast between baptism of water and baptism in the Spirit. What he does, in fact, is to baptize them again, 'in the name of the Lord Jesus'. This must mean baptizing them in a fuller confession of faith than they had when first baptized. Essential to this full confession of faith would be that Jesus is the Messiah who sends the Spirit that is poured out in the latter days. On that basis Paul could not just baptize them but also lay his hands on them for the receiving of the Spirit. They are initiated into the eschatological community of the Church, in which Paul is now recognized to be an apostle: the Holy Spirit comes upon them and they speak in tongues and prophesy (v. 6). They can then be counted as members of the Church: 'There were about twelve of them in all' (v. 7).

In the interests of finding scriptural roots for a tradition about Confirmation it seems fair to summarize the thought of Luke along the following lines. The Holy Spirit is that eschatological presence of the saving power of God that Jesus, the Messiah, brought about on earth. It is given when it is seen to be given in visible, tangible forms that are characteristic of the end times. It belongs in a primordial way to the community of men and women gathered under the leadership of the apostles of Jesus in Jerusalem. It is further given to those who, hearing the word about Jesus, believe in him, repent and have their faith and repentance ritualized by baptism. It does not coincide with baptism, and may precede as well as follow it. In whatever form it is manifested it is an entitlement as well as a guarantee for being admitted to the fellowship of the Church of the apostles. In this sense, manifest reception of the Spirit is a required part of Christian initiation. The manifestation may come as a surprise to the leadership of the Church (as in Cornelius), in which case it is accepted by them and they provide the other elements of initiation. Or it may come at their initiative (Samaria), as a result of prayer and a ritual gesture with which they complete an initiation already begun. The form in which the manifestation of the presence of the eschatological, messianic Spirit is given varies: it may be charismatic behaviour, especially that connected with preaching; it may be, as in the case of Paul, the preaching itself, which is a convincing sign no less than an effect of the coming of the Spirit; it may be the prayerfulness and joy and security evidenced in the community ('the comfort of the Holy Spirit' as Luke calls it in Acts 9:31, using the same word that will give the Spirit a personal name — Comforter/Paraclete — in John's account of the farewell discourse of Jesus).

If Luke seems to always require some such visible manifestation that the gift of the eschatological, messianic Spirit is being received by those who are being admitted to the community, one is justified in putting forward the hypothesis that this aspect of the giving of the Holy Spirit is what is being given ritual visibility in the part of initiation that eventually came to be called Confirmation. Its effect would be the effect that Luke attributes to all such manifestations of the Spirit: to make those who believe strong enough to take their faith into public places and play their part in the coming-of-age of salvation, which is the proclamation of Jesus as the only Saviour, with the conflicts that this inevitably provokes.

7.1.2   St Paul

St Paul is less interested in the manifestations of the Spirit than in the inner reality of the gift received by Christians. He sees the Spirit not as a transient, spectacular act of the power of God working through humans but as an abiding divine reality that is given for a permanent possession to those who believe in Christ, dying and rising with him in baptism and thenceforward living in him. By the Spirit people are drawn out of the domain of the flesh, are reborn in Christ and become new spiritual creatures, holy and belonging to the heavenly world, children of God. Men and women enjoy this spiritual quality, this access to the wisdom and power of God solely because they have received the gift of God's Holy Spirit; left to themselves, in the flesh, they have nothing to glory in (Rom 8:1–17; 1 Cor 2). The Spirit is given in the Church, which is the body of Christ, within which it is the bond of unity (1 Cor 12:4–11; Eph 4:3–7). Paul, no less than Luke, sees the Spirit as inspiring and giving strength to the Church's preaching of the Gospel (Rom 15:18–19; 2 Tim 1:6–9). He sees it as the source of a marvellous variety of spiritual gifts, charismatic in every sense of the word, that build up the Church (1 Cor 12; 1 Thess 5:19–21; Gal 3:2–5; Rom 12:6). It is also the source of prayer, in its interior depth (Rom 8:26–27) and in its external expression in 'psalms and hymns and spiritual songs' (Eph 5:19). However, while recognizing as Luke does the significance of all these gifts and the value of the ecstatic behaviour in which they are sometimes expressed, Paul is more impressed by what he calls 'the higher gifts' (1 Cor 12:31). Charity holds the highest place (1 Cor 13; Rom 5:5); the deep insight which faith gives into the mystery of God is another major gift of the Spirit (1 Cor 2); the fruit of the Spirit that he celebrates 'is love, joy, peace, patience, kindness, goodness, faithfulness, gentleness, self-control' (Gal 5:22–23). These gifts are not without relevance to the eschatological status and task of the Church in Paul. But Paul, even more than Luke, is careful about eschatological expectations. He is writing to communities that are already outgrowing any illusions there may have been that the coming of the eschatological age meant that the return of the Lord was imminent, to the point of making the world of time irrelevant. For Paul the inner, long-term gifts are more important for the Church and its mission in the midst of the world than the more spectacular but short-lived enthusiasm of the ecstatic charisms. He sees the Spirit that abides within Christians as the first-fruit of the new creation, the permanent guarantee that the work of God will be completed in a resurrection that has already been realized in Christ (Rom 8:18–26). This beginning of the new, eschatological creation shows in the abiding gifts of love and peace, and in the inner strength of faith and prayer, more than in transient gifts like tongues and prophecy.

The significance of Paul's teaching about the Holy Spirit for an eventual theological understanding of Confirmation must lie in the way it establishes the inner, abiding strength that the Spirit gives to those who must live and proclaim their faith publicly and build up the Church in the eschatological age. Luke does not deny this inner strength that comes from the Spirit but does not give it much attention. The difficulty that Paul's theology of the Spirit raises for a theology of Confirmation is that the giving of the Spirit is so closely related to Baptism that there does not seem to be much room left for postulating another rite for the giving of the Spirit. It is true that Paul does not give any descriptions of Christian initiation. The nearest he comes to it is in Romans 6:1-11, and one might make something of the fact that there he speaks about Baptism without any mention of the Holy Spirit. But in 1 Corinthians he does say: 'you were washed, you were sanctified, you were justified in the name of the Lord Jesus Christ and in the Spirit of our God' (6:11) and 'For by one Spirit we were all baptized into one body — Jews or Greeks, slaves or free — and all were made to drink of one Spirit' (12:13). The 'higher gifts' of the Spirit that he so emphasizes are gifts and effects that he commonly associates with Baptism. Nor does he refer to any rite that could become Confirmation. When the laying-on of hands is mentioned in the Pauline corpus it is for the giving of ministry. He does speak of Christians being anointed and sealed and given the Spirit as a guarantee (2 Cor 1:21–22; Eph 1:14) but the general opinion is that this language is metaphorical rather than a reference to anything in the rite of Christian initiation.

7.1.3   St John

The teaching about the Spirit in the Johannine writings is closer to the tradition of Paul than it is to Luke. It presents the Spirit as an abiding reality more than as a force manifested in action. In the gospel and epistles of John there is no mention of charismatic, ecstatic behaviour resulting from the presence of the Spirit. The book of Revelation, on the other hand, is entirely an account of prophecy 'in the Spirit' (1:10; 4:2; 17:3; 21:10) that reveals and guides, in apocalyptic images, the destiny of the Christian community in the conflicts of the eschatological age. In being with the Church ('the Spirit and the Bride say' — 22:17) in these enlightening visions and messages the Spirit is the kind of Counsellor (Paraclete, Comforter) that Jesus promised he would be. However, the abiding of the Spirit with the community that is presented in the gospels and epistles goes deeper and is more pervasive than what is manifested by the gift of prophecy. The Spirit is first in Jesus (John 1:32–34). Given the way John's Christology sees the unity of Jesus with the Father as a oneness of being, the Spirit must be conceived as belonging to the very reality of this oneness, rather than simply as a divine power that takes possession of the man Jesus and makes him Son of God. After he has been glorified Jesus can give the Spirit to those who believe in him (7:37–39). What the Spirit is and does for the disciples is explained in the discourse and prayer of Jesus at the Last Supper (John 14 – 17). The Spirit is from the Father on the level that Jesus is from the Father and relates to him as Son. He is another Counsellor, on the level that Jesus is himself Counsellor. As Jesus does, so does the Spirit make the disciples of Jesus live in the real world of God, instead of in the world of appearance and unreality associated with the flesh and the world. The Spirit reveals the ultimate truth about the world, convincing it of sin and of righteousness and of judgement. He admits the disciples to the truth of things, especially as this is contained in the words of Jesus. So Jesus can pray the Father to keep them safe and united in the midst of the world and its hostilities, sanctifying them in the truth, so that through their word others may come to believe that Jesus himself is the one sent by the Father. It is the Spirit who will be with them in this mission: 'But when the Counsellor comes, whom I shall send to you from the Father, even the Spirit of truth, who proceeds from the Father, he will bear witness to me; and you also are witnesses, because you have been with me from the beginning' (15:26–27). Jesus gives them this Spirit on the day of his resurrection (20:21–23). There is no 'waiting in the city' for a Pentecostal experience. The Spirit will give standing to what they do in the community, specifically to their forgiving of sins.

It is in Baptism that John sees the Spirit being given to those who believe in Jesus (John 3). John does not describe the rite of Baptism, as he does not describe the rite of the Eucharist in his account of the Last Supper. He is noted for dealing with the rites of the Church symbolically and theologically rather than ritually. He takes water as a symbol of the Spirit. People drink of the Spirit (7:37–39). What he sees in Baptism is rebirth in water and the Spirit (3:5–6) into the real world of God, beyond the flesh and the sinfulness that belongs to it. The reality that John wants people to see symbolized in their Baptism is the reality that the Spirit gives witness to (cf. also 1 John 5:6–9). Breath, or the wind is also a symbol of the Spirit: when John describes Jesus giving the Spirit by breathing upon the disciples (20:22) he is drawing attention to a symbolic rather than to a ritual action. The symbolical language of anointing is used in 1 John 2:20. It is used to contrast those who 'went out from us, but they were not of us' (v. 19) with those who 'have been anointed by the Holy One'. The issue is not unlike that raised by Peter in his rebuke to Simon the magician. It has to do with belonging or not belonging to the community of true believers. The true believers are 'anointed by the Holy One'. Although the anointing is not attributed to the Spirit, the consequence of it, 'you all know . . . the truth', is a characteristic work of the Spirit in John. A later verse points in the same direction: 'the anointing which you received from him abides in you, and you have no need that anyone should teach you; as his anointing teaches you about everything, and is true, and is no lie, just as it has taught you, abide in him' (v. 27). The text goes on to develop the idea of abiding in terms of being children of God, avoiding sin, and living in the truth about Jesus and in love, before eventually relating it explicitly to the Holy Spirit: 'By this we know that we abide in him and he in us, because he has given us of his own Spirit' (4:13). By this assurance of our abiding in God that comes from the Holy Spirit 'is love perfected with us, that we may have confidence for the day of judgement, because as he is so are we in this world . . . perfect love casts out fear' (vv. 17–18). From a different standpoint (that of inner experience) the text reaches a conclusion that has affinities with the teaching of Luke: the Spirit is strength for the Christian in the eschatological era.

Johannine literature speaks symbolically rather than descriptively of Christian rites: if the Eucharist is not described in the account of the Last Supper, the imagery of it does permeate the theology of the Eucharist that is expounded in John 6. One might wonder if the symbolical language about the Holy Spirit in terms of anointing does not likewise depend on a real rite that was practised in the Church as part of Christian initiation. But as there is no corroborative evidence for such a rite in the New Testament, as there is for the rites of Baptism and Eucharist, one cannot claim with any confidence that the fine theology of the Holy Spirit in 1 John is a reflection on an actual part of the rite of initiation that would eventually be recognized as Confirmation.

7.1.4   From Scripture to its tradition

The distinction that has been made within the New Testament between a theology of the Holy Spirit found in Luke and another that comes from Paul and is further developed in John has consequences for a reading of the subsequent tradition and for a theology of Confirmation. There are uncertainties and apparent divergences in the tradition about how and in what particular rite the Spirit is given in Christian initiation. There is a view that it is given in the act of baptizing. There is also a view that links it with an anointing or laying-on of hands that follows Baptism and which eventually identifies these rites as being a sacrament, distinct from Baptism, for the giving of the Holy Spirit. It is tempting to propose that the theology of the Spirit that is being transmitted in the first of these traditions is derived from Paul/John, whereas the second represents Luke. One might suggest that, in the early centuries, the more developed, Hellenistic theologies of Paul and John, centred on Baptism, supplanted the more primitive Jewish theology that had survived in Luke, but that there was a subsequent revival of Luke's ideas, especially in relation to the rites of laying-on of hands and anointing which had become part of the rite of Christian initiation. These hypotheses are certainly of some help for a reading of the tradition. But they can also be misleading. While Luke does not give great attention to the inner sanctifying presence of the Holy Spirit in Christians he in no way excludes it. His repeated reference to prayer as the setting in which the Spirit is given, and the reasoning he attributes to Peter about why Simon the magician could not give the Holy Spirit, show that he believes the Spirit belongs to holy people who live in the faith and love of Christ. To say that he does not make the Spirit be the direct principle of holiness does not mean that he thinks the gift of the Spirit is irrelevant to it. There is no trace in Luke of an Old Testament idea that the spirit of God could take hold of people against their wills, or that it could use evil people for God's purposes (oddly enough, it is John who says that Caiaphas prophesied without knowing it because he was high priest — John 11:49–51). Paul and John do highlight the inner sanctifying presence of the Spirit. But they also see the presence of the Spirit as affecting the mission of the Church to preach the Gospel. Their emphasis on the interiority and abiding reality of the gift of the Spirit gives a new depth to that self-confidence and sense of being chosen and gifted to bring about the saving work of God in the world of the last days that Luke attributes to the Holy Spirit. They put the Spirit-given strength of Christians on a firmer basis by locating it in their faith and love, in their knowing and doing the truth in love, rather than merely in their charismatic gifts. They deepen rather than discount the mission-centred theology of the Holy Spirit that Luke champions.

From such a starting point the theological issue to be traced in the tradition is not so much whether or how a particular New Testament theology of the Holy Spirit gave rise to a rite and theology of Confirmation, as one of how the full richness of all the theologies took sacramental shape in a complex rite made up of Baptism and Confirmation. The Spirit is given in Christian initiation, with all the effects that Luke and Paul and John assign to it. The theological question about Confirmation is about there being a particular aspect of this gift, that is consistently revealed in the New Testament, and is subsequently recognized in the Church as being symbolized and realized in a part of the rite of initiation other than baptizing in water, even if it takes some centuries for this other rite to find a settled and independent form.

7.2   THE FATHERS

In the Apostolic Fathers and Apologists the Spirit is commonly 'the prophetic Spirit'. It is not particularly connected with initiation, except to the extent that the Holy Spirit is named in the formula of Baptism (which Justin explains in *First Apology*, 64 by saying '. . . in the name of the Holy Spirit, who through the prophets foretold all things concerning Jesus'). Irenaeus, however, has a rich theology of the Holy Spirit which has a distinct bearing on initiation. The following text is a sample of how he weaves together different themes, images and theologies of the Holy Spirit.

the Spirit of God descended like a Dove upon Him; that Spirit, of whom it was said by Isaiah, 'and the Spirit of God shall rest upon him' . . . . And again, 'The Spirit of the Lord is upon me, because he hath anointed me'. The same Spirit of whom our Lord saith, 'For it is not ye that speak, but the Spirit of your Father that speaketh in you'. And again, giving his disciples power to regenerate into God, he said unto them, 'Go and teach all nations, baptizing them in the name of the Father, and of the Son, and of the Holy Ghost'. For him he promised by the Prophets to pour out in the last times upon servants and handmaidens, that they may prophesy. Whence also he came down upon the Son of God, made Son of Man, using himself to dwell with him in mankind and to rest among men, and to reside in the work of God's hands, working the will of the Father in them, and renewing them out of old age into the newness of Christ. This Spirit David sought for mankind, saying, 'And stablish me with thy principal Spirit'. Of whom Luke also saith, that after the Ascension of the Lord, he came down on the disciples in Pentecost, having power as concerning all nations, that they should enter into life, and to open the new Testament. For which cause also they breathed out in all languages one harmonious hymn unto God, the Spirit bringing back distant tribes into unity, and offering to the Father the first-fruits of all nations. Wherefore also the Lord promised to send the Paraclete, to unite us to God. For as out of dry wheat one mass or one loaf cannot be made without moisture; so neither could we many be made one in Christ Jesus, without the water which is from Heaven. And as dry earth, except it receive moisture, bears no fruit; so we also, being in the first place a dry tree, could never have become fruitful of life, without the spontaneous rain from above. For our bodies by the laver received that unity which leads to incorruption, but our souls by the Spirit. And so both are necessary, since both are profitable for the life of God: even as the Lord had pity on that sinful woman of Samaria . . . and promised living water . . . the drink which springs out to eternal life. This the Lord receiving as a gift from the Father, gave himself also to those who participate of him, when he sent the Holy Spirit into the whole earth . . . the Spirit of God who descended upon the Lord, — 'the Spirit of wisdom and understanding, the Spirit of counsel and might, and the Spirit of knowledge and godliness, the Spirit of the fear of God'. And this same Spirit he again gave to the Church, sending the Paraclete from Heaven into all the earth: whither also the Devil, as lightning, was cast out . . . and that where we have an accuser, there also we may have an advocate. Even as the Lord commits to the Holy Ghost that man of his, who had fallen among thieves; whom he did himself pity, and bound up his wounds, giving two royal pennies, that we receiving by the Spirit the image and inscription of the Father and the Son, might cause the penny entrusted to us to bear fruit, accounting for it to the Lord with manifold increase (*Adversus Haereses*, III, 17; trans. Keble).

There are obvious references in this text to the water of Baptism and to the action of the Spirit in it. The Spirit is at one and the same time the gift poured out at the end of time and manifested in prophecy, and the principle of regeneration to new life. There is no discontinuity between the action of the Spirit who brings back distant tribes into unity and the action that moistens us and makes us fruitful of life. The Spirit abides and inaugurates the New Testament. The interpretation of what the Lord did for the man fallen among thieves is curious. There is no particular justification in the gospel text for saying, as Irenaeus does, that the Lord 'commits him to the Holy Spirit', unless it is in the phrase 'pouring on oil' in the description of how the Samaritan took care of the injured man (Luke 10:34). Is the remark of Irenaeus an allusion to a ritual anointing with oil for the giving of the Holy Spirit in the rite of initiation? He has a reference in *Adversus Haereses*, I, 14 to the use of such a rite in initiation by a Christian Gnostic sect. It is also worth noting that he goes beyond the scriptural text in arguing from the fact that the two 'royal' pennies have an image and inscription to the statement that the Spirit stamps the image of Father and Son on the Christian. This stamping of an image by the Holy Spirit would make more sense if Irenaeus were referring even obliquely, to some rite of marking or sealing in Christian initiation. (Other texts of Irenaeus and analysis in Milner, pp. 19–22 and Fisher, *Confirmation*, pp. 21–25.)

Tertullian sees the Spirit of God in the waters of Baptism but says it is actually given to the Christian at the laying-on of hands that follows the water rite and the anointing with chrism: 'At this point that most Holy Spirit willingly comes down from the Father upon bodies cleansed and blessed' (*De Baptismo*, c. 8; cf. c. 4). However, when he is explaining the difference between Christian Baptism and the baptism of John he says clearly that even the remission of sins is given by the Holy Spirit (c. 10). He recommends that those who are baptized should pray for the charisms of the Holy Spirit (c. 20) but does not give charismatic gifts any special attention. His views on the Spirit and on the charisms surely changed when he joined the Montanists. They gave a central place to prophecy and other ecstatic forms of behaviour, which they attributed to the Spirit. Against them, and all other sects and schismatic groups, various writers of the third century contended that the Holy Spirit was received and given only within the unity of the catholic Church. The accent came to be put on the unifying work of the Spirit within the existing Church more than on the strength for missionary expansion that the Spirit also gave to the Church. Cyprian was a major proponent of the unity of the Church against heretical and schismatic groups. He argued that these groups did not have the Spirit because they were cut off from the unity of the Church. Because they did not have the Spirit they could not give it. Cyprian used this principle in making his case for rebaptizing heretics. He argued that because heretics did not have the Holy Spirit the Baptism they gave was no Baptism. The assumption is that there is no Baptism without the gift of the Holy Spirit. And yet it is with the laying-on of hands that follows the rite of baptizing that Cyprian normally associates the giving of the Spirit. He argues his case about Baptism on that basis. He notes that the opponents of rebaptism in the Church do, in fact, lay hands on converted heretics for the giving of the Spirit. Later theology might have called this the Sacrament of Reconciliation, but Cyprian takes it to be the first ritual giving of the Spirit. He sees in this practice of his opponents an admission that heretics did not have the Spirit. He accuses them of inconsistency in allowing that Baptism given by heretics could have value and should not be repeated, whereas their imposition of hands was being given no value and had to be repeated. His thinking can be followed in this text:

> For if the Church is therefore not with heretics, because it is one and cannot be divided, and if the Holy Ghost is therefore not with them, because He is One, and cannot be with profane persons and strangers, surely Baptism also which consists in the same unity, cannot be with heretics, because it cannot be separated either from the Church or from the Holy Ghost. Or if they attribute the effect of Baptism to the Majesty of the Name, so that they who are wheresoever and howsoever baptized in the Name of Jesus Christ, must be deemed to be renewed and sanctified, why should not also hands be by them laid on the person baptized, in the Name of the Same Christ, for the receiving of the Holy Ghost? Why does not the same Majesty of the Same Name avail in the laying on of hands, which they contend hath availed in the sanctification of Baptism? For if any, born out of the Church, can become the temple of God; why cannot the Holy Ghost also be poured on this temple? For he who has been sanctified, his sins being laid aside in Baptism, and has been spiritually formed into a new man, is made fit for receiving the Holy Ghost; for that the Apostle says, 'As many of you as have been baptized into Christ have put on Christ'. He then who being baptized among heretics can put on Christ, much more can he receive the Holy Ghost, whom Christ has sent. Otherwise he that hath been sent will be greater than Him That sent, if one baptized without may come indeed to put on Christ, but could not receive the Holy Spirit; as if either Christ could be put on without the Spirit, or the Spirit be separated from Christ. How unmeaning too were it, that whereas the second birth, whereby we are born in Christ through the laver of regeneration, is spiritual, some say that man may be spiritually born among heretics, with whom they deny the Spirit to be. For water alone cannot cleanse sins and sanctify a man, unless it have also the Holy Ghost. Wherefore they must needs concede either that the Spirit is there, where they say Baptism is; or that that is not Baptism, where the Spirit is not, in that Baptism cannot be without the Spirit . . . heresy, which is not the spouse of Christ, nor can neither be cleansed or sanctified by His washing, cannot bear sons to God. Moreover a person is not born by the laying on of hands, when he receives the Holy Ghost, but in Baptism; that so being already born he may receive the Spirit, as was done in the first man Adam. . . . For the Spirit cannot be received, except there is first one to receive it. But since the birth of Christians is in Baptism, and the generation of Baptism and sanctification are with that one spouse of Christ who can spiritually conceive and bear sons to God, where and of whom and to whom is he born, who is not a son of the Church, so as to have God for his Father, before he has the Church for his mother? (*Letter* 74, 6–8; trans. Carey).

The argument of Cyprian in favour of rebaptism can be answered with the help of distinctions worked out in later theology between a valid and a fruitful Baptism. These will also throw light on the ambiguity in his thought about whether the Spirit is given in the baptizing or in the laying-on of hands. Cyprian was probably so conscious of the unity of Christian initiation and so insistent that one could only be initiated in the one true Church that the assigning of the gift of the Spirit to one or other of the rites would not mean the exclusion of it from the other. The laying-on of hands is an episcopal and manifestly ecclesial ritual action. It makes the gift of the Spirit decisively visible because it manifests admission to the one and only Church. But it is meaningless without Baptism. Cyprian also mentions an anointing with chrism in Christian initiation (*Letter* 70) and says that those who join the Church from heresy are 'perfected with' the Lord's seal as well as having hands laid on them (*Letter* 73).

Cyprian's arguments in favour of rebaptizing heretics did not convince the Western church. The tradition affirmed by Pope Stephen against Cyprian was eventually sanctioned by the Council of Arles (AD 314), which ruled that those who had been baptized and confessed the Catholic Creed in an heretical or schismatic sect were to be admitted to the Church by having the bishop lay hands on them 'for the receiving of the Holy Spirit' (DS 123). The theological reflection about Christian initiation provoked by the question of the admission of heretics into the Church gave prominence to the rôle of the Holy Spirit in building up the internal unity of the Church. Unity was becoming a critical issue in that third century, as the pressures that could give rise to heresy and schism multiplied within the growing complexity of the communion of faith. The Church was also sufficiently public for it to become sensitive to the effect which its internal divisions could have on what the world thought of it. It would make more sense to see the Spirit that was received at initiation as the Spirit that gathered people together in the Church more than as the Spirit that sent them out in missionary expansion. The unity of the Church was, no doubt, seen in relation to its mission to the world. But a phrase like Cyprian's famous 'outside the Church no salvation' suggests a conception of unity that would make mission be a drawing of people into the Church, within which they would receive the Spirit, rather than an outward expansion of a Spirit-filled Church. In such a view the Spirit given in initiation is for the security of salvation more than for the adventure of mission.

The theology of the Holy Spirit and of the place of the Spirit in the life of Christians in the Church is marvellously developed in the writing of the Greek Fathers during the fourth century. One touches only the fringes of it in the mystagogical catecheses of Cyril of Jerusalem, John Chrysostom and Theodore of Mopsuestia. What they have to say, however, links the pneumatology of the East to the rites of Christian initiation and has an important influence on the theology of Confirmation. Cyril gives his teaching especially when commenting on the anointing with chrism that comes after baptizing in the rite of initiation (*Sermon* 3; Yarnold, pp. 79–83). Although he associates the gift of the Spirit with the anointing rather than with the baptizing, the natural continuity between bathing and anointing allows him to join the Christ-effect and the Spirit-effect closely. The baptizing is putting on Christ; the anointing also makes the baptized be 'christs' (anointed ones). At the same time, by referring the anointing to what happened at Christ's baptism he can say that 'the anointing is the Holy Spirit'. The Spirit is the messianic Spirit promised by Isaiah, with which the Father anointed Jesus when he 'chose him to be Saviour of the whole world'. It is the messianic 'oil of gladness' foretold by David, given to Christ, 'the author of spiritual joy', and by him to those who have been anointed. Cyril draws a daring parallel between the bread of the Eucharist and the chrism which 'after the invocation is no longer ordinary ointment but Christ's grace, which through the presence of the Holy Spirit instils his divinity into us'. The grace of Christ, the presence of the Holy Spirit, divinization — these are different aspects of what is given in the anointing. After explaining to the neophytes why they were anointed in different parts of the body he reminds them that Christ, after receiving the Spirit, went forth to do battle with the enemy, 'so you also, after your holy baptism and sacramental anointing, put on the armour of the Holy Spirit, confront the power of the enemy, and reduce it saying: "I can do all things in Christ who strengthens me"'. It is the theme of strength and of battle against the enemy that will become classical in the theology of Confirmation. Cyril continues to explain it in messianic terms, playing on the equivalence of Christ, Messiah, Anointed One: by the anointing the neophytes are entitled to be called Christians; they are the ones in whom the typological anointings of Aaron and Solomon are fulfilled ('not in figure but in truth, for you were truly anointed by the Holy Spirit'); they are taught all things, in the Johannine sense; and the salvation promised to all nations is being worked out in them: 'so the blessed Isaiah prophesied long ago: "The Lord shall make provision for all nations on this mountain" (by mountain he means the Church . . .). "They will drink of wine and gladness, and be anointed with chrism." To convince you utterly, hear what he says about the sacramental nature of this chrism: "Give all these things to the nations, for the Lord's counsel is to all nations"'.

Explanations of how the Holy Spirit is given in Christian initiation that come from the tradition of Antioch are affected by the peculiarities of the Antiochean rite of initiation: the anointing with chrism precedes the act of baptizing, the laying-on of hands is done at the moment of baptism and there is no anointing afterwards, at least until the late fourth century and then it is not associated with the gift of the Spirit (see above, 6.2). John Chrysostom comments on the anointing with chrism in a way that will become standard in later theology of Confirmation. The anointing makes one be 'a soldier . . . signed on for a spiritual contest'. The anointing has just been preceded by renunciation of the Devil. The anointed persons, 'renouncing him, . . . have changed their allegiance and publicly enlisted with Christ . . . the bishop anoints you on your forehead and marks you with the seal, to make the devil turn away his eyes . . . you will confront him in battle and this is why the bishop anoints you as athletes of Christ before leading you into the spiritual arena' (Homily 2, 22: Yarnold, pp. 166–167). However, John does not attribute any of these effects of anointing and sealing to the Holy Spirit. It is only at the moment of baptizing that the Spirit is given: 'Then by the words of the bishop and by his hand the presence of the Holy Spirit flies down upon you' (ibid., 25: p. 168). According to John's account the baptism is followed immediately by the welcome of the community, with a kiss, and the Eucharist, which he does associate with the Spirit: 'For as soon as they come up from the font, they are led to the awesome table which is laden with all good things. They taste the body and blood of the Lord and become the dwelling place of the Spirit' (ibid., 27: p. 169). But further on, near the end of his homily, he mentions something else that comes between Baptism and Eucharist. It is a prayer for others, in the Church and in the world. In the *Apostolic Constitutions* Hippolytus also prescribes prayer with the assembled community ('The Prayer of the Faithful') at this point of the rite of initiation. The quality of it that John Chrysostom recommends corresponds to the other title it would have in later times, 'The General Intercessions'. It is a prayer that looks forward to the Eucharist, but it also looks backwards to the gift that has been given in Baptism. John does not relate it particularly to the Holy Spirit. But his exhortation does recall the battle with the devil that he had associated with anointing and appeals to the self-confidence proper to those who have been made friends and children of God; he also highlights the unity of the Church and the salvation of the world, both of which are characteristic works of the Spirit:

> As you step out of the sacred waters and express your resurrection by the act of coming up from them, ask for alliance with him so that you may show great vigilance in guarding what has been given to you, and so be immune from the tricks of the Enemy. Pray for the peace of the Churches. Intercede for those who are still wandering. Fall on your knees for those who are in sin so that we may deserve some pardon. You were once diffident; God has given you great assurance. You were once slaves; he has enrolled you among the chief of his friends. You were once captives; he has raised you up and adopted you as sons. He will not refuse your demands; he will grant them all, true again in this to his own goodness. In this way you will draw God to still greater kindness. When he sees you showing such concern for those who are your own members and anxious about the salvation of others, because of this he will count you worthy to receive great assurance. Nothing so warms his heart as our compassion for our members and the affection that we show for our brothers, the great forethought we show for the salvation of our neighbour (ibid., 29–30: Yarnold, pp. 170–171).

Theodore of Mopsuestia is inclined to speak in general terms about the action of the Holy Spirit in initiation rather than to locate the giving of the Spirit in any particular rite. The Spirit is in the water by reason of the blessing of the bishop (*Homily* 3, 9: Yarnold, pp. 194–195); it is the principle of new birth in the womb of the water (*ibid.* and 3, 3); it is the principle and guarantee of resurrection and immortality (3, 7–9) and will have its full effect only at the resurrection (3, 10). Theodore stands apart from all previous writers in the Antiochean liturgical tradition in commenting on a sealing which is done after baptizing and in relating it explicitly to the Holy Spirit (cf. Yarnold, p. 208 and footnote 65). He seems to see this rite as a kind of resumé of the gift of the Spirit given throughout initiation rather than as the rite in which the Spirit is actually given. It recalls the messianic Spirit that came on Jesus and stayed with him as an anointing. It is this abiding, definitive quality of the gift of the messianic Spirit rather than the gift itself that he reads into this post-baptismal sealing and anointing of Christians:

When Jesus came up out of the water, he received the grace of the Holy Spirit, which came and remained on him in the form of a dove. This is why he too is said to have been anointed by the Holy Spirit . . . (Luke 4:18 and Acts 10:38) . . . . This shows that the Holy Spirit never leaves him, just as the anointing attaches to those who are anointed by men with oil and never leaves them. You too, then, must be sealed on the forehead. *While the bishop is putting the seal on you, he says: 'N. is sealed in the name of the Father, etc.'* This sign shows you that, when the Father, the Son and the Holy Spirit were named, the Holy Spirit came upon you. You were anointed by him and received him by God's grace. He is yours and remains within you. You enjoy the first-fruits of him in this life, for you receive now in symbol the possession of the blessings to come. Then you will receive the grace in its fullness . . . (*Homily* 3, 27: Yarnold, pp. 208–209).

St Ambrose attributes the work of Baptism to the Holy Spirit who descends and consecrates the water; the Spirit comes because Jesus first went down into the water at his baptism and the Spirit came upon him (*Sermon* 1, 15–19: Yarnold, pp. 105–107). In his second sermon, reflecting on the coming of the Spirit on Jesus, he interprets the dove as a sign given 'to call the incredulous to faith' (2:14: Yarnold, p. 114). This leads him to a general reflection about signs that is an important component of his sacramental theology: 'In the beginning there had to be a sign; in the ages which followed there has to be fulfilment'. He illustrates this distinction with a comment on the outpouring of the Spirit at Pentecost:

there was a loud roaring as though a fierce wind was blowing, and parted tongues were seen, as of fire. What does this signify, except the descent of the Holy Spirit? He wished to show himself corporally to unbelievers; corporally by a sign, but spiritually by the sacrament. This was an evident proof of his coming; but now in our case the privilege of faith is offered. In the beginning there were signs for the sake of unbelievers; but for us who live in the time of the Church's full growth the truth is to be grasped, not by signs but by faith.

He appears to be saying that what the spectacular manifestations of the Spirit at Pentecost once did for unbelievers the sacrament now does for believers. Both are manifestations that establish the coming of the Spirit: one does it by way of proof, the other by way of faith. The sacrament to which he refers is still, at this point of his commentary, the water-rite of baptism. When he comes later to explain the post-baptismal sealing he says that 'after the ceremonies of the font, it still remains to bring the whole to perfect fulfilment. This happens when the Holy Spirit is infused at the priest's invocation' (3, 8: Yarnold, pp. 124–125). The Spirit that is received is the Spirit of the seven messianic gifts read about in Isaiah. For Ambrose, 'These are the seven virtues you receive when you are sealed. For . . . the Holy Spirit is multiform and has a whole variety of virtues' (*ibid.*, 9–10). Ambrose was probably playing on the fact that the Latin word for 'virtue' is the same as the word used in Acts 1:18 for what the apostles are said to receive when the Spirit comes upon them (translated 'power' in RSV). It is to this variety of gifts that he returns when, at the end of his catechesis, he wants to show how the sanctifying action in Christian initiation is common to the three Persons of the Trinity, and yet that special aspects of it are peculiar to individual Persons (6, 9: Yarnold, p. 152). Neither there nor elsewhere does he relate these gifts of the

Spirit to any kind of public or missionary activity in the Church. Still less does he see anything charismatic about them. His earlier remark about Pentecost seems to suggest that the era of 'signs' is now past and has given way to the era of faith in which the Church has reached full growth. He seems to be presenting the sacraments, and the faith which perceives the truth and reality within them, as an alternative to the charisms in manifesting the presence of the Spirit, and indeed as something more appropriate to what he calls 'the time of the Church's full growth'. It is an idea that is not without interest for a theology of sacraments and particularly for the theology of Confirmation.

St Augustine must have imbibed some of his theology of Christian initiation from Ambrose when he was baptized by him. He uses the distinction between sign and sacrament when discussing the anointing with chrism that follows Baptism. But he uses it to distinguish between the external rite of anointing with oil, which is what he calls the sign, and the internal anointing with the gift of the Spirit, which is the sacrament (cf. *In Psalm. 44*, 19: *PL* 36, 505). Augustine is also influenced by the experiences and problems of the church of Africa. He identifies the gift of the Spirit given in Christian initiation with charity. There can be a true Baptism without it. In that case the Spirit is given to those who convert by the laying-on of hands. It is not altogether clear whether this is the rite that will come to be recognized as the Sacrament of Reconciliation, in which sins are forgiven through the power of the Holy Spirit, or the completion of Christian initiation in which the Spirit is given for the first time. However, in the normal process of initiation within the Catholic Church it is in the anointing with chrism that Augustine sees the Spirit being given. He recognizes that since the forgiveness of sin cannot be given in Baptism without the action of the Spirit, there is already a gift of the Spirit before the anointing. What is given by the anointing is the special gift foretold by the prophets and promised by Christ (*Sermon* 71, 19: *PL* 38, 454–455). It is the messianic Spirit:

> He is invoked, therefore, over the baptized so that God may give them, as the prophet says, the Spirit of wisdom and understanding . . . counsel and force . . . knowledge and piety . . . the Spirit of the fear of the Lord (*Sermon* 249, 3: *PL* 38, 1162).

But these, like all gifts of the Spirit, are for growth in charity. Augustine does not see anything charismatic about them. Charity, of course, is a very powerful concept in Augustine, both for the building-up of the Church and for its rôle in the salvation of the world. The gift of the Spirit given by anointing with oil in Christian initiation is certainly not a private preserve.

7.3   WESTERN THEOLOGIANS

As a separate rite of imposition of hands for the giving of the Spirit, that could be done only by the bishop, developed in the Latin West during the fifth century (see 6.2 above), it became necessary to preach about it and to explain it theologically. Of the many sermons that must have been preached on the subject one came to have a special influence on the whole of Western theology, and even on the magisterial statements that accompany it. It was preached by a certain Faustus once Abbot of Lérins and then Bishop of Riez in the south of France, on a feast of Pentecost sometime during the second half of the fifth century (Milner, p. 44; for original text see van Buchem). The text of it survived. Much later, in the ninth century, segments of it, carrying the name and authority of various early Popes, were incorporated in the False Decretals — a canonical collection put together to justify various liturgical and disciplinary reforms of the Frankish church — which became an important authority in theological discussion during the Scholastic period. In the original sermon Faustus explains what this rite of laying-on hands does. Beginning with the quotation 'I will pour out my Spirit upon all flesh' he says that the laying-on of hands now does what Pentecost did for the first assembly of the faithful. He then has to explain what this gift could add to the gift already received in Baptism. He does so by using an analogy that was already well established in explanations of Christian initiation. It is the military image of the Christian as soldier of Christ. It had often been used to explain the anointings and signings that occur in initiation. Faustus stretches it because what he has to explain is a rite of laying-on of hands by the bishop, rather than an anointing (translation from Milner, pp. 44–47):

> Military proceedings require that when a commander receives a man into the number of his soldiers, he should not only put his mark upon him, but also equip him with arms suitable for fighting with. So for a baptized man the blessing [of Confirmation] is a giving of arms. You have given a soldier; give him also the implements of warfare. What good is it for a parent to bestow great wealth on a small child unless he also provides him with a guardian? The Paraclete is precisely such a protector, counsellor and guardian of those who are reborn in Christ. Therefore the divine word says: 'Unless the Lord guard the city, in vain do the watchmen keep vigil'.

He softens the military image with the somewhat problematical one of child and guardian. But when he goes on to pin down more precisely the continuity and complementarity of Baptism and Confirmation, it is the image of battle that prevails:

> So the Holy Spirit, who descended upon the baptismal waters bearing salvation, gave at the font all that is needed for innocence: at confirmation he gives an increase for grace, for in this world those who survive through the different stages of life, must walk among dangers and invisible enemies. In baptism we are born again to life, after baptism we are confirmed for battle. In baptism we are washed, after baptism we are strengthened.

Confirmation is a strengthening. This is an idea that will be canonized by the use the False Decretals make of the text of Faustus, and will find its way into most Western theology, as well as into documents of the *magisterium*. The idea of strength can be related to that 'power from on high' that Luke says the Holy Spirit would give the disciples. But that is not quite what Faustus was thinking of. He uses the Latin word *robur* rather than *virtus*, which was the word used in the texts of Luke in the Latin Bible. With a different word goes a different idea. The strength that Faustus sees given by Confirmation is not so much for preaching the Gospel to the ends of the earth as for living the Christian life in the midst of conflicts and battles of this world. The monastic background of Faustus would certainly make this theme dear to him. Using it to understand Confirmation leads him to say, against most of the tradition, that those who die immediately after Baptism do not need Confirmation:

> Thus for those who die at once the benefits of rebirth are sufficient, but for those who survive the aids of confirmation are necessary. The rebirth of itself saves those who are soon to be received into the peace of the blessed age, confirmation arms and equips those who are reserved for the conflicts and battles of this world. He who after baptism comes to death immaculate in the innocence he has acquired is confirmed by death itself — for after death he is no longer able to sin.

The remainder of the homily expands Faustus's view that the gift of the Holy Spirit is given in Confirmation, as it was given to the apostles at Pentecost, for personal spiritual growth and strength.

Three centuries later, when Charlemagne was having the Roman rite of episcopal Confirmation imposed in his domains, one finds a solution being given to the question about Baptism and Confirmation which differs from what Faustus proposed. Charlemagne's ecclesiastical mentor Alcuin (d. 804) has a pithy statement of the effect of Confirmation in one of his letters: whereas in Baptism the Christian is endowed with grace for eternal life, in Confirmation 'he receives the Spirit of sevenfold grace so that he may be strengthened by the Holy Spirit to preach to others' (*Letter* 134: quoted in Milner, p. 58). The thought is more fully developed by his pupil Rabanus Maurus (d. 856). Like all the Carolingian reformers he is emphasizing that it is the episcopal laying-on of hands that brings the gift of the Spirit for the completing and perfecting of initiation. The anointing with chrism and the gift of the Spirit that it undoubtedly brings belongs rather with the grace of Baptism. On the episcopal rite of Confirmation he says:

> Finally the Holy Ghost, the Paraclete, is conferred upon him by the chief priest through the laying on of the hand, that he may be fortified by the Holy Spirit to preach to others the gift which he himself gained in baptism when he was endowed by grace with eternal life. For the baptized is signed by the priest on the top of the head, by the bishop on his forehead. The first anointing signifies the descent of the Holy Spirit upon him to consecrate a dwelling for God; by the second it is declared that the sevenfold grace of the same Holy Spirit has come upon the man with all the fullness of sanctity for the knowledge of the truth. On the former occasion, the Holy Ghost himself, when the bodies and souls are cleansed and blessed, willingly descends from the Father to sanctify his own vessel by his visitation. On this latter occasion he comes into the man with this intent, that the seal of faith, which he has received on his brow, may make him replete with the heavenly gifts, and strengthened by his grace to bear the name of Christ fearlessly before the kings and rulers of this world and preach it with a free voice (*De Clericorum Institutione*, I, 30: quoted in Milner, p. 60).

In the prominence given to messianic, eschatological words and images ('fortified by the Holy Spirit', 'sevenfold grace', 'fullness of sanctity', 'knowledge of the truth', 'seal', 'strengthened', 'bearing the name of Christ fearlessly before kings' . . .), and in centring the special gift of the Holy Spirit that comes with Confirmation on preaching the Gospel to others, Rabanus and Alcuin are recovering the Lucan emphasis in teaching about the Spirit. The Fathers had maintained the Lucan tradition, although in a somewhat scaled-down form because of their interest in the inner sanctifying work of the Spirit and his rôle in building up the unity of the Church, as well as because of the priority they give to faith and charity over prophecy and the other charisms. There is little trace of the outgoing, missionary interpretation of the gift of the Spirit in Faustus: the battle he is concerned with is the personal battle against sin rather than the battle against those who oppose the preaching of the Gospel in the world. As a background to the views of Alcuin and Rabanus it is worth noting that the Carolingian churches were quite missionary-minded. They sent preachers among the pagan barbarians and had the experience of forming and initiating adult converts. Rabanus was a noted evangelizer when he became Archbishop of Mainz and his *De Clericorum Institutione*, from which the above quotation is taken, was written for the training of monks and clerics who would be active in the evangelization of Germany.

Mediaeval scholastic theology of Confirmation is adequately represented by St Thomas. He deals with Confirmation in a single question in the *Summa* (IIIa, q. 72). He is influenced by some passages from Faustus that by his time had become authoritative canonical and even dogmatic statements under the name of the phantom Pope Melchiades. However, he manages to put his finger on some key themes of the tradition that go beyond what came to him through the texts of Faustus. In IIIa, 72, 6 s. con., he quotes as authoritative the words of Rabanus Maurus: 'Last of all the Paraclete is given to the baptized person by the bishop through the imposition of hands in order that he be strengthened by the Holy Spirit to proclaim the faith (*ut roboretur per Spiritum Sanctum ad praedicandum*)'. It is a text that seems to have had considerable influence on Thomas's theology of the sacrament. He presents Confirmation as the sacrament of the fullness of the grace of the Holy Spirit (a. 1 ad 1). This fullness is the reality that was given at Pentecost: there it was given visibly but not in a sacramental rite (a. 2 ad 1; a. 4 ad 1). It is now given in the Church by the rite of anointing with chrism (a. 2). It is in this anointing rather than in the laying-on of hands that Thomas sees the sacrament. He evokes many of the traditional themes in his explanation of why chrism is a suitable material for a sacrament that gives the fullness of the Spirit. He relates its symbolism to the requirements of human life that are met by different sacraments. Baptism, he says, corresponds to birth, and is the beginning of life. The life begun in Baptism has then to grow and increase (*augmentum*) to a certain point of fullness before it is perfectly human. It is this entry into 'perfect age', into being fully human, that provides Thomas with his analogy for what Confirmation does in the life of grace. Significantly, he says that the distinctive thing about perfect age is that then one 'begins to live in communication with others, whereas previously one lived as it were solely for oneself' (a. 2). In using the analogy of 'perfect age' for Confirmation Thomas is not saying anything about the age at which people can or ought to be confirmed. He is quite sure that infants can and ought to be brought into this 'perfect age' by being confirmed. His argument for doing so is that it is God's intention to bring everyone who is born to perfection and that infants are capable of the perfection given in Confirmation (a. 8). Confirmation, then, has to do with an objective quality of grace — its being perfect — rather than with a subjective stage of development of the person being confirmed. The grace that Christians are initiated into is grace come-of-age. It is this fullness, perfection, coming-of-age of grace that was revealed at Pentecost. The perfection of grace is characteristic of the New Covenant. This is the reason Thomas gives for saying there was nothing corresponding to Confirmation in the Old Law: 'Confirmation is the sacrament of the fullness of grace and therefore there could not be anything corresponding to it in the Old Law because "the law made nothing perfect"' (a. 1 ad 2). Thomas also uses the word *robur* (strength), which had been canonized in the text of Faustus, to characterize this perfect age. It is a spiritual strength coming from the Trinity within, and from the mark or sign of Christ that distinguishes those who do battle under the leadership of Christ (a. 4). Among the modalities of the strength given by Confirmation is the sacramental character. Thomas had been somewhat uncertain about the distinction between the character of Confirmation and that of Baptism in IIIa, 63, 6. What he has to say in q. 72, 5 is more decisive, although it still leaves some questions unanswered. In Confirmation the Holy Spirit gives the power (Thomas uses the Latin *potestas*, which comes from the Aristotelian categories in which he analyses the character, rather than the biblical word *virtus*) to perform sacred actions, not just for one's own salvation (which is what is given in Baptism) but for battle against the enemies of faith; the model of this power is what the apostles received at Pentecost (a. 5). There is a personal battle that all the baptized have to fight against invisible enemies; but the confirmed have to take a stand against the external enemies of the faith in confessing the name of Christ (a. 5 ad 1). All the baptized are called to profess faith personally by living the sacramental life of the Church; when they are also confirmed they are given power to profess the faith publicly in words, and by a kind of commission (*quasi ex officio*) (a. 5 ad 2). Thomas had likened Confirmation to Ordination in IIIa, 65, 3 ad 2, in that they both confer special offices. In IIIa, q. 72 he notes the difference between them. He bases the distinction on the different effects which the Holy Spirit had at Pentecost on the apostles and on the other disciples: it made the apostles be 'teachers of the faith', whereas it made the others be able to do those things which are needed for 'the building-up of the faithful' (a. 2 ad 1; a. 8 ad 1). He is not very specific, in fact, about what the confirmed are equipped or commissioned to do. That makes theological sense if one is seeing Confirmation as a normal part of all Christian initiation, expressing the fullness of grace and perfect age that all Christians ought to have because they belong to an age in which the Spirit has been given. Thomas does not follow up a thought he had in q. 63, 6 about Confirmation being somehow a power to receive other sacraments, nor does he try to go beyond what he said about sacramental characters being sharings in Christ's priesthood in q. 63, 3 with, for example, any kind of suggestion about a sharing in Christ's prophetic office through Confirmation. However, he does consistently describe the effects of Confirmation in terms of confessing the faith, in words, publicly, in the face of opposition, for the building-up of the faithful. This is in keeping with his original intuition about 'perfect age' being characterized by communication with other people.

7.4 FROM FLORENCE (1439) TO VATICAN II

The first doctrinal statement about Confirmation in the Catholic *magisterium* is in the Decree for the Armenians of the Council of Florence (1439). It is a résumé of the Latin tradition, expressed in the Scholastic framework of numbered sacraments, matter and form, minister and effects. The matter is chrism; the form is 'I sign you with the sign of the cross and I confirm you with the chrism of salvation in the name of the Father and of the Son and of the Holy Spirit'. The ordinary minister is the bishop: the reason given is that 'we read that only the apostles, whose place the bishops hold, imparted the Holy Spirit by the laying on of hand . . . (Acts 8:14–17). Confirmation given by the Church takes the place of that imposition of hand'. After admitting that in the past 'through a dispensation of the apostolic See' simple priests have been known to confirm, with chrism prepared by the bishop, the text states: 'The effect of this sacrament is that in it the Holy Spirit is given for strength (*robur*), as He was given to the apostles on the day of Pentecost, in order that the Christian may courageously confess the name of Christ. And therefore the one to be confirmed is anointed on the forehead which is the seat of shame, so that he may not be ashamed to confess the name of Christ, and chiefly his cross, which, according to the apostle, is a stumbling block for the Jews and foolishness for the Gentiles (cf. 1 Corinthians 1:23). This is why he is signed with the sign of the cross' (ND 1416–1418).

Many of the Reformers retained a rite corresponding to Confirmation, consisting of a laying-on of hands with a prayer for the giving of the Spirit; but, in keeping with their general theology of justification, they usually refused to recognize it as a sacrament in the sense defined by the Council of Florence. It was seen as a public profession of faith, to be made by those who had been baptized in infancy; it was preceded by a period of more intensive study of catechism, and was itself the immediate preparation for First Communion. The Council of Trent condemned this view of Confirmation in three canons (ND 1434–1436), but did not itself give any positive teaching about the sacrament. The Anglican Church kept the rite of Confirmation or 'Laying on of Hands upon Those that are Baptized and Come to Years of Discretion' in its Prayer Book, but without an anointing with oil. Its theologians also kept a lively interest in the meaning of the rite and its relationship with Baptism, especially as regards the giving of the Holy Spirit. Over the past century much scholarly work has been done by Anglicans on the question (details in Fisher, *Confirmation*, pp. 142–152) and the works of Lampe, Dix, and Fisher have offered rich, though contrasting theologies of the sacrament. Roman Catholics also joined in the debate, especially when it became clear that biblical and historical evidence to which standard Catholic theologies appealed was not always as straightforward as had been thought. But more importantly, the theology of Confirmation became caught up in the general renewal of sacramental theology and in the sensitivities that developed in pastoral liturgy over the past half-century. The teaching of Vatican II about Confirmation reflects these developments — both the progress that has been made and the uncertainties that remain.

Baptism and Confirmation are kept closely together in the teaching of Vatican II. *Lumen Gentium* attributes the priesthood of all God's People to their Christian initiation, saying: 'The baptized, by regeneration and the anointing of the Holy Spirit, are consecrated . . . ' (*LG*, n. 10). In n. 11 it separates Baptism and Confirmation as distinct sacraments, but describes their effects in a way that emphasizes the continuity and progression of the process of initiation. Having said that the faithful are already incorporated in the Church and its worship by Baptism, and are bound to confess the faith they have received, it adds: 'By the sacrament of Confirmation they are more perfectly bound to the Church and are endowed with the special strength (*robur*) of the Holy Spirit. Hence they are, as true witnesses of Christ, more strictly obliged to spread and defend the faith by words and deed'. This is the most decisive statement of the Council about the meaning of Confirmation. It is in terms of three things: relationship with the Church ('more perfect' status than what is established by Baptism); special strength of the Holy Spirit (central idea in the tradition); witnessing to Christ, spreading and defending the faith by word and action (public responsibility for faith). The idea of witness and responsibility for the faith is further developed in n. 12, as a sharing in Christ's prophetic office. Although there is reference to 'The whole body of the faithful who have an anointing that comes from the Holy One' and to their 'appreciation of the faith aroused and sustained by the Spirit of truth', the sharing in the prophetic office is not linked with any sacrament. Indeed, when the text goes on to speak of the special charisms of the Holy Spirit it presents them as something additional to what the Spirit does 'through the sacraments and ministrations of the Church'. No special attention is given to Confirmation in what *Lumen Gentium* has to say about the status and ministry of the laity in its ch. 4; and the Decree on the Apostolate of the Laity does not go beyond the theological statements of *Lumen Gentium*.

There are passages about the Holy Spirit in the documents of Vatican II which, although they do not refer explicitly to Confirmation, must guide a Catholic theology of the sacrament. Chapter 7 of *Lumen Gentium*, on 'The Pilgrim Church', has a fine statement on the Holy Spirit in the Church of the eschatological age. Having spoken of Christ as the saviour of all and of the Church, set up through the life-giving Spirit sent upon the disciples, as the universal sacrament of salvation, and about how the restoration of all things has already begun in Christ, the text continues:

> It is carried forward in the sending of the Holy Spirit and through him continues in the Church in which, through our faith, we learn the meaning of our earthly life, while we bring to term, with hope of future good, the tasks allotted to us in the world by the Father, and so work out our salvation (cf. Philippians 2:12). Already the final age of the world is with us (cf. 1 Corinthians 10:11) and the renewal of the world is

irrevocably under way, for the Church on earth is endowed already with a sanctity that is real though imperfect. However, until there be realized new heavens and an new earth in which justice dwells (cf. 2 Peter 3:13) the pilgrim Church, in its sacraments and institutions, which belong to this present age, carries the mark of this world which will pass, and she herself takes her place among the creatures which groan and travail yet and await the revelation of the sons of God (cf. Romans 8:19–22). So it is that, united with Christ in the Church and marked with the Holy Spirit 'who is the guarantee of our inheritance' (Ephesians 1:14), we are truly called and indeed are children of God . . . (*LG*, n. 48).

In this chapter of the Constitution on the Church the tradition of Paul and John about the Spirit predominates. But the missionary drive is very strong in the teaching of Vatican II and the Lucan tradition about the Holy Spirit is well represented. There is a good expression of it in the doctrinal section of the Decree on Missionary Activity (*Ad Gentes*):

Christ, whom the Father sanctified and sent into the world (cf. John 10:36), said of himself: 'The Spirit of the Lord is upon me, because he anointed me; to bring good news to the poor he sent me . . . ' (Luke 4:18). . . . Now, what was once preached by the Lord, or fulfilled in him for the salvation of mankind, must be proclaimed and spread to the ends of the earth (Acts 1:8), so that what was accomplished for the salvation of all men may, in the course of time, achieve its universal effect. (4) To do this, Christ sent the Holy Spirit from the Father to exercise inwardly his saving influence, and to promote the spread of the Church. Without doubt, the Holy Spirit was at work in the world before Christ was glorified. On the day of Pentecost, however, he came down on the disciples that he might remain with them forever (cf. John 14:16); on that day the Church was openly (*publice*) displayed to the crowds and the spread of the Gospel among the nations, through preaching, was begun. Finally, on that day was foreshadowed the union of all peoples in the catholic Church which speaks every language, understands and embraces all tongues in charity, and thus overcomes the dispersion of Babel. The 'acts of the apostles' began with Pentecost just as Christ was conceived in the Virgin Mary with the coming of the Holy Spirit, and was moved to begin his ministry by the descent of the same Holy Spirit who came down upon him while he was praying. Before freely laying down his life for the world, the Lord Jesus organized the apostolic ministry and promised to send the Holy Spirit, in such a way that both would be always and everywhere associated in the fulfilment of the work of salvation. Throughout the ages the Holy Spirit makes the entire Church 'one in communion and ministry; and provides her with different hierarchical and charismatic gifts', giving life to ecclesiastical structures, being as it were their soul, inspiring in the hearts of the faithful that same spirit of mission which impelled Christ himself. He even at times visibly anticipates apostolic action (Acts 10:44–47), just as in various ways he unceasingly accompanies and directs it (*Ad Gentes*, nn. 3–4).

In the Apostolic Constitution on the Sacrament of Confirmation *Divinae consortium naturae* (1971) Paul VI is mainly concerned with explaining and justifying the decision about the sacramental rite (see 6.2 above). He does, however, provide some theological refinements of the teaching of Vatican II on Confirmation. He says it is the rite 'through which the faithful receive the Holy Spirit as a Gift'. It is not the gift or gifts of the Spirit that are given but the Spirit himself, whose personal trinitarian name is Gift. When St Thomas analyses this name of the Spirit in Ia, q. 38 he takes it to mean total, irrevocable, final. Paul VI expounds the Gift as messianic, which comes to the same thing, using familiar scriptural texts. He sees the apostles laying on hands 'to complete the grace of baptism'. He has a fine paragraph in which he situates Confirmation within the three sacraments of initiation. He uses the Pauline notion of incorporation into Christ and into the Church to express the reality that he sees progressively brought to fullness in initiation. He uses the idea of character in both its Christological and ecclesiological cal senses to state the effects of Baptism and Confirmation; and it is with the character that he associates what *Lumen Gentium* said about the faithful when they are confirmed being 'bound more intimately to the Church' and being 'more strictly obliged to spread and defend the faith both by word and deed as true witnesses of Christ'. The passage reads:

> . . . the specific importance of confirmation for sacramental initiation by which the faithful 'as members of the living Christ are incorporated into him and made like him through baptism and through confirmation and the eucharist'. In baptism, the newly baptized receive forgiveness of sins, adoption as sons of God, and the character of Christ, by which they are made members of the Church and for the first time become sharers in the priesthood of their Saviour (see 1 Peter 2:5 and 9). Through the sacrament of confirmation, those who have been born anew in baptism receive the inexpressible Gift, the Holy Spirit himself, by which 'they are endowed . . . with special strength'. Moreover, having received the character of this sacrament, they are 'bound more intimately to the Church' and 'they are more strictly obliged to spread and defend the faith both by word and by deed as true witnesses of Christ'. Finally, confirmation is so closely linked with the holy eucharist that the faithful, after being signed by holy baptism and confirmation, are incorporated fully into the body of Christ by participation in the eucharist (*Rites*, p. 292).

The theology of Confirmation expounded by Paul VI would probably be accepted as a valid expression of the tradition of faith, if not the only one, by most Orthodox churches, by Anglicans, and by some Lutheran and Reformed churches. Many evangelical churches and communities, however, would still refuse to accept Confirmation as a rite that could be linked on any level of equality with Baptism. In contemporary ecumenical dialogue the BEM text of the World Council of Churches attempts to build a consensus among Christians in the following paragraph, entitled 'Baptism — Chrismation — Confirmation':

> In God's work of salvation, the paschal mystery of Christ's death and resurrection is inseparably linked with the pentecostal gift of the Holy Spirit. Similarly, participation in Christ's death and resurrection is inseparably linked with the receiving of the Spirit. Baptism in its full meaning signifies and effects both. Christians differ in their understanding as to where the sign of the gift of the Spirit is to be found. Different actions have become associated with the giving of the Spirit. For some it is the water rite itself. For others, it is the anointing with chrism and/or the imposition of hands, which many churches call confirmation. For still others it is all three, as they see the Spirit operative throughout the rite. All agree that Christian baptism is in water and the Holy Spirit (*Baptism*, n. 14).

Catholic difficulties with this text come from its failure to identify Confirmation as a sacrament. Underlying that failure is the unsatisfactory nature of BEM's understanding of sacrament already alluded to (see above, 2.10). The issue is not just one of discovering where 'the sign of the gift of the Spirit is to be found' but whether or not the Spirit is actually given in and by the sign; and whether the sign thus understood is distinct from the sign of Baptism; and whether it is an integral rather than an optional part of initiation.

7.5   SYSTEMATIC ESSAY

7.5.1   *The theological question*

A systematic theology of Confirmation should follow the same lines as a systematic theology of Baptism. The tradition out of which it must come is a tradition about Christian initiation which has often, especially at its origins, been simply called Baptism. Much of the earlier part of the theology of Baptism that was offered in 5.8 above is about Christian initiation and to that extent holds for Confirmation as well as Baptism. And, of course, the general theology of sacraments offered in Chapter 3 must also underlie a theology of Confirmation. The point where one has to begin to deal with what is distinctive about Confirmation was identified in 5.8.6 above. The question there was about God's action in giving the Holy Spirit. It is with this divine action that one ought to begin the specific study of Confirmation. It is too late to start looking for what is specific to Confirmation, and at how it differs from Baptism, when one has come to discuss the effects of the sacrament. Effects that one would want to assign to Confirmation will be found to have been already claimed for Baptism. One will be left struggling to work out the difference between the two sacraments in terms of modalities and degrees of the same effect. Sacraments are signs: one must begin to look for what is distinctive about a particular sacrament, not on the level of its effects but in its symbolism; the effects follow on the symbolism (*efficiunt quod figurant*, as the Scholastics said). The originality of sacraments is not so much in what they do — God can do all that is needed for human salvation without them — but that they make what God is doing visible in a human symbol. What is symbolized first and foremost in a sacrament is the salvific action of God. Human prayer and human response is also symbolized, but that is always relative to the particular way in which God is believed to act in the rite. As a sacrament of initiation Confirmation must symbolize the salvific action of God through Christ and in the Spirit as it first takes hold of humans. From the tradition about the rite it is clear that it symbolizes in a particular way the action of God in giving the Spirit. The problem is that the living and life-giving waters of Baptism already symbolize the divine action of giving the Spirit. The theological question then must be: is there anything in the divine giving of the Spirit that is not clearly symbolized in Baptism and is important enough for human salvation to require symbolizing in another rite? If one can identify such a distinctive feature of God's salvific action, and show how it is well symbolized in the rite of Confirmation, one will have a theological insight into the essence of the sacrament of Confirmation and a reason for its distinction from Baptism. The identification of a second sacrament of initiation does not postulate any new salvific action of God. It refers rather to something in that unique saving action that is manifested and communicated to humans in another ritual. The theological question about Confirmation is not just about the gift of the Holy Spirit but about *something distinctive in the gift of the Spirit that is made visible in the rite.*

7.5.2   *The messianic, eschatological Spirit*

As God's People tell their story, God has been sending his Spirit upon his world from the first instant of creation. In the Old Testament the coming of the Spirit was often visible and palpable in things, events and people (for example, in ecstatic prophecy and charismatic leadership). One of the lines of messianic hope developed by the prophets looks beyond these partial, provisional manifestations to a definitive, full outpouring of the Spirit in the day of the Lord at the end of time. The prophets see the gift of the Spirit being experienced both in a perfect interiorizing of relations with God and in spectacular external manifestations of his power. The Spirit would be at the heart of the messianic transformation of all things. The New Testament tells how this promise is manifestly fulfilled. It is fulfilled visibly in Jesus himself. The Spirit is seen to come upon him in the form of a dove, and is seen to stay with him in the way he sets about preaching the good news that messianic salvation has arrived in his own person, and that the end times are at hand. He promises and visibly gives the messianic Spirit to his disciples, sending them to preach salvation to the ends of the earth. The events of the day of Pentecost are the most spectacular manifestation that the day of the Lord has arrived and that the eschatological outpouring of the Spirit has occurred. There are other manifestations recounted by Luke in Acts — prophecy, speaking in tongues, a house shaking, daring missionary enterprises undertaken; and the visibility of the coming of the Spirit is also associated with a rite of laying-on hands with prayer. As well as Luke's account of these colourful and noisy manifestations that the reality of the messianic Spirit has arrived, there is the other tradition, told by Paul and later by John, that pays more attention to the way the prophetic hope for an interiorizing of relations with God through the inner gift of the Spirit is seen to be realized: here the gift that has been given to those who believe in Jesus shows in the faith they profess, in the love they practise, and in their peace and strength and joy and prayer. There is no rite associated with the visibility of the messianic Spirit in John or Paul, but the images of anointing and sealing are there, even if only as metaphorical language, to describe what the gift of the messianic Spirit looks like. The use of these images, which can easily be turned into actual rites, as well as of the rite of laying-on hands described by Luke, entitles one to advance the suggestion that the rite which was eventually recognized as Confirmation is a sacramental way of making visible the messianic, eschatological quality of the gift of the Spirit in the New Testament: it does in ritual form what the spectacular events of Pentecost, on the one hand, and the inner experience of ultimate salvation enjoyed by the first Christians, on the other hand, do in a prototypical way.

inner experience of ultimate salvation enjoyed by the first Christians, on the other hand, do in a prototypical way.

One can explore the suggestion further. With the coming of the messianic Spirit something changes radically in the relationship between God and his People. The giving of the messianic Spirit is the final salvific act of God in human history. No other divine act is needed for the salvation of the world. Only the Parousia remains, to close the series of 'the wonderful works of God'. The last times have arrived and the Parousia is at hand. In the time of waiting for it, people draw on the gift that God has already given. The world and the people who make its history are being transformed by a power of God that is already at work in it. The necessary resources are already in the world and in human hearts. The people on whom the Spirit has come visibly are made aware, by personal experience, of this radical change in the dispensation of grace. They are made aware that they have within themselves the full resources to complete the work of salvation. The Spirit is always an enabling gift. The eschatological Spirit enables people to do 'the last things', to do everything necessary to make themselves and their world ready for the coming of the Lord. They do not have to look outside themselves, individually or as community, for anything that might be needed for the day of salvation. The time for pedagogues and being led by the hand and childish religion is ended. The régime of grace has come of age. The adult phase of salvation has arrived. It is not that the children of God are automatically turned into adults. What Pentecost manifests is not immediately something about people but something about the quality of grace. It proclaims that the grace now available, because it is eschatological, is adult grace, which, if taken on its own terms, will find expression in adult attitudes towards God and his work in the world. It will be lived with the self-confidence and maturity that comes from the experience of having been given within oneself all that is required for salvation. It will be a life of interiority, of self-motivation, of self-reliance, of freedom and creativity. It will have to cope with conflict and opposition but will have the inner and outer strength and self-assurance to deal with them. These qualities belong to the grace of the New Testament because it is the grace of the messianic, eschatological Spirit. It seems reasonable that those who are being initiated into grace should have the messianic, eschatological quality of the gift of the Spirit manifested to them in a special rite, called Confirmation, as it was manifested to the first Christians at Pentecost. An anointing with perfumed oil has emerged as an appropriate rite. It has been recognized by the Church as actually giving the grace that it signifies. It is a sacrament.

7.5.3   For the salvation of the world

The régime of grace inaugurated by Pentecost is for people whose inner strength and adult behaviour mark their relationship with other people no less than their individual relationship with God. People who are aware of receiving the eschatological fullness of the Spirit are, of necessity, public people. The coming of the

Spirit concerns all peoples and all creation. It raises an issue that no one can ignore or be neutral about. All people are caught up in the eschatological reality of the Spirit, whether they know it or not. Sooner or later they must say where they stand about Christ and the Spirit he has sent. Those who have received the Spirit in some visible way cannot, then, confine their lives to private issues and relationships, or allow their Church to be a private club. They have responsibilities in the great public issue that dominates the final stage of human history. The Spirit has, indeed, been poured out on all flesh but the manifestation of the Spirit was given from the first only to some. It is they who are to tell the rest of the world what is happening in this final stage of human history. They are spokespeople of the Spirit, gathering together those who accept salvation, and standing firm against those who oppose it. They tell how the Father has sent his Son, Jesus, to be the Saviour of the world, and how that salvation is being worked out through the action of the Spirit who has been sent into the world. If they do not do the telling, it will simply not be done. This is the missionary meaning of the gift of the Spirit, the side of it brought specially to light by Luke in his account of Pentecost, and all through Acts. It is another aspect of the coming-of-age of the plan of salvation, of the mature adult phase of grace which has been reached. God can now trust men and women to save the world, because he has given them in this manifest way the resources that match this responsibility. The gift and its responsibilities are made visible in the tongues of fire seen at Pentecost, as well as in the behaviour of the disciples on whom they came. Men and women who were timidly minding their own business behind closed doors come out compulsively into the streets and begin to talk to everyone they meet. They find themselves suddenly strong enough in their convictions and articulate enough in their speech to be able to proclaim publicly the faith that is in them. They overcome the barriers of language in a way that symbolizes the overcoming of all barriers of communication that might impede the world-wide preaching of the message of salvation. They also overcome mockery, opposition and persecution. They become effective public people. The Lucan account of the manifestation of the Spirit is quite consonant with, and is very much enriched by, the accounts of Paul and John. The power from on high that Luke speaks about is a power that is also from within. The disciples take a public stand from inner conviction and strength. They are not just empty vessels being used by the Spirit. They act responsibly out of personal faith and love, which is what Paul and John so emphasize. The difference between the two traditions is not about the gift of the Spirit, which is seen as messianic and eschatological in both, but about its manifestations: in Paul and John these are connected predominantly with personal salvation and the inner building-up of the community of salvation; in Luke the main accent is on those that show the bringing of salvation to the whole world. The tradition of faith about what is sacramentalized in the rite of Confirmation has veered at different times and places towards one or other set of manifestations. It can be claimed that the steadying and unifying factor in the tradition about Confirmation is that what defines the sacrament is not this or that manifestation of the Spirit, but the messianic, eschatological quality of what is being manifested.

7.5.4 Confirmation, Baptism and other sacraments

In understanding Confirmation as the sacrament of the messianic, eschatological quality of the gift of the Holy Spirit, one has a good basis for distinguishing it from Baptism, and from other sacraments. The specific distinction from Baptism does need clarification. Some of the words used about Confirmation in the theological tradition can give the impression that the difference between the two sacraments is almost one of quantity or degree: Confirmation adds more of the same to what is already given in Baptism; or at most it completes and rounds off what is already there. Such words as 'completion', 'perfection', 'fullness', 'strengthening', 'maturing', 'increasing', 'sealing', and even 'anointing' can seem to be defining Confirmation by such a relationship with Baptism: it is the completing of, strengthening of . . . Baptism. However, these terms can be taken in another, more absolute sense: they can stand for an ultimate, definitive state of things that is qualitatively different from anything that may have gone before. The Christian tradition has, in fact, even outside the context of Confirmation, given an eschatological flavour to these words: they can describe a state of things that belongs to the end times. When they are used about Confirmation they can have this distinctive sense, rather than be simply describing further grades of what is already given in Baptism. It is true that Baptism gives the Spirit, as do all the sacraments. What is distinctive about a sacrament, however, is not what it gives but what aspect of the gift it makes visible. The Spirit is shown forth in the water-rite of Baptism as the principle of new creation and new birth. Although this Spirit is none other than the messianic, eschatological Spirit, it is not shown forth precisely as messianic and eschatological in the rite of Baptism. Because the recognition of this truth about the Spirit, with an appropriate response to it in faith, is necessary for Christian life, another rite is given to show it forth and to draw an appropriate response to it from those who are becoming Christians. Confirmation gives the same Spirit and the same grace as Baptism does. But to the extent that it sacramentalizes an aspect of it that Baptism does not, it gives a distinctive sacramental grace. It is a grace that should show in Christian life.

The specification proposed for Confirmation also helps to clarify its relationship with the Eucharist. The Eucharist is the sacrament of the eschatological banquet, celebrated in the Church until the Lord comes. The Spirit is poured out in it, both on the bread and wine and on the assembled community. What the Eucharist symbolizes about the Spirit is its relationship with the Body of Christ, both as sacramental reality and as ecclesial unity. The Spirit is seen to transform people, and the things of their world, into the Body of Christ, uniting everything in him. This is the goal towards which all the action of the Spirit is directed. It is a goal that is now possible because the Spirit is present in the world in that final fullness given by Christ. The Eucharist sacramentalizes the return of all things to God: they are gathered together in the eschatological Spirit, made one with Christ their Head and High Priest, and presented by him to the Father. The people who make such a sacrament should be seen to have been initiated into a life that is not only of Christ but also of the Spirit that is poured out at the end of time. The people who can make the Eucharist be and be seen to be the anticipation of the eschatological banquet are people who have been both baptized and confirmed.

The rite of Orders also sacramentalizes the giving of the Spirit. It even uses the same ritual elements as Confirmation — laying-on of hands and anointing. Like Confirmation it is connected with mission. The distinction between it and Confirmation is particularly important because it is the sacramental correlative of the ecclesiological distinction between hierarchy and laity. There is a kind of ecclesiology which instinctively puts hierarchy before People of God in its vision of the Church. When it thinks about the gift of the Spirit, it has a way of telling the story of Pentecost as the coming of the Spirit *on the apostles* rather than on the whole community gathered with the apostles. It sees the Spirit being then given to others by the apostles through the imposition of hands and in other ways. When this ecclesiological model is transferred to the sacramental order it tends to see the Spirit being given in the first place to the ordained, who are successors of the apostles; they are then able to give the Spirit to others through their ministry. Among the consequences of this approach is that any responsibilities that lay believers are recognized to have for the building-up of the Church and for its mission will be seen as a participation in and concession from the power that the Spirit has given to the ordained. A different ecclesiological model emerges when the story of Pentecost is told as the coming of the Spirit on the whole community, as it came later on the whole community of believers at Samaria, on the household of Cornelius and on the whole group at Ephesus. The community would not, of course, have been the community of believers without the apostles, because it would not have had a secure witness to the story of Jesus without them; it was gathered under their leadership and in a communion of which they were the foundations. But the eschatological Spirit, with everything that it stands for in the relationship of humans with God, was given to all believers. The special gift of the Spirit that the apostles received found its place within this eschatological community and the total gift of the Spirit that filled it. Those who were appointed to carry on in various ways the work of the apostles were given a special gift of the Spirit for particular ministries that were necessary for keeping the community, in its words and in its rites, faithful to the truth about Jesus that had been proclaimed by the apostles. This gift also took its place within the already gifted community, and was in keeping with the eschatological quality of its life. When one transfers this ecclesiological model, which is that adopted by Vatican II in *Lumen Gentium*, to the sacramental order (as is done in *LG*, ch. 2) one can understand the priority of Confirmation over Orders in the giving of the Spirit and how what is sacramentalized in Orders is conditioned by what has already been sacramentalized in Confirmation. Orders is for people who are already confirmed. It is for a particular service which only gets its meaning within the community of the confirmed. The quality of that service manifests the gift of the Spirit when it respects the status which has been given to the members of the community it serves by their Confirmation in the eschatological Spirit.

7.5.5   Necessity of Confirmation for salvation

The claims being made for Confirmation raise the question of whether it is necessary for salvation. It is a standard theological question about any sacrament. The answer depends on the relationship between Confirmation and saving grace. Now that Christ has come and the Spirit has been poured out, only one kind of grace is salvific. It is messianic, eschatological grace. This is a statement about the objective definition of grace rather than about the people who live in it. They can still be childish and immature, as Paul told some of them in no uncertain fashion. But the grace they are living in is, by definition, adult grace, as is proper to the eschatological age. This quality of grace has to be proclaimed, if those called to salvation are to benefit from it; this is what they have to respond to in faith and sacrament. In the community of salvation it is proclaimed by word and by rite. As well as being proclamation, the rite gives shape to the response of the one being saved and gives it visibility in the eyes of the Church: a confirmed person has been confronted with the messianic, eschatological quality of saving grace, has presumably said yes to it and is recognized in the Church as having the status that it confers. Perhaps in the early years of the preaching of the Gospel the rite was less necessary. There may not even have been a consistent distinctive rite, other than something implicit in the water-rite of Baptism. The manifest fervour of the first communities and the charismatic gifts that were common could have given sufficient external visibility to the reality of the messianic Spirit to leave aspiring Christians in no doubt about the kind of grace they were being called to and the kind of response they would have to make to it in Christian initiation. When the rite of anointing/laying-on of hands did become a distinctive part of Christian initiation it came to be recognized as a sacramental proclamation of this particular aspect of Christian grace. It required a particular response. Without that response people would not be opening themselves to the only kind of grace that now gives salvation. Nor would they be accepting the particular status and responsibility that is now required of those who are members of the community of salvation. On this basis one can say that Confirmation is now necessary for salvation.

Obviously, many people are saved without being confirmed. To make theological sense of this one has to appeal to the kind of distinctions that are made about the necessity of Baptism for salvation. What saves in Baptism is the reality (*res*) of the sacrament. It can be gained from the desire of the sacrament when the rite cannot be received (Baptism of desire). When people know about Baptism the desire includes the intention actually to be baptized. Were they to exclude it they could scarcely claim to have Baptism of desire. One may also say that when they know about Confirmation their desire includes the intention of being confirmed. What they desire is saving grace. This is messianic, eschatological grace, given through Christ and in the Spirit. It must be desired as such. Confirmation sacramentalizes this quality of it. Hence to desire it is to desire to be confirmed. To exclude the intention of being confirmed would be to desire something other than Christian grace. It would be to do deliberately something like what the group that Paul came across at Ephesus did through ignorance: to desire a grace other than the Spirit-filled grace of Christ that alone brings salvation. The further distinctions that are made about Baptism of desire (explicit and implicit, etc.) to account for the salvation of those who know nothing about the sacraments can also be applied to the necessity of Confirmation. There are many ways in which the reality of the sacrament is gained apart from its actual reception. But the reality that is gained, and that saves, will always be the reality that needs Confirmation to be adequately sacramentalized. To that extent Confirmation remains necessary for salvation. It has to be admitted that the tradition of faith does not affirm this necessity with anything like the force that it shows in affirming the necessity of Baptism. The obligation to be confirmed has not been stated with the same canonical decisiveness as the obligation to be baptized. The sacrament can at times seem to belong to those things that are good and desirable for Christian life rather than to what is absolutely necessary. Hence the desire for it is not cultivated with the same urgency or required with the same degree of necessity. Perhaps theological uncertainties about the nature of the sacrament also made it difficult to promote effectively the desire for it. The recovery of the best traditions about Christian initiation in the Church of Vatican II, and the accompanying pastoral insistence on confirming everybody who is baptized, including infants, in danger of death, lends support to a theological position that regards the grace of Confirmation, and therefore at least the desire of the sacrament, as necessary for salvation. There is also a theological teaching of St Thomas about desire for the Eucharist that fits well with the necessity of at least some desire for Confirmation for salvation. Thomas sees the grace of salvation coming ultimately through the Eucharist; in giving salvation Baptism includes the desire for Eucharist (IIIa, 73, 3). The tradition about the sequence and unity of the three sacraments of Christian initiation suggests the movement of desire from Baptism towards Eucharist should pass through a desire for Confirmation; and that the one desire is not possible without the other. There is only one saving grace. Those who desire it must desire it as it is. If it takes three rites to sacramentalize it in an orderly way, the desire for salvation might be reasonably required to include a desire for all three of them.

7.5.6   The effects of Confirmation

In sacramentalizing the messianic, eschatological quality of the action of God in Christ and the Holy Spirit, Confirmation also sacramentalizes its own proper effects. It makes those effects visible and in doing so actually causes them. The Catholic tradition has analysed them on the twin levels of character and grace. As has been explained above, this pattern reflects a sacramental ecclesiology: people receive and give the grace of Christ by being qualified and empowered to act in and for the visible community of the Church; Christ makes the actions of such qualified people to be his own salvific actions, communicating to those who do them a share in his own messianic offices of Prophet, Priest and King;

a Church made up of such people becomes his sacrament; it remains so even when the people who form it at a particular place and time are not actually living in grace. The character qualifies people to give and receive in a Church that is the eschatological community of salvation. They have to represent in their persons the fact that the messianic Spirit has been poured out. The baptismal character is a qualification to receive: it marks and qualifies people to receive all the gifts of the Spirit; it is the badge of and title to total receptivity in the grace of the end times. The eschatological outpouring of the Spirit requires that the people who form the Church should be also empowered in Christ to be givers of the Spirit. They are signed and sealed as eschatological prophets, priests and kings. There is an activity of giving that has to be exercised by all members of the Church, which is prior to those specific ministries which are exercised by some and provided for by the character of Orders. There is a particular way of carrying out this activity which manifests that the Church is both Christ-like and Spirit-filled. When all members of the Church are recognized as having something to give — towards their own salvation, towards the salvation of their fellow-believers, towards the salvation of those who are to be evangelized — the Church is seen to be what the Spirit has made God's People to be. The character of Confirmation is, then, a qualification and an empowering to be this kind of person in the Church. In confirming all its members the Church is saying that it has to be made up of such people. Its teaching spells out what it expects of its members, and its legislation structures their relationships with one another, lays down patterns of authority and obedience, and organizes the conduct of its mission to the world. But all this has to reflect and be judged against the peculiar dignity and responsibility that belongs to every Christian because he or she is marked with the character of Confirmation. If people do not treat one another within the Church itself with the respect due to those who are sealed with the messianic Spirit and participate in the come-of-age phase of grace, the Church cannot be recognized as the eschatological community of salvation. The character of Confirmation thus understood qualifies people for any activity that is required for the life of the Church. Attempts to link it exclusively with the prophetic rôle of the Church, or with the lay apostolate, have the value of highlighting certain aspects of what it is to be a Christian but perhaps at the expense of other aspects of Christian life that the tradition associates with Confirmation. For example, the character of Confirmation clearly comes into play in participation in other sacraments: it has a priestly as well as a prophetic function. It seems more helpful theologically to look for the specification of the character of Confirmation, not in particular ecclesial functions that would be proper to the confirmed, but in that eschatological quality of Christian life that has to be found in all Christian activities. The character of Baptism says that people have the power to be alive in Christ and to receive every gift that he offers. The character of Confirmation says that such people belong to the end times, are empowered to take an adult, public part in everything that needs to be done for their own salvation, for that of their fellow-Christians and for that of the whole world.

The grace of Confirmation, like the grace of every sacrament, is sanctifying grace. Those who have received grace in Baptism receive an increase in that grace from Confirmation. But that grace also receives a new set of virtualities that correspond to what is symbolized in the sacrament. They are a special richness of sanctifying grace that makes Christians do, in faith and love, what the character of Confirmation calls them to do. With the tradition, this special richness of grace can be called 'strength'. It is the adult moral strength of those who act from inner conviction, who pray because the Spirit is welling up within them, who can deal with inner conflict, who trust their own spiritual gifts and the gifts of others and are neither embarrassed nor exalted if these should take spectacular charismatic form, who can take their place comfortably and maturely in the community life of the Church in obedience but not subservience to their ordained ministers, who are not afraid to be recognized in public as Christians and indeed are at ease and joyful and communicative about their Christian faith in public situations, who can be counted on to do whatever the community under the direction of its leaders judges good for the preaching of the Gospel to the world, who will have the courage and ingenuity to overcome all forces that oppose the preaching of the Gospel and, when necessary, be prepared to suffer and die under persecution. All this seems more than enough to justify the standard statement, that confirmation makes a person 'a strong and perfect Christian'. However, it needs to be understood that the fullness and perfection in this phrase refer to the quality of the grace of Confirmation rather than to the degree in which grace is realized: it is full and perfect because it is definitive, eschatological grace. The actual degree of grace depends on the progessively fuller and more perfect human response that it produces. An infant who is confirmed has full and perfect grace, as have a seven-year-old and an adult convert; but they only become fully and perfectly graced through exercising and appropriating the grace that they have been given. Each sacramental grace contributes to an overall growth in sanctifying grace. It is specified by the sacramental rite; it is operative as soon as it is desired; it is taken hold of bodily in the actual celebration of the sacrament; it continues to grow under the retrospective influence of the sacrament; and in doing so it enters into the growth of sanctifying grace towards the degree of fullness proper to each person. It is the Eucharist, rather than Confirmation, that sacramentalizes this growth and this fullness. If it is true that each of the sacraments is directed towards the Eucharist it is also true that the growth potential of each of them is gathered into the sacramentality of the Eucharist. The completing of initiation by the Eucharist shows, with particular clarity, how it does this for the grace of Baptism and the grace of Confirmation. As the nourishment of life, the Eucharist is a constant call to the Christian to renew the original acceptance of life in Christ that was sacramentalized in his or her Baptism. As eschatological banquet it is a call to accept once again the eschatological gift of the Spirit, with all its consequences, that was originally sacramentalized in Confirmation. The proper grace of each sacrament grows, and grows repeatedly, within the comprehensive sacramental grace of the Eucharist.

7.6   A SUITABLE AGE FOR CONFIRMATION

Confirmation can be received at any age. It is given today in the Church, as it has always been, to infants, to seven-year-olds, to teenagers and to adults. Theology can make sense of Confirmation at any of these ages. It can explain how it works differently according to the different stages of personal development enjoyed by those who receive it. In doing so it can suggest advantages and disadvantages in being confirmed at one age rather than another. However, the theological balancing of advantages and disadvantages will probably never yield a decisive argument in favour of any one age. The best it can do is to give the theological criteria that should inform the judgement of pastoral prudence which is what eventually decides when and how a person or group of persons ought to be offered Confirmation in the Church.

The judgement about a suitable age for Confirmation belongs within a judgement about Christian initiation. There are strong theological reasons in favour of initiating infants into Christian life. Although in Western theology they are usually given as arguments in favour of baptizing infants (see above, 5.9.2), most of them could also be used in favour of confirming and admitting infants to the Eucharist; indeed, it would make sense to do so in view of the theological arguments that can be put forward in favour of maintaining the unity of the process of Christian initiation. There are satisfactory theological explanations of how any sacrament can work in infants. While they are generally worked out by Western theology in discussions about infant Baptism, they hold just as well for Confirmation and Eucharist. Over against these arguments in favour of initiating people to Christianity in infancy there is another set of arguments for delaying initiation: they are based on the value, and even necessity, of informed personal faith and decision on the part of the one being initiated. They can be put forward about the whole process of initiation but also about any of the three sacraments that make it up. The Eastern tradition has never accepted the weight of these arguments, neither for the whole of initiation nor for any of its parts. The Western tradition agreed for over a thousand years. However, its liturgical tradition developed in a way that allowed it to think of the three sacraments of initiation as separate, if connected, issues. In the thirteenth century it began to accept the force of the arguments for delaying initiation with regard to Confirmation; and soon also with regard to the Eucharist. The argument for delaying Confirmation was not that those who received it should be adults; it was rather based on the general premiss that sacraments should be an exercise of personal faith and discretion which, it was thought, could be expected at the age of seven years. This argument was never accepted as a ground for delaying Baptism. The way the necessity of Baptism for salvation was conceived, especially for infants, made such a delay unthinkable for any reason. And yet, one concession has been always made to the argument about the need for personal faith and decision regarding Baptism. If there is no assurance that, through Christian education, infants can be brought to personal faith as soon as they reach the age of discretion, their Baptism will be delayed. The effectiveness of the sacrament is recognized as being bound up with the convictions and intentions of their parents and educators. If these are not faith-bearing for the child, they will negative the faith of the Church and Baptism will not be given. It is recognized that there is an element of risk in initiating an infant — the risk of sacramental nonsense and therefore of profanation. The Eastern tradition takes the risk with the whole process of initiation. The Latin does with Baptism but, helped by its liturgical tradition, feels free not to take it with Confirmation and Eucharist. Positively, it seems to be reasoning that there is more to be gained by having personal faith and decision in Confirmation and Eucharist than there is to be lost in delaying the two sacraments and breaking up the unity of initiation. To delay the two sacraments is not to deprive the infant entirely of their grace. If the analysis given above of the way in which Baptism includes the desire for Confirmation and for Eucharist is correct, the grace of both sacraments is already at work in a baptized infant, reaching forward through the process of Christian education to the expression it will receive in actual Confirmation and Eucharist. However, there is a real loss of sacramentality involved in breaking up the unity of initiation. It is more than a matter of liturgical propriety. Baptism alone does not express sacramentally the full reality of Christian grace: it does not express its Pentecostal fullness. By separating it from Confirmation one risks offering an inadequate sacramental statement about Christian life. The absence of the Eucharist is even more problematical: the full meaning of incorporation into the Body of Christ, which occurs in initiation, is left without its strongest sacramental expression. Of course, preaching and Christian education compensate for the diminished sacramentality of initiation by Baptism alone. The Eastern practice also requires this preaching and education because the sacraments given to infants are only fully operative when they have been appropriated by personal faith and decision at the age of discretion. In both cases there is a waiting for personal faith to realize initiation. In putting all three sacraments of initiation at the beginning of the process the Eastern tradition strongly emphasizes the priority of God's action in it. The Western tradition does this, if a little less emphatically, by putting Baptism at the beginning. It gives greater prominence to the rôle of personal faith in the process by delaying Confirmation and Eucharist until the age of discretion.

In many parts of the Latin Church Confirmation is delayed even beyond the age of seven years. One can argue in favour of this practice on the grounds that personal faith is likely to become more developed as the years of childhood go by. To this are sometimes added other arguments that associate Confirmation with entry into adulthood. It has been claimed above that there is no real justification for seeing Confirmation as a sacrament of entry into adult life: what Confirmation sacramentalizes is the coming of age of the history of salvation with the gift of the Pentecostal Spirit, rather than the becoming adult of individual Christians. However, it is true that the kind of behaviour proper to the adult age of grace can normally be exercised only by adults. On that grounds one can make a theological case for delaying Confirmation until children are entering adult age. There can be a real gain in doing so. The personal commitment to being an adult in an adult Church, which is the effect of the distinctive grace of Confirmation, can be made in the celebration of the sacrament itself rather than worked towards as something to be fully entered into at some future date. There is some difficulty about deciding what criterion should be used for determining entry into adulthood. One could set the age by analogy with civic life, making it correspond to the age when young people begin to vote, or are free to marry, or can get a driver's licence. However, young people are often forced to take a stand on matters of religious faith rather earlier in their teens, if not in a fully public way, at least among their peers. They are also confronted with choices about serious moral issues (for example, in attitudes towards their parents, or in dealing with the sexual factor in relationships) earlier than the age at which they are admitted to public civic responsibility. The appearance of such religious and moral issues are telling theological indicators about the age for Confirmation. To be able to take an independent and even a public stand on such issues is characteristic of the confirmed.

The judgement about the appropriate age for Confirmation is also affected by the need to get the best balance between divine gift and human response in the sacrament. If there is reason to believe that the sacrament will be more effective when God's action is highlighted, the sacrament will be put early in the years of discretion; subsequent catechesis and religious formation will be experienced as a development of the sacramental gift and directed towards an eventual fully adult response. If it is thought better to highlight the human response, catechesis will be a preparation for and a build-up towards adult response in the sacrament itself, which will therefore be delayed until the candidate is ready to make such a response. The decision about which aspect of the sacrament to highlight depends to a large extent on the religious climate in which the young persons are being educated and to the extent to which the Church is present in their lives through parents and school. Where Christian faith is strong and pervasive in the world of young people, and particularly in their schooling, it makes theological sense to confirm them early. Otherwise it seems better to wait until their personal decision can be beyond reasonable doubt.

The criterion of personal faith and decision might seem to suggest that ultimately the best age for Confirmation is that set by the one to be confirmed for himself or herself: people are ready for Confirmation when they ask for the sacrament, for the right reasons. There is something to be said for this point of view; those who prepare candidates for Confirmation nowadays often require them to make a personal request for the sacrament. But educators and those who have a sense of how complex are the decision-making processes of young people hesitate to make too much of the criterion of personal choice in determining the age for Confirmation. Theologically speaking they have some good grounds for preferring to set an age and to guide and form young people towards acceptance of Confirmation at that time of their life. Confirmation is delayed in order to allow the candidate to accept it in an act of personal faith. Faith is a gift of God and of the community. No Christian community will let its respect for freedom of choice turn into indifference about the choice which one of its baptized members makes for or against being confirmed. It will have a view and a discipline about the best age for offering this gift to its members. It will educate young people towards and prompt their decision to be confirmed with the confidence that it is communicating a gift of God, in which human freedom is fully realized, rather than interfering with freedom of choice. It is, indeed, continuing to follow the same logic that led it in the first place to baptize this person as an infant.

The major theological difficulty about the Latin practice regarding the age of Confirmation is that many children are not confirmed before they are admitted to the Eucharist. The problem is one of sacramentality. If, as has been argued above, the grace of Confirmation is included in the grace of the Eucharist, children are not really (i.e. on the level of *res*) being deprived of grace by having their Confirmation delayed, any more than catechumens are by having their Baptism delayed. But the reality of that grace is not being given sacramental visibility in the way the overwhelming tradition of Christian liturgy and doctrine has wanted. Concern for the correct sequence of the sacraments of initiation is not a matter of liturgical faddism. Grace is given in a sacramental order, which is of God's designing. Sacramentally, the Eucharist is the eschatological, messianic banquet celebrated for and by those who belong to the final age of grace. It is brought about by the Holy Spirit who transforms bread and wine into the messianic body of Christ and those who receive it into the eschatological community of salvation, which is the Body of Christ. The Eucharist is the food of the strong, not of the childish. Sacramentally speaking, it is for the confirmed. There is a real loss of sacramentality in not preparing children for it by confirming them. There is at least as much reason for confirming them as there is for submitting them to the sacrament of Reconciliation. A theological alternative would be to accept that the reasons for delaying Confirmation beyond the age of discretion are equally valid for delaying full participation in the Eucharist. That was a much more common view in the Latin church before Pius X than it is today. However, while one can give a reasonable, if not peremptory, theological justification for delaying Eucharist until the age of discretion, the arguments for delaying it further are of comparatively little weight. Is one to say then that, in the interests of keeping a proper sacramental sequence, the arguments for delaying Confirmation beyond the age of discretion should give way to the arguments for having First Communion at that age? This would be in keeping with the general prescription of Canon Law: Confirmation at the age of discretion, Eucharist at the age of reason (which must mean the same thing). However, there are Episcopal Conferences who take advantage of the freedom given in Canon Law to delay Confirmation to a later age, but without delaying First Communion. The theological problem then is not so much about Confirmation as about Eucharist. Sacramentally there is something lacking in the participation of unconfirmed people in the Eucharist. Perhaps this is one of the reasons why 'Children's Masses' have gone out of favour. The sacramental incongruity is lessened when unconfirmed children participate in the Eucharist with their parents. When children do receive Communion before they are confirmed the practice of 'Solemn Communion', or some special solemnizing of their Communion at the Mass that follow their Confirmation would go some way towards restoring full sacramentality to their Christian initiation.

STUDY QUESTIONS

1   Study what 'the spirit of God' means in the Old Testament, with a view to understanding the account given in Acts 2 of the coming of the Spirit at Pentecost.
2   How does the Hellenistic concept of spirit differ from the Semitic one, and what influence does the difference have on the development of Paul's and John's thought about the Holy Spirit?
3   Reflect on the significance of the Last Discourse of Jesus in John 14–17 for a theology of Confirmation.
4   Study the laying-on of hands for the gift of the Spirit in the reconciliation of heretics, as described by Cyprian and Augustine, in relation to the sacrament of Confirmation.
5   To what point can one recognize Confirmation as a sacrament distinct from Baptism in the mystagogical catecheses of St Cyril of Jerusalem?
6   Examine the use of the word *robur* in relation to Confirmation from Faustus of Riez to Thomas Aquinas.
7   What have been the principal issues in Anglican theology of Confirmation over the last half-century?
8   In what sense can Confirmation be presented as a commission to evangelize?
9   Why does the Latin church insist nowadays that infants in danger of death should be confirmed?

FURTHER READING

Articles on the Holy Spirit can be found in dictionaries of the Bible; particularly helpful for an understanding of Confirmation is:

E. Schweizer and others, *'Pneuma'* in *Theological Dictionary of the New Testament*, ed. G. Friedrich, vol. VI (Grand Rapids, 1964), pp. 332–452.

There is also biblical material on the Holy Spirit and discussion on Confirmation in:

G. M. H. Lampe, *The Seal of the Spirit* (2nd ed.; London, 1967).
Y. M.-J. Congar, OP, *I Believe in the Holy Spirit* (trans. from French; 3 vols, London/New York, 1983); cf. also his *Un peuple messianique* (Paris, 1975).
F. X. Durrwell, *Holy Spirit of God* (in French 1983; Eng. trans., London, 1986).

Patristic texts on the Holy Spirit in:

J. Patout Burns, SJ, and G. M. Fagin, SJ, *The Holy Spirit* (Message of the Fathers of the Church 3; Wilmington, 1984).

Doctrinal tradition and systematic study in:

L. S. Thornton, *Confirmation, Its Place in the Baptismal Mystery* (Westminster, London, 1954).
B. Neunheuser, *Baptism and Confirmation* (New York, 1964).
A. Milner, OP, *The Theology of Confirmation* (Cork, 1971).
L. Ligier, *La Confirmation* (Paris, 1973).

J. D. C. Fisher, *Confirmation Then and Now* (London, 1978); also *Christian Initiation in the Mediaeval West* (London, 1965) and *Christian Initiation, the Reformation Period* (London, 1970).

T. A. Marsh, *Gift of Community. Baptism and Confirmation* (Wilmington, 1984); and 'A Study of Confirmation', *Irish Theological Quarterly* 39 (1972), 149–163 and 40 (1973), 125–147.

For ecumenical questions:

C. Argenti, 'Chrismation' in *Ecumenical Perspectives on Baptism, Eucharist and Ministry* (Geneva, 1983), pp. 46–67.

D. R. Holeton, 'Confirmation in the 1980s', *ibid.*, pp. 68–89.

On a suitable age for Confirmation:

Y. M.-J. Congar, *I Believe . . .* III, pp. 217–227.

J. Roberto (ed.), *Confirmation in the American Catholic Church* (Washington, 1978).

M. Gwinnell, 'Confirmation: Sacrament of Initiation', *The Clergy Review* 69 (1984), 126–135.

8

Eucharist: the rite

8.1 DESCRIPTION

The rite of the Eucharist is celebrated in the Roman liturgy in the form prescribed by the Roman Missal promulgated by Paul VI in 1969 (Apostolic Constitution *Missale Romanum*; text in Flannery, pp. 137–141). The detailed ordering of the rite (called *Ordo Missae*) is preceded in the Missal by a *General Instruction*, which carefully explains the structure and parts of the rite, as well as giving some of the doctrinal and pastoral principles that underlie it. The study of this *Instruction* is indispensable for entering into the sacramentality of the eucharistic rite.

The rite is presented in the *General Instruction* as a calling-together or assembly of God's People in one place, under the presidency of a priest: 'they assemble to celebrate the Memorial of the Lord, which is the sacrifice of the Eucharist' (n. 7). The celebration has two parts, called Liturgy of the Word and Liturgy of the Eucharist: the first provides the 'table of the word', the second the 'table of Christ's body'. The gathering, in fact, takes place around or before a table, which is also an altar, and there is bread and wine available for eating and drinking. Before the Liturgy of the Word begins there are some introductory ceremonies. They have to do with the act of assembly and the kind of community that is being assembled. There is movement and singing and praying that create a sense of being together as a community of Christian faith and repentance gathered in the presence of God. It is an ordered community. There are formal entrances for those who have special ministries in the celebration, and they are identified by the clothes they wear and the places they occupy. The president of the assembly is clearly identified and wears the insignia of priesthood. He is the bishop or one of the presbyters of the community. Nowadays there is no noticeable restriction on attendance. But the rite is clearly meant for Christian believers. They alone can take an active part in it. Those who believe but have not yet been baptized can take an active part in the Liturgy of the Word but, if they remain for the Liturgy of the Eucharist, do not receive the consecrated bread and wine. There may be other members of the assembly who, though baptized, do not receive from the table of the Lord's body. Their abstention has some significance, but what that is does not appear from the rite itself.

Once the community is assembled in an orderly way it listens to readings from the Scriptures and to a homily given by the president or another priest or deacon.

The homily is an address about the significance that what has been read has for the present life and situation of the community; it is an exhortation to live out the demands that the word makes on those who celebrate it in the Eucharist. This Liturgy of the Word is a working-out of the principle that word is always twinned with rite in the celebration of God's People. It is God's word to his People, repeating his covenant promises and guarantees and the response they require. It is the ongoing story of God's People, brought up to date for the celebrating community in the preaching addressed to it and projected forward in the prayers for their salvation and that of the whole world that end the Liturgy of the Word. The whole Bible is meant to be read at successive Eucharists, over a period of time (currently three years). The movement of the story that the Bible tells is conveyed by having two or more readings, taken from different parts and always ending with the climax of the story which is found in one of the four gospels. Sometimes the continuous reading of the Bible is interrupted and special passages are chosen in order to bring the word of God to bear on some particular event of salvation that is being celebrated by the community.

The transition from Liturgy of Word to Liturgy of the Eucharist can seem somewhat abrupt and the continuity may be obscured by the terminology; there may be an impression that the Eucharist proper only begins when the Liturgy of the Word has ended. But, in fact, the whole celebration, from the assembling of the community right through to its dismissal, is a unified action of word and rite, which in its totality is called Eucharist. The word obviously predominates in the first part, and the distinctively eucharistic ritual elements are found in the second. A Liturgy of the Word can, indeed, be celebrated independently of the Eucharist or within the celebration of another sacrament. But when a community assembles to celebrate the Eucharist its Liturgy of the Word is already eucharistic and is being affected by the rite of which it is part. The rite, in turn, gets an essential element of its significance from its connection with the word. It becomes a response to the covenant word of God and as such a sacrifice of covenant renewal. The General Instruction insists that the two parts of the Eucharist (Liturgy of Word, Liturgy of Eucharist) 'are so closely connected with each other that together they constitute but one single act of worship' (n. 8).

The 'single act of worship' continues, then, with a taking and putting on the altar of bread and wine. These are seen as gifts made by members of the community for common use. They are taken from them in some symbolic way and received with prayer as gifts of God. Other gifts that the participants bring for the needs of the Church, including money, are gathered at this time, but only bread and wine are put before the presiding priest. What they are put on is called a table, because they are food for eating and drinking. It is also called an altar, because what will be done with the food by the presiding priest is an act of sacrifice. He does it in the form of a prayer of thanksgiving said over the bread and wine. He associates the community with the prayer by an introductory dialogue, by having them see and hear what he is doing, by inviting them to chorus their acclamation at various points and by drawing them to approve the prayer with a final Amen.

The Eucharistic Prayer nowadays follows a formula fixed and approved by the Church. It includes the following elements (*General Instruction*, n. 55): (a) *Thanksgiving*, which is the dominant note of the prayer and gives its name to the whole rite ('eucharist' comes from the Greek word for thanksgiving); the thanksgiving is for the gifts of bread and wine, because the prayer is said over them, but it broadens out to be for the total gift of God evoked by them, which is the giving of his own glory in the work of creation and redemption; sometimes a special work of salvation that is being commemorated and that has been proclaimed in the Liturgy of the Word is highlighted in the thanksgiving; (b) *Acclamation* by the whole assembly of the holiness of God, and of the blessedness of the one who comes in his name; to say God is holy is to proclaim the disinterestedness of his giving, and the impossibility of giving him anything in return other than by making his gifts holy as he is holy; (c) *Epiclesis*, from the Greek word for 'calling down', which calls down the power of God on bread and wine to make them holy; the transforming divine action called for is usually attributed to the Holy Spirit; the making holy or consecration that is called for is that the bread and wine would become the body and blood of Christ; (d) *Narrative of Institution* which justifies the request made in the epiclesis and guarantees the efficacy of the Eucharistic Prayer by proclaiming that at the Last Supper Christ said that the bread and wine which he was giving to his disciples was his body and his blood that was being offered for the salvation of the world, and that the disciples were to do what he had done in memory of him; (e) *Anamnesis*, from the Greek word for 'remembering', which is a bringing to mind of all that was done and will be done in the body and blood of Christ — death, resurrection, ascension, second coming; because of what the bread and wine now are, the thanksgiving for them has become thanksgiving for the saving gift of God that is given in the body and blood of Christ; (f) *Oblation*, in which the remembering community lets its thanksgiving (and the self-offering that thanksgiving implies) be taken over by the self-offering that Christ, its Head, makes in his body and blood, so that what it offers to God with thankfulness is the sacrifice of Christ; in that sacrifice the community offers itself, praying that the Spirit, who makes its bread and wine be the body and blood of Christ, will make it itself be one in his Body; (g) *Intercession*, in which the solidarity which the assembled community enjoys in the Body of Christ reaches out to all those who form the Body of Christ, asking for a sharing with those who are already with Christ in glory, for the unity of all the communities that form the Church of Christ on earth, for the faithful departed that they may enter into eternal rest, and for all those who are being saved in Christ; (h) *Doxology*, in which the prayer returns to the dominant mood of praiseful thanksgiving offered to the Father through Christ and the Spirit whose presence and action have been invoked throughout the prayer to transform the gifts of the Church and its thankful acceptance of them into a holiness that is acceptable to God. The ritual gestures and the way of treating the bread and wine have shown the movement towards this holiness. What has been treated as bread and wine at the beginning is being treated before the end as the divine reality that it has become.

When the Eucharistic Prayer is finished preparations are made for the eating and drinking of the consecrated bread and wine. The Lord's Prayer is said: it resumes, in the Lord's own words, what has been said in the Eucharistic Prayer about the holiness of God, the bond between heaven and earth, the meaning of his gifts and how they meet the needs of human life. The members of the community exchange a gesture of reconciliation and peace. The consecrated bread is broken into portions and given to the participants to eat. The cup of consecrated wine is given to them for drinking. (However, in the Latin rite it became common practice, and still remains so in many celebrations, that only the presiding priest and the presbyters and deacons who minister with him at the altar drink from the chalice.) The distribution and receiving of the Body and Blood of Christ is accompanied by prayers and gestures of reverence and song.

The rite ends with prayer and with a formal act of adjournment or dismissal by one of the presiding ministers. The people are sent out with a final blessing.

8.2   HISTORY

The rite of the Eucharist is, even in its present form, highly complex. Its history is correspondingly complex. As every detail of the rite has some significance, so every bit of information about the history of the rite is valuable for understanding it. But even a less than meticulous history can throw a great deal of light on the rite. One can find certain patterns of worship in the Old Testament that recur in the Eucharist; one can see the form these patterns took at the Last Supper and in the 'breaking of bread' of the apostolic communities in the New Testament; one can see the liturgical shape of the Eucharist developing in descriptions of the Eucharist in the texts of the early centuries; and one can follow in broad terms the evolution of those first forms of the Eucharist through the particular liturgical tradition of the Roman church, in a way that throws light on how and why that tradition has been given the form it has today in the Missal promulgated by Paul VI.

8.2.1   Rites of the old covenant

As the life of God's People has been dominated from its beginning by the covenant which God made with them, so their rites have been connected in one way or another with covenant making and covenant keeping and covenant renewal. Covenant making and renewal follow a consistent ritual pattern in the Old Testament: there is a summoning by God of certain chosen people to come into his presence; God speaks in some way, and his words are of promises, of guarantees of his fidelity and of conditions to be met by those for whom the promises would be fulfilled; those who have been called accept the promise and guarantees, and undertake to fulfil its conditions; that belief gives them their existence as a group; they give some tangible expression to their decision to let themselves be taken by God as his People, which is commonly some form of ritual sacrifice; by sharing in that rite they are affirmed as God's People and the inheritors of his promise. The pattern is already visible in the account of the covenant that God made with Abraham (Genesis, chs 12 and 15): God calls Abraham, makes a promise to him and gives certain guarantees, Abraham believes and expresses his acceptance of God's covenant in various sacrificial rites; and all this is done within a palpable experience of the presence of God.

The pattern is more developed in the making of the Mosaic covenant at Mount Sinai during the Exodus (Exodus 19–24). God has summoned his People and, by the dramatic events of the Exodus, brought them out of Egypt and into his presence at this holy mountain. Their leader and prophet Moses goes apart and has the word of God revealed to him. He tells this word to the assembled People: it is a word of promise, centred on the gift of being God's own People, from which all other blessings will flow; it is a word of command about how the covenant People should live (which includes timeless laws like those that came to be called the Ten Commandments, details of social organization and the requirements of justice appropriate to the life-situation of a people who would have to travel through the desert and take possession of the land they had been promised, arrangements for worship and its priesthood); and it is a word of reminding which recalls what God has already done for his People, from the time of their ancestors to the more recent events of the Exodus, as a guarantee of God's fidelity to his promise. It is this covenant word that the People assent to: 'Moses came and told the people all the words of the Lord, and all the ordinances; and all the people answered with one voice, and said, "All the words which the Lord has spoken we will do"' (Exod 24:3). Their acceptance of the covenant is not just verbal; it is also ritualized in sacrifice. The link between word and rite is facilitated by the fact that 'Moses wrote all the words of the Lord' (24:4). The word is now a book, which is called the Book of the Covenant. The hearing of the word of God will from then on include listening to the reading of a book. The book itself is incorporated into the ritual-making of the Mosaic covenant. An altar is set up and animals are sacrificed to God. Moses takes the blood of the sacrificed animals and sprinkles half of it on the altar. Then he takes the Book of the Covenant and reads it to the People. It tells them what they are committing themselves to. Their assent is put into words in Exodus 24:7: 'All that the Lord has spoken we will do, and we will be obedient'. This is the verbal equivalent of the rite of sprinkling the blood of sacrificed animals on the altar: to do that was to put one's life (symbolized by the blood of an animal that one had once owned) into the hand of God (symbolized by the altar, which consecrated to God whatever was put on it). It is the God-ward movement of the sacrifice. Once the People had agreed to the covenant, Moses could sprinkle the other half of 'the blood of the covenant' on the assembled People. This is the human-ward movement of the sacrifice: it is the receiving from God, in ritual form, of the mark and the gift and the bonding of being his very own People.

When the second book of Kings tells, in chapter 22, how King Josiah set about renewing the life of his People in accordance with the covenant, it sets the story in the framework of covenant ritual. First there is a new giving of the word of God through the discovery of the Book of the Covenant in the Temple and the interpretation of its significance, in which priests and prophets and king are involved. Then, in chapter 23, the People are summoned to solemn assembly in the house of the Lord. The king 'read in their hearing all the words of the book of the covenant which had been found in the house of the Lord'. Then, standing by the pillar (a recognized place for performing solemn, official actions) he 'made a covenant before the Lord, . . . to perform the words of this covenant that were written in this book; and all the people joined in the covenant'. No ritual action is mentioned in connection with the making of the covenant at this point, but later, when the trappings of worship that were contrary to the covenant have been purged from the holy places the People are called to 'keep the passover to the Lord your God, as it is written in this book of the covenant'. The Passover included the fundamental covenant sacrifice.

There is another covenant renewal at the beginning of the restoration after the Exile, described in Nehemiah, chapters 8 and 9, which is ritualized according to the same pattern. There is an assembly of the People, led by Nehemiah the governor, and Ezra who was scribe and priest, and the Levites. There is a reading from 'the book of the law of Moses which the Lord had given to Israel', which goes on from early morning until midday. The People weep at what they hear but are told by their leaders to 'Go your way, eat the fat and drink sweet wine and send portions to him for whom nothing is prepared; for this day is holy to our Lord; and do not be grieved, for the joy of the Lord is your strength'. The reading continues on successive days and the People keep feast for seven days and live in tents, as they did during the Exodus. On the eighth day there is a solemn assembly. The People fast and wear sackcloth and ashes; they separate themselves from foreigners and confess their sins. These are cultic preparations for entry into the presence of God. Once assembled they listen again to the book of the law of the Lord. Then comes a new element: they pray ('for another fourth of it [the day] . . . they made confession and worshipped the Lord their God'). The text of the prayer said by Ezra the priest is given. It is a prayer of praise of God and of remembering the wonderful things he has done for his people in spite of their infidelity. It concludes with the words: 'Because of all this we make a firm covenant and write it, and our princes, our Levites and our priests set their seals to it'. There could be no sacrifice to ratify the covenant because the Temple had not yet been rebuilt. The prayer, however, takes the place of ritual sacrifice in ratifying the covenant.

There was already a connection between sacrifice and prayer in the Jewish ritual tradition. Among the sacrifices prescribed in the Book of Leviticus is the *todah*, which is variously translated as 'sacrifice with or of thanksgiving' or 'sacrifice with or of praise'. It is suggested that it was a kind of communion sacrifice accompanied by expressions of praise or thanks (see H. Cazelles, 'L'Anaphore . . .'). Many of the psalms of blessing, praise and thanksgiving are associated with the sacrificial worship of the Temple. Psalm 50 represents God as assembling his People 'who made a covenant with me by sacrifice' (v. 5), and telling them that what really counts in his eyes is not the sacrifice of animals but the sacrifice of praise/thanksgiving (vv. 14 and 23; cf. Ps 119:108). During the exile in Babylon the Jews were deprived of the Temple and the ritual sacrifices that could be offered only there. They developed in its place the synagogue form of worship. They assembled in groups (and it was the Greek word for 'assembly' that gave the name 'synagogue' to the kind of community they formed and the place where they met) to hear the word of God and to respond to it by prayer. The prayer of Ezra in Nehemiah, chapter 9 is an example of the type of prayer that came to be used in synagogue services. It follows a fundamental Jewish prayer form that is called *berakah* and usually translated as 'blessing'. To pray is to bless and praise God for who and what he is. It is to bless him for his gifts. The prayer of blessing is also a prayer of thanksgiving. One of the Greek translations of the Hebrew words for this type of prayer is the word for 'thanksgiving', *eucharistein*, from which comes 'eucharist'. Thanksgiving is a form of praise. As in the prayer of Ezra the blessing of God can include remembering the wonderful things he has done for his People throughout their history. It expresses the experience of 'making a memorial' (*zikkaron, anamnēsis*) that is at the heart of Jewish worship. It can also be a remembering of the infidelities of the People, finding in them the reason for their present difficulties. The prayer of blessing is also a prayer about the present (see the typical transition to the present made with the words 'Now therefore . . .' in v. 32 of the prayer of Ezra). It calls on God to repeat the wonders of the past here and now for a People who are pledging themselves once again to obey the covenant.

The prayer of blessing was also part of the ritual of all Jewish meals. It was the form taken by what would today be called Grace at Meals. The following is a reconstruction by L. Finkelstein of what such a prayer might have been in the tradition of Judaism, before the destruction of the Temple:

> Blessed are you, Lord our God, King of the universe,
> you who feed the whole world with goodness, with grace and with mercy.
> We thank you, Lord our God, for giving us as our inheritance a desirable, good and ample land.
> Have mercy, Lord our God, on Israel, your people, and on Jerusalem, your city, and on Zion, dwelling place of your glory, and on your altar and on your temple.
> Blessed are you, O Lord, who build up Jerusalem.
> (quoted in translation by Moloney, 'The Early Eucharist', p. 37; other texts and analysis in Bouyer, *Eucharist*, ch. 4).

While all Jewish meals were religious events that, in various ways, affirmed the covenant and its blessings, there were, in post-exilic Judaism, special meals that were held for specifically religious purposes. What exactly they were, what patterns of worship they followed, and how those patterns influenced the New Testament and the development of the Christian Eucharist is the subject of a good deal of speculation. Joachim Jeremias has done a careful critique of the speculation (*Eucharistic Words . . .*, ch. 1) and concluded that much of it goes beyond what the evidence warrants, if it is not actually in conflict with it. Nevertheless it does seem possible to say at least this much: meals were used to commemorate important occasions in the life of the covenant People and provided a form of covenant worship; they were sacred occasions in which the presence of God was experienced (Nielen, p. 37 quotes a phrase from the Talmud: 'When they sit at table and the words of the Torah are the subject of their conversation, then the Shekinah comes down upon them'); they provided an occasion for some speaking of or about the word of God; the blessing said over the food (which was commonly associated with the distribution of bread and a festive cup of wine) would express the sense of occasion and the hopes of those who were celebrating.

It is not altogether unfounded speculation to think that this form of worship would lend itself particularly well to the needs of those communities of people who were drawn together, as the disappointing years of post-exilic Judaism went on, by a strong faith in the prophecies about the new covenant and who saw themselves as the poor, or remnant of Israel, with whom that new covenant would be made. The meal form lent itself particularly well to messianic and eschatological hopes, and to the new assembling of God's People that it would bring. The image of a banquet in which people feasted together in a shared, God-given abundance was common in prophetic descriptions of the messianic age. Table-talk lent itself to sharing the hopes and dreams and demands which different people were hearing in the word of God, especially as it looked towards the future. The blessing prayer lent itself to that more interior, spiritual worship that was to characterize the new covenant. It also lent itself to expressing the contrast between promise and present reality that is always the pain of prophetic people. The form of the blessing prayer allows for a passage from praise and thanks for the wonders God has done in the past to a consideration of the present misery and need of his People. At that point the community could put some of its own pain, especially what it was suffering because of its fidelity to God, into the blessing prayer. The prayer would give their situation something of that sacrificial value in the sight of God which the great prophecies of Isaiah about the Suffering Servant of the Lord had seen in human pain that was accepted in dedication to God for the taking-away of sin. That sacrificial view of present sufferings would give confidence to the petitions with which the blessing prayer ends for a new and definitive fulfilment of the promises of the covenant.

There is less need for conjecture about the ritual of the Passover meal, which was part of the official annual commemoration of the Exodus and the Covenant. The basic rite is reflected in the account given in Exodus 12 of what the Jews were commanded to do at the original Passover in Egypt. The form of the rite that would have been in use in Jerusalem at the time of Jesus is known with reasonable accuracy (details in Jeremias, pp. 84–88). A family or family-sized group gathered at table on the evening of the feast to eat the Passover lamb, as their ancestors had done on the eve of their liberation from Egypt. The lamb had been slaughtered ritually by priests in the Temple during the day. It was eaten with bitter herbs and with unleavened bread, and various ritual cups of wine were drunk. During the meal the head of the household explained, in response to questions from the younger members of the family or group, the meaning of the different kinds of food and drink that were being taken. There was also singing of psalms of praise. At the beginning of the meal — as of every Jewish meal at that time — the head of the household would break the loaf of bread into portions which he distributed to those at table. The action was accompanied by a prayer of blessing, such as 'Blessed be thou, JHWH, our God, king of the universe, who bringest forth bread from the earth' (Bouyer, *Eucharist*, p. 80). The blessing prayer said over the different cups of wine and over the bread when it was being broken were particularly solemn. A text that might have been used for the blessing said over the final cup of wine at the time of Jesus has been reconstructed from later sources. Here is the version given by Bouyer (*Life and Liturgy*, pp. 124–125; cf. also Jaspers and Cuming, pp. 9–10):

> Blessed be Thou, O Lord our God, King of all eternity, Thou Who dost feed the whole world by Thy goodness, Thy grace, Thy mercy and Thy tender compassion. Thou dost give to all flesh its food, for Thy mercy endures for ever. Through Thy great goodness, food has never failed us: may it never fail us, for the love of Thy great name, for Thou dost provide for and sustain everything that has life; to all Thou doest good, and Thou dost provide with food every creature that Thou hast created. Blessed be Thou, O Lord, Who givest this food to all things.
>
> Blessed be Thou, O Lord, because Thou hast given to our fathers as an inheritance a vast, good and desirable land; and because Thou hast brought us, O Lord, out of Egypt, and delivered us from the house of bondage; and also for Thy covenant which Thou hast sealed in our flesh, for Thy Law which Thou hast taught us, for Thy statutes which Thou hast made known to us; for the life, grace and mercy which Thou hast poured out on us, and for the food with which Thou dost feed and sustain us always, every day and at all times and hours. For all this, O Lord our God, we give Thee thanks and we bless Thee. Blessed be Thy Name from the mouth of all the living, now and forever, according to what is written: thou shalt eat and be filled, and thou shalt bless the Lord thy God for the good land which He has given thee. Blessed be Thou, O Lord, for this food and for that land.
>
> Have mercy, O Lord our God, on Israel Thy people, on Jerusalem Thy city, on Sion the dwelling of Thy glory, on the Kingdom of the house of David, Thine anointed, and on the great and holy house which has been called by Thy name. O God our Father, feed us, maintain us, sustain us, support us, relieve us, and grant us soon, Lord our God, that we should not need the gifts of men or their alms, but only the gifts of Thy helping hand, which is always full, open, holy and giving freely, so that we might not be ashamed or confounded forever . . . .

8.2.2   The rite of the new covenant

The meal which Jesus took with his disciples on the night before he suffered is presented by the Synoptics as a Passover meal. There have been some hesitations among exegetes about accepting the historical accuracy of this statement because of the chronology of the Passion given in the gospel of John. In John's account the official Jewish Passover meal should have been eaten on the evening of the day that Jesus died rather than the evening before (see John 18:28). His death would then have corresponded to the sacrificial slaughtering of the Paschal lamb in the Temple. Whatever the historical value of the different chronologies (see

Jeremias, ch. 1), there seem to be adequate grounds for holding that the accounts of the Last Supper are to be interpreted against the background of Passover ritual and ideas. Remaining on the level of rite and reserving questions about the full theological meaning of the New Testament texts for Chapter 9, one can use the Passover background, and the general Jewish tradition about ritual meals, to develop a sense of what Jesus wanted to evoke and fix for the future in the rite that he performed at the Last Supper. The meal represents Jesus *assembling* the nucleus and leaders of the new covenant people; it is the setting in which he speaks his final *word* to them to explain how his leaving them would be a new exodus; its solemn prayer of blessing over the bread and the cup is used by Jesus as a *sacrifice of praise* to accompany the sacrifice that he would make on the following day as Suffering Servant, offering himself in his body and blood on the cross; the expression it gives to festive togetherness is being established as the rite that would give assurance to the disciples of being already with Christ in the definitive kingdom of God.

When the accounts of the Last Supper were being written down the Church already had some decades of experience of regularly practising the rite of 'the breaking of bread' in memory of Jesus. The accounts select those elements of the Passover meal that justify and explain the practice. What was being done was patterned on the distinctive words and actions of Jesus rather than on the full rite of the Passover meal that he had used. The Passover was a once-yearly celebration of the former covenant. The disciples of Jesus met to remember him and wait for his coming every day, or at least on the first day of the week, which they celebrated as the day he rose from the dead. They were listening to the story about Jesus proclaimed in the testimony of the apostles. They were celebrating a new Passover and the making of a new covenant. They were doing it in the 'breaking of bread', that is to say, in a meal that had a special significance for them because of the way the ritual breaking of bread, which was a normal feature of Jewish meals, was done. The Last Supper was not the only meal that affected the meaning that the disciples found in their 'breaking of bread' in memory of Jesus. Some of them had eaten with him regularly during his ministry of preaching and doing good. Once they had begun to recognize him as the Messiah sent by God these meals took on something of the character of the messianic banquet promised by the prophets. This impression had been confirmed by miraculous multiplications of their food, which had allowed them to share it with multitudes of people. They had also seen Jesus eat with people who were considered to be sinners and outcasts, and perhaps shared that experience with him. That must have brought it home to them that meals at which Jesus was present and accepted were events of reconciliation and fellowship that knew no human barriers. Some of them had also shared food with him after he had risen from the dead, which was a powerful reinforcement of the sense they had of his presence with them when they were gathered for the breaking of bread.

The Emmaus incident reflects, in a rather beautiful way, the paradigm of the eucharistic rite (see Dupont in Delorme). It happens away from Jerusalem, away from the Temple and its sacrality, to people who are on a journey. It begins with a conversation which grows, on the one hand, out of the lived experience of the two disciples — their hopes for salvation and their troubled reaction to the death of Jesus and the stories of the women that he was alive — and on the other hand out of the Scriptures. The passages of Scripture selected and explained by Jesus give the disciples new light on the death of Jesus and their own reactions to it, which makes their 'hearts burn within them'. Their acceptance of the word and of the one who has expounded it to them impels them to insist that he stay with them and share their meal. But it is he who becomes the host of the meal. He takes bread, says the prayer of blessing, breaks it and gives it to them. In these ritual actions they recognize Jesus for who he is. He then disappears from their sight, as if to say that as long as they can break bread together in the distinctive way that he had of doing it, they do not need his visible presence. The two disciples, powerfully confirmed in their faith in the resurrection, go back to join the community of disciples gathered with the Eleven in Jerusalem. They are able to confirm one another in their faith that Jesus is alive. Once again he appears to them, and once again he eats with them.

The nearest one gets to a description of what a Christian community actually did at the 'breaking of bread' in memory of Jesus is in 1 Corinthians 11. Paul is describing what happens, or rather what ought to happen, 'when you assemble as a church' (v. 18). Earlier in the chapter he had been laying down the discipline that should regulate praying and prophesying (v. 4) in the Christian assembly. Now he talks about the meal that is taken. It seems to be a full meal, at which people could eat and drink their fill. What Paul reproves them for is that in this meal 'it is not the Lord's supper that you eat' (v. 20). The reason he gives for saying so is not a matter of ritual but of life: they do not share the meal together, but divide up into separate parties, at which some have too much to eat and drink and others do not have enough. Paul does not say that they should not eat together but simply that, if it is a private party they want, they should have it at home. Only if they are sharing their food in true fellowship can they be celebrating the Lord's Supper. But he then gives a reason drawn from the ritual that they should be following, and from its meaning. The ritual is the one given by the Lord at the Last Supper and handed on in the Church. If Paul repeats the traditional account of the Last Supper it is presumably to tell the Corinthians that at some point in their meal bread should be taken and a blessing said over it which proclaims it to be the body of Christ, and that it should be broken and distributed to all; likewise with the cup. He does not say who should do this or at what point of the meal it should be done. A Jewish community would hardly need to be told. When Christian communities became less homogeneous and the Jewish tradition diluted it would be necessary to regulate these matters. Before the end of the first century the taking of bread and wine in remembrance of Jesus was being separated from the meal of fellowship (the *agapē*) and being celebrated as a distinct rite.

The prophesying and praying that Paul regulates before dealing with the Eucharist in 1 Corinthians 11 was a normal part of the assemblies of the Corinthians. Paul deals with the subject in detail in subsequent chapters, but without connecting it explicitly with the Eucharist. He deals in those chapters with other matters that are subsequently associated with the Eucharist, including the collecting of contributions for the saints to be made on the first day of the week and fellowship with other Christian communities (ch. 16), but again without mentioning the Eucharist. A connection between the word of God and the breaking of bread is, however, made in two texts from the Acts of the Apostles. In Acts 20:7–11 Luke recounts: 'On the first day of the week, when we were gathered together to break bread, Paul talked with them . . . and he prolonged his speech until midnight . . . . And when Paul . . . had broken bread and eaten, he conversed with them a long while, until daybreak'. The capsule description that Luke gives in Acts 2:42 of the new life of those who had received the word, been baptized and joined to the Christian community puts together very neatly the elements that structure the eucharistic rite: ' . . . the apostles' teaching (the word) and fellowship (communion with the Church of the apostles), the breaking of bread (ritual meal) and the prayers (a setting of worship that could not but have included the prayer of blessing over the bread and the cup)'.

8.2.3   The second and third centuries

There are some indications in the documents of the second and third centuries that Christians took some meals together that were not modelled on the Lord's Supper. There are hints of meals taken with bread but without any particular attention to what was drunk, meals with bread and salt, meals with fish (Cullmann, p. 10). Some of these practices have some basis in the New Testament. Then, there were meals of fraternal *agapē* which cannot be said with certainty to have included the rite performed by Jesus at the Last Supper. The *Didachē* (trans. Kleist) provides the most outstanding example of this ambiguity. It prescribes prayers for 'the eucharist', one 'concerning the cup', another concerning 'the broken bread'. It follows these with a general prayer of thanksgiving to be said 'after you have taken your fill of food' (9–10). Later (14) it prescribes: 'On the Lord's own day, assemble in common to break bread and offer thanks; but first confess your sins, so that your sacrifice may be pure. However, no one quarrelling with his brother may join your meeting until they are reconciled; your sacrifice must not be defiled . . . '. The prayers of the *Didachē* are of the Jewish blessing type, with Christian content. They do not include the narrative of institution.

Traces of the kind of love-feast Eucharist represented by the *Didachē* can be found in some later liturgical traditions. But the tradition coming from the Last Supper dominates. It is found in St Justin's descriptions of the Eucharist, written in his *First Apology* about AD 150. His first account is part of his description of Christian initiation. After the newly baptized have been admitted to the assembly,

> . . . bread and a chalice containing wine mixed with water are presented to the one presiding over the brethren. He takes them and offers praise and glory to the Father of all through the name of the Son and of the Holy Spirit, and recites lengthy prayers of thanksgiving to God in the name of those to whom he granted such favours. At the end of these prayers and thanksgiving, all present express their approval by saying 'Amen'. This Hebrew word, 'Amen', means 'So be it'. And when he who presides has

celebrated the Eucharist, they whom we call deacons permit each one present to partake of the Eucharistic bread, and wine and water; and they carry it also to the absentees. We call this food the Eucharist, of which only he can partake who has acknowledged the truth of our teachings, and who has been cleansed by baptism for the remission of his sins and for his regeneration and who regulates his life upon the principles laid down by Christ (nn. 65–66; trans from Palmer).

There follows a theological explanation in which Justin appeals to the accounts of the Last Supper in order to show that the Eucharist is no 'ordinary bread' but the flesh and blood of Jesus. The term 'Eucharist' has passed by now from being the kind of prayer said at the breaking of bread to being the name for the whole action. It is also the word used to describe the bread and wine that has been prayed over. There is no suggestion that the Eucharist is part of an ordinary meal. The fact that Justin thinks of a possible comparison with the Mithraic mysteries in the course of his explanation (only to exclude it; see 2.3 above) suggests he sees the Eucharist as a kind of cultic rite. His description of the Sunday assembly adds some details. There is a Liturgy of the Word, including a homily and general intercessions:

> On the day which is called Sunday we have a common assembly of all who live in the cities or outlying districts, and the memoirs of the Apostles or the writings of the Prophets are read, as long as there is time. Then when the reader has finished, the president of the assembly verbally admonishes and invites all to imitate such examples of virtue. Then we all stand up together and offer up prayers . . . (n. 67).

After repeating his description of what is done with the bread and wine he adds: 'The wealthy, if they wish, contribute whatever they desire, and the collection is placed in the custody of the president . . . '.

The next oldest description of the Eucharist is in the *Apostolic Tradition* of St Hippolytus, written about AD 200. He describes the Eucharist that is celebrated at the Ordination of a bishop (III, 4) and the Easter Eucharist that completes Christian initiation (XXIII). The structure is that which was described by Justin. Distinctive ministries are now assigned to the bishop, who presides and says the Eucharistic Prayer, to presbyters who assist the bishop and with him lay hands on the 'oblation', and to deacons. The Baptism, and presumably the Ordination, have been preceded by a 'Liturgy of the Word', and are followed immediately by the properly eucharistic part of the rite. It begins with the bringing of what is called the 'oblation' before the bishop. This consists of bread and wine mixed with water, which are set apart from other foods that are to be shared (milk and honey at the paschal Eucharist of initiation and oil, cheese and olives at the ordination of a bishop). The bishop says a prayer of thanksgiving, by which he is said to 'eucharistize first the bread into the representation of the Flesh of Christ; and the cup mixed with wine for the antitype of the Blood which was shed for all who believed in him' (XXIII, 1). This prayer is distinct from the prayer said over the other foods. It is said by the bishop. Hippolytus gives a text, but as a model rather than a fixed and binding formula. It is in recognizable continuity with the Jewish form of blessing prayer but has a distinctively Christian content. In the following translation of Hippolytus's account of the Eucharist at the Ordination of a bishop the headings have been added by the editor, Dom Gregory Dix:

Kiss of Peace

IV. 1. And when he has been made bishop let every one offer him the kiss of peace, saluting him, for he has been made worthy.

Offertory

2. To him then let the deacons bring the oblation and he with all the presbyters laying his hand on the oblation shall say, giving thanks:

Preface

3. The Lord be with you. And the people shall say: And with thy spirit. Lift up your hearts. We have them with the Lord. Let us give thanks unto the Lord. It is meet and right. And forthwith he shall continue thus:

Eucharistic Prayer or Canon

4. We render thanks unto Thee, O God, through Thy Beloved Child Jesus Christ. Whom in the last times Thou didst send to us [to be] a Saviour and Redeemer and the Messenger of Thy counsel; 5. Who is Thy Word inseparable, through Whom Thou madest all things and in Whom Thou wast well *pleased*; 6. Whom Thou didst send from heaven into the Virgin's womb and Who conceived within her was made flesh and demonstrated to be Thy Son being born of the Holy Spirit and a Virgin; 7. Who fulfilling thy will and preparing for Thee a holy people stretched forth His hands for suffering that He might release from suffering them who have believed in Thee; 8. Who when He was betrayed to voluntary suffering that He might abolish death and rend the bond of the devil and tread down hell and enlighten the righteous and establish the ordinance and demonstrate the resurrection:

Words of Institution

9. Taking bread and making eucharist [i.e. giving thanks] to Thee said: Take eat: this is my Body which is broken for you. Likewise also the cup, saying: This is my Blood which is shed for you. 10. When ye do this, ye do my 'anamnesis'.

The Anamnesis

11. Doing therefore the 'anamnesis' of His death and resurrection we offer to Thee the bread and the cup making eucharist to Thee because Thou hast bidden us [or, found us worthy] to stand before Thee and minister as priests to Thee.

The Epiclesis

12. And we pray Thee that [Thou wouldest send Thy Holy Spirit upon the oblation of Thy holy Church] Thou wouldest grant to all Thy Saints who partake to be united to Thee that they may be fulfilled with the Holy Spirit for the confirmation of their faith in truth, 13. that we may praise and glorify Thee through Thy Beloved Child Jesus Christ through whom glory and honour be unto Thee with the Holy Spirit in Thy Holy Church now and for ever and world without end. Amen.

It is in his description of the paschal Eucharist with the newly initiated that Hippolytus tells about the ritual of communion:

XXIII. 5. And when he breaks the Bread in distributing to each a fragment he shall say: The Bread of Heaven in Christ Jesus. 6. And he who receives shall answer: Amen. 7. And the presbyters — but if there are not enough the deacons also — shall hold the cups and stand by in good order and with reverence: first he that holdeth the water, second he who holds the milk, third he who holds the wine. 8. And they who partake shall taste of each thrice, he who gives saying: In God the Father Almighty; and he who receives shall say: Amen. 9. And in the Lord Jesus Christ; 10. And in the Holy Spirit in the Holy Church; and he shall say: Amen. 11. So shall it be done to each one.

8.2.4   The Roman rite

Although there are no other descriptions of the Eucharist contemporaneous with that of Hippolytus with which to make a comparison, it seems certain that there were other liturgical forms of the Eucharist already in existence. Those different forms can be documented from the fourth century onwards. Notable differences have emerged between East and West; and within both East and West several distinct traditions, associated with the great primatial sees, have established themselves. Although the liturgy of Hippolytus is not some kind of common ancestor of these different traditions, it does represent something primordial about the rite of the Eucharist in which later liturgical families can recognize something of their origins, and in which they can find a common bond. That sense of continuity with the forms of the past and of a basic sameness underlying contemporary variations is essential for the functioning of the Eucharist as a rite, especially in a community that lives with the historical and geographical complexities of the Catholic Church. Those who celebrate in the Eucharist a ritual renewal of the covenant that binds them together as God's People need to be able to sense that continuity and communion in the rite itself. The history of the different liturgical forms taken by the Eucharist and the ability to compare them is invaluable for developing this sense. One can discover how each form of the rite came to be what it is today, and why it differs from other forms, and one can see how those differences do not break the unity of a common tradition.

For a Christian church the Eucharist is, indeed, something received in the tradition that comes from the apostles. But it is also something in which a church expresses itself in its relationship with the world. The Christian community is, in one sense, set over against the world and stands for the eternal in face of the temporal. There is, correspondingly, a certain quality of apartness, of timelessness, of the heavenly in its rites, especially in its Eucharist. But a church is also set in the midst of the world of time, with a mission to transform it and move it in a God-ward direction. Its members are citizens of the world. When new members are drawn into a particular church in Christian initiation they leave something of the world behind but, of necessity, bring a lot of it with them. They will be required as members of the church to transform their world in Christ. When the local church expresses itself in the Eucharist it will inevitably express itself in relation to the world from which its members are drawn, which is the world that it is in, if not of. It must also express itself in relation to other churches throughout the world. It is only in communion with them that it forms the Church in the world. It will want its Eucharist to be like theirs by being rooted in a common tradition. And yet it must be different from theirs if it is really to express the Church in relation to the world of its own members. The variety of liturgical families that have grown up in the Church since the fourth century is due to this need of particular churches to celebrate the Eucharist in their own way while maintaining the bond of a common tradition about the rite.

The Roman liturgy of the Eucharist embodies the particular historical experience of the Roman Catholic Church, and the way its self-understanding as Church has developed in that experience. The way it embodies it today is the product of the way it has been embodying it over the centuries. The Roman rite of the Eucharist has taken on certain characteristics that have become a permanent part of the self-expression of the Roman church; it could hardly be recognized as itself without them. Some of the features it has taken on can now be seen to have been a response to particular historical situations, and have been, or can be, discarded when the situation changes. Still other peculiarities are seen to be the result of a certain decadence or neglect, which the church itself has eventually tried to remedy. The remedies have been sought in, on the one hand, an appeal to the tradition about the Eucharist common to all the hurches and, on the other hand, a judgement about how the Church's self-awareness in relation to the contemporary world of its members can best be expressed in the Eucharist.

One can learn the history of the Roman rite in a factual way. There is no substitute for knowledge of the facts. But when one is doing history in order to cultivate a sensitivity to the significance of the contemporary rite one also needs to absorb the sense of the facts. Supposing that one has some knowledge of the historical facts (from Jungmann or some other documented history of the Roman Mass), one can try to absorb their significance for the present celebration of the Eucharist in the Roman rite by reflecting on them in the light of: (a) the cultural and socio-political factors that were at work in the world to which the church was addressing itself in developing its rite of the Eucharist; (b) the self-understanding which the Roman church manifested in those developments; (c) particular positions in theology and spirituality that show how the Eucharist was being understood at different stages in the formation of the Roman rite.

(a) Cultural and political factors: The first people who were called together in the new covenant and who assembled week by week to ratify it in the Eucharist were Jews. Soon they were joined by Greeks and Romans and later by those they called barbarians. The culture of each group which accepted the call of the new covenant left a mark on the rite. The original Jewish core remained, canonized forever in the New Testament. The Greeks took the rite from the biblical sources, which were already in their own language, and enriched it creatively out of their own literary and philosophical resources. They filled out the Jewish prayer forms and added new ones. They introduced their human conventions of reverence into the action of the rite. They built and decorated places of assembly suited to the Eucharist, according to their own artistic taste. Eventually, when the Greek world became predominantly Christian, the liturgy became one of the principal carriers of their culture (on the Greek liturgies in relation to the Roman cf. Jungmann, pp. 22–32).

Rome drew on the Greek cultural tradition and its oldest known liturgies of the Eucharist are in Greek. When the Latin language came to be used it carried with it into the rite the peculiar genius and values that characterized Roman culture. The people in the western provinces of the Roman Empire did not just translate the Greek liturgy into the Latin language: they Latinized it through and through. Texts and forms were not yet fixed authoritatively, so they had a good deal of freedom in composing their own texts and shaping their ritual forms. The most creative work of which there are records was done in Rome itself from the fourth to the seventh century. The rite of the Eucharist has always been affected by the way the community assembled, and particularly by the kind of building chosen for the assembly. The church at Rome assembled in the type of building that was commonly used for public business, the basilica. The fact that it was in a 'secular' building rather than a religious one, such as a temple, that Christians housed their celebration is paradigmatic for the whole 'inculturation' of the rite. The meeting was with the world of men and women, not with the world of the gods. The arrangement of space in the basilica already gave a certain shape to the rite. For example, it gave the ministers their proper place and spatially defined their relationship to the faithful. The community was no longer seated around a table. The act of assembling was solemnized with processions and movement, and enlivened with singing. Special forms of dress, copied from civil life, were adopted to identify rôles; the conventions of reverence for persons (bows, kisses, genuflections, incense, lights) were introduced; arrangements were made for an orderly reading of the Scriptures and the actual reading was done by special ministers and surrounded with ritual; the preparation of the gifts became an elaborate ceremonial; the prayers, and particularly the Eucharistic Prayer, were given fixed forms in a Latin that was of the best literary quality available. (Description in Jungmann, pp. 37–56.)

The form of eucharistic rite that was developed in Rome was only one of several Latin liturgies that emerged during those centuries. There was an African form that was very close to the Roman; there were Gallican, Celtic, Spanish and Milanese types that were rather more different (Jungmann, p. 33). However, the creation of new liturgical families slowed down towards the end of the patristic period. Eventually it stopped altogether. New communities of Christians, instead of creating a new form of liturgy suited to their own human situation, simply copied the existing liturgies of other churches. There were ecclesiological reasons for this halt to the growth of new forms in the rite of the Eucharist. But there were also sociological and political ones. The effect of these was also to relate the Eucharist to a given human situation, but one that was being controlled by various centralizing and standardizing forces. The development of the Roman rite was profoundly affected from the late eighth century onwards by the political decisions of Charlemagne. One of the strategies he used to bring order and unity into his turbulent territories was to require that the churches throughout his empire should reform their liturgy according to the model of the Roman rite. Since the only Roman books available were those that described the rite of the Papal Mass it was that form of the rite that began to have a dominant influence on the way the Eucharist was celebrated throughout Europe. However, the

Frankish and Germanic peoples did leave their imprint on the Roman Mass (Jungmann, pp. 56–71). They added many prayers to the rite, which are quite different in character from the Roman prayers: they are individualistic, emotional and repetitious. Several of them became a permanent part of the Roman tradition. The *Ordo Missae* that was codified in these Germanic and Frankish lands, sometimes called generically the Gallican form, was eventually taken back to Rome and was in use there by the eleventh century. It was the form in which the Roman rite was handed on to the mediaeval world (Jungmann, pp. 71–77).

The countries that were responsible for the colonial expansion of Europe into the New World, and into Africa and Asia, saw the value of missionaries for their colonial enterprises. The missionaries brought Latin rites of the Eucharist, and particularly the Roman rite, with them. The few brave efforts to let new Christian communities develop rites in keeping with their own culture were opposed for political as well as theological reasons. The political interests of the Papacy were not altogether irrelevant to the maintenance of the Roman rite. The standardization was not always experienced as oppressive. It often suited the political and even the cultural interests of people among whom new churches had been founded to have a liturgy that put them in touch with European culture. It was of no value to them politically — apart from any ecclesiological considerations — to have the church in their midst develop its own way of celebrating the Eucharist. The political effects of the Reformation also affected the fortunes of the Roman rite. Countries which remained Catholic saw the maintenance of it as a symbol of their national identity as Roman Catholic. In Protestant countries fidelity to the Roman rite became, apart from any theological considerations, a symbol of political disloyalty. The secularizing of social life and culture has, in recent times, liberated the life of the Church, and its way of celebrating its rites, from many of these presssures. At the same time the very secular cult of pluralism has not been without influence in the Church's move towards a certain liturgical pluralism. Indeed, as long as the celebration of the Eucharist remains the action of a community of people who live in the world and are caught up in its history, it will never be entirely free from socio-political and cultural influences. Even today one finds those who cherish a certain tradition of classical culture pressing for forms of celebration which they call more traditional; and right-wing political movements patronize liturgical conservativism. Left-wing political groups favour another style of celebration, which would accent the significance that the rite has for human liberation; contemporary revolutionary forms of expression are incorporated in the rite. The Church's understanding of itself in relation to the world, which must somehow be expressed in the way the Eucharist is celebrated, is never a simple matter of benevolent, politically-neutral inculturation.

   (b)   Self-understanding of the Church: When a group of people 'assemble as a church to celebrate the Lord's Supper' their way of doing it is bound to be affected by the way they understand what it is to be church. There has been development in the self-understanding of the churches, and it is reflected in the way they have celebrated the Eucharist. The community of believers that

gathered in Rome at the home of one of its better-off members during the centuries when Christianity was an unlawful and persecuted religion had a different self-image from the community that gathered in the basilica of St John Lateran around their Pope and bishop in the century after the peace of Constantine. The difference is reflected in the different way they celebrated the Eucharist. The later community could be so much more self-confident in its belief that in itself the world was being transformed and won for Christ. The world and its ways, and, best of all, its leaders were becoming Christian. Leaders of the church were being accepted as civic dignitaries. Assemblies of Christians were public events; their celebrations were celebrations of the public good. The eucharistic assembly had, from the beginning, been understood to represent the coming of God's kingdom. When those who formed it were no longer a persecuted minority but a dominant majority they could afford to let their Eucharist be a triumphant celebration of the society in which they lived. As the church came to see itself as the religion of a Christian society it could begin to fill out its eucharistic rite with forms taken from the cultic practices of society. There were already good reasons for adopting the forms of Roman culture. The fact that they may have at one time been associated with the worship of the emperor or the mystery cults was no longer felt to be a threat to faith. More importantly, there was a precedent in the tradition of faith itself for this kind of relationship between forms of worship and the state of society. In the theocratic world of the Old Testament religious worship had reflected the reign of God over every detail of life. In the New Testament the rites of Christians are contrasted sharply with those of the Old Law, and during the first three centuries analogies between Christian liturgy and the rites of the Old Testament are handled very discreetly. But once the church has an established position in a world that was predominantly Christian there is a more conscious modelling of Christian liturgical forms on the Old Testament. The Temple begins to overshadow the Upper Room. Fixed forms of prayer and stylized sacred actions take the place of calculated improvisation. There is a sanctuary, with its holy of holies, there are priests and orders of priests who do cultic things and wear priestly vestments . . . . As the church sees itself mirrored more realistically in the relationship between religious institutions and society that is described in the Old Testament, it has a theological justification for the use of Old Testament images and forms, and for giving an Old Testament interpretation to forms borrowed from civil life, in its celebration of the Eucharist.

The development of ecclesiology in the Roman church was affected by the sheer size of the Christian community in a world that had become Christian, and by the need to organize it internally and in relation to civil authorities. The structures of ministry and authority received from the New Testament became more formal and the distinction between clergy and laity more carefully thought out. The form of eucharistic celebration developed in the Roman church reflected an ecclesiology that gave prominence to the hierarchical structure of the Christian community. When it was taken over by the churches of the Frankish empire under Charlemagne it found itself being influenced by an ecclesiology that added a clerical emphasis to the hierarchical. For all sorts of sociological reasons the church was being thought of as being adequately represented by the clergy. For example, when conflicts between church and state were seen as conflicts between the *sacerdotium* and the *regnum*, the priesthood in question was that of the clergy, who were opposing the power of the emperor and other civil authorities. The people of Europe belonged to both priests and kings, and were expected to do what they were told by both. When they let the clergy direct matters they were in the church. Acts of the church were acts of the clergy. The celebration of the Eucharist reflected this ecclesiology. In the Middle Ages the rite was done by the clergy. The faithful could do little more than attend and watch what was being done for them. The clergy did their part in a language which the people no longer understood and much of it in a voice that was not supposed to be heard. The singing was done by choirs of clerics. The reading of the Scriptures had become a formal exercise because the people could not understand what was being read. When the Reformers protested against Roman ecclesiology they protested particularly against what it had done to the celebration of the Eucharist. Their calls for a return to a simpler, biblical form of celebration were, simultaneously, calls for a return to a biblical ecclesiology and theology of ministry.

Another element of the ecclesiology of the Roman Catholic Church criticized by the Reformers had an important bearing on the development of the rite of the Eucharist. From the earliest times the church of Rome had been recognized by all other churches as having a ministry of unity within the whole Church. It was recognized that it exercised this ministry by watching over the faith of the churches and their celebration of the sacraments. In keeping with the nature of ritual the Roman church had confined its care for the Eucharist of other churches to the essential core of the rite; the liturgical form given to the rite in particular churches was their own business. The Roman liturgy did, indeed, have considerable authority among the churches of the Latin West, and the work of Popes like St Leo the Great and St Gregory the Great had been accepted as normative. But in the Middle Ages, when the Roman liturgy was imposed as a standard for many churches of the West, the initiative seems to have come from the emperor rather than from the Pope. Papal initiative in favour of liturgical reform and pressure towards standardization according to the usages of the Roman church did become insistent as the Middle Ages went on. But up to the Council of Trent there was still no obligation on particular churches to conform their celebration of the Eucharist to a form determined by the Pope. The authority of the Pope to do so was generally recognized but it only became an undisputed part of Catholic ecclesiology at the Council of Trent.

(c) Theology and spirituality: As well as being influenced by the general self-understanding of the church that produced it, the Roman rite of the Eucharist was influenced by particular theological teachings and spiritual experience that developed over the centuries in the Western church. What the church thought about the grace of God, about the way it is given in sacraments and specifically about how it was given in the Eucharist affected the form given to the rite. The spiritual experience that accompanied doctrinal developments,

and was sometimes more responsible than intellectual considerations for its moving in a particular direction, also moulded the rite.

The Eucharistic Prayer that a church uses is always a good indicator of what it thinks about the mystery of grace, about sacramentality and about the Eucharist. The way it is said and the rituals that accompany it give a good sense of how the Eucharist is being spiritually experienced by the celebrating community. There is a common Christian teaching about the grace of salvation inherent in every Eucharistic Prayer that is faithful to the broad tradition of faith. Particular churches find one or other aspect of it more spiritually and intellectually congenial, and accent it accordingly in the text they develop. At the heart of every Eucharistic Prayer, as of the Jewish *berakah* on which it is modelled, is a sense that everything is grace from God; creatures have nothing to do but bless and thank him. There is also in it a sense of the justice of things: God is right to punish us for our sins, but at the same time he ought now to show us his favour because we are committing ourselves anew to obeying his covenant. It appears that a sense of justice was something that appealed strongly to the people of the Roman world. In the civil sphere they worked out a rather admirable system of law and procedures for the administration of justice. In theology they had a special interest in how that sense of justice could be maintained within an understanding of the grace of God. Most of the early doctrinal debates about grace occurred in the Western church. Special attention was given in the theology of grace to the place of human action, and to the experience of give and take that marks human reception of God's gifts: how is it that we can do nothing to establish a claim on God's gifts, and yet we must do everything to please God and make ourselves worthy of his grace; what is the gift within us that allows us to be our human selves in receiving the gifts of God? The Scholastic theology of grace and justification gave particular attention to these typically Western concerns.

The Roman Canon begins to appear in Rome in the fourth century, has existed substantially as it is now since the sixth century (Jungmann, pp. 38–42), and was adopted by all Western churches between the ninth and eleventh centuries (Jungmann, pp. 71–77). While it embodies the classical tradition of Eucharistic Prayer it has the distinctive Western accent on the give and take of grace. It is not afraid to speak of the offering that the faithful, and the priest on their behalf, make in the Eucharist as 'these gifts we offer you in sacrifice', and to ask that they be accepted by God as were the gifts of Abel and the sacrifice of Abraham and the bread and wine of Melchizedek; it sees the taking of 'this sacrifice to your altar in heaven' as being connected with our being 'filled with every grace and blessing'; it offers 'this sacrifice of praise for ourselves and those who are dear to us . . .'. The Eucharist is the sacrifice of God's people and they expect results from it. According to the intentions of a Western, and especially a Scholastic, theology of grace, the certainty that the only offering now acceptable to God is the sacrifice of Christ (which is a fundamental presupposition of every Eucharistic Prayer) is not in the least compromised by this attention to the human offering. The whole effort of that theology was to understand how the work of salvation could be entirely the gift of God, realized by the sacrificial death of Christ and communicated by the grace of the Holy Spirit, while being at the same time a genuinely human work that had meritorious, satisfactory (propitiatory) and intercessory value in the sight of God. That theology found a congenial expression in the Roman Canon. However, if that Scholastic theology were badly understood it could make the Roman Canon seem to be saying that the gifts of God were somehow the result of a claim which humans established by their sacrifice. The Reformers challenged the Scholastic theology of grace on the basis of their understanding of the biblical doctrine of justification: they were convinced that to attribute any meritorious and satisfactory value to human action was to negate the grace of God given only in Christ. From their perspective the Roman Canon was not only uncongenial but un-Christian. It made the Eucharist to be a work of the law. In their attack on the Catholic doctrine of justification they could hardly avoid raising the issue of the Roman Canon, because it truly does express the characteristic Roman Catholic theology of grace and justification.

The Western theology of grace is also at work in the way the Roman Canon prays for the consecration of the bread and wine so that they will become the body and blood of Christ. In most other Eucharistic Prayers, ancient and modern, this takes the form of a calling on God to send the Holy Spirit to sanctify the offerings (it is an epiclesis). The Roman Canon reflects a theology and a spirituality that is more interested in the created effect of God's sanctifying action than in the divine Person to whom the action is to be attributed. From the *De Sacramentis* of St Ambrose onwards one can find explanations in Latin theology that such actions, although they may be attributed in some of their aspects to one or other of the divine Persons, involve a joint causality, a single sanctifying action of the whole Trinity (Ambrose, VI, 5; Yarnold, p. 150). The effect of the action involves some kind of real change in created reality (habitual or sanctifying grace in humans, transubstantiation in the bread and wine). The petition for consecration in the Roman Canon is simply that the offering itself may be 'blessed, approved, acceptable . . . may become an offering in spirit and in truth'. It is a prayer for sanctification that is more concerned with the effect of sanctification than with the personal identity of the Sanctifier. It accords with a general reticence of Latin theology about the Holy Spirit and its volubility about the created effects of the Holy Spirit.

The theology of sacraments that was worked out in the Latin church (see above, 2.6 and 3.7) inevitably influenced the Roman rite of the Eucharist. The thesis that each sacrament has an essential matter and form, for example, made it necessary to identify these two components in the Eucharist. Bread and wine were obviously the matter. The words of Jesus, 'This is my body . . . this is the chalice of my blood', were identified as the form. The moment when these words were said was identified as the moment when the sacrament came into existence. The theology of the Eastern churches was less interested in defining the exact moment of consecration, but when it did ask the question it looked rather to the epiclesis than to the saying of the words of Jesus for an answer. The Latin theology made the moment of consecration be the climax of the celebration.

Correspondingly the rite came to surround that moment with special solemnity and gestures of reverence, such as genuflections, burning of incense, ringing of bells. The theological analysis of how the consecration happened also had its effect on the rite. The relationship between the sacramental bread and the body of Christ was worked out in terms of substance and transubstantiation (see 9.3 below). It became clear to the church that the consecrated bread was no longer substantially bread. It became clear, too, that every fragment of the consecrated bread is the body of Christ. This kind of theological clarification, allied to a deep reverence for the body of Christ truly present in the sacrament, had an influence on the practice of preparing special bread and wine for use in the Eucharist. White, wafer-thin bread, already separated into particles suitable for individual communion, gradually began to take the place of loaves of unleavened bread from the ninth century onwards (Jungmann, p. 64); and 'altar wine' eventually became a special commodity. The taking of bread from the faithful at the offering of the gifts, and the breaking of the loaf for distribution in communion were no longer needed. The doctrine of what is called 'concomitance' — which explained that, while sacramentally the bread becomes the body and the wine the blood of Christ, nevertheless the whole Christ, body, blood, soul and divinity, is really present in the species of bread alone, as it is in the species of wine — gave a theological justification for the practice of giving the faithful communion only under the form of bread (Jungmann, p. 512). A spiritual need to see and adore the body of Christ present in the consecrated species was met by introducing the elevation of the host and chalice at the consecration; the practice of exposing the consecrated host in a monstrance allowed this act of eucharistic devotion to be prolonged outside the celebration of the Eucharist (Jungmann, pp. 90–92). A spirituality of the real presence brought to the Roman celebration of the Eucharist a distinctive quality of adoration and a sense of reverence for the wonder of God's coming to be present with his people. Later, during the Baroque period, this found expression in a way of celebrating the rite that had something of the theatrical about it (Jungmann, pp. 111–113). Even though the official rite still provided for participation of the faithful by sacramental communion and various responses, these were often sacrificed to the interests of a more solemn performance of the rite by the clergy, and by the choir and musicians who gave a splendour to the celebration worthy of the divine manifestation that occurred within it.

There were other theological and spiritual factors contributing to the acceptance of celebrations of the Eucharist in which the faithful did not partake of the body and blood of Christ. A case came to be made for expressing a sense of wonder at the gift of the Eucharist by abstaining from receiving it. The tradition of faith had recognized that a sense of unworthiness and a confession of sinfulness had its place in the celebration of the Eucharist. It had expected sinners who were not reconciled to God in and by the community to abstain from the Eucharist until they had been absolved from their sin. But only special kinds of sinful situation required this exclusion from the Eucharist. Indeed the Eucharist itself was recognized as expressing repentance, bringing God's forgiveness, and effecting reconciliation within the community. A confession of sinfulness and various prayers for forgiveness had found a place in the Roman rite from the ninth century onwards. The rituals of adoration that expressed Western devotion to the real presence accentuated feelings of unworthiness and an appreciation of the spiritual value of excluding oneself from receiving the Eucharist until one was really ready and worthy. The very abstention was reckoned to be a good way of improving the quality of one's participation in the Eucharist. Theology taught that one could receive the grace of the Eucharist by the desire of receiving it, without actual sacramental reception. Once ritual form was given in the Eucharist to a strong theology and spirituality of the real presence, acts of seeing and adoring the host could be treated as a form of spiritual communion which would do as much for one's growth in grace as sacramental communion. Saints no less than sinners regularly took part in the Eucharist without receiving communion, and it was not unknown from the late Middle Ages to have the Eucharist celebrated in the Roman rite without any provision for communion of the faithful.

There was another line of theological justification for celebrating the Eucharist without provision for communion, and even without provision for attendance by the faithful. The general tradition about the Eucharist, and the Roman tradition in particular, had always recognized the Eucharist as a sacrifice. Mediaeval theologians introduced a distinction between the effects which the Eucharist had as sacrifice and those that it had as a sacrament received in communion (see 9.4 below). Late mediaeval preaching and practice made much of the fruits of the Eucharist as sacrifice, in a way that made them seem independent of the reception of communion (Jungmann, p. 97). To be present at the Eucharist and join in it as the offering of the sacrifice of Christ was a value in itself, and had fruits both for oneself and for others for whom it was offered. The theology of the fruits of the Mass, and the spirituality that accompanied it, had other effects on how the Eucharist was celebrated. The tradition of faith was that the rite is designed for celebration by and for an assembled community of believers. But a theological case could be made for saying that the fruits of the sacrifice do not depend on the presence of a congregation. When an ordained priest performed the rite, using the essential matter and form, one had a real Eucharist with its sacrificial effects. The effects could be directed by the intention of the priest towards those for whom he was offering the sacrifice, whether they were present or not. Thus a Mass without an actual congregation could be given theological sense. The prescribed rite of Mass was not deprived of its communitarian features, but many of them were incongruous without an assembled community. These 'private' celebrations of the Eucharist became more frequent and acceptable in the Roman rite through being associated with devotion to particular mysteries of the life of Christ, or to the saints (Votive Masses), and with promises of special favours that could be gained through various combinations of them, for the dead as well as for the living (Jungmann, pp. 97–99). They also became an important source of income for the priests who celebrated them. But there was some incongruity between the multiplication of 'private' Masses (and of the reasons for which they might be celebrated, such as special intentions of benefactors, special devotional exercises, votive offerings) and the basic meaning that continued to be embodied in the rite which was the gathering together of an ecclesial community to renew the covenant that bound them together to God and to one another in the body of Christ.

The offering of the Eucharist for particular intentions or in connection with needs of individuals not shared with the community also affected the relationship between the two parts of the eucharistic rite, which are nowadays called the Liturgy of the Word and the Liturgy of the Eucharist. The reading of the word was done with impressive solemnity in the original Roman rite. It became a somewhat formal ritual, however, when it continued to be done in Latin even where that was no longer the vernacular language of the communities who were celebrating. The choice of passages to be read was determined in the classical tradition of Roman liturgy by the intention of having the whole Bible heard, if not in all its pages at least in a representative selection, over a certain period of time. While that principle was never abandoned its effectiveness was gradually blunted by the many other criteria of choice that began to operate. Feasts of saints, votive celebrations, Masses for the dead and many other particular occasions had their own proper readings which interrupted the continuous reading of the Bible. The result was that many Christian communities heard a quite haphazard selection of readings. They were not exposed to that full story of God's People in the Old and New Testaments which gave them their identity as God's Covenant People, and to which their Eucharist was a response in Christ. Their Eucharist was affected more by the occasions and intentions for which it was celebrated than by the pedagogy of God's word. The general neglect of the homily during the Middle Ages left the Scripture readings often without controlled application to the life of the community, and left the community without direction as to how it should offer itself to God in the eucharistic part of the rite.

8.2.5 The Missal of Pius V

It is undeniable that by the beginning of the sixteenth century many celebrations of the Eucharist in the Western church distorted the rite that had been received from the apostles, had been given a classical Roman shape in the period from the fourth to the seventh century, and then adapted to the new Europe of the Middle Ages with a good deal of sensitivity to the culture and historical reality of its people. The Council of Trent knew all about the situation. It had before it detailed catalogues of ritual and other aberrations in the way the Eucharist was celebrated (Jungmann, pp. 100–113). A special commission was set up at the Council to deal with what were called *abusus Missae*. However, before the Council of Trent met, the Protestant Reformers had been having their say about the *abusus Missae*. They had fulminated against the Mass as they experienced it. The forms they knew were not always in the rite of Rome itself, because there was as yet no uniformity of rite in the Latin church, but they were close enough to it to let Rome and its rite of Mass be the legitimate target of Protestant outrage.

The Reformers generally attributed the abuses they found in celebrations of the Eucharist to bad theology: they saw them as the outcome of erroneous, unbiblical Catholic thinking about justification, about the relationship between faith and sacraments, about the Eucharist as sacrifice and about the presence of Christ in the consecrated elements. That left the Council of Trent with a dilemma. It may have wanted to make some of the reforms in the celebration of the Eucharist that Protestants were proposing or already making. But the Protestants were giving theological reasons for their reforms which the Catholic Church could not accept. In their new liturgical creations they were doing some things which Catholics might have considered to be the right things, but for what Catholics judged to be the wrong reasons. (They were also judged, of course, to be doing some wrong things for those same wrong reasons.) The Council of Trent believed it had to define Catholic doctrine unambiguously in the face of erroneous Protestant teaching and practice. It had to state that the Catholic tradition as it had been expressed in the faith-statements of the mediaeval councils and doctors was the tradition received from the Scriptures and the Fathers. It would have been pastorally difficult to do this while at the same time making radical changes in the sacramental practice that accompanied this teaching. If it made reforms in the celebration of the Eucharist that had already been pre-empted by the Protestants it risked giving the impression that the Protestants were right not just about the reforms but about the reasons for them. To give that impression would be to obscure the firmness of the dogmatic positions which the Council was taking. It could also have weakened the authority of the Church and of the Pope on which the dogmatic value of the teaching of the Council depended. If Popes and Councils had been wrong about so many things in the celebration of the Eucharist . . . . Hence the reforms in the celebration of the Eucharist enacted by the Council of Trent are modest and cautious. Its *Decretum de Observandis et Evitandis in celebratione Missae* (1562) is a call for the elimination of obvious abuses stemming from 'avarice, irreverence and superstition' (Jungmann, p. 101). It does not provide for any changes in the rite itself. Neither did it take a decisive line on the much debated question (Jungmann, p. 100) of whether the rite should be standardized and centrally controlled in the Western church.

The Council of Trent left the whole question of rites to be dealt with by the Pope. Work on the Mass was begun immediately after the Council and it resulted in the promulgation of a *Missale Romanum* by Pope St Pius V in 1570. The arrangement of the rite (*ordo missae*), the calendar and the selection of Scripture readings which it contained was made obligatory for the Latin church, but not for those dioceses and religious orders that could demonstrate they had been using a stable rite of their own for more than 200 years. The form of rite chosen was the one that was then in use in the Roman Curia. While the commission did make some attempt to examine the original sources of the Roman rite in such documents as were available to scholars at the time, and whereas the Pope stated in his Bull of Promulgation that the intention had been to restore the celebration of the Eucharist *ad pristinam sanctorum Patrum normam ac ritum* ('in conformity with the original norms and rite laid down by the holy Fathers'), what the compilers of the Missal settled for was, in fact, a well-established mediaeval form of the Roman rite which respected the essentials of the original biblical and patristic tradition, and the particular stamp that had been put on the tradition in Rome when a Latin liturgy was created there. Although it went beyond Trent in the degree of standardization and centralization it imposed on the Latin church, the Missal did generally obey the intentions of Trent: it provided a good standard form of the rite according to which the celebration of the Eucharist could be restored; it retained mediaeval forms which corresponded well with the doctrinal definitions of the Council; it refused reforms such as the use of vernacular languages and communion from the chalice for the laity, thus avoiding the doctrinal ambiguity to which they could give rise, as well as the pastoral risks that changes in well-established custom would have entailed.

8.2.6   The Missal of Paul VI

The Missal that was promulgated by Pius V in 1570, with a few very minor changes, remained binding on Catholics of the Latin rite until it was replaced by the Missal of Paul VI in 1969 (see above, 8.1). The new Missal is presented in the Apostolic Constitution that introduces it as a revision of the old. The revision is said to be based on the experience of the liturgical movement and on scholarly research, and to complete 'the adaptation of the Roman Missal to the new outlook and spiritual mentality of our own times' which was already begun by Pope Pius XII. While praising the Missal of Pius V as 'universally acknowledged to be among the most useful of the many fruits which that Council [of Trent] brought forth for the good of the whole Church of Christ', Paul VI readily admits that it needed revision. He obviously approves the claim made for the new Missal in the Foreword to its *General Instruction* that it is 'a considerable improve-ment' on the old one (n. 6). At the same time he has no doubt that the rite he is promulgating embodies one and the same tradition that is represented by the Missal of Pius V. The analysis of the development of the Roman rite given in 8.2.4 should help one to appreciate what the Pope means. Cultural, ecclesiological and theological factors were at work in bringing the Roman rite to the point it reached in the Missal of Pius V, and in the way that Missal was subsequently used. They operated within the transmission of a traditional rite, guiding its adaptation to changing circumstances of human life over the centuries. The rite given in the Missal of Pius V is not identical with the rite celebrated by St Gregory the Great. There is no reason why it should have been. Neither is there any good reason why it should be identical with the rite celebrated by Paul VI. There are very good reasons why it should not be. Human culture, ecclesiology, theology are still at work. As they evolve they are forces for change within the tradition. It is not surprising that some people found the changes introduced in the Missal of Paul VI to be rather abrupt and were upset by them. For one thing the very nature of rite requires stability and a sense of the familiar; any change is upsetting in ritual. But the changes made after Vatican II had to be particularly severe. There had been no change of any consequence in the Roman rite since 1570. In other periods of history the factors of change had been allowed to work gradually and almost imperceptibly. During the centuries after the Council of Trent, however, it was judged better to maintain the rite in a fixed form. Inevitably, when change could be allowed again and a beginning was made in the courageous reforms of Pius XII, a lot of ground had to be made up and changes were experienced as abrupt and surprising.

The rite of the Eucharist in the Missal of Paul VI was designed on the paradoxical principle that the best way to be progressive in reforming an institution like the Eucharist is to look backwards. The criterion of authenticity in relation to sources is more fundamental than the criterion of relevance in liturgical reform. The authors of the rite went back to the biblical and patristic sources of the eucharistic rite and to the classical origins of the Roman rite. They had better historical information than did the compilers of the Missal of Pius V. They knew what could and should be omitted if the Roman rite were to be given a chance to be contemporary. What they omitted from the Missal of Pius V was mostly from the mediaeval stratum; what they restored to it came from the patristic and early Roman level. The restoration of the essential Roman rite was the most positive thing they did to make the rite relevant to the life of the Church in the world of the present. They did not add contemporary new features to the rite. They made certain choices which would free the rite so that contemporary human culture, ecclesiology and theology — those factors that have always influenced the development of the eucharistic rite — could be brought to bear on it and give the Church the kind of celebration of the Eucharist it needs in the contemporary world.

The Second Vatican Council articulated its sensitivity to contemporary human culture and society in its Constitution on the Church in the Modern World; it expounded the Church's self-awareness as Church in the Constitution on the Church; it gave its theology of sacraments in the Constitution on the Liturgy. What the Council taught in each of these areas was respected in the design of the rite of the Eucharist prescribed in the Roman Missal. Contemporary culture wants to be pluralistic, in spite of the pressures that tend towards the global village. The present form of the Roman rite does have a certain classical flavour, but also has a built-in demand for adaptation to local cultures. It is in the Latin language and shows a certain affinity with Latin ritual and Latin church music. But it is open to translation not just into contemporary languages but into the music, conventions of assembly and movement, expressions of reverence, prayer forms of any contemporary culture. If the intentions of the Missal are respected it would be difficult any more to use the rite for any kind of cultural, still less political domination.

There are limits to the cultural adaptation allowed for in the present Roman rite. Here the ecclesiological factor begins to come into play. In Catholic belief the church of Rome is at the centre of the unity of the Church of God. Anything that helps its mission of unity is good for the whole Church. Introducing the Missal in his Apostolic Constitution, Paul VI expresses a hope that in spite of the variations that it allows for in obedience to Vatican II, 'this book will be received by the faithful as an aid whereby all can witness to each other and strengthen the one faith common to all, since it enables one and the same prayer, expressed in so many different languages, to ascend to the heavenly Father through our High Priest Jesus Christ in the Holy Spirit — a prayer more fragrant than any incense' (Flannery, p. 141). Obviously this appeal for liturgical unity is addressed only to Catholics of the Latin rite, because the book is intended for them alone. Those who follow an Oriental rite of the Eucharist are not calling the unity of the Church into question by attachment to their own rite. One must take the Pope's words to mean that Catholics of the Latin rite will have a deeper experience of unity among themselves, and give a more effective witness of unity to the rest of the Church when their celebration of the Eucharist is in accordance with the prescriptions of the one Roman Missal. Dogmatically it would be quite permissable for a local church to want to develop a new rite of the Eucharist according to its own cultural and ecclesiological perceptions which would go beyond the adaptations allowed for in the Roman Missal. There is no dogmatic reason why new rites should not emerge in the Church of today as they did in the early centuries, provided they respect the essentials of the common tradition of faith and the fundamental structure of the rite that comes from the apostles. The discipline of communion between the churches, and the special liturgical authority which the Roman church has over churches that are historically of the Latin rite would, however, be called into question by such a step. For a church which is historically of the Latin rite to want to opt out of it would put some strains on the bonds of communion. However, disciplinary requirements for communion have not always been the same in the Church. The hope expressed by Paul VI is expressed within the terms of a particular phase within the tradition of ecclesiology. Perhaps future developments in the understanding of the disciplinary requirements of communion — affected, for example, by the reuniting of churches now separated — could result in a Roman Missal that would be even more Roman than that of Paul VI, but less binding on local churches that, although historically of the Latin rite, would want to develop liturgical forms more in keeping with their own non-Latin cultures.

The ecclesiology of Vatican II constructs the Christian community from the People of God, on the basis of the sharing that all its members have in the priestly and prophetic offices of Christ, before it puts in place the ordained hierarchy of ministers by which it is served. The rite of the Eucharist reflects this view of the Church. Its primary form is designed for participation by the full ecclesial community. It diversifies rôles so that many persons can contribute to the rite according to the particular ministry and gift they have in the community. It highlights the special priesthood of the one who presides, and provides for concelebration by a number of priests in a single celebration; but this does not downplay the general priesthood of believers or the ministries of deacons, readers, acolytes, singers etc. The structured hierarchical character of the eucharistic assembly is fully maintained, but the virtual monopoly of ritual action which clerics had in the former Roman rite is broken. The rite is an action of the whole church in the variety of its members. This is how the Foreword or Introduction to the *General Instruction* presents the eucharistic community that the rite is designed for:

> But the very nature of the ministerial priesthood sheds light upon another kind of priesthood of great dignity, namely, the royal priesthood of the faithful whose spiritual sacrifice is accomplished through the ministry of the priest in union with the sacrifice of Christ, the One Mediator. For the celebration of the Eucharist is an act of the whole Church. Everyone at Mass is to do all of, but only, those parts which pertain to his office according to his status within the people of God. A consequence of this principle is that certain features of the celebration are now receiving greater attention than was formerly accorded to them during some of the preceding centuries. The celebrating people are in fact the people of God, purchased by the Blood of Christ, convened by their Lord, nourished by his word, a people called on to lay before God the entreaties of all mankind. They are a people who give thanks to God for the mystery of salvation in Christ by offering his sacrifice; a people who grow together in unity by being united with his Body and Blood, a people, holy by origin, who continually grow in holiness by active, conscious and fruitful participation in the eucharistic mystery (n. 5; Flannery, p. 156).

The Foreword gives special attention to the doctrinal issues about sacraments and about the Eucharist itself which affected the form of the rite standardized by Pius V. It notes that Vatican II had made its own the definitions of the Council of Trent on the questions about the Eucharist that were at issue with the Reformers: the Eucharist is a sacrifice; Christ is really present under the eucharistic species through transubstantiation of the elements; the celebrant is a ministerial priest who offers the sacrifice in the person of Christ (nn. 2–4). The Foreword states these truths, however, in a way that draws on the renewed and ecumenically sensitive sacramental theology that had been adopted by Vatican II. It suggests that the caution required by the dogmatic disputes of the Reformation is no longer necessary. It was for dogmatic reasons that Pius V found it necessary to stand by the form which the Roman rite had come to take during the Middle Ages (n. 7). But now one can give liturgical recognition to the priesthood of all believers without compromising the ministerial priesthood of the ordained (n. 5). There is no longer a risk of casting doubts on the objective efficacy of the Eucharist by having it in the vernacular, by having the Eucharistic Prayer said aloud, and by other things that may be done to heighten the pastoral and catechetical value of the rite (nn. 11–13). One does not call the Tridentine doctrine of the real presence of the whole Christ under the appearance of bread into question by re-introducing communion under both kinds (n. 14). Nor, one might add, is transubstantiation put in danger by requiring that the bread used in the Eucharist should look like food and be in a form that allows it to be broken into pieces for distribution (*General Instruction*, nn. 282–283). It must also be said that what has been done to restore sacramental communion as the normal way of participation by all the community in the Eucharist does not call its sacrificial values into question. The theology of salvation and grace inherent in the Roman Canon is, of course, affirmed and the Prayer is retained with only minor modifications. It has been relativized, however, by the introduction of new Eucharistic Prayers which, according to the Apostolic Constitution, 'emphasize different aspects of the mystery of salvation' (Flannery, p. 139). All the new Eucharistic Prayers have an epiclesis of the Holy Spirit. Theological traditions other than the Roman and Scholastic are at work, then, in the rite, as they are throughout the teaching of Vatican II. Even when Paul VI stipulates in the Apostolic Constitution that the 'words of our Lord shall be the same in all forms of the Canon' the reason he gives does not come from the Scholastic sacramental theology of matter and form but from 'pastoral reasons and so as to facilitate concelebration'.

Vatican II has a theology of the word of God and of its relationship to sacraments that puts the debate with the churches of the Reformation about faith and sacrament in justification on a much more promising level. It also brings a deeper understanding of the relationship between Liturgy of Word and Liturgy of Eucharist in the eucharistic rite. The liturgical reforms since Vatican II have done much to make the eucharistic action be experienced once again in the Roman rite as a response to the great events of the new covenant and the telling of them in the Bible. The re-arrangement of the calendar, the setting of limits to the number of feasts of saints to be celebrated, the control of celebrations for special and private occasions, as well as a new lectionary, have allowed the continuous reading of the Scriptures to be re-established, so that the history of salvation and its fulfilment in Christ is put before the covenant people in an orderly way. The celebration of the Word of God, read and sung and then applied to concrete situations of the community in the homily, gives meaning and reality to the covenant sacrifice of praise which God's assembled people make in Christ, in their meal of bread and wine which is his body and blood.

8.3   RITUAL MEALS

The rite of the Eucharist has precedents and parallels throughout human life. Ritual meals mark or recall significant moments in family and civil life. Sacred meals are celebrated in many of the world religions. Reflection on the human significance of meals can help to develop a sensitivity to the sacramentality of the eucharistic rite.

People eat because they need food to sustain life. They eat together because they usually do things better when they do them together and the human quality of life is enriched by company. The food is likely to be better for being provided, prepared and shared by several. When people are happy to be together it affects the way they eat. Their meals become festive. They use them to identify the things that make them happy. When, for example, they are particularly aware of one of their members because it is the anniversary of his or her birth they turn their meal into a birthday party. The party says that their life together is richer because that person is with them. When one of their group marries they have a wedding feast. It becomes a way of saying that they have a future as a family. Those who belong together in professional associations, sports clubs, business firms have their annual dinner. It is good for morale and fellowship and dedication to a common purpose. On a more intimate scale people invite friends, or those they want to have as friends, to their home for a meal; or friends go out to eat together. People eat together, eventually, because they have some life-giving common bond, which is important to them and which they want to last. The meal renews the bond, deepens it and becomes a promise that it will continue. When they are happy about the bond their meal becomes a celebration.

People do not take festive meals just because they are hungry. And yet hunger, even the hunger of the world, is an issue in every meal, be it festive or just functional. No meal is entirely private. Having a table to sit down to goes along with being in a family, having friends, belonging to a socially productive group. Each of these circles provides some guarantee that one will not go hungry: people go hungry because they do not belong to any of them. Good people who eat together with joy and thankfulness think readily enough of those who have no table at which they are welcome and who go hungry. They feel some responsibil-ity for feeding the hungry and welcoming the stranger. There is a built-in will to hospitality in a humanly good meal. In many cultures there had to be always a place at table for a traveller and extra food was prepared for the poor. Nowadays one expects those who eat well to have a certain social conscience about their responsibility to work for a society in which everyone would have a table at which they could feel at home and no one need go hungry. There are, of course, those whose meals are a celebration of their own selfish successes, and of values and events that actually make others be outsiders and go hungry. Their meals can become a flaunting of food in the face of the hunger of others. The meals of the generous are symbols of human hope and hospitality. The meals of the selfish may be festive to them but they can be an outrage to the hungry.

Festive meals easily become ritualized. Special food and drink are used to give a sense of occasion. In the Western world there has to be a cake at a birthday party or wedding, and champagne is a recognized festive drink. Sometimes the food is chosen to stir memories and maintain continuity. Americans eat turkey at their Thanksgiving meal because the Pilgrims did so and their descendants have been doing it ever since. Rôles become ritualized. Because food has to be provided and prepared by someone, and a table has to be set, those who give the meal are distinguished from those who are invited to receive it as a gift. The host, the 'breadwinner' and the cook are easily recognized as gift-givers. Guests are receivers, although they may also bring gifts of food or other things to a meal. Then there are ritual speeches at meals. At family festive meals they take the form of conversation, but even then there may be a somewhat formal toast. The toasts and the speeches are more ritualistic in the meals of less personally intimate groups. On solemn occasions the speeches will proclaim what the group stands for, tell of its origins, boast of its successes, thank those who have contributed, express hopes for the future. The toasts are more specific and personal. They are often associated with the taking of the distinctive festive food and drink — with the cutting of the cake and the opening and pouring of the champagne. Indeed the significance of the meal tends to be concentrated in such moments.

The human values of ritual meals were incorporated in the Jewish and Christian tradition out of which the Eucharist comes (see above, 8.2.1 and 8.2.2).

They are still present in the rite of the Eucharist, even though the expression of them is rather formalized. If they are to function sacramentally they must give those who take part in them a credible experience of eating and drinking together. For this it is not necessary that the Eucharist should become an imitation of one or other of the festive meals that are experienced in family or civil life. That could make the human communion seem to be the very purpose of the Eucharist rather than a part of the sacramentality through which more profound communion is achieved. Ritual elements should indeed produce some real human experience. But they are meant to work on many other levels of significance besides the obvious and immediate. They normally work better when they are somewhat formal and exotic. By being formal they allow people to manage emotions that might otherwise be rather overpowering; by being exotic they allow them to recognize that something special is happening. Champagne and cake might not be as real as tea and toast but they work much better as rituals. To try to make the Eucharist like any other meal, and to think that any food and drink would do just as well as bread and wine, would be, apart altogether from strictly theological objections, to weaken its ritual power. The sacramental sign is a ritual meal and must be experienced as such. It helps to have the bread and wine look and taste like the food and drink they are. But they need to be presented as establishing continuity with the food and drink that Jesus used at the Last Supper, and that Christians have used always and everywhere since. Eating and drinking them is to be likened, not to the hearty consuming of the main course, but to the nibbling of the wedding cake and the sipping of champagne that comes at the end. The meal character of the rite can also be made to envelop the Liturgy of the Word by hearing the Scripture readings and homily as the kind of family speeches and conversation, and messages from absent friends, that are listened to at festive meals. The Eucharistic Prayer can be likened to a solemn toast, followed and endorsed by eating and drinking the bread and wine. Humanly speaking, the whole rite can be experienced as the festive celebration of a community of people who have a common bond and are happy to be together. And because it is a matter of shared food and drink it can touch the consciences of the participants with a concern about whether this meal is a sign of hope or of desperation for the hungry of the world.

Meals become an experience of God when the food and the fellowship is recognized as his gift. Then the speech becomes a prayer in which the divine significance of the meal is expressed. The meal does not become any less a human experience for being an experience of the divine. Once the bond that it expresses is recognized as a gift of God the meal becomes a dedication of the community to God. The life of its members and their future lies with him. It is only in belonging to him that they will never go hungry. Their eating together becomes a guarantee of life. These ideas can be expressed in table prayers. They provide the general theological and human foundation which underlies the Eucharistic Prayer.

Various religions of humanity practise sacred meals (see van der Leeuw). One can find parallels to the Eucharist in them. They are often sacrificial meals, which provides a useful analogy for an essential aspect of the Eucharist. However, the Christian tradition, especially in its early centuries, was rather chary of analogies between its rites and any religious practices. Too many of those practices did violence to the values, especially that of love and fellowship, that Christians stood for, and projected a God who could not be the Father of Our Lord Jesus Christ. It turned rather to the simple rites of human togetherness, such as bathing, anointing and taking food together, for its experience of God and of the effect his coming has on human life. In fact it is sometimes hard to know whether what is being described in the early texts is a simple fellowship meal or is also the Eucharist. It still seems more profitable for Christians to draw on their human experience of ordinary festive meals, rather than on anthropological studies of sacred meals, for developing the kind of imagination and sensitivity that contributes to a fruitful celebration of the Eucharist (see 1.2(a) above).

STUDY QUESTIONS

1   Write a description of a parish Sunday Mass for someone who is not a Christian and has never seen a Mass.
2   Analyse the 'Roman Canon' (Eucharistic Prayer I), and any modern Eucharistic Prayer on the basis of the constituent elements of the Eucharistic Prayer listed in the *General Instruction of the Roman Missal*, n. 55.
3   Do an exegesis of one of the covenant renewal accounts in the Old Testament.
4   Study table prayers in the Jewish tradition.
5   Follow the history of any one significant action of the Roman rite of the Eucharist (e.g. the preparation of bread and wine, manner of giving communion . . .).
6   Note the ritual and verbal expressions of oblation in the Roman rite of the Eucharist.
7   Examine a liturgical form of the Eucharist created by one of the major Reformers; compare it with the form of the Roman rite established in the Missal of Pius V, and then with the form given in the Missal of Paul VI.
8   Show how the doctrinal positions of the Council of Trent are expressed in the rite of Mass established by the Missal of Paul VI.
9   Describe some ritual meals from a contemporary culture, and show how they might throw some light on the rite of the Eucharist.

FURTHER READING

The rite of Mass:

Ordo Missae promulgated 26 March 1970 (includes the Apostolic Constitution *Missale Romanum* promulgated 3 April 1969).
Published in ICEL English translation as *The Roman Missal*, 1973.

The rite as given in the Missal of Paul VI is presented in general works on liturgy dating from after 1970; also:

J. D. Crichton, *Christian Celebration: The Mass* (London, 1971; repub. London, 1981).
J. Emminghaus, *The Eucharist: Essence, Form, Celebration* (trans. from German; Collegeville, 1978).

Biblical origins (covenant assemblies, Passover, blessing prayers, table liturgies) in:

L. Bouyer, *Life and Liturgy* (London, 1956)/*Liturgical Piety* (Notre Dame, 1956); and *Eucharist. Theology and Spirituality of the Eucharistic Prayer* (trans. from French; Notre Dame, 1968).

J. P. Audet, 'Esquisse historique du genre littéraire de la "bénédiction" juive et de l' "eucharistie" chrétienne', *Revue Biblique* 65 (1958), 370–399; trans. as 'Literary Form and Contents of a Normal *Eucharistia* in the First Century' in *The Gospels Reconsidered* (Oxford, 1960).

J. Jeremias, *The Eucharistic Words of Jesus* (trans. from 3rd German ed.; London, 1966).

L. Ligier, 'From the Last Supper to the Eucharist' in *The New Liturgy*, ed. L. Sheppard (London, 1970), pp. 113–150.

R. Moloney, SJ, 'The Early Eucharist: the Jewish Background', *Irish Theological Quarterly* 47 (1980), 34–42.

Sources of the Roman as well as other rites in:

P. Palmer, *Sacraments and Worship* (London, 1957).

L. Deiss, *Early Sources of the Liturgy* (New York, 1967).

R. C. D. Jaspers and G. J. Cuming, *Prayers of the Eucharist: Early and Reformed* (London, 1975).

On the general history of the Roman Mass:

J. A. Jungmann, SJ, *Missarum Sollemnia. The Mass of the Roman Rite* (4th German ed. 1958; English trans., 2 vols, New York, 1951/55; revised and abridged in 1 vol., New York/London, 1959).

G. Dix, *The Shape of the Liturgy* (London, 1945).

On the Eucharistic Prayer, with particular reference to the Roman Canon:

G. Vagaggini, OSB, *The Canon of the Mass and Liturgical Reform* (trans. from Italian; London, 1967).

J. B. Ryan, *The Eucharistic Prayer* (New York, 1974).

R. Moloney, SJ, *Our Eucharistic Prayers* (Wilmington, 1986).

For the rites developed by the Reformers:

B. Thompson, *Liturgies of the Western Church* (Cleveland/New York, 1962).

On ritual meals:

G. van der Leeuw, *Religion in Essence and Manifestation* (London, 1938).

T. Guzie, *Jesus and the Eucharist* (New York, 1974).

M. Hellwig, *The Eucharist and the Hunger of the World* (New York, 1976).

9

Eucharist: the word

Because the Eucharist is the climax of Christian initiation, and the regularly repeated celebration of Christian living, the word that accompanies it in the Church is uniquely comprehensive. No word of the Church is out of place in the celebration of the Eucharist and, indeed, every word that is truly of the Church must sooner or later be spoken there. The entire Bible is read, the whole tradition of God's People is remembered in feasts and anniversaries, the full range of human experience is dealt with in preaching and in prayer. The Liturgy of the Word is designed specifically to bring this comprehensive word of God and this breadth of human life right into the midst of the eucharistic rite. The Eucharistic Prayer is a celebration of the word that is being heard by the assembled community, an application of it to their life-situation, a response to its demands that is incorporated into the sacrifice of Christ, a petition for unity of faith in the same word which is fulfilled in the unity of the Body of Christ.

There is, of course, a specific theological word about the Eucharist itself that is present, at least implicitly, in every celebration. It deals with the sacramental reality of the rite itself and with the way it gives life to God's People. It explains why it is that the Eucharist embodies the fullness of God's saving action and the full taking hold of it by his People. These are the truths that make it possible for the Christian community to find in the Eucharist a sacramentalizing of its entire life. But it is important to see the specific theology of the Eucharist as a word open to the comprehensive hearing of the word of God that is done in the Eucharist. A theology of the Eucharist that is just about the Eucharist carries the risk of making the Eucharist seem like one among the many gifts of God. There is much to marvel at and contemplate with deep prayerfulness in the Eucharist. One can celebrate the Eucharist itself in the Eucharist, as one does on the feast of Corpus Christi. But in itself the Eucharist is a gift to be used rather than to be merely admitted. It is a daily bread taken and eaten to satisfy living hunger and to sustain the hunger for life of those who hear the Word of God in all its fullness and keep it in their lives.

It is important for another reason to establish this almost functional perspective when one is embarking on a theology of the Eucharist. Historically, Western theology has had to deal with two critical issues about the Eucharist — real presence and sacrifice. They are questions about the Eucharist itself. One cannot understand the Eucharist without getting at the truth about them. But if they are the only issues dealt with in a theology of the Eucharist, or if they loom so large that everything else seems trivial, the impression may be given that the Eucharist exists for its own sake and not for the sake of the life it gives to God's People. A theology of the Eucharist has to be about the Eucharist, about the Eucharist as it realizes the presence of the body and blood of Christ in bread and wine, about the Eucharist as the sacrifice of Christ, but about all this as it is the sacrament of the fullness of eternal life for the Church of God. It has to be a real sacramental theology, that appreciates the place of this particular rite in the whole sacramental economy. The real presence and the presence of Christ's sacrifice make it possible for the Eucharist to be at the centre of the sacramental economy, but their purpose and finality is to bring God's People to the fullness of life through listening to the entire word of God and consecrating themselves to him in the ongoing course of their daily life. A theology of the Eucharist must keep this broad sacramental perspective. It must not reduce its examination of the Scriptures and of the patristic and other witnesses to the tradition of faith to a search for material on real presence and sacrifice — although these will inevitably present themselves as major issues. And when it comes to systematic constructions it must attempt to find a framework for thinking about the Eucharist that will situate these two questions within a full, life-centred theology of the sacrament.

9.1   THE NEW TESTAMENT

9.1.1   Accounts of institution

Scriptural material from the Old and New Testament was examined in Chapter 8 with a view to understanding the form which the rite of the Eucharist takes in the Church. The passages that had the most immediate bearing on the rite are the accounts of the institution of the Eucharist which are found in the Synoptics and in Paul. Even while holding that they are a historical record of what happened at the Last Supper, one must recognize that they are inevitably also a theological statement about the Eucharist. They reflect what the Church had been thinking about the place of the Eucharist in its life during the years that passed between the resurrection and the writing of the accounts of the Last Supper in the form they now have in the gospels and in Paul. Christians had been living as the People of the new covenant, gathered under the leadership of the apostles of Jesus, saved from the slavery of sin by a new passover in his blood, already enjoying a place in the eschatological banquet of his kingdom while they waited for him to come again. All these scriptural words in which they describe their experience belong to a full biblical theology of the Eucharist. The great themes of salvation that resonate in the eucharistic words find their clearest expression in passages that deal with the death, resurrection and coming again of Jesus. Those passages provide the immediate context for the eucharistic words. The accounts of institution are saying, in the language of covenant, passover, salvation and estin   hisra/dama   basar/dam

ultimately of the cross, what the Church believes God is doing for his world in the Eucharist. The Eucharist is what it is because of all that God has been doing, is doing and will do for the salvation of the world.

At the core of the Synoptic accounts of the Last Supper, and highlighted by Paul's résumé of what happened at it, are the words that Jesus spoke about the bread and wine that he took and gave to his disciples (Matt 26:26–29; Mark 14:22–25; Luke 22:19–20; 1 Cor 11:23–27). He said that the bread was his body and the wine in the cup was his blood. There is no convincing reason for not taking his words literally. Jesus can be presumed to have spoken in Aramaic, or, if not, in Hebrew (Jeremias, *The Eucharistic Words*, pp. 196–198). Although there would have been no verb corresponding to 'is' in the phrases about the bread and the wine in either of these languages, the simple juxtaposition of the words bread and body, wine and blood was sufficient to affirm identity between 'this (bread)' and 'my body', between 'this cup (of wine)' and 'my blood'. The Greek of the New Testament text makes the 'is' explicit with the verb *estin* (Benoit, p. 65). Given the Semitic idiom and ideas being employed, 'body' in the context means something like 'me in my concrete personal reality'. 'Body' stands not just for part of a person (to be distinguished from 'soul') but for the whole person in the reality of physical existence and presence. Jesus is saying in effect, 'what I am giving to you is myself'. When he adds that the cup of wine that he is passing around is his blood he is still talking about himself. Blood is the life of the body. A person's life is in his/her blood. In the cup, Jesus is with his disciples in the reality of his life. He is a living person for them. But if he is living he is also capable of dying. In Luke and Paul the bread is said to be not just 'my body' but 'my body that is given for you'. One gives one's life by dying; one can do it by shedding one's blood. The blood that the cup of wine is said to be in the texts is 'my blood of the (new) covenant, which is poured out for many for the forgiveness of sins' (Matt 26:28).

The words of Jesus that come to be translated 'body' and 'blood' in the accounts of institution are thought to be a pair of words, *bisra/dama* in Aramaic or *basar/dam* in Hebrew, drawn from the vocabulary of ritual sacrifice (Jeremias, pp. 198–201). They evoke the Passover lamb (Jeremias, pp. 220–225). The word 'given' that accompanies them is likewise sacrificial. The blood is 'poured out' as it was in the ritual sacrifices of animals in the Temple. It is the 'blood of the covenant', likened to the blood of sacrificed animals that Moses sprinkled on the people and on the altar when the covenant of Sinai was being ratified. Jesus is presenting himself as one who, like the Suffering Servant foretold by Isaiah, gives himself in sacrifice for many, bringing the forgiveness of sins and the coming of the Kingdom (Benoit, pp. 54–58). The Aramaic word that Jesus is thought to have used about the bread could be translated 'flesh' and as such could evoke the dead flesh of animals slaughtered in sacrifice. But the Greek text translates the word used by Jesus about the bread as 'body' (*sōma*), not 'flesh' (*sarx*). The Jesus who is present in the Eucharist is alive, in the body. And that life is in the blood, which, although it is poured out in the death of Jesus, becomes living and life-giving in the resurrection.

The words of institution in Luke and Paul contain the phrase 'Do this in remembrance of me'. Those who did what Jesus had done would be remembering him as he had presented himself in what he said about the bread and wine. They would be remembering him in his dying for the salvation of many. The custom of remembering in a ritual meal those who had died was common in the Greek and Roman worlds of the first century. However, it seems certain that the remembering of Jesus that was done in the Christian Eucharist was an exercise of a much more profound kind, that came out of the Semitic and biblical experience of God in prayer and in ritual. To make a 'memorial' (*zikkaron* in Hebrew, *anamnēsis* in Greek) of the events in which God had acted in human history for the benefit of his covenant People was somehow to call on and allow God to do that wonder again in a new, present situation that had some similarity with the past. When Christians did the eucharistic rite in memory of Jesus they were making a memorial of the event in his life in which God had performed the definitive work of human salvation. They were remembering the death and resurrection in which his life reached its climax. In their remembering, he was present with them in the reality of his body and blood, in which he had died and was now risen. In that presence God is even now realizing the forgiveness of sins and the making of the new covenant in the blood of Jesus for those who are celebrating the Eucharist. The bread which is his body and the wine which is his blood are life-giving for the assembled community and their fellowship is in that life.

9.1.2   St Paul

Because of the literary form they were using, the Synoptics had to keep their theological reflection about the Eucharist within the limits of a narrative about the Last Supper. Paul is also faithful to the narrative method when giving his account of the Lord's Supper in his first epistle to the Corinthians. However, the literary form of an epistle allows him to add some explicit theological thinking about the relationship between the Last Supper and actual celebrations of the Eucharist. He does it in chapter 11, but also in other places in the epistle. 1 Corinthians 11 has already been discussed for its significance in general sacramental theology (see above, 1.2) and for the information it yields about the rite of the Eucharist (see above, 8.2.2). Here it needs to be examined, along with other passages of the epistle, for the theology of the Eucharist they contain (Barrett, pp. 258ff.).

Paul's theology of the Eucharist in 1 Corinthians is the fruit of his concern for the relationship between participation in the Eucharist and the life of Christians. He argues that the realism of what occurs in the rite has definite imperatives for Christian living. He bases the realism of his thinking about the Eucharist itself on the account of institution which has been handed on to him. If he adds the strong phrase 'For as often as you eat this bread and drink the cup, you proclaim the Lord's death until he comes' at the end of the account, it is to make quite explicit something that is already stated clearly in the words of institution; but it is also to support his theological reflection about what participation in the Eucharist means for Christian life. Paul sees the Lord's Supper touching life on different levels. It is a community celebration in the form of a meal. It therefore concerns the level of life that is nourished by taking food and that is offended against when people are left hungry or eat and drink too much (vv. 21–22, 33–34). It is also about the level of life that is nourished by people being together in community (vv. 2–16: each one knowing and keeping his or her place; vv. 21–22, 33–34: sharing resources and 'waiting for one another'), and therefore it is flouted when people are 'contentious' (v. 16) about rôles and divide into factions (vv. 18–19). But ultimately the Supper touches the level of life that corresponds to its being the commemoration and proclamation of the saving death of Christ until he comes again. What the Corinthians are doing is not just being selfish and contrary to the spirit and order of Christian assembly. They are taking the same attitude to the death of Jesus, proclaimed in the Supper, as those who condemned and crucified him, and hence they are 'guilty of . . . the body and blood of the Lord' (v. 27). If they are not measuring up to the reality that is given in their eating and drinking, the Supper itself condemns them (v. 29). Indeed, the Lord himself, whose Supper this is and who is therefore the real host, condemns them (v. 32). Instead of drawing life from the Supper they are left a prey to illness and death (v. 30).

Paul had already used the line of reasoning that he follows in 1 Corinthians 11 to deal with another issue of Christian life. How were Christians to relate to the world of pagan worship that surrounded them? In 10:14 he tells them to 'shun the worship of idols'. He does not give a moral or dogmatic reason for his command. He tells the Corinthians that they ought to be able to see the point for themselves if they but remembered the reality that was inherent in their own assemblies: 'The cup of blessing which we bless, is it not a participation in the blood of Christ? The bread which we break, is it not a participation in the body of Christ? Because there is one bread, we who are many are one body, for we all partake of the one bread' (1 Cor 10:16–17). His argument appeals to the significance of drinking from a single cup and eating from a single loaf. It is, on one level, a demand for loyalty toward those with whom one shares the table of the Lord. But the force of the argument comes from the reality communicated by that cup and that loaf. The reality is the body and blood of Christ. The body and blood of Christ, given in a loaf that is shared and a cup that is shared, brings with it the reality of Christian fellowship ('we who are many are one body, for we all partake of the one bread'). The body of Christ is found in Christian fellowship. If one belongs there one does not belong at the table of demons (v. 21). If Paul had spoken only about the body of Christ in this passage, without mentioning the blood, one might wonder if the reality he was arguing from was simply the fellowship and solidarity that is experienced in a common meal and expressed by calling the Christian community a body. However, the twinning of body and blood, cup and loaf, and the reference to the blessing of the cup, make it clear that it is the Eucharist as body and blood of Christ that is at the heart of his argument. The community is body of Christ because it eats of a loaf and drinks of a cup that are his body and blood. This eucharistic realism makes much more sense of the way Paul presents the Christian community as body of Christ in 1 Corinthians 12 (Benoit, pp. 72–73; Boismard in Delorme, pp. 97–99).

There is already a hint of the connection between partaking of the Eucharist and membership of the body of Christ in 1 Corinthians 6:12–20, where Paul argues against sexual immorality on the principle that 'your bodies are members of Christ'. He says: 'The body is not meant for immorality, but for the Lord, and the Lord for the body. And God raised the Lord and will also raise us up by his power. Do you not know that your bodies are members of Christ? Shall I therefore take the members of Christ and make them members of a prostitute? Never'. While he does not mention the Eucharist explicitly in this passage it is hard to believe that the ideas about being united to and in the body of Christ that he expounds later in the epistle are not already present to his mind. The model of reasoning is the same: because one is joined to the body of Christ one ought not to have any part with behaviour or institutions or persons who are contrary to what Christ stands for in his dying and rising. To know what the Eucharist is, is to know what one is oneself, and what kind of company one should keep. Here, as in the phrase about 'eating and drinking without discerning the body' in 1 Corinthians 11:29, there would be a two-sided discernment corresponding to the two-sided meaning of 'body'. The eucharistic act makes the bread to be the body of Christ and at the same time makes the community to be his body. If one is not seeing oneself and one's fellow-Christians as members of the body of Christ one can hardly claim to be accepting the word of Jesus that the bread and wine are his body and blood given for the salvation of others.

Paul does not speak about the Eucharist in any of his letters other than 1 Corinthians. And in 1 Corinthians his teaching about it is almost incidental: it occurs within a teaching about Christian life. He is clearly more interested in life than in rite. And he was a man of the word, a preacher, before being a man of rites (see 1 Cor 1:17). The fact that Paul does not refer to the celebration of the Eucharist in his letters to other churches does not mean they did not have the rite, or did not understand it in the way Paul did (*pace* Leitzmann: see below, 9.5), or that Paul considered it unimportant. But it does suggest that he was much more aware of the reality that was within the rites than of the rites themselves. He talks much more often, then, about what Christ did and is in the body, and what Christians are and do in the body of Christ, than he does about the bread which is his body. The rite, in fact, must have been a rather ordinary and un-self-conscious act of life for the earliest Christians. It was an exercise of that simple, familiar worship in spirit and in truth that distinguished the new covenant from the old. It was surely dominated by the sense of the reality and influence of the risen Christ that marked the life of the first Christian communities. Their rites of worship must have had a kind of transparency that allowed faith to go right through them to the reality of Christ himself, present in his own body, and in his body which was the living Christian community. The fact that it was being celebrated with a strong sense of waiting for the coming again of Christ ('until he comes' in 1 Cor 11:26) increased the transparency. The captivity epistles never mention the rite of the Eucharist. But they are full of the reality of the Eucharist that was expounded in 1 Corinthians. They are about the mystery of what God does in Christ, of how Christ has become life-giving and Spirit-giving in the body in which he died and rose again, of how he is joined as head to his body which is the Church, of how that Church is life-supporting through the diversity of ministries and gifts with which it is endowed, and of how Christians ought to live in this Church and in the world as they wait for the coming of the Lord.

9.1.3   St John

If Paul does not feel the need to draw attention explicitly to the rite of the Eucharist each time he addresses a Christian community, John seems to want to avoid doing so altogether. He tells the story of the Last Supper without describing the meal rite or giving the 'words of institution' on which the Christian Eucharist seems to be based. There are allusions to the rite in the discourse on the bread of life in chapter 6 of the gospel, but in the form of hints that would only register with people who already knew about the rite. The reticence about the rite has to find its explanation in the purpose and character of the fourth gospel and the other Johannine writings. The general position of R. Brown in *The Gospel According to John* and *The Community of the Beloved Disciple* offers a reasonable explanation. The author of John was, it seems, primarily concerned with the truth about Jesus, with his origin as pre-existent Word from the Father, with his being made flesh, with the divine works (signs) that he performed, with his glorification and the consequent sending of the Spirit from him. Life comes to the world from Jesus and is received by faith in him. There is reason to believe that the author of John thought that some of the institutions of the Church — teaching ministries and rites among them — were developing in a way that could obscure the centrality of Jesus himself. He was concerned to overcome this danger by showing that it is the divine power of Jesus alone that is saving and life-giving; and that the life that he gives is the life that he himself receives from the Father. Belief in him and in the truth about him is the only way to receive life. In Brown's view there are no solid grounds for saying that John is anti-sacramental. What he wants to ensure is that the ministerial structures and rites which Christian communities have (notably Baptism and Eucharist) do not obscure the centrality of Jesus and the profound truth about his relationship with the Father. He speaks about sacraments but in the language of symbolism rather than of ritualism. By this he invites believers to raise their minds to the divine realities that are signified by familiar rites and institutions that may have become settled and formal, or may have remained weighed down by a residue of Old Testament ritualism among those Christians who retained some allegiance to Judaism. He wants to tell them how life can be found in these activities by telling them how Jesus can be found in them through faith (cf. Brown, *Gospel*, I, cv–cxiv; *Community*, pp. 186, 78 and note 145, 157 and notes).

If John does not tell about the institution of the Eucharist at the Last Supper, he does tell about Jesus washing the feet of the disciples (John 13:1–20). The story of the washing of the feet may have some ritual references, particularly in relation to Baptism. However, what is interesting about it for a theology of the Eucharist is not any reference to rite but what it says about Jesus and about the life of those who would 'have a part in him' (v. 8). Jesus takes an initiative which shows the kind of life he wants to give to his disciples. They were to be together in a fellowship of service to one another. Their service was to be of the kind Jesus gave to them. He, though Lord and Master, became the servant of all, by washing their feet. In that service he was acting as host, providing the courtesies of hospitality to those he had invited to his table, but doing it himself rather than having a servant do it. He humbled himself before them. By accepting his service they 'had a part in him'. People who associated the Eucharist with the Last Supper should have been able to see the message. When they gather for the eucharistic meal the real host is not the one who presides at their table but Jesus himself. He gives people a 'part in him' by an act of becoming their servant, which he did pre-eminently by giving himself to death on the cross for their sake: in the Eucharist he is remembered in this humiliated, servant state of dying. Those who partake of the Eucharist must live together in a fellowship of mutual service in imitation of Jesus: not to do so is to have oneself judged by Jesus who gave himself for others (which is precisely what Paul said in other terms to the Corinthians).

One can find further teaching about the Eucharist in John's account of the Last Supper. There is something about the place of the word in it. John puts a long discourse and a prayer on the lips of Jesus. The rite of bread and wine is accompanied in the Eucharist by words of discourse and prayer. They are not just about the bread and wine but about the whole gift of life that the Father gives through Christ and the Spirit to those who believe and live together in his love, waiting in the midst of the world until he comes again. These are the themes of the last discourse of Jesus in John. There may even be a eucharistic reference (through a symbolic evocation of wine) in the parable/allegory of the vine (cf. Brown, *Gospel*, II, pp. 672–674). It is not that the discourse and prayer provide a model for a liturgical celebration of the Eucharist, but they do expound the great truths and hopes that the words and prayers of the Eucharist must be about if the rite is to be life-giving and bread of life.

Jesus is presented as the bread of life in chapter 6 of John's gospel. What has been said about the purpose and character of the fourth gospel, and about the distinctive way that John has of talking about rites and institutions, entitles one to read the whole chapter as a theology of the Eucharist. Later dogmatic disputes about the relationship between faith and sacrament in justification have sometimes been projected on to this chapter of John. Attempts have been made to establish that all of it is about receiving Jesus by faith in the word, which is what bread stands for, and that there is nothing in it about the sacrament of the Eucharist. There have been other attempts to divide the discourse that makes up most of the chapter into sections, some of which deal exclusively with the word and others with the sacrament. However, theology, least of all the theology of the New Testament, does not require one to choose between faith and sacrament: all receiving of Jesus is by faith, and faith is always response to the word of God; but when God makes that word concrete in a rite such as Baptism or Eucharist, faith of necessity takes the form of receiving him in that rite. A case can, indeed, be made for saying that the chapter is a putting together of different literary units, some of which were not originally eucharistic. But as the chapter, and particularly the discourse on the bread of life, now stands there is good reason to think that it is all directed towards a Christological understanding of the Eucharist (Brown, *Gospel*, I, pp. 284ff.; note his suggestion on p. 290 'that the juxtaposition of the sapiential and the sacramental themes is as old as Christianity itself. The two forms of the Bread of Life Discourse represent a juxtaposition of Jesus' twofold presence to believers in the *preached word* and in the *sacrament* of the Eucharist. This twofold presence is the structural skeleton of the . . . Roman Mass . . . '). The chapter, then, can be read from the beginning as being about Jesus and about recognizing and receiving him for who he is; as being about the life he has come to give, about how he gives it to those who receive his word in faith, and about how that word is food; about how receiving that food requires eating the flesh and drinking the blood of Jesus in what can only be the rite of the Eucharist; and finally about recognizing that what Jesus is saying is not understood by everyone: those who understand the rite in the way Jesus has explained remain with him in the fellowship of his disciples and there receive from him the gift of eternal life.

The eucharistic theology of John 6 is worked out with an extraordinary richness of detail. The author situates the events he is describing at the Passover (v. 4), thus giving them an Exodus and covenant and ritual flavour. He presents Jesus as the one who works signs (v. 2). These signs identify him as the Messiah, in the specific Johannine sense of the one sent from heaven by the Father and endowed with power to do things that only God does. The sign that Jesus performs is the feeding of a multitude with five loaves and two fish (vv. 5–14). The miraculous giving of food to the People wandering in the desert is an Exodus theme. Jesus gives food, not because he has been reminded by the disciples that the people are hungry (which was how the Synoptics told the story) but on his own initiative (v. 5). The formula used to describe what he did with the loaves echoes descriptions of what he did with the bread at the Last Supper and what Christians do at the Eucharist: he '*took* the loaves, and when he had *given thanks*, he *distributed* them . . . ' (v. 11). What Jesus provided is recognized as a kind of messianic banquet by the people (vv. 14–15). If, as Brown suggests, John sees Christian sacraments as a prolongation of the signs which Jesus worked while on earth, this messianic banquet given by Jesus can be a symbolic statement about the Eucharist: the one who is at work in the Eucharist is the one sent by the Father and manifested in signs and works. After another incident that symbolically manifests his divine power and identity (walking on the water as an evocation of the power that brought the Israelites safely across the Red Sea; 'It is I' evoking the name 'I am who am' revealed to Moses), Jesus provokes a discussion about food with the people who had followed him, and explains the real significance of the sign he had worked (vv. 22–26). He wants them to think of 'the food which endures to eternal life' (v. 27). There follows an extended discourse on 'the bread of life'. It is a Christology in which Jesus is presented as coming from the Father to give eternal life. It uses the imagery of bread and the typology of the Exodus to describe what the Father is doing in Jesus. The Father gives true bread from heaven. It is true by comparison with the manna that Moses gave in the desert which gave life but not eternal life. When Jesus has got his hearers to the point of asking (v. 34) 'Lord, give us this bread always' (John had Jesus provoke a similar request for water from the Samaritan woman in a passage of chapter 4 that is clearly about Baptism), he announces that he himself is the bread from heaven that gives eternal life: 'I am the bread of life' (v. 35). Those who believe in him, recognizing that he comes from the Father, will never hunger or thirst; they will receive eternal life and Jesus himself will raise them up on the last day. He can do so because he comes from the Father (vv. 35–50).

If the discourse on the bread of life ended at v. 50 it would be a statement of profound Christological truth but not necessarily have a bearing on the theology of the Eucharist. Verse 51, however, carries the thought forward in a way that allows all that has preceded in chapter 6 to be taken as part of a theology of the Eucharist. John wants Christians to understand the rite of the Eucharist in a Christological and theological way: by developing his Christology in terms and images of bread he has prepared it for use in a theology of the Eucharist. The first half of verse 51 is a résumé of what he has already said: 'I am the living bread which came down from heaven; if anyone eats of this bread he will live forever'; the second half opens up the question of the Eucharist: 'and the bread which I shall give for the life of the world is my flesh'. The incredulous reaction of the Jews, described by John in v. 52, leaves no doubt about how the statement is to be understood. To their question 'how can this man give us his flesh to eat?' Jesus answers: 'Truly, truly, I say to you, unless you eat the flesh of the Son of man and drink his blood, you have no life in you; he who eats my flesh and drinks my blood has eternal life, and I will raise him up on the last day. For my flesh is food indeed, and my blood is drink indeed. He who eats my flesh and drinks my blood abides in me, and I in him' (vv. 53–56). Jesus is now talking about drinking as well as eating, about blood as well as flesh. Unless the intention is to refer to the Eucharist it is hard to see why drinking should now be mentioned along with eating. If people do not eat the flesh of Jesus and drink his blood they will not have life. This is how the bread of life has now to be received. What is taken as food is the flesh of Christ, what is taken as drink is his blood. John uses the Greek *sarx* (translated 'flesh') rather than *sōma* (used by Paul and the Synoptics and translated 'body'). 'Flesh' is a key word in the Christology of the Johannine writings. 'The Word became flesh . . . ' (John 1:14). In eating his flesh Christians are receiving the one sent by the Father in all his reality, and they are recognizing him for who he is. When 'flesh' is twinned with 'blood' the words evoke the cross. In 19:34 John will describe how blood and water came from the pierced side of Jesus; and 1 John 5:8 talks about the threefold witness of the Spirit, the water and the blood. It is because he died in obedience to the Father's will that Jesus can give life, can give the Spirit. The life that he gives is the life he himself receives from the Father. It is eternal life, and those who have it will be raised up by Jesus on the last day. Already by eating his flesh and drinking his blood they abide in him and he in them. This is the deep meaning and purpose of the eating and drinking that Christians do in the rite of the Eucharist.

The final section of the discourse on the bread of life in John 6 deals with the fact that not everybody accepts what Jesus has been saying about the bread of life (vv. 60–71). It has a statement of Jesus that can cause some difficulty for the eucharistic interpretation of the whole discourse: 'It is the spirit that gives life, the flesh is of no avail; the words that I have spoken to you are spirit and life. But there are some of you that do not believe' (vv. 63–64). Brown thinks these words refer not to the specifically eucharistic part of the discourse but to what Jesus had been saying about the bread of life in vv. 35–50, which may not have originally referred to the Eucharist (Brown, *Gospel*, I, pp. 229–303). He claims that vv. 60–71 originally formed a single literary unity with vv. 35–50. The final editor of John inserted the eucharistic material of vv. 51–59, drawing out the eucharistic implications of vv. 35–50, but without adjusting the final section to eucharistic doctrine. If one does not accept Brown's hypothesis one can still understand the words of Jesus in a way that does not call into question the realism of what he had been saying about the Eucharist in vv. 51–59. Jesus prefaces his words about the flesh being of no avail with the words: 'what if you were to see the Son of Man ascending where he was before?' (v. 62). If John is writing for people who may have been celebrating the rite of the Eucharist but missing its full Christological meaning, the words of Jesus would be telling them that it was no good remembering Jesus as he was in the flesh during his earthly life if one does not believe that he is the Son of Man who came from the Father and is now glorified and sending the Spirit: it is this Jesus that gives life in the Eucharist. The eucharistic reference is possibly confirmed by the final verses of the section, which evoke the Last Supper. The twelve remain with Jesus because, as Peter confesses, he has 'the words of eternal life; and we have believed and come to know that you are the Holy One of God' (vv. 68–69). But among the twelve is Judas (vv. 70–71). The reference to the twelve and to the betrayal by Judas seems to be intended as a link between what Jesus has been saying, and indeed the whole of chapter 6, and the Last Supper.

9.1.4   *The letter to the Hebrews*

There is no clear reference to the Eucharist in Hebrews. However, the doctrine of the letter about the priesthood of Christ has a profound bearing on the theology of the Eucharist. If the rite is to be of any value for the salvation of God's People it must come through some kind of identification that it has with the high priestly offering that Jesus made in his own blood, by which the new covenant is established. Priesthood, altar, sacrifice, liturgy are unique and once for all in the new covenant. The use of covenant and sacrificial language about the Eucharist, which has been noted in the Synoptics, and in Paul and John, can never contradict the primary reference of that language, which is to Christ's own priestly person and work. Hebrews requires Christians to assemble together. The passage in which it does so must say something about the sense to be given to their assembly:

> Therefore, brethren, since we have confidence to enter the sanctuary by the blood of Jesus, by the new and living way which he opened for us through the curtain, that is, through his flesh, and since we have a great priest over the house of God, let us draw near with a true heart in full assurance of faith, with our hearts sprinkled clean from an evil conscience and our bodies washed with pure water. Let us hold fast the confession of our hope without wavering, for he who promised is faithful; and let us consider how to stir up one another to love and good works, not neglecting to meet together, as is the habit of some, but encouraging one another, and all the more as you see the Day drawing near (10:19–25).

The word of God is the great gathering force of the community of believers and the purpose of their assembly would certainly be to hear it. Hebrews is not concerned with any rites the community might perform at its assemblies (cf. 6:2). The exhortation that concludes the letter (chs 12 – 13) does, however, talk about the life of Christians in rather down-to-earth terms of daily life. Whether or not the author had thoughts about the Eucharist in his mind, what he had to say is not without relevance to whatever form of worship Christians practise. If the following passage does not refer to the Eucharist in Hebrews it certainly has applications to it which the later tradition will not miss:

> Remember your leaders, those who spoke to you the word of God; consider the outcome of their life, and imitate their faith. Jesus Christ is the same yesterday and today and for ever. Do not be led away by diverse and strange teachings; for it is well that the heart be strengthened by grace, not by foods, which have not benefited their adherents. We have an altar from which those who serve the tent have no right to eat. For the bodies of those animals whose blood is brought into the sanctuary by the high priest as a sacrifice for sin are burned outside the camp. So Jesus also suffered outside the gate in order to sanctify the people through his own blood. Therefore let us go forth to him outside the camp and bear the abuse he endured. For here we have no lasting city, but we seek the city which is to come. Through him then let us continually offer up a sacrifice of praise to God, that is, the fruit of lips that acknowledge his name. Do not neglect to do good and to share what you have, for such sacrifices are pleasing to God. Obey your leaders . . . . Pray for us . . . . Now may the God of peace who brought again from the dead our Lord Jesus, the great shepherd of the sheep, by the blood of the eternal covenant, equip you with everything good that you may do his will, working in you that which is pleasing in his sight, through Jesus Christ; to whom be glory for ever and ever. Amen (13:7–21).

9.2   THE TRADITION OF THE FATHERS

Beginning with the *Didachē*, there is regular reference to the Eucharist in the earliest literature of Christianity. It also appears very early in Christian art. There are texts that describe the Eucharist, and later there are catechetical commentaries on it. It is in these that one gets the first theological reflection on the Eucharist. There is also theological reflection on the Eucharist to be found in discussions about the incarnation and about the Church. In the patristic age the theologies of the Eucharist are the fruit of spontaneous reflection on the experience of faith rather than a deliberate discussion of technical questions. There are few if any intellectual problems about the Eucharist. One has to be careful then not to expect clear answers in these texts to the theological and dogmatic questions of later ages. One can indeed find witness to belief in the real presence and in the sacrificial character of the Eucharist in those early texts. But one does not find it in the theological terms of a later debate. The theology of the Eucharist in the Fathers, as already in the Scriptures, is more comprehensive than a theology of real presence and sacrifice. It deals with these questions and with other aspects of the Eucharist within broader questions about the work of God in Christ and in his Church.

9.2.1   The Apostolic Fathers

It is within a theology of the incarnation, directed against Docetists who deny the reality of the flesh of Christ, that Ignatius of Antioch speaks about the Eucharist in the letter *To the Smyrnaeans* (*Epistles* . . . ; trans. Kleist). Belief 'that the Eucharist is the Flesh of our Saviour Jesus Christ, which suffered for our sins, and which the Father in His loving-kindness raised from the dead' (n. 7) is so bound up with belief in the incarnation (nn. 3–4) and in 'the Passion which effects our resurrection from the dead' (n. 5), and with 'faith in the blood of Christ' (n. 6) that those who deny those truths inevitably deny the truth about the Eucharist. It is Johannine Christology brought into explicit relationship with eucharistic realism, as John himself had done in the discourse on the bread of life. Ignatius speaks more explicitly about the rite than John did. He calls it 'the Eucharist', which from the beginning of the second century comes to be used as a technical term for what the New Testament called the breaking of bread or the Lord's Supper. In his letter *To the Philadelphians* Ignatius relates the Eucharist to ecclesiology. Those who believe in Jesus are gathered into unity in the Church around the Bishop (nn. 1–3). The Eucharist expresses and guarantees this unity:

> Take care, then, to partake of one Eucharist; for, one is the Flesh of Our Lord Jesus Christ, and one the cup to unite us with His Blood, and one altar, just as there is one bishop assisted by the presbytery and the deacons, my fellow servants. Thus you will conform in all your actions to the will of God (n. 4).

The same thought, with the precision that only a Eucharist presided over or authorized by the bishop is valid, is found in *To the Smyrnaeans*, n. 8. Ignatius has several other references to the Eucharist that show its bearing on Christian life. The most beautiful expression of how the reality of the Eucharist pervades his Christian spirituality is in the way he speaks about his own coming death:

I am writing while still alive, but my yearning is for death. My Love has been crucified, and I am not on fire with the love of earthly things. But there is in me a *Living Water*, which is eloquent and within me says: 'Come to the Father'. I have no taste for corruptible food or for the delights of this life. *Bread of God* is what I desire; that is, the Flesh of Jesus Christ, who *was of the seed of David*; and for my drink I desire His Blood, that is, incorruptible love (*To the Romans*, n. 7).

St Justin follows up the description of the Eucharist which he gives in his *First Apology* (n. 65; see 8.2.3 above) with an explanation of why the Eucharist is different from ordinary food and drink. He uses an analogy with the incarnation to show how the prayer said over the bread and wine make them to be the flesh and blood of Christ:

We call this food the Eucharist, of which only he can partake who has acknowledged the truth of our teachings, who has been cleansed by baptism for the remission of his sins and for his regeneration and who regulates his life upon the principles laid down by Christ. Not as ordinary bread or as ordinary drink do we partake of them, but just as, through the word of God, our Saviour Jesus Christ became Incarnate and took upon Himself flesh and blood for our salvation, so, we have been taught, the food which has been made the Eucharist by the prayer of His word, and which nourishes our flesh and blood by assimilation, is both the flesh and blood of that Jesus who was made flesh (n. 66; trans. from Palmer).

In his *Dialogue with Trypho* Justin argues that those who believe in God, have their sins taken away in the name of his Son and are called by his word 'are now of the true priestly family of God'. As priests they offer everywhere those pure and pleasing sacrifices foretold by the prophet Malachi. Justin identifies these sacrifices as those

which Jesus Christ commanded to be offered, that is, in the Eucharist of the Bread and of the Chalice, which is offered by us Christians in every part of the world (nn. 116–117).

Admitting for the sake of argument that the prophet Malachi may have been talking about the prayers of the Jews of the Diaspora, calling them sacrifices and saying they were more acceptable to God than the sacrifices offered in the Temple, Justin makes the point:

Now, I also admit that prayers and thanksgiving, offered by worthy persons, are the only perfect and acceptable sacrifice to God. For Christians were instructed to offer only such prayers, even at their thanksgiving for their food, both liquid and solid, whereby the passion which the Son of God endured for us is commemorated . . . (n. 117).

The Christian Eucharist is here being presented as the sacrifice of the new covenant. It takes the form of a prayer said over bread and wine, at the command of Christ, in commemoration (*anamnēsis*) of his passion, on behalf of the true priestly people in whom the promises made in the old covenant are fulfilled.

St Irenaeus also sees the prophecy of Malachi fulfilled in the Eucharist (*Adversus Haereses*, IV, 17, 4). The pure offering that God wants from people is 'faith and obedience and justice for their own salvation', not burnt offerings and sacrifices. And yet, Irenaeus argues, this does not exclude the things of creation from the worship of God. In being received with thanks they are offered to God. This is what Jesus wants done in the Eucharist:

> And yet, when counselling His disciples to offer to God the first fruits from among His creatures — not as if He needed them, but lest they themselves should be unfruitful and ungrateful — He took that which is from creation, bread, and gave thanks, saying: 'This is my body'. And likewise the cup, which is of the same creation as ourselves, He confessed to be His blood, and taught a new oblation of the New Testament. This the Church receives from the Apostles and offers [it] to God throughout the world, to Him who gives us nourishment, as the first fruits of His own gifts in the New Testament. In reference to this oblation, Malachias, in the twelve Prophets, attached the following meaning in advance: 'I have no pleasure in you, says the Lord Almighty, and I will not receive a sacrifice from your hands. For, from the rising of the sun even to the going down my name is glorified among the Gentiles, and in every place incense is offered to My name, and a pure sacrifice; since great is My name among the Gentiles, says the Lord Almighty' [Malachi 1:10–11] (trans. from Palmer).

That passage is part of Irenaeus's ongoing argument about the goodness of the material world against the Gnostics. He is particularly concerned with affirming that, in the human make-up, flesh is as much the creation of the goodness of God as spirit, and that it shares in eternal life by resurrection. He argues this point on the basis of a very realistic understanding of what the Eucharist teaches about human flesh and blood because it is itself the flesh and blood of Christ:

> How can they [the Gnostics] say that the flesh yields to corruption, and does not partake of life, that flesh which had been fed on the body and blood of the Lord? Let them either change their doctrine or cease to make the aforesaid offerings. But our doctrine is in perfect accord with the Eucharist, and the Eucharist in turn confirms our doctrine. For we offer to God that which is His own, and in so doing we proclaim the union of flesh and spirit, and confess our belief in the resurrection of both flesh and spirit. For just as bread from the earth, receiving the invocation of God, is no longer common bread but a Eucharist consisting of two elements, an earthly and a heavenly, even so, our bodies, partaking of the Eucharist, are no longer corruptible, possessing as they do the hope of resurrection unto life eternal (*Adversus Haereses*, IV, 18, 6).

In a further argument about the flesh against the docetism of the Gnostics, he appeals again to the realism of the Eucharist and has a beautiful explanation of how it fits into the creative action of the Spirit and of the Word of God in the world of matter and flesh:

> When, therefore, the mixed chalice and the bread that is made receive the word of God and become a Eucharist, the body of Christ, by which the substance of our flesh grows and subsists, how can they [the Docetists] deny that the flesh is capable of the gift of God, which is life eternal, seeing that it is nourished with the body and blood of Christ, and is His member? For when the blessed Paul says in his letter to the Ephesians 'that we are members of his body, of his flesh and of his bones' [5:30], he is not speaking of spiritual and invisible man — 'For the Spirit has neither bones nor flesh' [Luke 24:39] — but of a truly human organism that is made of flesh, and nerves, and bone. It is this which is nourished by the cup, which is His blood, and by the bread, which is His body. And just as a cutting from the vine, planted in the earth, bears fruit in due season, and a grain of wheat, falling on the ground, therein dissolves, and rises again with large increase by the Spirit of God who sustains all things, and thereafter, by the Wisdom

of God, becomes fit for man's food, and at last receives the Word of God and becomes a Eucharist, which is Christ's body and blood, so too our bodies, nourished by the Eucharist, and laid in the earth there to suffer dissolution, will in due season rise again. This resurrection will the Word of God grant them to the glory of God the Father, who clothes mortality with immortality, and grants to the corruptible incorruption, God's power thus being perfected in weakness [1 Corinthians 15:43] (*Adversus Haereses*, V, 2, 3).

The description that St Hippolytus gives of the paschal Eucharist (see 8.2.3 above) includes remarks that indicate some theological reflection on how the bread and wine are made to be the flesh and blood of Christ. He uses a verbal form that Dix translates 'eucharistize' to describe what is done by and in the Eucharistic Prayer over the bread and wine. It is not the last of the strange words that will be coined throughout the history of theology to define this unique action! What the bishop does is to

eucharistize first the bread into the representation of the Flesh of Christ; and the cup mixed with wine for the antitype of the Blood which was shed for all who believed in Him (*Apostolic Tradition*, XXIII, 1).

The words translated 'representation' and 'antitype' are an attempt to explain the relationship of the bread and wine to the body and blood. They are from the language of symbolism and imaging, from a thought-pattern which accepts that some obvious things are not really what they seem to be but stand for deeper hidden realities. Some such analysis of the Eucharist has to be done sooner or later, because on the level of sense-experience the body and blood of Christ will still look and taste like bread and wine. The language of Hippolytus is a recognition of what later theology will express by saying that the flesh and blood of Christ are taken in the Eucharist sacramentally. It is in no sense a denial that the Eucharist is the body and blood of Christ. That is confirmed by the way Hippolytus contrasts 'blessed bread' with the Eucharist (i.e. bread that has been 'eucharistized' to be the body of Christ), and by the care that he expects people to take of the Eucharist when they receive it in their homes, precisely because it is the body of Christ (XXVI, XXXII).

Hippolytus uses the word 'oblation' several times to talk about the bread and wine and other gifts brought to the Bishop in the Eucharist. It is an indication of the spiritual attitude in which Christians met for the Eucharist and shared their gifts. In the text which he gives for a Eucharistic Prayer the words of institution are followed by this *anamnēsis*:

Doing therefore the 'anamnesis' of His death and resurrection we offer to Thee the bread and the cup making eucharist to Thee because Thou hast bidden us [or, found us worthy] to stand before thee and minister as priests to Thee (IV, 11).

The putting together of 'anamnesis', 'offering', 'making eucharist', 'ministering as priests' in this text gives expression to the heart of the mystery of the Eucharist. The connection between the ideas is not articulated; but taken together they leave little doubt about the sacrificial quality being attributed to the Eucharist (Bouyer, *Eucharist*, pp. 177–179). The final passage of the Prayer expresses the effect of the

Eucharist as union with God and the outpouring of the Holy Spirit (the words in square brackets may be a later addition):

> And we pray Thee that [Thou wouldest send Thy Holy Spirit upon the oblation of thy holy Church] Thou wouldest grant to all Thy Saints who partake to be united to Thee that they may be fulfilled with the Holy Spirit for the confirmation of their faith in truth, that we may praise and glorify Thee through Thy Beloved Child Jesus Christ through whom glory and honour be unto Thee with the Holy Spirit in Thy holy Church now and for ever and world without end. Amen.

9.2.2   The Eastern Fathers

It is in liturgical catechesis and occasionally in scriptural commentaries that the Fathers of the Eastern churches deal with the Eucharist. There were no real dogmatic problems about it during the patristic age, nor any issues on which churches were divided. True to their catechetical and exegetical methods, Origen and Clement of Alexandria give a highly spiritual and mystical interpretation to the eucharistic words and rites. But there is enough evidence in their writings to reassure one that they also gave them a realistic meaning, in accordance with the general faith of the Church of their time (Quasten, II, pp. 28–31, 85–87). Teaching on the Eucharist is still being expressed in predominantly scriptural and liturgical terms into the fourth century. However, there are theological developments. Some are derived from the more refined theologies of the incarnation that were worked out during those centuries. Others arise from catechetical reflection on the Eucharist itself. It is noted, for example, that if what was bread and wine at the beginning of the celebration is later the body and blood of Christ it must somehow have been changed. People were entitled to ask why and how. A fragment from a sermon of St Athanasius (d. 373) notes the fact of change and attributes it, as Irenaeus did, to the coming of the Word on the bread and wine (PG 26, 1325; quoted in Quasten, III, p. 79). St Gregory of Nyssa (d. 394) deals with the question of change in *Oratio Catechetica Magna*, chs 37ff. (PG 45, 9–106): to the idea that the change is brought about by the coming of the Word in the Eucharistic Prayer he adds a peculiar theory that Christ somehow 'digests' the bread and wine to make it his own body and blood. *Sermons* 4 and 5 of the mystagogical catecheses of St Cyril of Jerusalem are a quite full statement of the tradition of faith about the Eucharist. They raise some theological issues and offer explanations. It is to reassure the newly initiated that they themselves 'are now "of the same body" and blood of Christ' that Cyril insists on the realistic understanding of Christ's words 'this is my body . . . blood' (4, 1). He argues that if Christ could change water into wine it is credible that he could change wine into his blood (4, 2). He is thinking about the Eucharist, then, in terms of some kind of miraculous change. But immediately he recognizes that, in one sense, nothing is changed. The 'body has been bestowed on you in the form of bread and his blood in the form of wine' (4, 3). 'Form' (*tupos*) here belongs to the language of symbolism (on this terminology of Cyril cf. Yarnold, p. 93, note

23). Symbols, in the mind of Cyril, are not opposed to reality. The symbol allows the reality to be received and to transform the receiver:

> So let us partake with the fullest confidence that it is the body and blood of Christ. For his body has been bestowed on you in the form of bread and his blood in the form of wine, so that by partaking Christ's body and blood you may share with him the same body and blood. This is how we become bearers of Christ, since his body and blood spreads throughout our limbs; this is how, in the blessed Peter's words, 'we become partakers of the divine nature' (4, 3; trans. Yarnold).

Sermon 5 of the mystagogical catecheses is a commentary on the rite of the Eucharist and particularly on the Eucharistic Prayer. Cyril attributes the change of bread and wine into the body and blood of Christ to the Holy Spirit invoked in the *epiklēsis*: 'for clearly whatever the Holy Spirit touches is sanctified and transformed' (5, 7). He introduces the petitions that are made in the Eucharistic Prayer with the remark: 'When the spiritual sacrifice — this worship without blood — has been completed, we beg God over the sacrifice of propitiation for . . . ' (5, 8); and he later describes these prayers for the living and the dead as being made 'while the holy and most awesome sacrifice is being offered' (5, 9). When he is justifying praying for the dead in the Eucharistic Prayer he says that it is effective because 'we offer Christ, who has been slain for our sins, and so we appease the merciful God on their behalf and on ours' (5, 10). His commentary on the words 'Taste and see that the Lord is good', which are used to invite the faithful to come forward to receive the body and blood, is:

> Entrust this judgement not to your bodily palate, but to faith which knows no doubt. For those who taste are bidden to taste not bread and wine but the sign (*antitupos*) of Christ's body and blood (5, 20).

Cyril's description of how the body and blood of Christ are actually received is full of a sense of 'homage and reverence' (5, 22): one must be careful not to drop a particle of the body for 'to lose any of it is clearly like losing part of your own body' (5, 21). But worse still would be to 'cut yourself off from communion . . . deprive yourselves of these holy and spiritual mysteries through stain of sin' (5, 23).

Theodore of Mopsuestia deals with the Eucharist in his *Catechetical Homilies* (the last four of the sixteen homilies are edited in English translation in Yarnold, pp. 211–263; the last two, dealing with the Eucharist, are numbered IV and V). *Homily* IV begins with some reflections that connect the Eucharist with Baptism. The new birth of Baptism is an anticipation in symbol of the real new birth of resurrection when 'you will eat another kind of food which is wonderful beyond description; you will feed upon the grace of the Spirit, which will make your bodies immortal and your souls unchanging' (IV, 2). The symbolic anticipation is a real 'advance payment' of that life of the resurrection. To nourish it while we wait for the resurrection 'we need a food which is suitable for our life in the world to feed us symbolically with the grace of the Holy Spirit' (IV, 3). The Eucharist is this eschatological food. Theodore makes this thesis the cornerstone of his theology of the Eucharist.

The food that nourishes us in the life of the resurrection comes from the risen Christ. He entered into resurrection through his death. The Eucharist becomes the food of resurrection in proclaiming the death of Christ. Theodore interprets Christ's words about the bread and wine as meaning 'that by his death he will give us the world to come where our sins will be forgiven'. From this he concludes:

> It is our duty to take part in the sacrament and symbolically proclaim his passion, which will procure for us the possession of the future blessings, together with the forgiveness of our sins (IV, 7; trans. Yarnold).

He explains why this should be done in sign and symbol (IV, 8–9; cf. 13–14 for the symbolism). He insists that the bread and wine really are the body and blood of Christ, not merely symbols:

> When he gave his apostles the bread he did not say, 'this is the symbol of my body . . . ' (IV, 10).

And yet bread and wine do have a symbolic rôle. They represent another reality, which they become by the grace of the Holy Spirit. Christ

> wanted us to turn our attention from the nature of the bread and the chalice once they received the grace and the presence of the Holy Spirit and to receive them as the body and blood of our Lord (*ibid.*).

Theodore develops this thought by drawing an analogy between what happens to the bread and wine in the Eucharist and what happened to Christ himself in his death and resurrection. The argument suffers from the ambiguities of Theodore's Christology (cf. Yarnold, pp. 173 and 216, note 11), but is a brave piece of theological reasoning — Pauline rather than Johannine — that is open to an orthodox interpretation. It runs:

> For even our Lord's body did not enjoy immortality and the power to confer immortality by its own nature, but by the gift of the Holy Spirit. It was by resurrection from the dead that his body was united with the divine nature and so became immortal and the source of immortality for others (IV, 10).

Citing the words of John 6, 'It is the spirit that gives life, the flesh is of no avail', he reasons:

> He would undergo this change, he [Christ] meant, by the nature of the life-giving Spirit, which would transfer him to this state in which he would become immortal himself and confer immortality on others (IV, 11).

Theodore then applies the Christological analogy to the Eucharist:

> But if the life-giving Spirit gave our Lord's body a nature it did not possess before, we, too, who have received the grace of the Holy Spirit by sacramental symbols should not regard the offering as bread and chalice any longer, but as the body and blood of Christ. It is the descent of the grace of the Holy Spirit that transforms them, obtaining for those who receive them the gifts which we believe the faithful obtain by means of our Lord's body and blood (*ibid.*).

Because Theodore runs together in this sentence the coming of the Holy Spirit on the faithful and his coming on the gifts the logic of the argument is not quite clear. But he is obviously seeing a continuity between the transforming action of the Holy Spirit on the personal body of Christ at the resurrection, on the bread and wine in the Eucharist and on those who are nourished for immortality by receiving the Eucharist. One could have Christological difficulties about his claim that the Spirit gave 'our Lord's body a nature it did not possess before' but the analogy with the Eucharist makes it clear that he is not saying Christ ceased to be human at the resurrection. In the Eucharist the bread and wine do, indeed, receive a 'new nature', which is the body and blood of Christ; but the body and blood exist and are received in the bread and wine which now serve as sacramental symbols:

> To keep alive we take nourishment in the form of bread . . . because God decreed that it should have this power. This fact should convince us that we shall receive immortality when we eat the sacramental bread. For although it is not the nature of bread to produce this effect, once it has received the Holy Spirit and his grace, it can bring those who eat it to the enjoyment of immortality . . . . So too it is with our Lord's body, which the bread signifies: it received immortality and conferred it on others through the power of the Holy Spirit, even though it was quite devoid of immortality by its own nature (IV, 12).

Theodore's explanation of how the Eucharist is 'a kind of sacrifice we perform' tries to balance the truth that it is a memorial of the passion of Christ, and as such is his unique sacrifice, with his conviction that it is a sacrifice offered by the priestly Church. He begins his rather extended treatment of the subject in this way:

> The most important point to grasp is that the food we take is a kind of sacrifice we perform. It is true that we commemorate our Lord's death in food and drink, believing that these are the memorials of his passion, since he said himself: 'This is my body which is broken for you'. But it is evident also that what we perform in the liturgy is a kind of sacrifice. The duty of the High Priest of the New Covenant is to offer this sacrifice which revealed the nature of the New Covenant. It is clearly a sacrifice, although it is not something that is new or accomplished by the efforts of the bishop: it is a recalling of this true offering (IV, 15).

Sacrifice and priesthood go together. To show how the Eucharist is 'a kind of sacrifice we perform' Theodore explains how the bishop, who presides at the liturgy, represents Christ the High Priest. The bishop is related to Christ as the earthly to the heavenly. What he does on earth is a symbol of what is done in heaven: 'Since the bishop performs in symbol signs of the heavenly realities, the sacrifice must manifest them so that he presents, as it were an image of the heavenly liturgy' (IV, 15). Christ exercises the true (in the Platonic sense) high priesthood in heaven, where he 'is High Priest of the heavenly things, and will bring us all up there when the right time comes' (IV, 17). In the meantime, we receive the food of immortality by approaching the first fruits of these blessings, the risen Christ, in the symbols of the liturgy (IV, 18). Theodore argues that the relationship of the eucharistic liturgy to the high priestly work of Christ is ensured by the fact that it is presided over by ordained priests, and in the course of his argument gives a remarkable statement of the relationship between the kind of sacrifice that the Eucharist is and the sacrifice of Christ:

> It follows that, since there needs to be a representation of the High Priest, certain individuals are appointed to preside over the liturgy of these signs. For we believe that what Christ our Lord performed in reality, and will continue to perform, is performed through the sacraments by those whom divine grace has called to be priests of the New Covenant when the Holy Spirit comes down on them to strengthen them and ordain them [literally, 'establish them as sons of the sacrament']. This is why they do not offer new sacrifices, like the repeated immolations prescribed by the Law . . . . With priests of the New Covenant it is just the reverse: they continue to offer the same sacrifice in every place and at every time. For there is only one sacrifice which was offered for us all, the sacrifice of Christ our Lord . . . (IV, 19).

It has to be noted that, in all this development about the Eucharist as sacrifice, Theodore is relying on his basic thesis about the Eucharist being the food of immortality, symbolically anticipated in bread and wine. That is its essential relationship to the risen Christ, who became food of immortality by giving himself to death in his body and blood. It is what makes the Eucharist be the symbolic, earthly representation of the sacrifice of Christ. Being a sacrifice in this sense it gives access to the heavenly reality that is the fruit of the priestly action of Christ.

After working out his theoretical theological explanations Theodore proceeds to apply them in a step-by-step commentary on the rite of the Eucharist. His discussion on the preparation of the offerings makes much of the sacrificial nature of the Eucharist. To the idea that the bishop is minister of Christ he now adds the idea that the bishop acts on behalf of the whole community:

> For although it is the bishop who stands up to make the offering [i.e. by saying the Eucharistic Prayer] he is only acting as the tongue on behalf of the whole body (IV, 41).

He is able to call the Eucharist 'the community sacrifice' in a strong statement that comes near the end of this *Homily*:

> For the ceremony which is about to take place is a community affair. The community sacrifice is immolated and the community offering is presented on behalf of all, for those absent as well as those present, in as much as they have shared the faith and been numbered as members of God's Church and lived out their lives in it. It is evident that 'to present the offering' and 'to immolate the offering' are synonymous terms, for what is immolated and offered to God is, as it were, a dread victim. Thus St Paul says Christ 'did this once for all when he offered up himself', 'it is necessary for this priest also to have something to offer'. So, since our sacrifice is a representation of Christ's sacrifice, we call it the 'offering' or the 'presenting of the offering' (IV, 44).

In the last of his sixteen *Homilies* (Yarnold, V) Theodore continues his commentary on the rite of the Eucharist. As an example of the kind of theological question that the rite raises one may note the comment he makes about the breaking of the bread:

> When we receive one little mouthful we each receive Christ whole (V, 19);

and the example he gives to illustrate this truth, which seems like an anticipation of contemporary personalist theologies of the Eucharist:

> when we kiss, we ordinarily do so with the mouth; it is a small part of the body, but by means of it we intend to embrace the whole body. We often walk in pairs hand in hand, taking this part of the body as a sign of our fellowship (*ibid.*).

He sees the receiving of 'the divine food' as communion both in the sense of union with our Lord's body and blood and in the sense of making us part of the community of the baptized, that is, the body of Christ (V, 24). He seems to be reasoning against people who abstain from communion although present at the Eucharist when he says:

> Our Lord showed by his words that the efficacy of the sacrament lay in the eating and drinking: 'He who eats my flesh and drinks my blood will live forever'. He does not say 'He who celebrates', but 'He who eats' . . . (V, 25).

He explains at length the spiritual and moral attitudes expected of those who receive the Eucharist. But he insists that those who sin through human weakness, far from abstaining from communion, should find forgiveness and strength to overcome sin by receiving it. He recognizes that:

> If we have committed a serious sin of any kind which implies the rejection of the Law once for all, we must abstain from communion, but we should not allow ourselves to stay away from it indefinitely (V, 39).

The penitential discipline of the Church is available to bring such sinners back to the Eucharist (V, 39–44).

St John Chrysostom (d. 407) deals with the Eucharist frequently in homilies and scriptural commentaries (references in Quasten, III, p. 480). His teaching about how the Eucharist is related to the once-only sacrifice of Christ resembles that of Theodore (they studied together in Antioch). He joins the sacrificial action of Christ in the Eucharist to the action by which he makes the bread and wine become his body and blood, attributing a permanent actuality to the words he said at the Last Supper:

> It is not man who causes what is present to become the Body and Blood of Christ, but Christ Himself who was crucified for us. The priest is the representative when he pronounces those words, but the power and the grace are those of the Lord. 'This is my Body', he says. This word changes the things that lie before us; and as that sentence 'increase and multiply', once spoken, extends through all time and gives to our nature the power to reproduce itself; even so that saying 'This is my Body', once uttered, does at every table in the Churches from that time to the present day, and even till Christ's coming, make the sacrifice complete (*Hom. 1 de proditione Judae*, quoted in Quasten, III, p. 481).

The Alexandrian tradition of eucharistic theology reaches a high point in St Cyril of Alexandria (d. 444). He brings his theology of the Trinity, of the Incarnation and of grace as divinization to bear on his understanding of the Eucharist. In his commentary on the gospel of John, for example, he discusses the return of those who were once sinners to union with God through Christ and the Holy Spirit. What is restored is 'union and harmony of mind among the faithful [that] ought to be modelled on the divine unity and essential identity of the Holy Trinity, and on the perfectly interwoven accord of the persons with one another'. This being 'one in body and spirit with one another and with God' is brought about by the Only-begotten who 'mixed himself, so to speak, with this body of earth in a union of oneness that defies all telling . . . . He who is by nature God truly became a heavenly man'. He did so 'that He might invest man with the glory of fellowship and a sharing in the divine nature. For fellowship in the abiding presence of the Spirit has passed on to us, after first taking its beginning through and in Christ, who, as man like unto us, was anointed and sanctifies . . . '. It is in that powerful dogmatic synthesis that Cyril finds the meaning of the Eucharist. He continues:

> That we might attain to union with God and with one another, and that we might be made one despite that fact that we differ so peculiarly in both body and soul, the Only-begotten, with the wisdom that is proper to Him and with the counsel of the Father, devised a kind of plan. With one body, and that His own, He blesses through mystic communion those who believe in Him, and makes them one body with Himself and with each other. For who shall separate those who are joined through that sacred body in union with Christ; who shall detach them from the natural union that they have among themselves . . . . United then as all of us are to Christ through His sacred Body — since we receive the one and indivisible Christ in our own bodies — we owe the service of our members more to Him than to ourselves . . . (*PG* 74, 553–561; trans. Palmer).

9.2.3   The Latin Fathers

One can find witness to the basic faith of the church of Africa about the Eucharist in St Cyprian, as already before him in Tertullian. It is in Cyprian's *Letter* 63 to Caecilius, where he is arguing against a practice of using not wine but only water in the Eucharist; it is in his commentary on the Lord's Prayer, where he gives a eucharistic interpretation to 'our daily bread' (n. 18); and it is in various discussions about the unity of the Church. However, there is little by way of theological development in these passages. In Africa that will only come with Augustine. Meantime, St Ambrose (d. 397) contributes some important ideas to the Latin tradition. One can study them especially in his catechetical sermons collected in *De Sacramentis* (Yarnold, pp. 97–153). There, after explaining Baptism and the sealing with the Spirit in the rite of Christian initiation, he creates a dramatic build-up, at the end of *Sermon* 3 and the beginning of *Sermon* 4, about approaching the altar: 'You went there [to the baptismal font], you washed, you came to the altar, you began to see what you had not seen before: that is to say through the font of the Lord and the preaching of the Lord's passion your eyes were opened. Before, you seemed to be blind of heart; but now you began to perceive the light of the sacraments' (III, 15). The term 'altar' is explained by means of types from the Old Testament and a reminder that the baptized are a priestly people (IV, 3). What they see on the altar is the sacraments, i.e. bread and wine, things common and familiar in themselves but with a symbolism more ancient and profound than the sacraments of Judaism, because derived from Melchizedek and actually established by Christ who is a priest according to the order of Melchizedek (IV, 8–13). There is something of a theology of the Eucharist as sacramentalizing the priesthood of Christ in these allusions.

There is a more straightforward piece of theological explanation in the answer that Ambrose goes on to give to a supposed objection, that the Eucharist is just ordinary bread:

> Perhaps you say: 'The bread I have here is ordinary bread'. Yes, before the sacramental words are uttered this bread is nothing but bread. But at the consecration this bread becomes the body of Christ. Let us reason this out. How can something which is bread be the body of Christ? Well, by what words is the consecration effected, and whose words are they? The words of the Lord Jesus. All that is said before are the words of the priest: praise is offered to God, the prayer is offered up, petitions are made for the people, for kings, for all others. But when the moment comes for bringing the most holy sacrament into being, the priest does not use his own words any longer: he uses the words of Christ. Therefore, it is Christ's word that brings this sacrament into being. (15.) What is this word of Christ? It is the word by which all things were made. The Lord commanded and the heavens were made . . . . If, then, there is such power in the word of the Lord Jesus that things begin to exist which did not exist before, how much more powerful it is for changing what already existed into something else (IV, 14–15).

Ambrose is inviting his hearers to reason things out. There is no reasoning about the fact that the bread and wine are the body and blood of Christ. That is a given of faith. The reasoning is that if they were not the body and blood from the beginning, then they must have *become* it. That becoming is called a consecration: to be made the body and blood is to be made holy. A becoming has to have some cause. Ambrose assumes that the cause must have something to do with the words said by the priest, 'this is my body . . . blood'. These are the words that consecrate and bring the sacrament into being. The question then is, how can words do such a thing? The answer of Ambrose is that these words are the words of Christ. He proves that by noting that the priest speaks them, not as his own words but as the words of Christ. Ambrose then makes a theological identification between words (*sermones*) of Christ in the plural and word (*sermo*) in the singular. This is the principle which allows him to argue that the words of consecration can make bread and wine become the body and blood of Christ: they have within them the power of the Word by which all things were made, so they can very well change what already exists into something else. Western theology of the Eucharist will make much of this idea of changing what already exists into something else.

Indeed, the whole line of reasoning followed by Ambrose in this text became standard in Western theology up to the time of the Reformation. Sometimes the final part of it (connecting the words with the Word) would be forgotten and the words of consecration would seem to be given a power within themselves. At other times, when a predominantly juridical judgement was being made about the Eucharist, it would seem that their power was thought to consist simply in their being the fulfilment of a command: if one said the words one was supposed to say the Eucharist would be valid and the consecration would follow. For Ambrose, however, as for the Fathers generally, the words consecrate because the divine, creative Word of God is present and acting in them. The Eucharist truly is a mystery. Ambrose is not particularly concerned about identifying the exact moment of consecration. He pays attention to the whole Eucharistic Prayer in the sermon (V, 21–29). However, his argument does, in fact, link the consecration with the saying of 'the words of consecration'. This becomes a standard position in Western theology, and later puts it in some conflict with the Eastern tradition which came to associate the consecration with the invocation of the Holy Spirit on the gifts more than with the saying of the Lord's words.

Having affirmed the reality of the change in the sacrament Ambrose has to face the difficulty that the bread-made-body and the wine-made-blood do not look like body and blood. His explanation is that 'I do not see the appearance (*species*) of blood. No, but the likeness (*similitudo*) is there' (IV, 20). This is his way of saying that the blood is received in a symbol, 'in order that nothing of the horror of blood may be there and at the same time that the price of our redemption may become operative' (*ibid.*). He returns to this theme in his final homily where, having recalled what he had said about the power of the word of God 'to change and transform (*convertere*) the fixed natural species (*genera instituta naturae*)', he shows how the realism of body and blood, that is required in order to preserve 'the grace of redemption' in the Eucharist, can be maintained without provoking the natural 'horror of blood': 'you receive the sacraments in symbolic form (*in similitudinem*) but you receive the grace and efficacy of Christ's real . . . nature (*verae naturae*)' (VI, 3).

Finally, one may note that Ambrose is satisfied to let the liturgy of the Eucharist speak for itself about its being a sacrifice. He quotes the prayer of offering that follows the *anamnēsis* of the death, resurrection and ascension (in a text which is almost identical with the corresponding part of the Roman Canon):

> And we offer you this spotless sacrifice (*hostiam*), this spiritual sacrifice, this bloodless (*incruentum*) sacrifice, this holy bread and chalice of eternal life, and we beseech and pray you to take up this offering (*oblationem*) by the hands of your angels to your altar on high, just as you were graciously pleased to receive the gifts of your just servant Abel, and the sacrifice of our father Abraham, and the offering the high priest Melchizedek made to you (IV, 27).

The eucharistic offering heralds the remission of sin because it heralds the death of the Lord; and what it heralds it actually does:

> What is it the apostle says about every time you receive it? 'As often as we receive it, we herald the death of the Lord.' If we herald his death, we herald the remission of sins. If whenever his blood is shed, it is shed for the remission of sins, I ought always to receive him so that he may always forgive sins. Since I am always sinning, I always need the medicine (IV, 28).

At the risk of over-systematizing the rich and abundant material about the

Eucharist that can be found in the writings of St Augustine (texts in Lang; Palmer, pp. 208–213, 215–216, 281–288), one can deal with it successively in relation to his Christology, to his ecclesiology, to his general sacramental theology, and finally to his theology of sacrifice. Much of what Augustine says affirms the general tradition of faith and need not be repeated. What needs to be looked at are the points on which he showed some theological originality, and those which had a significant influence on later Latin theology.

Since Christology teaches that Christ is the divine Son of God who took flesh for our salvation it requires that he be adored in that flesh which is given to us to eat for our salvation:

> For He assumed from earth — since flesh is of the earth, and from Mary's flesh He took flesh; and because in His very flesh He walked on earth, and because His very flesh He gave us to eat for our salvation — and no one eats that flesh unless he has first adored it — we find how that footstool of the Lord may be adored, and not only do we not sin by adoring, but we sin by not adoring (*Comm. on Ps.* 98: *PL* 37, 1264; trans. Palmer).

Christ is mediator between God and humans, a priest who offers himself in sacrifice:

> Hence that true Mediator, inasmuch as He was made the mediator between God and man by assuming the form of a servant, the man Christ Jesus — although in the form of God He receives sacrifice along with the Father, with whom He too is God — yet, in the form of a servant He preferred to be rather than to receive a sacrifice, lest anyone should take occasion from this to believe that sacrifice is to be offered to any creature whatever. For this reason He is also priest, the very one who offers and the very offering. And He willed that the sacrifice of the Church should be the daily sacrament (sign) of this. Since she is the body of this head, through Him she is taught to offer herself . . . . To this supreme and true sacrifice all false sacrifices have given way (*The City of God*, 10, 20: *PL* 41, 281ff.).

Christ is now risen, and that is the key to understanding what he means when he says 'unless you eat my flesh and drink my blood you will not have life in you'. Among the many commentaries which Augustine made on this text is this characteristic passage:

> Do you think that I am speaking of this body which you see, as though I were about to make it into pieces by cutting up my members and giving them to you? What 'then, if you shall see the Son of Man ascending to where He was before?' Surely He who can ascend in His entirety cannot be consumed. Thus He gave us His body and blood for our salutary refreshment, and at the same time solved in a few words the great problem of His own integrity (wholeness). Therefore, let those eat who eat, and drink who drink; let them hunger and thirst: life let them eat, life let them drink. To eat thereof is to be remade; but you are remade in such a way as not to unmake that by which you are remade. To drink thereof, what else but to live? Eat life, drink life; you will have life, and life remains whole and entire. Then shall it come to pass that the body and blood of Christ will be life to each one, when that which is received visibly in the sacrament is in very truth spiritually eaten, spiritually drunk (*Sermon* 131: *PL* 38, 730).

When Augustine thinks about the body of Christ that is given in the Eucharist he is thinking at the same time of the body of Christ that is made by the Eucharist. His ecclesiology — which is worked out predominantly in terms of the body of Christ — pervades his eucharistic theology. 'Body' draws together Christ, the Church and the Eucharist in his thinking:

> . . . the whole redeemed city, that is to say, the congregation and community of the saints is offered as a corporate sacrifice through the great Priest, who also offered Himself in his passion for us, in the form of a servant, that we might be the body of so glorious a head. As a servant He offered Himself; in this form was He offered, because in this form is He mediator, in this form priest. Now therefore the Apostle, having exhorted us to present our bodies a living sacrifice, holy and acceptable to God, our spiritual worship . . . says, ' . . . so we though many are one body in Christ, and individually members of one another . . . ' (Romans 12:5). This is the sacrifice of Christians: we the many are one body in Christ. And this also is the sacrifice which the Church continually celebrates in the sacrament of the altar — which is known to the faithful. In it the Church learns that in the offering which she makes she herself is offered . . . (*The City of God*, 10, 6: *PL* 41, 281ff.).

The Eucharist is the source of unity, especially when seen in continuity with Baptism and Confirmation:

> If you receive well, you are what you have received. For the Apostle says: 'one bread, one body, we the many' (cf. 1 Corinthians 10:17) . . . . In this bread you are reminded how you ought to love unity. For is that bread made from a single grain? Were there not many grains of wheat? But before they came to be bread, they were separate. By water and a process of pulverization (*contritionem*) they were united. For unless wheat is crushed and sprinkled with water, it can in no way take on that form which is called bread. In like manner, you too were first crushed under the humiliation of the fast and the sacrament of exorcism. Then, baptism in water was added. You were, as it were, wetted down that you might take on the shape of bread. But until there is fire there is no bread. Where then is the symbol of fire? It is in the anointing. For oil is the sacrament of the Holy Spirit, our fire . . . . After water, then, the Holy Spirit is added, fire; and you become bread, which is the body of Christ. In this way, so to speak, unity is symbolized (*Sermon 227: PL* 38, 1099–1100).

Augustine makes much of the symbolism of bread and wine — of their making and of their eating and drinking. That, combined with his repeated insistence that one must eat 'spiritually', can give the impression that he thinks the Eucharist to be only a symbol of the body of Christ. Later theology, during the Middle Ages and at the Reformation, was able to quote him on both sides of the debate about what had then become the issue of the real presence. It is here that one needs to interpret his theology of the Eucharist in the light of his general sacramental theology. The rites of the Church do belong to the world of sign and symbol. To call them sacraments is to say so. But it is also to say that they hold within themselves a reality (*res*) which they bring about. The effect of a sacrament is complex. Augustine had to establish against the Donatists that a sacrament can bring about a certain reality — and therefore be a real, true sacrament — even when it does not bring about its ultimate effect, which is the grace of the Holy Spirit. While he worked out that theory mainly with reference to Baptism, there is also room for it in his understanding of the Eucharist (Camelot, pp. 405, 409).

In the celebration of the Eucharist there is a level of sheer symbolism: it is exploited freely by mind and imagination. Underlying this, and brought about by the celebration, there is a level of sacramental reality: the Eucharist really is the body and blood of Christ. Because this level is not yet itself the ultimate reality of the Eucharist but points forward to it, Augustine can still call it the sacrament (later theology will call it the *res et sacramentum*): it is the real body and blood of Christ, but acting, in the form of bread and wine, as a sign of an even deeper reality. That deeper reality is still the body of Christ, but now uniting to itself in a single body those who are receiving the grace of the Holy Spirit: the ultimate reality (*res*) of the Eucharist is the unity of the Church as body of Christ. It is to this body of Christ that most of Augustine's attention is directed in his eucharistic theology. He is interested in the sacramental body and blood as a sacrament of the unity of the mystical body, more than as a reality to be thought about in its own right. To eat only of the sacrament (which sinners can do) profits nothing. One must eat spiritually. To eat spiritually is to eat in faith and love, recognizing and accepting the reality of the unity of the body of Christ that is signified and brought about by the Eucharist.

There is nothing novel about Augustine's clear statements that the Eucharist is a sacrifice or about the way he identifies it with the one true sacrifice of Christ. What is distinctive, and had considerable influence on later Western theology, is the general theory of sacrifice he applied to the Eucharist and the way his idea of sacrament affects the application. Augustine develops a teaching on sacrifice in Book 10 of *The City of God*. He is contrasting the beliefs and practices of Christians with those of the pagan world. In chapters 4 and 5 he stresses the interiority and spirituality of what Christians understand by sacrifice. In a phrase that will be much used in mediaeval theology he says that 'visible sacrifice is a sacrament, that is to say a sacred sign of invisible sacrifice'. Another definition of sacrifice that will be prized in the Middle Ages appears at the beginning of chapter 6: 'Now, a true sacrifice is every work done that we may cleave to God in holy fellowship, a work that is related to that supreme good in which we can find our true beatitude'. This definition allows him to explain how Christians offer true sacrifice by living in the service of God, how all these sacrifices are offered to God by Christ the High Priest who offered himself in his passion to make us members of his body (see above). It is this reality of Head and members, offering and being offered together, 'which the Church continually celebrates in the sacrament of the altar'. The Eucharist is a sacrifice because it is the sacrament or sacred sign of that one reality, which is the self-offering of Christ, head and members. The Eucharist can be a sign of Christ's sacrifice because it has some similarity with it:

> Christ was immolated in himself only once, and yet sacramentally (*in sacramento*) he is immolated not only in every celebration of Easter but every day for the people: if one is asked about it one will not lie in saying that he is immolated. If sacraments did not have some similarity with the things of which they are sacraments they would not be in any way sacraments (*Letter* 98: PL 33, 363).

Thus, while Augustine uses a technical analysis of sacrifice, drawn from the meaning the word has in general religious language, to talk about the Eucharist as sacrifice, he transforms it profoundly by working into it his concept of sacrament.

9.3   MEDIAEVAL THEOLOGY

There is reciprocal influence between theological thinking about the Eucharist and its liturgical celebration. Some of the features of liturgical practice that go hand in hand with theological development in the Latin church during the Middle Ages are: an increasing passivity of the lay members of the congregation, who tended to look on the Eucharist as something which the clergy did for them rather than as something in which they joined actively with the clergy; the gradual silencing of the word component of the celebration, because of the continuing use of a Latin language that was less and less understood, and also of the use of a subdued tone of voice in the saying of many of the prayers, including the Eucharistic Prayer; the gradual disappearance of communion from the chalice for the faithful, and the substitution of loaves of bread by wafers of unleavened bread already divided into particles; increasing abstention from communion by those who were present at the Eucharist; the development of forms of devotion to the reserved sacrament, and a spiritual fascination with Christ present in it; the multiplying of Masses celebrated without a congregation for private intentions and occasions. The theological questions that got most attention during the Middle Ages reflect these features of liturgical practice; and the theological answers proposed influenced practice. The question of the relationship between the body of Christ and the bread which was consecrated and eaten and reserved in the Eucharist was debated at length. There were also some questions about the use or reception of the Eucharist and about how it produced its effects. The tradition that the Eucharist is a sacrifice got some attention in that context (it produced effects as a sacrifice even for those who did not receive it sacramentally) but was not really a major issue in mediaeval theology. The questions that were asked about the body of Christ and its relationship to the bread of the Eucharist had, obviously, also to be asked about the blood of Christ in relation to the wine; and answers had to be along the same lines. Quite frequently the discussion was just about body and bread. To some extent this was a form of theological shorthand: if one said something basic about body and bread one was not expected to repeat it each time about blood and wine. But it must also have reflected a certain concentration on the body of Christ apart from the blood, both in theology (corpus Christi was by itself a bridge with ecclesiology and Christology in a way that sanguis Christi was not) and in devotion (when communion was taken only under the form of bread and the reserved corpus Christi became an object of devotion in the way sanguis Christi did not). The concentration on certain questions does not mean that the broad tradition of faith about the Eucharist was altogether absent during the Middle Ages. It continued to be carried by the Scriptures, by the liturgy itself, and by the writings of the Fathers that were known. It sometimes found expression in allegorical commentaries on the liturgy which, for all their lack of discipline, transmitted a sensitivity to the mystery of the Eucharist that the better mediaeval theologians never lost, for all their stern reasoning.

9.3.1 Ninth to twelfth centuries

The first questions about the Eucharist arose when the scholars of the ninth century began to apply the rules of grammar and logic to statements about the sacrament that were to be found in the Scriptures and in texts of the Fathers, particularly of Augustine. There were texts that said quite simply that the bread taken in the Eucharist was Christ's body and that the wine was his blood. On the other hand there was John 6:63: 'It is the spirit that gives life, the flesh is of no avail'. Augustine had commented enthusiastically on that text, saying that in the Eucharist the body of Christ was eaten spiritually, or sacramentally, or *in figura*; it was not eaten carnally or 'capharnaitically' (a word coined from Capharnaum where, according to John 6:59, the carnal, almost cannibalistic caricature of what was meant by 'eating the flesh' of Jesus was first put forward and ridiculed). What was meant by these statements? Did the body of Christ that they spoke of refer to the flesh-and-blood body that was born of Mary and is now glorified in heaven? Or was it some kind of spiritual body that was being received spiritually? Or was it the body of Christ that is the Church (which was coming to be called by the originally eucharistic term 'mystical body' in those centuries)? Questions of this kind were launched by Amalarius of Metz (d. 850) in the course of a commentary on the Mass. They were taken up by Paschasius Radbertus (d. 860) in his *De Corpore et Sanguine Domini* (*PL* 120, 1267–1350). He takes what has been called a 'realist' position (in contrast to the more symbolical, if not allegorical, position of Amalarius). The body that is said to be eaten in the Eucharist is identical with the body born of Mary, because that is the only body that can give salvation and that can be head of the body of the redeemed which is the Church. The Eucharist is the *veritas* (truth, reality) of the body of Christ, whereas the rites of the Old Testament were simply its *figura*. However, this real body of Christ is present in the Eucharist in signs; it is eaten mystically (*in misterio*) and not in a way that is perceptible to the senses. There is nothing 'capharnaitic' about the eating. But the realism is strong in the thinking of Paschasius. When he wants to explain how the body of the risen Christ could be present within a host, and in so many hosts, he postulates a miraculous multiplication of the flesh of Christ analogous to the multiplication of the loaves recorded in the gospels. He seems to suggest that the bread is replaced by the flesh of Christ: the *veritas* (reality) of the Eucharist is the body of Christ; the bread is only an appearance, serving as a *figura* of the body of Christ. He attributed this change of reality in the bread to the miraculous work of the Holy Spirit, putting it in line with his work of uniting the divine to human flesh in the incarnation, and seeing it as preparing humans for the final miracle of their transformation in the resurrection (text from Paschasius in Palmer, p. 223).

The position of Paschasius seemed novel and exaggerated to Rabanus Maurus (d. 856). He had no doubts that the bread consecrated in the Eucharist is really the body of Christ. But he and others questioned the simple identification of what was eaten in the Eucharist with the historical body of Christ. He thought, for instance, that this would suggest that Christ actually died each time the Eucharist was celebrated. The opponents of Paschasius distinguished between the historical body of Christ, the ecclesial body and the eucharistic body. Although these three were *naturaliter* identical they were *specialiter* distinct. That meant for these grammarians and logicians that one could not talk about one the way one talked about the other. They thought Paschasius was confusing different kinds of language and so saying things that were false (text from Rabanus in Palmer, p. 226). Ratramnus of Corbie (d. 868) was one of those who opposed Paschasius. In his *De Corpore et Sanguine Domini* (*PL* 121, 125–170) he tries to work out what can and cannot be said about the Eucharist by introducing a type of analysis that today might be called epistemological. He takes the common Augustinian terminology of *veritas/figura* as referring to the way things are known rather than to what is known: *veritas* is what is attained in direct perception; what is known *in figura* is what is known through the symbolism of what is directly perceived. According to this terminology the *veritas* of the Eucharist is bread; the body of Christ is in the bread *in figura*, because it is perceived through the symbolism of the bread. The *veritas* of the body of Christ is now in heaven. That body is present in the Eucharist, not *corporaliter* or *in veritate* (i.e. not precisely as a body) but *in figura*. In the terms proposed by Ratramnus this presence *in figura* is the only way that the body of Christ could be present and life-giving in the Eucharist. He thinks that the explanation of Paschasius, in affirming that it is the risen body of Christ, which was born of Mary, that is truly present in the Eucharist, is affirming a corporeal presence of the sort that the tradition of faith, especially as expounded by Augustine, said was of no avail. The *veritas* of the body of Christ is what was present on earth during his life, on the cross in his dying, and is now in heaven; it is a body animated by physical, biological life. It is not that corporeal life that is communicated in the Eucharist, says Ratramnus, but spiritual life. The presence of the body of Christ in the Eucharist is spiritual, the eating of it is spiritual, the life that it gives is spiritual. The eucharistic body, like the ecclesial body, is, indeed, identical with the body born of Mary, but not with the corporal form that it took on earth and now takes in heaven (text from Ratramnus in Palmer, pp. 224–226).

The approach of Ratramnus was taken up with even greater dialectical rigour two centuries later by Berengarius of Tours (d. 1088) in his *De Sacra Cena* (ed. Beekenkamp). For his pains he has the distinction of being the first theologian to be condemned, by a Synod of the Roman Church, for a teaching on the Eucharist. The question he raised was, once again, the relationship between the consecrated bread and the body of Christ. His thinking on the question was founded on faith but was affected by certain elements of philosophical analysis that were then being introduced into theology by the dialecticians. In particular, he assumed that the reality of a thing was known by its appearances, and therefore that a thing must really be what it seemed to be. If what was on the altar seemed to be bread it must be bread (Powers, p. 28). Berengarius believed that what is received in the Eucharist is the body of Christ. He took from the Augustinian tradition that it was received and eaten spiritually. For Berengarius the qualification 'spiritually' meant that the body of Christ was there not in a bodily way, not materially, not as an object of sensation. His philosophical position would not allow for any change in the bread: if it seems to be bread then it is bread, not merely its appearance. Nor did he see any reason why it should change. In his view what happens at the consecration is that, while continuing to be what it is, the bread begins to be the sign of the life-giving body of Christ that is thus present and eaten spiritually. Neither does this involve any change in the body of Christ. It does not come down from heaven, nor is it multiplied in many hosts as Berengarius understood the proponents of the realist position to be saying. It is active and life-giving in the Eucharist, but present only spiritually and in the sign of bread.

The opponents of Berengarius, the most prominent of whom was Lanfranc, Archbishop of Canterbury (cf. his *De Corpore et Sanguine Domini*: PL 150, 407–442), argued that his theory denied that the bread really became the body of Christ at the consecration; he was not therefore, they argued, confessing the faith of the Church that what is eaten in the Eucharist truly is the real body of Christ. They claimed that his theory said no more than that the bread is a sign through which the heavenly Christ is believed to be active and life-giving (texts from Lanfranc in Palmer, pp. 229–231). That, too, was the judgement of two Roman Synods that devised professions of faith that Berengarius was required to make by way of renouncing his errors. The way the faith is expressed in these texts shows the uncertain state of theological thinking and language about the Eucharist at that time. The first formula, imposed by a Roman Synod of 1059, states the faith of the Church in a language of rather extravagant realism that leaves little place for sacramentality: ' . . . the bread and wine . . . are not only the sacrament but the real body and blood . . . and in a tangible way (*sensualiter*), not just sacramentally but in truth are handled and broken by the priest and chewed by the faithful . . . ' (DS 690). It is a formula that St Bonaventure would later criticize as *nimis expressa* (*IV Sent*. d. 12, I, 3, 1), and St Thomas would feel the need to explain away (IIIa, 77, 7 ad 3). The second formula, which the recalcitrant Berengarius was required to sign by a Roman Synod of 1079, is more carefully worded. It avoids the epistemological ambiguities associated with *sensualiter* and *in veritate*, and the use of 'handling, breaking, chewing' in relation to the body of Christ. It uses language that allows it to state what the Eucharist is objectively rather than in terms of our perception of what it is; it is more metaphysical than epistemological. The profession of faith is:

I, Berengar, believe in my heart and confess with my lips that the bread and wine which are placed on the altar are, by the mystery of the sacred prayer and the words of the Redeemer, substantially changed (*substantialiter converti*) into the true and proper and life-giving body and blood of Jesus Christ our Lord; and that, after consecration, they are Christ's true body, which was born of the virgin and hung on the cross, being offered for the salvation of the world, and which sits at the right hand of the Father; and Christ's true blood, which was poured forth from His side; not only by way of sign and by the power of the sacrament (*non tantum per signum et virtutem sacramenti*) but in their true nature and in the reality of their substance (*in proprietate naturae et veritate substantiae*) (DS 700; ND 1501).

The suggestion that this text marks a concentration on the ontological reality of the Eucharist, and a shift away from the more epistemological concerns that were prominent in the debates of earlier mediaeval theology, is borne out by the appearance of the word *substantia* in it. The body of Christ is no longer said to be there *in veritate* but *in veritate substantiae*. The previous history of the word 'substance' had prepared it to serve in discussions about the ontological reality of the Eucharist (cf. Schillebeeckx, *Eucharist*, pp. 70ff.). It had been in Latin theological language from the beginning. It appears in Latin versions of the Scriptures: in Hebrews 11:1 ('faith is the *substantia* of things hoped for, the conviction of things not seen'), and in Matthew's version of the Lord's Prayer, where what is nowadays rendered in English as 'our daily bread' is *panis super-substantialis* (Matt 6:11). It played a prominent part in dogmatic debates about the Trinity (cf. *consubstantialis* in the Nicene Creed) and about the incarnation. While the word was given technical overtones and some philosophical honing in these debates it continued to be used in a general non-technical sense for what is solid and permanent in a given reality, for the abiding nature of a thing which holds steady when its appearances change, for the 'real thing' as distinct from what it might seem to be. It is found in a text thought to be from the fifth-century Faustus of Riez (*PL* 30, 272; cf. Schillebeeckx, *Eucharist*, p. 73) that speaks of a change of bread and wine into the substance of the body and blood of Christ. But it does not seem to have gained a significant place in the vocabulary of eucharistic theology until the time of the condemnation of Berengarius. From then on it is the key word in mediaeval theological discussion about the reality of the Eucharist. It was there before the introduction of Aristotelian philosophy into the mediaeval universities. The meaning given to it was eventually influenced by that philosophy; but it always kept a certain theological independence. In the profession of faith imposed on Berengarius it is used in a phrase that states the genuineness and realness of the body of Christ that the consecrated bread becomes. It is not yet strong enough to carry the meaning all by itself, but requires the support of other words: *in proprietate naturae et veritate substantiae*. But it has already been used in an adverbial form earlier in the text and it is this use that really makes its fortune in theology: the bread and wine are said to be 'substantially changed' (*substantialiter converti*) into the body and blood of Christ by the mystery of prayer, i.e. the Eucharistic Prayer for consecration and the words of institution. The change from bread to body is put on the level of substance.

The idea that bread and wine are changed into the body and blood of Christ in the Eucharist is already present in the Fathers (see above, 9.2). The change was variously attributed to the Holy Spirit and to the Word of God, and likened to what happened to human flesh in the incarnation. The Greek tradition developed various words beginning with *meta-*, corresponding to Latin words beginning with *trans-*, and to their English equivalents transform, transfigure, transmute etc. to describe the change (Schillebeeckx, *Eucharist*, pp. 65–67). The theological and philosophical horizon in which the Greeks used these terms was not quite the same as that in which the Latins used 'transubstantiation', especially after Aristotle had become a force in Western theology (Schillebeeckx, *Eucharist*, pp. 67–69). Although they affirmed the change every bit as strongly as the Latins they were not very much concerned about whether or how the bread ceased to be bread when the change occurred. For the Latins, however, that became a critical question. Berengarius thought the bread did not, and could not, cease to be bread and simply remain an appearance. The profession of faith required him to affirm that the bread was 'substantially changed'. That was not yet an explicit statement that the bread ceased to be bread. There is no direct reference in the text to the substance of bread. However, the qualification of the change as substantial, and the use of substance to affirm the kind of reality that the body and blood of Christ have in the Eucharist inevitably required reflection on the substance of bread. It is into that kind of reflection that the word 'transubstantiation' fits. It appears around 1140 in the works of Etienne de Baugé (*PL* 172, 1291–1293) and Roland Bandinelli (later Pope Alexander III) in his *Sententiae* (ed. J. Gietl, p. 231). It defined the change of bread and wine into the body and blood of Christ that is confessed in the tradition of faith as a change of the substance of bread into the substance of Christ's body, and of the substance of wine into the substance of Christ's blood. It measured up to the realism about the presence of the body and blood of Christ in the Eucharist required by the profession of faith of Berengarius. It also offered some explanation of how what seemed to be bread was no longer so, because it said that the substance under the appearances was no longer that of bread but of the body of Christ. It became a standard term in mediaeval theology of the Eucharist from the middle of the twelfth century onward. It found its way into the *magisterium* at the Fourth Lateran Council in 1215 (DS 802). At first it had no technical philosophical connotations, other than the general sense derived from what the word 'substance' meant in Graeco-Roman culture. When the philosophy of Aristotle won its way into Catholic theology in the thirteenth century it offered an analysis of reality in which the category of substance played an important part. That analysis was found useful by some theologians who wanted to push the understanding of transubstantiation to its intellectual limits with a view to a better understanding of the Eucharist. It was also found useful by them as a protection against a certain grossness that the theory of transubstantiation, badly understood, could leave in people's perception of how the body and blood of Christ were present and received in the Eucharist.

9.3.2 St Thomas Aquinas

There is much more to the eucharistic theology of the Middle Ages than a doctrine of transubstantiation (cf. Macy, Introduction). While the question of the sense in which bread and wine become the body and blood of Christ at the consecration was central from the beginning, and loomed large right to the end, it was not dealt with in isolation from the broad tradition of eucharistic faith and practice that the mediaeval world inherited from the Fathers. Earlier writings may be somewhat one-sided because they are occasional and controversial. The controversies and special interest remain noticeable even in the more systematic works and *Summas* that come to be written later, but there is in them, nevertheless, a better sense of balance. The treatment of the Eucharist in the *Summa Theologiae* of St Thomas Aquinas is a fine example of mediaeval systematic theology. Apart from its intrinsic worth as theology it also has to be studied because of its historical influence on the distinctively Catholic tradition about the Eucharist.

Thomas studies the Eucharist within his treatment of the sacraments of the Church. In his general discussion on sacraments he establishes that it is the most important (*potissimum*) of the seven and that all the others are somehow directed towards it (IIIa, 65, 3). He deals with it after Baptism and Confirmation, showing sensitivity to the liturgical appropriateness of following this order (cf. IIIa, 72, 12 ad 3). He organizes his thinking in a sequence of questions that is dictated by his general theory of the sacramental economy (see 2.6 above). Firstly, he asks whether and how the Eucharist is a sacrament (q. 73); then he analyses it in terms of the essential matter (qq. 74–77) and form (q. 78) that must come together in it to constitute the sacramental sign; then he looks at the effects produced in and by this sign (q. 79), and at the sacramental action and attitudes of the people who take these effects to themselves (qq. 80–81); finally, he asks about the minister of the Church who leads the making of the sacramental sign (q. 82) and about the full liturgical rite in which the Eucharist is celebrated (q. 83).

The first of this series of questions (q. 73) is crucial: in establishing that the Eucharist is a sacrament in the technical sense Thomas identifies the special kind of reality that it is and the peculiar categories that must be used to understand it. He builds his case for the sacramentality of the Eucharist from the outside inwards, going from the symbolic action to what is symbolized: the symbolic action is the taking of food and drink in a meal; what it symbolizes is the nourishing of that spiritual life that the whole sacramental economy is meant to cultivate (a. 1–2). In relating the Eucharist to life and seeing it as nourishment Thomas is drawing on the Johannine tradition about the Eucharist as bread of life. Next, Thomas asks if the Eucharist is necessary for salvation: it has to be so in some way in order to be recognized as a sacrament of the Church. In establishing its necessity for salvation he introduces the ecclesial symbolism of the Eucharist and the Pauline tradition about the body of Christ. As a meal of bread and wine the Eucharist sacramentalizes a life of unity with others in the mystical body of Christ, outside which there is no life or salvation. (Thomas takes advantage of his general sacramental theory at this point to show that the ecclesial reality of the Eucharist can be received by desire for the sacrament, and how that desire is included in Baptism.) The third step Thomas takes to establish the sacramentality of the Eucharist is to show that it has the threefold significance for past, present and future that is characteristic of the sacramental economy. He finds that reflected in three names which the tradition had given to the Eucharist — sacrifice, communion and viaticum (a. 4). The Eucharist looks to the past by commemorating the passion of Christ; the passion was a sacrifice; as the sacrament of that sacrifice the Eucharist is itself called *sacrifice*. From this early stage of his discussion on the Eucharist Thomas is seeing sacrament and sacrifice as interwoven: it is a sacrament because it symbolizes, among other things, the life-giving sacrifice of Christ; it is a sacrifice because it is a symbolic commemoration of the sacrifice of Christ. Thomas has no treatment of the Eucharist as sacrifice apart from his treatment of it as sacrament. He has no treatise on the Mass. All that he has to say about the Mass, and about its sacrificial nature, is said under the heading of the sacrament of the Eucharist and in the language of sacramentality. The Eucharist is a sacrifice because it is a sacrament of the cross. As well as looking to the past the Eucharist as a meal looks to the present by signifying and being called *communion*, that is, the unity of the Church. Thomas leaves the word open here to its full biblical and patristic meaning. As a banquet the Eucharist looks also to the future in which God is enjoyed in heaven. Here the tradition about the eschatological significance of the Eucharist is integrated in its sacramentality. The name *viaticum*, which Thomas appeals to here, had not yet come to mean the last communion before death. It referred to a quality there is in every Eucharist: it is always food for the journey, sustaining those who wait for the coming of the Lord and anticipating the joy of his coming. The final step taken by Thomas to establish the sacramentality of the Eucharist is a discussion about its scriptural origins (a. 5–6). It meets the requirements for institution as sacrament, in that it is rooted in the Scriptures of the Old and New Testaments. Thomas is not concerned with canonical institution here but with showing how the sacramentality of the Eucharist takes its origin from what was said and done by Jesus at the Last Supper, and how this was prepared for by the classical Old Testament types: Melchizedek, ritual sacrifices of expiation, the manna, and, pre-eminently, the Paschal lamb.

The theological method of Thomas in his first question about the Eucharist — giving intelligible shape to the tradition of faith about the Eucharist by applying the technical categories of sacramentality to it — has to be kept in mind for understanding all the rest of his eucharistic theology. Otherwise one will get things like his theory of transubstantiation and some remarks he makes about sacrifice quite out of perspective. His discussion about transubstantiation comes in the context of his study of the 'matter' of the Eucharist, that is to say, of the material element that, in the sense defined by the words with which it is used (the 'form'), carries the sacramental symbolism. In the mediaeval analysis of sacramentality, which is derived from Augustine, there is a level that is found in the symbolism of the matter and form themselves: this is the level of the *sacramentum tantum*. There is a further level which arises when the matter and form are actually used in a liturgical celebration: something real is produced (a sacramental character or some other ecclesial reality), which has a significant rôle in bringing about the final effect of the sacrament. It is called the *res et sacramentum*. It can exist and signify even if the final reality is for some reason blocked. It can do so because a sacrament is always an act of the Church, exercising its rôle as sacrament of Christ. The third level of a sacrament is its final effect, which is grace. It is called the *res tantum*. In IIIa, 73, 1 ad 3 Thomas notes that the Eucharist differs from the other sacraments in that its *res et sacramentum* is in the matter of the sacrament rather than in the person who receives it. What he proposes, in fact, is that the *sacramentum tantum* of the Eucharist is bread and wine; the *res et sacramentum* is the bread and wine consecrated to be the body and blood of Christ by the Lord's words spoken about them; the *res tantum*, or proper grace effect of the Eucharist, is unity in love between baptized Christians in the body of Christ (73, 6). The bread and wine are consecrated when the Eucharist is properly celebrated, even if those for whom it is being celebrated do not accept the proper grace of the sacrament (as the baptismal character is caused even when the recipient puts some obstacle in the way of the grace of the Baptism). But the whole purpose of the consecration of bread and wine, according to this analysis, is to signify and eventually cause the grace of the Eucharist.

Thomas carries his study of the sacrament of the Eucharist forward, then, by considering how bread and wine are suitable symbols of all that he has discovered the Eucharist to be in q. 73 (life, life for humans made of body and soul, life in the community of the Church, life coming from the passion of Christ, life that reaches fulfilment in the eternal enjoyment of God). In q. 74 he explores this symbolism in the liturgical usages of the Church as he knew them. Then he moves on to the level of the *res et sacramentum*, studying the bread and wine as they are consecrated to be the body and blood of Christ. He takes up the patristic idea of the changing (*conversio*) of the bread and wine to become the body and blood of Christ: in q. 75 he explains how the real presence of Christ's body and blood in the Eucharist is brought about by this change; in q. 76 he examines the kind of presence that the change gives; in q. 77 he considers what ontological status the bread and wine have after the change; and then in q. 78 he studies the words that, as sacramental form, bring about and give meaning to the change. In the thirty articles he needs to deal with these questions Thomas dutifully discusses the problems that mediaeval theology had been raising about the Eucharist since Amalarius, and the liturgical and devotional practices of his time that called for theological reflection. His explanation is grounded on the faith of the Church in the real presence (75, 1). The magisterial authority he appeals to is the condemnation of Berengarius. He does not cite the Fourth Lateran Council, nor does he use the word 'transubstantiation' to state the basic faith of the Church. He works towards it as a suitable theological term for explaining the kind of change in bread and wine that brings about the real presence. He argues that, to maintain the faith of the Church, one must hold that the substance of bread does not remain after the consecration, and that it is, in fact, changed into the substance of Christ's body (q. 75, 2). The tradition of faith was not decisive about whether or not the bread remained bread after the consecration, and earlier mediaeval theologians had disagreed on the question. Thomas puts the question not just about bread but about the substance of bread. The word 'substance' had been used for some centuries in the theology of the Eucharist to refer to the fundamental, stable, distinctive reality that was present in the sacrament. Taking it in that sense one could make a good, but not overwhelming, theological case for saying that the substance of bread did not remain in the Eucharist after the consecration: a thing cannot be two different realities at the same time; if it becomes the reality of the body of Christ it surely ceases to be the reality of bread. However, Thomas comes up with a much more decisive argument, and goes so far as to say that it would be heretical to say that the substance of bread remains (75, 2). The reason for his dogmatism is that he is taking 'substance' in a precise metaphysical sense, which he has worked out philosophically under the influence of Aristotle. In Aristotelianism a substance is that which exists independently of anything else. The substantial components of a reality are those which give it independent existent as a particular kind of reality. It may have other components which can come and go without changing its substantial nature. These are called its accidents. Of special importance for the theology of the Eucharist is that, epistemologically, substance and substantial components can only be perceived by intelligence and affirmed by the judgements of intelligence; they cannot be the immediate objects of sensation. What a thing is (its substance), as distinct from what it appears to be, can only be reached by mind. Putting the question about bread as a question about its substance, understood in this sense, Thomas can see no possible way that the consecrated bread could really be the body of Christ if the substance of bread continued to be present. If the independent existent that one is talking about is bread it cannot at the same time and on the same level be the body of Christ. It is not as if Thomas wants to get rid of the bread to make way for the presence of Christ. He rejects the hypothesis of some kind of local movement, that would bring Christ down from heaven into the bread, as being as contrary to the faith of the Church as a purely symbolic theory of presence would be. He refuses the hypothesis that the bread is annihilated. What he wants to show, in fact, is that it is precisely in allowing itself to be changed on the level of substance that the bread makes it possible for Christ to be really present in the sacrament of the Eucharist. This is the positive theological worth that he sees in the idea of transubstantiation. The bread and wine lend their symbolism to make the Eucharist a sacrament; they also lend their reality to make it a sacrament of the real presence of the body and blood of Christ.

At the risk of trivializing what is a profoundly metaphysical discussion one may offer the following hints towards a theological reading of Thomas's treatise on transubstantiation. Christ is an independent existent, and therefore a substance. This substance is personal, because Christ is an existent endowed with mind and freedom (Thomas would define 'person' as 'a substance of the thinking sort' — *rationalis naturae individua substantia*). Christ is now present in his total personal reality, with all the attributes of his being, at the right hand of his Father. If he is to be really present in the sacrament of the Eucharist, as Christian faith believes, it must be this independent existent that is present; not however with the visibility and tangibility that he has in his heavenly existence, but in a sign of bread and wine. Bread and wine are independent existents — substances. If they were to be changed on the level of what gives them independent existence into Christ on the level of what gives him independent existence, he, not they, would be present 'where' they had been. He would 'be there' as they had 'been there' before God changed their being there into his being there. God, because he acts on created reality at the most profound level on which things are, can bring about such a change. The divine power, acting through the Word and the Spirit in the eucharistic liturgy, changes the substance of bread into the substance of Christ's body, and the wine into the substance of his blood. The change being postulated is not the making of one thing out of another: the body of Christ is not being made out of the bread, since the body that is made present is the body that already exists. What is claimed to happen is that the existent that was once substantially bread is made to be substantially the body of Christ. There is not a common subject of change that is carried over from one substance to the other: what is changed is the total substance of bread, not just its substantial form. But there is continuity or succession in existence between the two substances (there is always something there, which once is bread and then is body) which justifies speaking of change from one substance to another. The accidents which remain also give a certain continuity in the process of change. Only God can operate change in the total substance of something; creatures always require a subject, or matter, to work on when they change things. In the Eucharist God changes the entire substance of the bread, making the act of existence that substantiated itself in bread become the act of existence that substantiates itself in the body of Christ. This is the change that is called *transubstantiatio*. The appearances (*accidentia*) of bread and wine remain in existence by divine power, unchanged in themselves. Because of the change, and because it has been done for the sake of making a sacrament, these appearances become the symbols of, and at the same time the point of presence and contact with, the independent existent who is Christ. Christ is not in any way changed in such a transition. He becomes, on the level of his substance, the term of a change worked in the bread and wine, as a result of which their accidents are now related (they have a *habitudo*) to him. Anything related to these accident/symbols is therefore related to Christ. Specifically, anyone who eats and drinks what they now contain is related to the substance of Christ, i.e. to Christ as person. When that eating is a personal act, done in faith by people endowed with mind and freedom, it gives them personal contact with Christ, as really as if they were seeing and touching him. Yet Christ is not touched, nor seen, nor moved around; he is present in the fullness of his personal being, but in the way that substance is present (*per modum substantiae*), since it was his substance that was the term of the change in the substance of bread and wine. Christ is only one substance, but the humanity in which he subsists has component parts, like body and soul and blood, which can be distinguished. In the interests of sacramentality (*vi sacramenti*) the substance of bread has been changed into the substance of his body, that of wine into the substance of his blood. This makes it possible for the appearances of bread to symbolize his bodiliness, in which he worked human salvation and gave himself in love to the Father and to his brothers and sisters. The appearances of wine symbolize his life's blood, which he gave for the sacrificial ratification of the new covenant. But as body and blood are now substantially one in the living divine person of Christ, wherever the body is there also (*vi concomitantiae*) is the blood and everything else that belongs to the personal reality of Christ; likewise with the blood. The division of bread and wine into parts for eating and drinking by many does not divide anything of Christ. Since each divided part is still the same substance as what was divided it is the substance of Christ, i.e. his full personal reality.

Thomas seems to think that transubstantiation is the only good explanation of the Church's faith that the Eucharist is the body and blood of Christ. It meets the needs of realism and of sacramentalism. It protects against crass and fanciful ways of understanding the Eucharist (q. 76, 5–8; q. 77, 3–8). It respects the mysteriousness of the eucharistic presence and its accessibility to faith alone because it sees it as brought about by an action that only God can perform by the divine power that works through the sacramental words of Christ, and that can only be recognized by the witness of those same words. The sacramental presence of Christ is, in fact, brought about by the 'form' of the Eucharist, which is Christ's own words spoken in his person by the ordained minister; it gets its significance from those same words. Thomas's discussion on the form of the Eucharist in q. 78 completes his doctrine of transubstantiation and confirms that his thinking about the presence of Christ in the Eucharist is, for all its realism, entirely sacramental.

Thomas follows up his discussion on the consecration of the bread and wine with a question on the effects of the Eucharist (q. 79). It is the standard movement of sacramental theology from the *sacramentum*, through the *res et sacramentum*, to the *res tantum*. However, there is a complication in the case of the Eucharist. Thomas had noted it in 78, 1: other sacraments exist only when they are in actual use; the Eucharist already exists (*perficitur*) before it is used (i.e. before the individual Christian receives it by eating and drinking). The sacrament of the Eucharist exists once the bread and wine have been consecrated to be the body and blood of Christ. One may be tempted to find here a theological justification for that separation of Mass from Holy Communion that so blighted the eucharistic life of the Church during the later Middle Ages. If one says that the Eucharist is complete once the consecration has taken place, one can be giving the impression that sacramental communion is something of an appendix to the celebration of the Eucharist as Mass. It is a historical fact that the kind of analysis that Thomas is doing here (and it was done by other mediaeval theologians as well) was used at times to justify a separation of Mass and Communion. But this was hardly the intention of Thomas's theology. He continues to assume that, in the Eucharist, the *usus sacramenti*, and therefore the distinctive purpose for which it is designed and celebrated, consists in the eating and drinking of the body and blood of Christ by the faithful (q. 74, 3; q. 80).

What Thomas is accounting for in making this distinction between the *perfectio* of the Eucharist in the consecration of the matter and its *usus* in communion is, in fact, something that lies deeper in the tradition of faith than the peculiarities of mediaeval practice. It is a sense that the celebration of the Eucharist responds to the reality of the Church itself, rather than simply to the demands of individual Christians for communion. While mediaeval Catholicism multiplied Masses without much reference to a celebrating, receiving community, and Protestant-ism, in reaction, directed the celebration of the Eucharist towards the needs of actual communicants, the main Christian tradition surely is that wherever there is a church (i.e. an ecclesial community) the Eucharist is celebrated regularly, especially on the Lord's Day, even if all the members do not assemble or if some of those who do so may not, for one reason or another, receive communion. The Eucharist is celebrated for the benefit of the Church: the ecclesial reality that is expressed in it and affected by it is wider than those who actually receive communion. Sacramentally, that ecclesial reality is ensured by the presence of at least some members of the community, some if not all of whom communicate; and by the ministry of an ordained priest who always communicates. But it is ensured above all by the fact that, when such a community celebrates and consecrates the Eucharist, Christ is present in the consecrated bread and wine as head of the Church and as its priest. He continues to be present in the bread that is reserved in the church for the benefit of its members who are ill or absent for some other reason, and who may want to receive the Eucharist later. This presence of Christ, sacramentalized in these different ways by the presence and action of the Church, is the sacrament of the Eucharist. The reality of the Eucharist, then, does not depend, as Thomas notes, on the use of the Eucharist by the faithful, in the way that, for example, the reality of Baptism depends on there being someone to baptize (nor does the consecration of baptismal water make a Baptism, in the way the consecration of bread and wine makes the Eucharist). By the consecration of the Eucharist Christ is present and acting and available as the giver of the specific grace of building-up the Church as his body. The people who take part in the Eucharist are already the body of Christ through Baptism. They are this, and can become it more fully in the Eucharist, even if not all of them actually receive the body of Christ sacramentally. Many other people who are not even present at the Eucharist are remembered there, as belonging to the body of Christ. There is an ecclesial reality in the Eucharist, therefore, that is not co-extensive with those who actually receive communion. This is the tradition that Thomas is allowing for when he says that the Eucharist is realized in the consecration of the matter rather than in its use by the faithful (78, 1; 80, 12 ad 3). At the same time it is clear from his treatment of the effects and the *usus* (i.e. receiving) of the Eucharist that he is also fully aware of the central truth of the tradition, which is that the Eucharist is made for reception by the faithful; that the building-up of Christians in the body of Christ is done by eating his body and drinking his blood.

The effects of the Eucharist are presented by Thomas in q. 79 as grace, charity and the taking-away of sin. His teaching organizes the great themes of the patristic tradition. In the course of it he works out a distinction between the Eucharist as sacrament and as sacrifice that builds upon what has already been noted in connection with *perfectio* and *usus*, and on the tradition that saw the Eucharist as a sacrifice. It is an important distinction in eucharistic theology, but one that has sometimes been badly used. Thomas introduces it in q. 79, 5 to explain how the Eucharist takes away the punishment due to sin. He says the sacrament of the Eucharist is both sacrifice and sacrament. The distinction is not between two different parts of the sacrament but between two different aspects (*ratio*) of it. One and the same Eucharist is a sacrifice precisely as offered (*offertur*); it is a sacrament as consumed (*sumitur*). There is a double movement — from humans to God in worship, from God to humans in sanctification — in every sacrament. The word 'sacrament' has, indeed, tended to be more associated with the sanctification movement (the giving of grace) than with the worship movement. When Thomas contrasts sacrifice with sacrament he is using 'sacrament' in this more restricted sense: he is setting it over against sacrifice, which is the specific upward movement of worship proper to the Eucharist. But the object that is being analysed as both sacrifice and sacrament is, in Thomas's own language, the sacrament of the Eucharist. In this sense the sacrifice is an aspect of the sacrament. It is, in fact, the passion of Christ, which is offered sacramentally in the Eucharist. Thomas takes the distinction up again in q. 79, 7, where he asks whether the Eucharist benefits others besides those who receive the sacrament. His answer begins with the observation that the Eucharist is not only a sacrament but is also a sacrifice: it is a sacrifice in so far as it represents the passion of Christ; it is a sacrament in so far as grace is given in it through symbols. Thomas has already explained that it is as a sacrament that the Eucharist represents the passion of Christ (73, 4). Therefore he cannot mean that sacrament and sacrifice are two separate things in the Eucharist: the whole reality of the Eucharist is sacramental, including its sacrificial reality; the sacrament, for its part, draws from the sacrifice, because all grace comes from the passion of Christ. In Thomas's view the sacrifice of Christ is sacramentalized in the twofold consecration, which sacramentally separates Christ's body and blood, thus representing his death (80, 12 ad 3). It is sacramentalized, too, in that it is offered by the Church in the Eucharistic Prayer, which makes Christ really present as victim. The prayer of offering includes intercession for those for whom it is being offered. Christ's body and blood were offered for everyone and everything on the cross. They are offered in the Eucharist in that same general way, but also for specific persons who are mentioned in the Eucharistic Prayer. Thomas quotes from the Roman Canon in 79, 7 to show that the first ones prayed for are those who receive the sacrament by eating the body of Christ and drinking his blood. Their grace is, therefore, the effect of the Eucharist as both sacrament and sacrifice. Others who are prayed for in the Eucharistic Prayer, but who do not communicate sacramentally, receive grace from that particular Eucharist as sacrifice but not as sacrament. Here Thomas is using the word 'sacrament' in a restricted sense. In his general sacramental theory grace is said to come from a sacrament when it is given in the application of the matter and form of a sacrament to a particular individual. In this sense it is true to say that only those who eat of the bread and drink of the cup receive grace from the sacrament. However, the terminology does carry the risk of setting up two independent ways in which the Eucharist gives grace. It would be so used later to justify multiplication of Masses without communicants and even without congregations. This could happen when the distinction was taken out of the context in which Thomas made it. He never suggests anything like an *usus* of the Eucharist purely as sacrifice. The Eucharist is a sacrifice within its sacramentality, not independently of it. The sacrament has eventually to be received, if by nobody else then by the priest. And those who receive grace from the Eucharist considered as sacrifice have at least a desire for eucharistic communion (q. 79, 1 ad 1). There is no sanctification without eucharistic communion, at least in desire (q. 73, 3).

In q. 80 Thomas discusses reception (*usus vel sumptio*) of the Eucharist. He deals with the requirements for fruitful reception and with the obstacles to it, especially sinfulness; and he discusses how often and in what form one should communicate. While his theology is well grounded in the patristic tradition it is marked by a certain apologia for new liturgical practices that were developing in the Middle Ages — for example, that of not giving the faithful communion from the chalice. It is the kind of judicious theological reasoning that tries to make the best of pastoral practice, even while recognizing that it is not always ideal (cf. q. 80, 12 regarding communion from the chalice). Even if it was sometimes used to justify liturgical vagaries of the late Middle Ages it is principled enough to have served to justify the cautious reforms of the Council of Trent; and most of it can sit quite comfortably with contemporary liturgical standards. A good example of its strengths and weaknesses is the distinction that Thomas draws between spiritual and sacramental eating of the Eucharist (q. 80, 1). To receive the sacrament in faith and love, and therefore to accept its grace, is to receive it spiritually; to receive the sacrament, but without its spiritual effects, is to receive it (merely) sacramentally. It is a distinction that can be traced back to the Fathers, especially to Augustine. But it is possible to have a spiritual eating that is only the desire for the Eucharist, without actual sacramental eating. Thomas allows for it in q. 80, 1 ad 3. If spiritual eating is taken in that sense it can become an alternative to sacramental. That makes it easier to justify Mass without sacramental communion: one can have the grace of the sacrament by a 'spiritual communion'. The distinction between spiritual and sacramental communion, made by Thomas for other reasons, came to be used in that sense during the late Middle Ages and subsequently.

The final questions devoted to the Eucharist in the *Summa* deal with the minister (q. 82) and the rite (q. 83). They are a systematic reflection on the liturgical practice and discipline of the Eucharist as Thomas knew it, in the light of the tradition of faith. He argues the need for a priest to consecrate the Eucharist from the dignity of the sacrament: the reality and the form of the Eucharist require that it be done *in persona Christi* (i.e. the words of consecration are Christ's own words and what is consecrated is his body and blood); to act *in persona Christi* in this way one must receive a special power from Christ, through ordination to priesthood; one must be put on the level of those to whom the Lord said at the Last Supper, 'Do this in memory of me'. Thomas does not, then, derive the priesthood of the consecrating minister from the sacrificial reality of the Eucharist, but from the need for someone to act *in persona Christi* in the sacrament. He correlates the power of the priest to consecrate the Eucharist with the power the baptized have to receive it. And he sees the distribution of communion as being integral to the power of the priest to act *in persona Christi* (q. 82, 3). Behind his thinking lies the tradition that there is a giving and taking in the Eucharist that has to be sacramentalized; there is a host and there are guests. Christ does the giving and that has to be sacramentalized in his priestly minister. The sacramental giving includes an act of sacrifice. This sacrificial movement of the Eucharist gets its clearest development in q. 83. There Thomas explains how Christ is immolated in the Eucharist (the sacrament ritually represents his passion and applies its fruits). The perspective is entirely sacramental. The sacrifice that is in the Eucharist is sacramental; and the sacrament is sacrificial. There is a giving to God (*oblatio*) and a receiving from him (*sumptio*). The giving, or offering, is a sacrifice because it represents the sacrifice of Christ. What is received is the fruit of this sacrifice. The offering is done sacramentally in the Eucharistic Prayer. The Prayer also sacramentalizes the receiving because those who will receive communion, and others who will benefit from the Eucharist, are interceded for in it. The sacramentality requires that at least the one who says the Eucharistic Prayer should eat and drink the consecrated bread and wine. It requires that those who are present, and on whose behalf he says the Prayer, should be brought, as far as is possible, to sacramental and spiritual eating and drinking. It allows that those of the congregation who are impeded from receiving communion, and others not present who are prayed for, can receive the fruits of the Eucharist without sacramental eating, provided they are living in faith and charity and thus united to the Body of Christ (q. 79, 7 ad 2), and, it may be added, by that very fact desiring eucharistic communion (see q. 73, 3).

9.4   THE REFORMERS AND THE COUNCIL OF TRENT

The main positions of mediaeval theology on the Eucharist were established by the early fourteenth century. They were carried on towards the controversies of the Reformation by commentaries on the *Sentences* of Peter Lombard, by the works of the masters like Thomas and Bonaventure and Scotus, and also by pastoral manuals and a more popular kind of theology. Such development as occurred in this later period of Scholastic theology were by way of logical analysis of texts of the earlier masters. What was clear and commonplace got less attention than what was difficult and controversial in such a method. As a result, technical philosophico-theological issues were sometimes made to seem more theologically important than the great themes of the scriptural and patristic tradition that filled the eucharistic theology of a master like Thomas. Nominalism did a critique of this kind of theological speculation, but the alternative it offered was inspired by a new set of philosophical and logical principles more than by a recovery of the biblical and patristic tradition. Indeed, its logical radicalism uncontrolled by tradition produced some strange variants of Scholastic theories about the Eucharist. The Reformers seem to have often judged Scholastic theology by the nominalist form of it that was prominent in the fifteenth and early sixteenth centuries (see Clark, ch. XIV).

Speculative developments in the theology of the Eucharist in the later Middle Ages were mainly on the question of the reality of Christ's presence in the sacrament and the explanation of it by transubstantiation. There was little theological speculation about the Eucharist as sacrifice. That was not a disputed issue. The biblical and patristic traditions about it, formulated in terms like those noted in Thomas, were routinely repeated. This may seem surprising when one considers the violence of the Protestant opposition to Catholic teaching on the Eucharist as sacrifice, but it can be documented from a study of Catholic theologians of the pre-Reformation period (Clark, ch. V; Lepin, pp. 213–240). What is harder to document is the way Scholastic theology of the Eucharist, for all its rectitude, was being used popularly in relation to the abuses that there undoubtedly were in Catholic eucharistic practice during the century before the Reformation (Jungmann, pp. 96–101; Clark, ch. IV; Power, ch. 2). At its best this theology could have kept liturgical practice on secure lines. At its worst, in the minds of people for whom distinctions easily justified separations, and possibilities thought about readily became permissions presumed, Scholastic theology could go hand in hand with decadent liturgical practice. There seems good reason to believe that the Reformers judged the theory to be saying what the practice was doing. Thus the Catholic theory of the Eucharist as sacrament and sacrifice was, for all its good intentions, judged to mean that there was nothing wrong with separating the Mass from communion, with multiplying Masses celebrated for private intentions without communicants or congregation, and with promising extravagant fruits from such Masses without much reference to the way people participated sacramentally and spiritually in the Eucharist. The preponderant and possessive rôle that ordained priests had in Catholic practice of the Eucharist was thought to be underpinned by the theological theory. The Catholic theory of transubstantiation was judged in relation to abuses in the way priests employed the power they alone had to consecrate the Eucharist, and in forms of devotion to the reserved sacrament. The doctrine of sacrifice was judged by the way priests used the power it gave them to produce and distribute fruits of the Eucharist and to be rewarded economically for so doing. The Reformers were prophets of the renewal of eucharistic celebration before they were theologians of the Eucharist.

9.4.1   The Reformers

The teaching of the Reformers on the Eucharist fits into their general theology of the justifying grace of God and its acceptance by faith, and of the way this is realized in sacraments. Their general sacramental doctrine, and particularly the prominence they gave to word in relation to rite, has been discussed already (see above, 2.7). Here attention is drawn to the more specific issues they raised about the Eucharist. Because it is one of the sacraments of the Lord, attested in

Scripture, they were much more positive about the Eucharist than they were about other rites of the Church that were claimed to be sacraments but did not have a clear biblical warrant. The biblical texts that were at the centre of its celebration made it already a proclamation of God's word. Some of the eucharistic theology of the Reformers was a recovery of elements of the biblical tradition of faith about the Lord's Supper that were not very operative during the later Middle Ages. More of it, however, was reformist and polemical, concerned with eradicating Roman 'superstitions' and 'idolatries'. The doctrine of sacrifice, with all the practices that seemed to depend on it, was the primary target. The doctrine of transubstantiation, as an explanation of the presence of Christ in the Eucharist, was the second major target. The liturgical form and manner of celebrating the rite — the Roman Canon, gestures of adoration made to the consecrated bread, neglect of the proclamation of God's word, the refusal of the chalice to the laity, Masses said without congregations and merely because a stipend had been offered for some private intention — were a third target, since they reflected a sacrificial understanding of the Eucharist and a doctrine of transubstantiation. While the critique was made on the authority of Scripture it inevitably produced new theological positions that were offered as alternatives to the Scholastic doctrines, and new liturgical forms.

John Wycliffe (d. 1384) had already rejected the doctrine of transubstantiation a century and a half before the Reformation. He had philosophical as well as theological difficulties with it; and he blamed it for fostering a worship of the consecrated host that he considered idolatrous. Drawing on Augustine, he thought that one should understand the presence of Christ in the Eucharist as being spiritual and in a sign, and that the substance of bread remained in it along with the substance of Christ (*consubstantiatio* rather than *transubstantiatio*). The theology of Wycliffe was summarily condemned at the Council of Constance in 1415 (DS 1151–1153). Transubstantiation was already being taken as a touchstone of eucharistic orthodoxy. However, it is worth noting that in the Papal *Bulla* of 1418 in which Martin V carried forward the work of the Council against the followers of Wycliffe and Jan Hus, he does not use the term 'transubstantiation' in formulating the questions that were to test their orthodoxy about the Eucharist (ND 1507).

The historical leaders of the Reformation (notably Luther, Zwingli, Calvin, Cranmer) gave particular attention to the theology and to the rite of the Eucharist. They wished to restore in the Church a scriptural understanding and practice of the Eucharist as the Lord's Supper. They read what the Scriptures had to say about the Lord's Supper in the light of what they understood it to say about justification by faith. Ultimately, it was their doctrine of justification, and their understanding of the rôle of sacraments in it, that required them to deny that the Eucharist is a sacrifice, in the sense they understood Catholic theology to be saying it was. The *ex opere operato* effectiveness that was being claimed for the Mass seemed to them to set it up as a 'work' which had some independent value for justification. They were particularly opposed to the idea that the Eucharist had any of the propitiatory value that they thought sacrifice must have. They had a deeply-felt sense of human sinfulness and of faith in the redeeming value of the cross of Christ as being the only way of forgiveness. Anything that seemed to claim that the forgiveness of sin could be gained for oneself or others by a human work (i.e. a sacrifice) was an intolerable denial of the all-sufficiency of the cross. In the theological development of this position of the Reformers Melanchthon had an important rôle. He argued that, since the Eucharist could not be propitiatory (only the cross was) it could not possibly be a sacrifice, because sacrifice in the strict sense is propitiatory and requires *immolatio* or the shedding of blood (Lepin, pp. 245–248). His argument set a challenge which Catholic theologians took seriously, both at the Council of Trent and in subsequent eucharistic theology.

What the Reformers contested, then, was something deeper than any eccentricities there may have been in late mediaeval theology about the Eucharist as sacrifice (Clark, chs V, VI). They wanted to affirm beyond any doubt that the Eucharist is a gift of God, not a work of man (in Luther's words a *beneficium* rather than a *sacrificium*; cf. B. Thompson, p. 100). The salvific movement it sacramentalizes is entirely from God to humans. It has some God-ward movement, in the sense that it has elements of praise and thanksgiving in it, and so can be metaphorically called a 'sacrifice of praise'. But the real business of the sacrament is the giving of the grace of God, in the face of which humans have nothing to offer but acceptance of justification in faith and repentance. What the rite does is to proclaim and pledge that this grace is being given, for the forgiveness of sin, in the bread and wine which Christ gave as his body and blood at the Last Supper. The Eucharist is a *testament*, or promise of what believers will inherit from the death of Christ. The words of institution that are the centre of the rite are a Gospel proclamation that Christ died for sinners. The bread and wine are the sign or pledge of the promise of salvation proclaimed in the words. Given as body and blood of Christ, they call forth faith from those who eat and drink and in that faith their sins are forgiven. There is no room for offering by humans in this view of the Lord's Supper. All words suggesting it must be eliminated from the prayer said over the bread and wine. It was for this reason that the Roman Canon, which has so much about the oblation being made by the Church, was so scornfully rejected by the Reformers. And with the rejection of a sacrificial Canon went the rejection of any special priesthood for the one who said the Canon. Ministers of the Eucharist did not make a sacrifice. They proclaimed God's word of promise, which was confirmed by the body and blood of Christ that they distributed to those who believed. In this view, a silent Canon, or a Canon said without a congregation, made no sense. The Reformers did affirm strongly that the Supper is a memorial of the sacrifice of Christ. But it is a remembering of the sacrifice of Christ, not as something that is being offered but as something from which the fruits of salvation are now being drawn. The movement from the divine (in Christ) to the human (in sinners) is recognized but not the movement from humans, caught up in the human sacrifice of Christ, to the divine (in the Father) (texts of the Reformers on the Eucharist as sacrifice in Palmer, pp. 293–304; Lepin, pp. 241–252).

The three principal leaders of the Reformation wanted to maintain the truth of the Lord's words that the bread and wine given in communion are his body and blood. They differed about the sense in which they were true. For Zwingli they meant that Christ was present in his body and blood to those who received the saving proclamation of his passion by faith: the bread and wine strengthened the proclamation and helped faith, because as used in the Lord's Supper they are signs of his body and blood. In this view there is no question of bread and wine being changed into Christ's body and blood: to say so would be to materialize Christ in the Eucharist, whereas what faith and philosophy call for is a spiritual, life-giving presence; transubstantiation is unthinkable. Luther had more realism in his understanding of how bread and wine are the body and blood of Christ. He argued rather vehemently against Zwingli on the subject. However, he rejected transubstantiation as an explanation of how the presence came about. He blamed Aquinas, schooled in the rationalism of Aristotle rather than in the faith of the Scriptures, for introducing it. He would have seen, too, how closely the theory was bound up with the doctrine that the Eucharist is a sacrifice. It concentrated attention on the act of consecration by which, according to mediaeval theology, the priest, and he alone, brought the sacrifice into existence. Transubstantiation was also, of course, the principal theological reason given for worship of the reserved sacrament. Luther provided an alternative theology of the presence, using an analogy with the incarnation, which is something many of the Fathers had done. He took up a form of the theory that had already appeared in the Middle Ages and goes by the name of 'impanation'. As the Word took flesh to himself in the in-carn(flesh)-ation, so in the Eucharist Christ, through his words, takes bread to himself in an im-pan(bread)-ation. The bread, in Luther's view, remains bread, while becoming the body of Christ; the two substances co-exist; instead of *transubstantiatio* there is what was called *consubstantiatio*. He also speculates that Christ can be present in many Eucharists at one and the same time because of his divine ubiquity, which is communicated to his body in the incarnation. Luther did not accept Zwingli's idea that consecrated bread and wine which is not consumed in the Eucharist simply reverts to being ordinary bread and wine. Reservation of the sacrament was, indeed, rejected by Lutheranism, as it was by Calvinism; but the care taken in both traditions to consecrate only as much bread and wine as was needed, and to consume any that remained, was a way of avoiding the extreme position of Zwingli about the duration of the presence.

Calvin's teaching about the presence of Christ in the Eucharist draws from both Zwingli and Luther, while being critical of both of them. He criticizes Zwingli for not giving sufficient force to the presence, by treating the bread and wine merely as symbols. He criticizes Luther for being still too close to what he thought was the crude realism taught by the proponents of transubstantiation. He thought that Luther's theories did not avoid a spatial view of the presence, and still gave the impression that Christ somehow came down from heaven. Calvin's own contribution to the theology of the presence was to see it as the power (*virtus*) of the heavenly Christ being made active in the bread and wine that are received in the eucharistic celebration. This power is the real substance of the sacrament. It is not something exercised from afar but constitutes a real, mysterious presence of Christ in the bread and wine. In his *Short Treatise on the Lord's Supper* he writes:

> We have then to confess that if the representation which God grants us in the Supper is veracious, the internal substance of the sacrament is joined with the visible signs; and as the bread is distributed by hand, so the body of Christ is communicated to us, so that we are made partakers of it. If there were nothing more, we have good reason to be satisfied when we realize that Jesus Christ gives us in the Supper the real substance of his body and his blood, so that we may possess him fully, and, possessing him, have part in all his blessings (p. 148).

It was Calvin's teaching more than that of Luther that influenced the Protestant current in the Anglican Reformation. It is in the thinking of Cranmer, in the liturgy of the Lord's Supper that he designed and in the Articles of Religion that deal with the Eucharist (texts of the Reformers on eucharistic presence in Palmer, pp. 240–250; liturgical texts with introduction in B. Thompson; also in Jasper and Cuming; analysis in Brilioth).

9.4.2   The Council of Trent

The doctrinal and disciplinary decrees of the Council of Trent on the Eucharist are the reaction of Catholic orthodoxy to the theology and ritual practice of the Reformers. Catholic doctrine is presented in a way that will protect the faith of God's People from what are considered to be untraditional and divisive doctrines. The dogmatic canons attached to the decrees are direct condemnations of what are judged to be the heresies of the Reformers. Theologians had prepared summaries of the doctrine of the Reformers, documented by extracts from their works, for use by the Council Fathers. These had an important influence on the agenda of the Council, and on its decrees and condemnations. The Council considered the Eucharist in two phases. During the first, which lasted from 1547 to 1551, it dealt with errors concerning the real presence. The outcome of this work was the approval, in Session XII (October 1551), of the *Decretum de ss. Eucharistia* and the *Canones de ss. Eucharistiae sacramento* (DS 1635–1661; ND 1512–1536). Work began immediately afterwards on the question of the Eucharist as sacrifice, but the Council was interrupted in 1552 and did not reassemble again until 1562. What amounted to a new beginning was made on the Eucharist. The results were a document, approved in Session XXI, on communion under both kinds and communion by children and, in Session XXII (September 1552), the *Doctrina de ss. Missae sacrificio*, with accompanying canons (DS 1738–1762; ND 1545–1563). The separation of sacrament and sacrifice, in treatment and in time, reflects the way the issues were seen at the Reformation: the Mass as sacrifice was one issue; the real presence understood as brought about by transubstantiation was another. The separate dogmatic treatment had the effect of giving a methodological and even a kind of dogmatic justification for a separation of the two issues in Catholic theology.

The doctrine on the Eucharist as sacrament is about the reality of the sacramental presence, about the worship due to the sacrament, and about its reception. It is presented in a rich setting of scriptural texts. The texts are interpreted in a sense and with a language that was considered to be justified by the tradition of the Church and necessary for the unambiguous affirmation of the faith at that point in time. Using the language of mediaeval sacramental theology, ch. 1 states that, in the Eucharist after the consecration, Christ is 'truly, really and substantially . . . contained' under the appearance (*species*) of bread and wine. There is no contradiction, it is explained, between the natural way of existing that Christ has at the right hand of his Father and his being present sacramentally (*sacramentaliter*) by his substance to us in many other places. Sacramentality qualifies the mode, not the reality of the eucharistic presence. The special quality of Christ's presence in the sacrament of the Eucharist 'as distinct from the other sacraments' is indicated by saying he is present there 'in his substance'. This doctrine is said to be the plain meaning of the scriptural texts about the institution of the Eucharist, and the way they have traditionally been understood in the Church. Chapter 2 presents the reasons why Christ gave this sacrament to the Church: they are the commonly accepted values and effects of the Eucharist, including that of being a memorial of the death of Christ, but without any reference to sacrifice. Chapter 3 explains that the Eucharist surpasses the other sacraments in that the author of holiness exists in it before it is used (*ante usum*), whereas the others only become sanctifying when in actual use. What is present in the Eucharist is the whole Christ, now risen, uniting in himself body, blood, soul and divinity. He is present under the appearance of bread and wine in the consecrated host and chalice and in every portion of them when they are divided. A distinction worked out by mediaeval theology is used to explain why, nevertheless, it is his body that is present under the appearance of bread and his blood under that of wine. His body is present in the bread 'by virtue of the words' (*vi verborum*), while his whole person is present 'in virtue of the natural connection and concomitance (*vi . . . -concomitantiae*) by which the parts of Christ the Lord, who has already risen from the dead to die no more (cf. Romans 6:9), are united together'. (This distinction is important for a sacramental understanding of how the Eucharist is a sacrifice, but Trent makes no reference to the sacrifice at this point.) Chapter 4 reads:

> Because Christ our Redeemer said that it was truly His body that He was offering under the species of bread (cf. Matthew 26:26 . . .), it has always been the conviction of the Church of God, and this holy Council now again declares that, by the consecration of the bread and wine there takes place a change of the whole substance of bread into the substance of the body of Christ our Lord and of the whole substance of wine into the substance of His blood. This change the holy Catholic Church has fittingly and properly named transubstantiation (cf. canon 2) (ND 1519).

The idea of change (*conversio*) is certainly well attested in the patristic tradition. The description of the change as being of 'the whole substance of bread into the substance of the body of Christ . . . ' comes from mediaeval Latin theology.

What Trent must be saying, then, is that it is the tradition that goes back to the Fathers that the mediaevals wanted to express by using the language of substance. In saying that the whole substance of bread was changed into the body of Christ they wanted to say clearly and unambiguously, in the language of their own time, what the Fathers had said about how bread became the body of Christ. Like their mediaeval masters, the Council Fathers of Trent knew of no way in which the issue of the reality of Christ's presence in the Eucharist could be stated other than in terms of substance. The only kind of change that would bring about the real, sacramental presence that they had defined in ch. 1 was a conversion of substance to substance. And they concluded that such a change was appropriately called 'transubstantiation' by the Catholic Church. 'Transubstantiation' is, then, (1) a term that is approved, for (2) an explanation that is required, for (3) maintaining the truth of the real presence. The three levels of definition are interconnected, but obviously the fundamental truth of faith that is being defined is the reality of the presence.

The remaining chapters (5–8) of the Decree on the Sacrament of the Eucharist deal with consequences of what has been defined in the first four: worship and veneration of the sacrament, its reservation and communion of the sick, its reception (*usus*). Paradoxically, it is in a paragraph of ch. 5 that defends solemn public processions of the Blessed Sacrament that the idea of availing of the Eucharist to represent the triumph and victory of Christ's death is put forward. The two ways of receiving the Eucharist distinguished by Thomas and others as *sacramentaliter* and *spiritualiter* had by the time of the Council become three, with the addition of a reception that was *tantum spiritualiter*. Trent approves this threefold distinction in its ch. 8, understanding the *tantum spiritualiter* to refer to ' . . . those who, receiving in desire (*voto*) the heavenly bread put before them, with a living faith "working through love" (cf. Gal 5:6), experience its fruit and benefit from it'. Spiritual communion can thus be presented as an alternative to sacramental communion. The Decree, however, concludes with an exhortation to frequent sacramental communion, that is at the same time a moving plea for the restoration of unity among Christians in the Eucharist:

> Finally, with fatherly affection the holy Council warns, exhorts, asks and pleads, 'through the tender mercy of our God' (Luke 1:78), that each and all who bear the name of Christians meet at last in this 'sign of unity', in this 'bond of charity', in this symbol of concord, to be finally of one heart. Keeping in mind the great majesty and the most excellent love of our Lord Jesus Christ, who laid down His precious life as the price of our salvation, and who gave us His flesh to eat (cf. John 6:48ff.), may all Christians have so firm and strong a faith in the sacred mystery of His body and blood, may they worship it with such devotion and pious veneration, that they will be able to receive frequently their 'supersubstantial bread' (cf. Matthew 6:11 Vulgate). May it truly be the life of their souls and continual health for their minds; strengthened by its power (cf. 1 Kings 19:8), may they, after journeying through this sorrowful pilgrimage, reach their home in heaven, where they will eat without any veil the same 'bread of angels' (cf. Ps 78:25) which they eat now under sacred veils (DS 1649; ND 1524).

Then, more soberly, the Council goes on to 'add the following canons so that all, already knowing the Catholic doctrine, may also realize what are the heresies that they must beware of and avoid'. The first two need to be quoted:

1.   If anyone denies that in the sacrament of the most holy Eucharist the body and blood, together with the soul and divinity, of our Lord Jesus Christ and, therefore, the whole Christ is truly, really and substantially contained, but says that He is in it only as in a sign or figure or by His power, *anathema sit*.

2.   If anyone says that in the holy sacrament of the Eucharist the substance of bread and wine remains together with the body and blood of our Lord Jesus Christ, and denies that wonderful and unique change of the whole substance of the bread into His body and of the whole substance of the wine into His blood while only the species of bread and wine remain, a change which the Catholic Church very fittingly calls transubstantiation, *anathema sit* (DS 1651/2; ND 1526/7).

The Doctrine on the Sacrifice of the Mass is introduced in the Foreword as being about 'the great mystery of the Eucharist . . . as true and unique sacrifice'. If the Eucharist is spoken of as 'mystery' it is never called 'sacrament' in this Decree. Indeed, it is called Eucharist only once more, when reception of communion is being dealt with in ch. 6. Otherwise it is spoken of as the Mass, or the sacrifice, or the sacrifice of the Mass. The question dealt with in ch. 1 is, nevertheless, a typically sacramental one — that of institution. The institution is established by an analysis of what Christ did at the Last Supper (which is how the institution of the Eucharist as sacrament had been established in the earlier Decree). The chapter begins with a Christological statement about the priesthood of Christ, based on Hebrews. This sets the perspective for the discussion: sacrifice is to be seen as an act of priesthood. The action of Christ at the Last Supper is analysed in what is, in Latin, one long, elaborately constructed sentence. The first clause presents a kind of Christological imperative for what Christ did: the priesthood that he would exercise by offering himself once for all to the Father on the altar of the cross was not to be extinguished by his death. It takes several clauses to get to what he actually did to perpetuate his priesthood: he offered his body and blood under the appearances of bread and wine to the Father. The sacramental fullness of what he did is conveyed by saying that, as well as offering his body and blood, he gave them to his apostles under the same signs (*sub earundem rerum symbolis*) to consume. He did this, by his own claim, as 'a priest according to the order of Melchisedech'. The reason he did so was to leave to his beloved spouse the Church a visible sacrifice, such as is required by human nature. It is a visible sacrifice of a very particular kind because it is one in which the bloody sacrifice that would be carried out once only on the cross would be represented (*representaretur*), its memory (*memoria*) preserved until the end of time, and its saving power applied (*salutaris virtus applicaretur*) for the forgiveness of the sins that we commit every day. In offering his body and blood and giving them to his apostles to consume Christ is said to have established them as priests of the new covenant. He commanded them, and their successors in the priesthood, to offer his body and blood, which he had given them under the appearance of bread and wine, by telling them 'Do this in memory of me'. This is how the Church would have its visible sacrifice, in which the priesthood of Christ would be perpetuated, because what was to be done by the apostles and their successors would represent and remember and apply the fruits of his once-for-all sacrifice of the cross.

Although it does not use the word 'sacrament', the text of Trent is giving what can legitimately be called a sacramental explanation of how the Eucharist is a sacrifice (Power, p. 130). The reality of it is Christ offering his body and blood to his Father; the symbolic representation, memorial and application of it is done in bread and wine that have become the body and blood of Christ that is being offered. The sacramental view is confirmed by the parallel that the text goes on to draw between the Eucharist and the Passover. Christ is said to have 'instituted a new Pasch, namely Himself to be offered by the Church through her priests under visible signs (*sub signis visibilibus immolandum*) in order to celebrate the memory of His passage from this world to the Father when by the shedding of His blood he redeemed us . . . '. The sacramental tradition right back to the Fathers had not hesitated to see Jesus symbolically immolated in the Eucharist, because of the representative, memorial and application relationship of the Eucharist to the cross. This is what Trent is affirming here. If it says that those who do the offering on behalf of the Church are priests, their priesthood can only be some kind of sacramental participation in the unique priesthood of Christ, which is what the Eucharist is meant to perpetuate. The offering/immolation is done under visible signs, which is what general sacramental theory means by a sacrament. The chapter ends with another typically sacramental concern: the sacrifice has its own intrinsic value, 'which cannot be defiled by any unworthiness or malice on the part of those who offer it'. This is established by identifying the Eucharist, as the tradition had done since Justin Martyr, with the 'clean oblation' promised by the prophet Malachi, and then by an argument from 1 Corinthians. One sees something of the dilemma created by the separation of sacrament and sacrifice in the way 1 Corinthians is used. A clear argument is available in 1 Corinthians 11:23–29 for the 'objective' reality of the Eucharist in relation to the death of Christ. But the accent there is on eating and drinking (sacrament in the Tridentine sense) rather than on offering (sacrifice). So 1 Corinthians 10:21, about those who partake of the table of the Lord not partaking of the table of the devil, is used: it is unmistakably cultic and sacrificial. Just to be sure that 'table' would not be misunderstood in a Protestant sense, Trent qualifies its reference by adding: 'By "table" he understands "altar" in both cases'. Finally, the Eucharist is said to bring to fulfilment and perfection all the sacrifices of the Old Law, which is what a sacrament of the New Law is expected to do.

Chapter 2 of the Doctrine on the Sacrifice of the Mass takes up a critical issue between Catholics and Protestants: was the Eucharist not just a sacrifice but a propitiatory sacrifice? 'Propitiatory' meant having value for the expiation and taking away of sin in oneself and in others. Many questions of theory and practice turned on the propitiatory value of the Eucharist. The doctrine of justification was involved: to say the offering of the Mass was propitiatory was to say that humans could do something that had meritorious and satisfactory value in the giving of grace and the forgiveness of sin. The practice of offering Mass, and having Mass offered for oneself and others, for the living and the dead, relied on it. The right of a priest to apply the fruits of the Mass to those from whom he had received a stipend depended on it. The issue of propitiation was debated with the help of two theological ideas: immolation and oblation. Oblation is the moral act of offering inherent in the very notion of sacrifice; immolation is the shedding of blood or other destruction of the victim in a sacrifice. The terms can be found in the Fathers, and they were used by mediaeval theologians in discussion about the Eucharist as sacrifice. They were not, however, given much technical definition in Scholastic theology before the Reformation. Paradoxically, it was the Protestants who forced Catholic theology to develop a theology of the Eucharist as sacrifice in terms of them. They were arguing from the Scriptures that there was no propitiation for sin without the shedding of blood; the shedding of blood in sacrifice is immolation; hence there could be no propitiation where there was no immolation; since there is no immolation in the Mass it cannot be propitiatory; it cannot, therefore, be offered (oblation) as a sacrifice of propitiation. The Fathers of Trent had no ready-made Catholic theology of the Eucharist as sacrifice that would answer these arguments precisely in the terms set by the Reformers. There was nothing comparable to what the doctrine of transubstantiation had been able to provide for dealing with the question of real presence. One can see the theology of sacrifice being worked out in the debates of the Council itself (analysis of the debates in Lepin, pp. 297–326). On some points (e.g. on whether there was an immolation of the body and blood of Christ at the Last Supper) the theological effort could not provide a sufficiently clear or convincing answer to be of any use for the formulation of conciliar teaching. The theological debate would continue long after the Council. But meanwhile the Council did find a way of stating the essential tenet of Catholic faith that it needed to affirm, and in doing so it gave a direction to future Catholic theology.

The essential teaching of ch. 2 is that 'the divine sacrifice which is celebrated (*peragitur*) in the Mass . . . is truly propitiatory'. It is so because 'the same Christ who offered Himself once in a bloody manner (cf. Hebrews 9:14, 27) on the altar of the cross is contained and is offered (the Latin word is *immolatur*) in an unbloody manner'. The one who is offered was immolated in a bloody manner (*cruente*) on the cross; he is immolated 'in an unbloody manner' (*incruente*) in the Mass. It is assumed that Christ's offering of himself on the cross is propitiatory; the Mass is propitiatory because it is that very offering of Christ. The realism of the identification is ensured by the realism of Christ's presence in the Eucharist (he is 'contained' and thus immolated). The sacramental quality of the real presence (i.e. that it occurs in the signs of bread and wine) is not, however, invoked to explain how the Mass realizes the identification. There was a lot of theological debate at the Council about how what is done with the bread and wine constituted an immolation, about how such an immolation satisfied the definition of sacrifice, and about how it makes the sacrifice propitiatory. Melanchthon had criticized the Catholics for not defining clearly what they meant by sacrifice. The theologians at Trent tried to work out such a definition and to make immolation part of it (Lepin, p. 312). They seemed to have been looking for a general definition that would be applicable both to the cross and to the Mass. They failed to agree on one. The Fathers of the Council eventually decided that the challenge of Melanchthon could and should be answered in another way. Their text does not adopt any definition of sacrifice, or any theory about how what is done with the bread and wine constitutes an immolation. Rather, it proceeds descriptively, comparing the Mass with the cross, and showing that it has the elements that make the cross be a sacrifice: Christ himself is offered and immolated in it, and Christ himself is the one who offers. The sacrificial nature of the Mass is not established, then, from its verifying of any moral or cultic definition of sacrifice, but simply from its identification with the sacrifice of the cross. The only difference stated between it and the cross is that the oblation/ immolation of Christ is done in an 'unbloody manner'. From the dogmatic point of view Trent is saying what essentially needed to be said at that time: the Mass is a real propitiatory sacrifice because it is really, though not realistically, the sacrifice of Christ on the cross. A theological question remains about how this 'not realistically' can be put into more positive terms. In ch. 1 the Council related the Mass to the cross as its representation, memorial and application. Theology ought to be able to identify what there is in the Mass that makes it a representation, memorial and application of the cross. Trent leaves the question to the theologians.

A propitiatory sacrifice has the effect of taking away sin and giving grace. Protestants charged that the Catholic teaching was giving the impression that the Mass itself forgave sin and conferred grace, and that it did so without faith and conversion on the part of those for whom it was offered. The text of Trent replies with an application of the Catholic doctrine of justification. It says that the propitiatory effects of the Mass are for those who 'draw near to God with an upright heart and true faith, with fear and reverence, with sorrow and repentance'. Grace is given in the Eucharist on one ground only: the Lord is pleased by the offering since it is of the same victim and by the same priest as was the cross, only the manner of offering being different. Understood thus, as the application of the fruits of the sacrifice of the cross, the sacrifice of the Mass could not, says Trent, possibly detract from the all-sufficiency of the cross. It is, therefore, 'rightly offered according to apostolic tradition, not only for the sins, punishments, satisfaction and other necessities of the faithful who are alive, but also for those who have died in Christ but are not yet wholly purified'.

Chapters 3–8 of the Doctrine on the Sacrifice of the Mass apply the doctrine of the first two chapters to issues that had been raised by the Reformers: Masses in honour of Saints (ch. 3); the Roman Canon (ch. 4); the ceremonial of Mass (ch. 5); Masses at which only the celebrating priest communicated (ch. 6); the mixing of water with the wine (ch. 7); the use of vernacular languages (ch. 8). Chapters 6 and 7 are quite sacramental, and there is an exhortation to the faithful to receive communion at every Mass, 'so that they may derive more abundant fruits from this most holy sacrifice'. Chapter 8 recognizes the need for instruction (eruditio) that is inherent in the Eucharist and 'orders that pastors and all who have the care of souls must frequently, either by themselves or through others, explain during the celebration of Masses some of the readings of the Mass, and among other things give some instruction about the mystery of this most holy sacrifice, especially on Sundays and feastdays'. It is a careful concession to something the Protestants were insisting on, but it is quite some distance from their theology of the Eucharist as proclamation. The use of the vernacular is not excluded as a matter of principle but is not considered expedient as a general practice. Each church was to maintain its own rite, including the traditional language of the rite. The Council was cautious about liturgical innovations and defensive about Catholic practice. Even if some reforms had seemed desirable, the fact that they had been pre-empted by the Protestants on the basis of an unacceptable sacramental and eucharistic theology discouraged the Council from adopting them.

The final chapter of the Doctrine on the Mass introduces the canons directed against Protestant errors. The most theologically significant of them, nn. 1–4, may usefully be quoted:

1. If anyone says that in the Mass a true and proper sacrifice is not offered to God or that the offering consists merely in the fact that Christ is given to us to eat, *anathema sit*.

2. If anyone says that by the words 'Do this as a memorial of Me' (Luke 22:19; 1 Corinthians 11:24) Christ did not establish the apostles as priests or that He did not order that they and other priests should offer His body and blood, *anathema sit*.

3. If anyone says that the sacrifice of the Mass is merely an offering of praise and thanksgiving, or that it is a simple commemoration of the sacrifice accomplished on the cross, but not a propitiatory sacrifice, or that it benefits only those who communicate; and that it should not be offered for the living and the dead, for sins, punishments, satisfactions and other necessities, *anathema sit*.

4. If anyone says that the sacrifice of the Mass constitutes a blasphemy against the most holy sacrifice which Christ accomplished on the cross, or that it detracts from that sacrifice, *anathema sit*.

9.5   FROM TRENT TO VATICAN II

The two dogmatic texts of the Council of Trent dominated Catholic systematic theology of the Eucharist during the centuries of what came to be called the Counter-Reformation. The broad tradition of faith about the Eucharist continued to be studied in the Scriptures, in the Fathers and in the mediaeval masters. But the material was organized systematically around the questions of real presence and sacrifice. It became common to present two separate treatises: one on the Eucharist as sacrament, which dealt with the real presence, communion, reservation and veneration of the Eucharist outside Mass; the other on the Eucharist as sacrifice, or on the sacrifice of the Mass. The agenda of these treatises was influenced very much by the agenda of the Council of Trent. The dogmatic definitions on which the various theses were constructed were the canons of the Council. Apart from the profession of faith imposed on Berengarius and a few references to transubstantiation in some mediaeval councils they were the only dogmatic texts available about the Eucharist. It was the canons rather than the doctrinal expositions of Trent that were given the status of dogma because, methodologically, it was held that when Trent condemned a proposition attributed to the Reformers it was dogmatically defining the opposite of the condemned proposition: what the heretics were condemned for denying was what Catholics were bound to believe. It would not have been claimed that the dogmas of Trent so understood exhausted Catholic teaching on the Eucharist. But when Catholic theology was conceived as an exposition of the dogmas of the Church it was difficult to justify giving a major place to other questions about the Eucharist that did not have the credentials of dogmatic definition. The dogmas also determined the categories and language of Catholic theology. Since what Protestants had been denying were generally the positions of Catholic mediaeval theology, their negative judgements were often formulated in Scholastic terms. The condemnation of their views by Trent was necessarily formulated in the same terms. When the canons were turned around to become dogmatic definitions their language was also canonized for dogmatic usage.

There were developments in Catholic theology of the Eucharist during the centuries after Trent. Some came from a better rooting of Catholic dogmatic positions in the tradition of faith through a more informed use of the Scriptures and the Fathers. Others came from systematic analysis and philosophical refinements of key concepts. These speculative developments occurred regarding both the sacrament and the sacrifice. The metaphysical niceties of transubstantiation were studied thoroughly. The theology of the Eucharist as sacrifice was worked at even more intensely and the developments are noteworthy. Trent had defined the tradition of faith quite clearly but had left many open theological ends. Catholic faith in the Eucharist as propitiatory sacrifice was intellectually vulnerable until an appropriate theology was worked out. A definition of sacrifice was sought that would be verified in the Mass but in a way that allowed for its being the same sacrifice as the cross. Explanations had to be given of how the immolation of Christ on the cross was represented, remembered and applied in the Mass, which would at the same time show the Mass to be a real sacrifice and not merely a representation or memorial. The relationship between Christ's offering and the offering made by the priest-minister, by the whole Church and by individual Christians, had to be unravelled. Proper distinctions had to be made between the fruits of the Mass that were available to different persons who offered the Mass or had the Mass offered for them. Reasons had to be given for these fruits being limited even though the cross from which they all flow in the Mass is infinite in value and efficacy. Because consideration of the Eucharist as sacrament usually belonged to a different theological treatise, questions about the Mass were rarely dealt with in the categories of sacrament. Use was made rather of the kind of theology of sacrifice that Scholastic masters like Thomas Aquinas had worked out in their analyses of the virtue of religion — something which, it is interesting to note, Thomas himself did hardly at all in this theology of the Eucharist (Lepin documents and analyses these developments in post-Tridentine authors: pp. 335–758; Clark deals with the way they are presented by more recent Catholic authors: pp. 249–268).

The Counter-Reformation model of eucharistic theology remained dominant among Catholics until the various movements that led up to the Second Vatican Council began to make their presence felt. From the end of the nineteenth century the renewal of general sacramental theology (see 2.8 above) was also at work in the theology of the Eucharist. The Mass began to be experienced in a different way under the influence of the liturgical movement. The tradition of faith about the Eucharist began to sound richer as the independent voices of biblical and patristic scholars came to be added to those of the neo-Scholastic theologians. While the renewal of eucharistic theology was a complex process, one of the key transforming factors must certainly have been the more profound understanding of the word 'sacrament' and the sense given to it when applied to the Eucharist. The image of key was, in fact, used by Dom Ansgar Vonier, OSB in the title of a remarkable book about the Eucharist which he published in 1925, *A Key to the Doctrine of the Eucharist*. The key he offers is the concept of sacramentality. Vonier took the concept from St Thomas. He was, as the editor of his collected works notes (vol. 2, p. 226), writing in the context of 'a good deal of controversy on the relation of the Mass to Calvary'. The controversy was being carried on by Catholic theologians in mainly Scholastic terms, with frequent appeal to St Thomas. Vonier believed, says his editor, that 'some of the protagonists, in spite of their elaborate display of scholarship had departed from the traditional concept of the Eucharist'. He considered that concept to be 'the essentially sacramental character of the Sacrifice of the Altar'. Vonier demonstrates his thesis from the text of Thomas and finds confirmation of it in the teaching of Trent about the Eucharist as sacrifice. He sees sacramentality as the key not just to the question of sacrifice but also to the question of presence. It is a unifying idea which requires that the ideas of sacrament and sacrifice should interpenetrate rather than go their separate ways. Other authors besides Vonier had been giving sacramentality a richer sense when applied to the Eucharist. Billot has it in his theology of transubstantiation; De la Taille has something of it in *Mysterium Fidei* (1921) and *Esquisse du Mystère de la foi* (1925). However, both these authors maintain the standard Counter-Reformation division of the treatment of the Eucharist into sacrifice and sacrament. The methodological distinction can probably never disappear entirely from the Catholic way of doing the theology of the Eucharist, but the separation of the two ideas can be overcome. The studies of Odo Casel and his school posed questions for systematic theology about the relationship between mystery/sacrament and cult/sacrifice, and about the presence in mystery of the Passover sacrifice of Christ, which required the drawing-together of sacrament and sacrifice in the theology of the Eucharist (cf. Filthaut). One can already see a wedding of these currents with the Thomistic tradition in C. Journet, *La Messe. Présence du Sacrifice de la Croix* (1957), and in M.-J. Nicolas, OP, *L'Eucharistie* (1959).

The controversies and schisms of the Reformation set up independent traditions of eucharistic theology in Lutheran, Calvinist and Anglican churches. They
continued to reflect the battles of the Reformation for almost as long as Catholic
theology did. Without the firm dogmatic framework which Catholics accepted
from the decrees of Trent, theologians of these other traditions often felt freer to
explore approaches to the Eucharist that might go beyond their own confessional
statements. They were, of course, also vulnerable to reductionist tendencies when
historical and psychological studies on the Eucharist from the standpoint of
comparative religion became common in the nineteenth century. But from the
beginning of the twentieth century one begins to get important biblical and
patristic theologies of the Eucharist from all the churches, which contribute to a
recovery of the full tradition of faith and to the possibility of a theology that
might approach the controversies of the Reformation in a new and reconciling
way. Significant works of this kind from the Anglican tradition are C. Gore, *The
Body of Christ* (1901) and E. L. Mascall, *Corpus Christi* (1953). From Lutherans
came the important work of the Swedish scholar Y. Brilioth, *Eucharistic Faith and
Practice. Evangelical and Catholic* (1926; English ed. 1930). Brilioth analyses the
Eucharist according to four characteristic and complementary aspects; Thanksgiving, Communion-fellowship, Commemoration, Sacrifice; and a fifth, Mystery, which embraces and unites the other four. He does a critical analysis of how
the mediaeval church and then the major Reformers and the churches issued from
them dealt with these different aspects in their eucharistic theology and practice.
An influential study from the Reform traditions was that of O. Cullmann, 'The
Meaning of the Lord's Supper in Primitive Christianity' (1936); this was published in English in 1958, along with F. J. Leenhardt, 'This Is My Body', under the
title *Essays on the Lord's Supper.* Cullmann's essay was a critique of another study
from the Protestant side that had raised troublesome theological issues about the
Eucharist: H. Lietzmann, *Messe und Herrenmahl* (1926; Eng. trans. 1953–76).
Leitzmann's studies of the early liturgies of the Eucharist led him to the hypothesis
that St Paul's teaching on the Lord's Supper, which relates the fraternal meal of
Christians to the death of Christ by interpreting it in the light of the Last Supper,
was distinct from another New Testament tradition which saw the fraternal meal
of Christians as a joyful, eschatological remembering of the fellowship the
original disciples enjoyed when they ate with Jesus during his lifetime on earth,
in meals that were messianic but had no connection with his death. Cullmann
shows from the New Testament, using especially the accounts of the sharing of
food which Jesus did with his disciples after the resurrection, that the Eucharist
as a joyful meal of Christian fellowship was also and at the same time a
commemoration of the Passover death of Jesus which, in the light of the
resurrection, is the source of that fellowship. His demonstration has important
theological consequences for understanding the Eucharist as a sacramental meal
and how that very sacramentality makes it be a real commemoration of the
sacrificial death of Christ.

The study of Leenhardt that accompanies Cullmann's essay is an ecumenical
attempt to interpret the doctrine of transubstantiation in a way that, while doing

justice to the Catholic dogma, would also be acceptable to Protestants. The effort became associated with, if it was not actually the inspiration of, attempts by some Catholic theologians to restate the doctrine of transubstantiation in personalist, phenomenological terms. The effort produced, in the years around 1960, theories of transfinalization and transignification as explanations of the real presence of the body and blood of Christ in the Eucharist. In simplified terms, the theories suggested that the 'final reality' of anything is determined by the finality intended for it by its maker, rather than by what it is made of. Bread and wine are made for the purpose of giving human nourishment and promoting human fellowship in a meal. In the Eucharist God changes the finality which, as Creator, he gave bread and wine, making it have the finality of the body and blood of Christ given for the salvation of all. The change in finality brought about by God is a change in the reality of bread and wine into the body and blood of Christ. One can thus speak of a transfinalization. The theory expressed by the term is claimed to be a faithful rendering of the Catholic dogma of transubstantiation, having the advantage of avoiding various philosophical and theological difficulties that the word 'substance', and the Aristotelian philosophy associated with it, carries with it in a theology of the Eucharist. Another form of the same basic theory goes by the name of transignification. It sees the reality of the things that eucharistic theology is concerned with in their signification or meaning. The reality of things is the significance or meaning that they have for human existence. In profane use bread and wine have a given human signification. In the Eucharist that signification is changed: what is signified now is all that is meant by the body and blood of Christ. The trans-signification is a change of reality because the reality of things that is at issue in the Eucharist is the signification they have in human life.

Some versions of transfinalization and transignification advanced in the early 1960s were quite superficial. They employed a simplistic reading of what the tradition of faith said about presence in sign to justify treating the eucharistic presence of Christ as a matter of signification; they gave careful enough attention to the anthropological process by which the meaning of things changes, but less thought to the action of God and its consequences for the reality of things, that has always been the primary referent of the words 'sacrament' and 'sign' in the tradition of sacramental theology. Transubstantiation was sometimes dismissed as being an 'outdated' concept without much reflection on the difference between being 'dated' and being 'outdated'. But there were theologians who did the kind of serious work that was needed to establish a theory of transignification. The texts of Trent were examined hermeneutically to discover the historical sense given to transubstantiation by the Fathers of Trent and the extent to which a contemporary grasp of that same meaning required the continued use of the term transubstantiation. The philosophical value and limits of the concept substance were examined (particularly in view of its associations with Aristotelian physics and philosophy of nature), and the ontological status of an analysis of reality in terms of meaning was defended (cf. for example, Schillebeeckx, *The Eucharist*). Pope Paul VI intervened in the debate in 1965 with the encyclical *Mysterium Fidei* to remind Catholics of the faith that had been defined at Trent and to warn about limitations in theories of transignification and transfinalization. He did not condemn these theories but set the conditions under which they might be incorporated in Catholic theology:

> It is not allowable . . . to exaggerate the element of sacramental sign as if the symbolism, which all certainly admit in the Eucharist, expressed fully and exhausted the mode of Christ's presence in this sacrament. Nor is it allowable to discuss the mystery of transubstantiation without mentioning what the Council of Trent stated about the marvellous change of the whole substance of bread into the body and of the whole substance of wine into the blood of Christ, speaking rather only of what is called 'transignification' and 'transfinalization' . . . . As a result of transubstantiation, the species of bread and wine undoubtedly take on a new meaning and a new finality, for they no longer remain ordinary bread and ordinary wine, but become the sign of something sacred, the sign of a spiritual food. However, the reason why they take on this new significance and this new finality is because they contain a new 'reality' which we may justly term ontological. For there no longer lies under those species what was there before, but something quite different; and that, not only because of the faith of the Church, but in objective reality, since after the change of the substance or nature of the bread and wine into the body and blood of Christ, nothing remains of the bread and wine but the appearances, under which Christ, whole and entire, in His physical 'reality' is bodily present, although not in the same way as bodies are present in a given place (ND 1577, 1580; cf. O'Neill, *New Approaches*, p. 110).

9.6   SECOND VATICAN COUNCIL

Vatican II confirmed the dogmatic positions of the Council of Trent on the Eucharist (*SC*, nn. 6, 7, 55). It is, however, sparing in its use of Tridentine language and of technical categories of the post-Reformation Scholastic theology that had for so long interpreted Trent for Catholics. It prefers the biblical and patristic language that had been earning its place in eucharistic theology in the half-century preceding the Council. It is not that the Council is itself doing a new kind of systematic theology — such is not the business of a council — but, nevertheless, the way in which it expresses the faith of the Church about the Eucharist has inevitable consequences for theology. The Council is telling the world about the mystery of the Eucharist rather than telling Catholics how to defend their faith against heresy on particular points. It is telling Christians of other churches what the faith of the Catholic Church is with a view to bringing about the union of Christians in the Eucharist, rather than with a view to condemning the views of others about the Eucharist. It is telling Catholics, then, to develop a theology of the Eucharist that would reflect the full biblical and patristic tradition in a balanced way rather than concentrate on the dogmatic issues settled by Trent against the Reformers.

There is no separation of sacrament and sacrifice in the formulations of Vatican II about the Eucharist. There are inevitable distinctions between offering the sacrifice and eating the Lord's Supper (*SC*, n. 10; *LG*, n. 11) but the aspects so distinguished are not dealt with apart from one another. Chapter 2 of the

Constitution on the Liturgy is entitled 'The Most Sacred Mystery of the Eucharist', and deals in a unified way with material that Trent separated into sacrament
and sacrifice. Attention was drawn in 2.9 above to the richness of the idea of
sacrament used by Vatican II, and to the way it recovers the biblical and patristic
tradition of *mysterium/sacramentum*. It is a conception that expects an interaction
between word and rite in the celebration of sacraments; it leads the Council to
say in the chapter on the Eucharist: 'The two parts which in a sense go to make
up the Mass, viz. the liturgy of the word and the eucharistic liturgy, are so closely
connected with each other that they form but one single act of worship' (*SC*, n.
56). In presenting the Eucharist as mystery/sacrament the Council is putting it in
series with the mystery of Christ and with the mystery of the Church as universal
sacrament of the salvation Christ is sent to give to the world in his human flesh.
The Christological reality of the Eucharist had been defined in its essentials by
Trent. Vatican II gives more attention to the ecclesiological reality that is present
in it. All that is said about the liturgy in ch. 1 of the Constitution is verified
pre-eminently in the Eucharist. All that will subsequently be done, in the
redesigning of rites and in pastoral strategy, to make the Eucharist be a real
expression of the life of the whole Church community is grounded on the
doctrinal statement that opens the chapter on the Eucharist:

47.   At the Last Supper, on the night he was betrayed, our Saviour instituted the
eucharistic sacrifice of his Body and Blood. This he did in order to perpetuate the
sacrifice of the Cross throughout the ages until he should come again, and so to entrust
to his beloved Spouse, the Church, a memorial of his death and resurrection: a
sacrament of love, a sign of unity, a bond of charity, a paschal banquet in which Christ
is consumed, the mind is filled with grace, and a pledge of future glory is given to us.

48.   The Church, therefore, earnestly desires that Christ's faithful, when present at
this mystery of faith, should not be there as strangers or silent spectators. On the
contrary, through a good understanding of the rites and prayers they should take part
in the sacred action, conscious of what they are doing, with devotion and full
collaboration. They should be instructed by God's word, and be nourished at the table
of the Lord's Body. They should give thanks to God. Offering the immaculate victim,
not only through the hands of the priest but also together with him, they should learn
to offer themselves. Through Christ, the Mediator, they should be drawn day by day
into ever more perfect union with God and each other, so that finally God may be
all in all.

Post-conciliar documents on the Eucharist, and particularly the *General Instruction of the Roman Missal* (see above, 8.1; 8.2.6), spell out the doctrinal and pastoral
orientations of the Council. A theology of the Eucharist that lets itself be
prompted by these texts will take a sacramental approach to the Eucharist; it will
relate the rite of the sacrament to the word that is proclaimed within it; it will
see the Eucharist as an action of the whole Church; it will consider the realism
of Christ's presence in the consecrated species in relation to the manifestations of
his presence that are given in the assembled community, in the word that is read
and preached, and in the ministry of the ordained; it will see the sacrificial reality
of the Eucharist as a unique (because sacrificial) realization of that movement of

worship that corresponds to the movement of sanctification in the whole sacramental system; it will take full sacramental participation, climaxing in the eating and drinking of the body and blood of Christ (i.e. communion under both kinds) to be the normal practice according to which the Eucharist has to be understood; it will refuse to see communion as a sacramental extra for which one has to give added explanations, considering that what needs the added explanation is rather the incongruity of Christians not receiving the body and blood of Christ when they assemble as Church to take part in the Eucharist; it will take account of the eschatological dimension of the Eucharist as the Church celebrates it within a world that is working out its salvation while waiting for the coming of the Lord.

9.7   ECUMENICAL CONVERGENCE

The kind of eucharistic theology patronized by Vatican II has made it possible for Catholics to have productive ecumenical dialogue with Christians from other ecclesial and theological traditions. Theologians of all churches have been drawing on the same general sources and using a similar methodology to think out the Church's faith about the Eucharist. Scriptural and historical studies are done ecumenically. The patristic theology of the Eucharist maintained in the Eastern churches is increasingly well known and appreciated in Western theology. The theology of the great Reformers is being looked at with a new appreciation for what it did to restore and transmit the tradition of faith and to challenge certain limitations of mediaeval theology. The work of the Council of Trent can be presented more persuasively in view of a general willingness to recognize certain exaggerations and omissions in the theology of the Reformers which needed correction. At the same time the historical situating of the decrees of Trent allows them to be used without that absoluteness that was commonly attributed to them in Counter-Reformation theology. The Eucharist is considered a central issue in most of the bilateral and multilateral dialogues that have been held between the churches over the last twenty years. The Anglican–Roman Catholic International Commission (ARCIC I) dealt with it at the very beginning of its work and produced *An Agreed Statement on Eucharistic Doctrine* (Windsor, 1971; Meyer and Vischer, pp. 68–77) which claims to represent substantial agreement on the issues that once divided the two churches. The statement is not meant to be a comprehensive theology of the Eucharist but at the same time its authors consider that it has not omitted anything essential. It uses the idea of *mystery* to state the most basic truths about the Eucharist; it uses the idea of *memorial/anamnēsis* to state the relationship between the Eucharist and the cross in a way that would meet Catholic dogmatic requirements about the sacrificial character of the Eucharist and Anglican concern about maintaining the all-sufficiency of the cross; in speaking of the presence of Christ it says that 'Communion with Christ in the eucharist presupposes his true presence, effectually signified by the bread and wine which, in this mystery, become his body and blood. The real presence of his body and blood can, however, only be understood within the context of the redemptive activity whereby he gives himself, and in himself reconciliation, life and peace to his own' (n. 6); it uses the concepts of sign and sacrament to affirm both the reality of the presence and its being ordered to communion (nn. 8–9); it also relates the consecratory prayer (*anaphora*) to communion by saying that 'Through this Prayer of thanksgiving, a word of faith addressed to the Father, the bread and wine become the body and blood of Christ by the action of the Holy Spirit, so that in communion we eat the flesh of Christ and drink his blood' (n. 10); 'transubstantiation' is described in a note as a word 'commonly used in the Roman Catholic Church to indicate that God acting in the eucharist effects a change in the inner reality of the elements. The term should be seen as affirming the *fact* of Christ's presence and of the mysterious and radical change which takes place. In contemporary Roman Catholic theology it is not understood as explaining *how* the change takes place'. ARCIC I issued a series of Elucidations on the intentions and meaning of its Windsor and other statements in 1979, by way of response to comments it had received on its texts. The fact that the Commission did not revise its original Statement shows the continued confidence that its members had in their formulation; the fact that the text of the Elucidations is longer than the text of the Statement is an indication of the complex process of critical reception that has to go on in the churches before real agreement is reached. The authorities responsible for doctrine in both churches have a decisive rôle to play in the process. It is likely that when they do make an official judgement on the ARCIC Statement about the Eucharist they will ask for some further work to be done on particular points. The Observations which the Congregation for the Doctrine of the Faith issued in May 1982 on the Final Report of ARCIC is a warning of what the concerns are likely to be on the Catholic side. For indications of what the Anglican judgement may be, cf. *Towards a Church of England Response to BEM and ARCIC*, a Report from the Faith and Order Advisory Group (London, 1985). However, the degree of agreement already reached by Anglican and Roman Catholic theologians about the Eucharist is still very striking. The Windsor Statement remains an essential document for the contemporary theology of the Eucharist. It is a kind of prophetic statement along lines that theology will certainly want to pursue.

Another important text for the theology of the Eucharist is the Final Report on the Eucharist issued by the International Lutheran/Roman Catholic Commission in 1978 (Meyer and Vischer, pp. 190–212). The Report comes in two parts. The first, called 'Joint Witness', is a statement of faith about the Eucharist that both churches are thought to agree on. It presents the Eucharist as the new Passover meal in which Jesus gives himself 'in order to bestow on human beings peace and communion with God and with one another' (n. 6); as the 'mystery of faith' (nn. 7–12), celebrated 'Through, with and in Christ' (13–20), 'In the unity of the Holy Spirit' (21–28), for the 'Glorification of the Father' (29–37), 'For the life of the World' (38–41), 'with a view to future glory' (42–45). The second part is called 'Joint Tasks'. It looks at the issues of doctrine and practice that have divided the churches, at the progress that has been made in resolving them, and at the work that remains to be done. It conveys a confidence that the difficulties can be overcome and a common doctrine and practice of the Eucharist achieved. The tasks it sets must be an integral part of any contemporary theology of the Eucharist.

A multilateral dialogue, involving Christians of several churches calling themselves the Groupe des Dombes, produced a statement of doctrinal agreement on the Eucharist in 1972 (*Modern Eucharistic Agreement*, London, 1973), in which it is claimed that 'the major difficulties concerning the eucharistic faith have been removed' (n. 36), although 'some clarification is still required in regard to the permanence of the sacramental presence and the precise place of the apostolic succession in the ministry' (n. 37). A more comprehensive theological effort to develop a common statement of eucharistic faith was begun by the Faith and Order Commission of the World Council of Churches as far back as its first conference in Lausanne in 1927. The study, along with parallel studies on Baptism and ministry, was carried on by commissions made up of Protestant, Anglican, Orthodox and, in due course, Roman Catholic theologians, through various consultations and meetings of the Faith and Order Commission, until it eventually became part of BEM, the document approved at the Lima Assembly of Faith and Order in 1982. The eucharistic theology of BEM is sacramental. It begins with the institution of the Eucharist by Jesus at the Last Supper, as a 'sacramental meal which by visible signs communicates to us God's love in Jesus Christ, the love by which Jesus loved his own "to the end"' (n. 1). The meaning of the Eucharist is expounded as it is discovered through its sacramentality, for 'The eucharist is essentially the sacrament of the gift which God makes to us in Christ through the Holy Spirit' (n. 2). Five aspects are considered: in 3–4, Thanksgiving to the Father (this includes a statement of the sacrificial movement of offering); in 5–13, Anamnesis or Memorial of Christ ('living and effective sign of his sacrifice . . . effective proclamation of God's mighty acts and promises', 'sacrament of the unique sacrifice of Christ', 'the sacrament of the body and blood of Christ, the sacrament of his real presence'); in 14–18, Invocation of the Spirit (by whose power, along with the living word of Christ, 'the bread and wine become the sacramental signs of Christ's body and blood' and 'remain so for the purpose of communion'); in 19–21, Communion of the Faithful ('demonstrates and effects the oneness of the sharers with Christ and with their fellow sharers in all time and places . . . inconsistent if we are not actively participating in this ongoing restoration of the world's situation and the human condition . . . responsible care of Christians for one another and for the world . . . '); in 22–26, Meal of the Kingdom ('Reconciled in the eucharist, the members of the body of Christ are called to be servants of reconciliation among men and women and witnesses of the joy of resurrection . . . participation of God's mission to the world . . . '). The final section is about the liturgical rite and actual celebration of the Eucharist.

The theology of the Eucharist in BEM is an attempt by contemporary theologians from all the major ecclesial traditions to state the full apostolic faith about the Eucharist in a way that will help divided Christians to come together in full communion. It draws on the biblical and patristic scholarship of the past half-century and organizes it in a classical framework of economic trinitarianism.

It avoids using the dogmatic and confessional language in which the churches have historically defined their differences, not in order to avoid the issues about the Eucharist that divide the churches but to try to resolve them by dealing with them differently. The Commentary which accompanies the main text notes these difficulties and gives some suggestions about how they might be overcome. There has been much positive reaction from the churches to the statements about the Eucharist in BEM. The reserves expressed by the Catholic Church (see 2.10 above) bear on ambiguities and inadequacies of expression rather than on anything that is actually affirmed. Among the inadequacies singled out are the use of the notion of intercession as a way of stating the sacrificial reality of the Eucharist, the optional status given to belief that there is a change in the elements in which the body and blood of Christ are made present in the Eucharist, the non-committal position adopted about the continuing presence of Christ in the eucharistic elements after the celebration.

9.8   SYSTEMATIC ESSAY

A good case can be made from the tradition that has been presented throughout this chapter for saying that a theology of the Eucharist does best when it is a theology of sacrament. What is offered here is some systematic sacramental thinking about the Eucharist. It supposes the theology of sacrament that was worked out in Chapter 3 above and later used to think systematically about Baptism (5.8) and Confirmation (7.5). The Eucharist builds on and completes what is begun in Baptism and Confirmation. A theology of it can profitably take up where the theology of Baptism and Confirmation left off and follow the same lines. In the categories of sacramentality it should be able to draw together in an orderly way and bring to light the intelligibility of the rich tradition of faith about the Eucharist that has been narrated throughout this and the preceding chapter.

9.8.1   A sacramental meal

What Baptism and Confirmation sacramentalize is God's giving of life to his People through Christ and the Spirit. They sacramentalize that giving of life at its beginning — the passage from death to life (Baptism) and the special quality of the life that is being entered into because it is to be lived in the final, eschatological phase of salvation history (Confirmation). What the Eucharist sacramentalizes is the solid and continuous possession of the life begun in Baptism and Confirmation. One is fully initiated when one has taken part in it for the first time and thereafter it is the regularly repeated nourishment that ensures survival and growth. Ritually the Eucharist is a community meal of bread and wine which are taken as food and drink after a prayer of thanksgiving has been said over them. The meal ritual should be the starting point of all theological reflection about the Eucharist. From the time of the Reformation until quite recently, Catholic theology was somewhat reluctant to think of the whole Eucharist as a meal; at most it would admit that one aspect of it could be called a meal. There seemed to be a fear that the idea of Eucharist as meal led inevitably to the Protestant view of the sacrament as a non-sacrificial Holy Communion service. Present-day sacramental theology ought to be able to speak about the Eucharist as a meal without generating such fears. The Eucharist is a meal in the sacramental sense, as Baptism is a bathing in the sacramental sense. It is a reality (body and blood of Christ, sacrifice, communion, viaticum, thanksgiving . . .) that is contained, conveyed, acted out, symbolized in and by a meal. The meal is the sign, not the reality. It is not just the bread and wine that are signs in the Eucharist but the bread and wine given and taken in a meal. The host of the meal is as much part of the sign as the food he gives, and the guests who receive the food contribute to its significance. There would be no Eucharist without an ordained minister to represent Christ in his rôle of host who gives himself as food and without some believing people (at the very least the minister himself) to eat and drink the food that is prepared and given.

To give a meal to people is to give them life. Any giving of food is recognized as life-sustaining. The first drops of mother's milk given to a child and accepted by it are an effective sign of the mother's desire to keep the new-born child alive and of the child's ability to go on living: one cannot be sure that a new-born child has a hold on life until it begins to take food. It is in this sense that the Eucharist enters into the sacramentality of Christian initiation. As the first giving and taking of food it is a sign that initiation into the life process is really complete. To continue giving food is to make life continue and grow. To give it in a meal is to give life in its distinctively human dimension. Taking a meal is more than just taking food. Humans cultivate food and prepare it, as well as just gathering it: it is 'fruit of the earth and work of human hands'. They prepare it together and give it to one another. To prepare food and invite someone to come and sit down at one's table is to express one's intention of being life-giving for them in a distinctively human way: it is to offer them food of the body but also of the spirit in the form of companionship and conversation; it is to be ready to draw life from them in return. To make the meal a festive one is to express the joy of host and participants in some shared life-experience, and in doing so to intensify their shared life. Meals are taken to remember people and events that have contributed to the life of those who eat and drink together. A special kind of food associated with the person or event being remembered may be used to reinforce the remembering. Meals are an occasion for remembering God the life-giver when food is recognized as his gift. People pray at meals and express their awareness that all life comes from God.

9.8.2   Sacrament of the gift of eternal life

What the eucharistic meal ritualizes is God's giving of eternal life to his People and their receiving of it. The first Eucharist that is received as part of initiation manifests and ensures that the initiate has a stable hold on eternal life and is ready for nourishment and growth towards the full enjoyment of it. When people continue to take part in the Eucharist in a regular rhythm, what is being sacramentalized is God's continuing care to maintain the life he has given and bring it to fullness, and their own acceptance of that growth. Every Eucharist, but particularly that which is received as a preparation for death, is a viaticum, sacramentalizing the fact that eternal life cannot be enjoyed in its fullness by those who live in time, so that what manifests and nourishes it on earth is always a looking forward to its fullness in heaven.

In sacramentalizing God's giving of eternal life and human reception of it, the Eucharist sacramentalizes Christ: he is the full, definitive giving of divine life to humanity and its perfect reception by humanity. It sacramentalizes Christ in his resurrection, by which his body was made fully alive and life-giving by God. It does so by sacramentalizing him in the death by which he gave his earthly life in witness to his acceptance that eternal life comes only from the God who is his Father: it was because of the way he died that he became totally open to receive that life from his Father at the resurrection. In sacramentalizing the Father's gift of life through, with and in Christ, the Eucharist sacramentalizes the Holy Spirit, who is given from the risen Lord as the transforming pledge of eternal life in the midst of the world. It is as a Spirit-filled meal that the Eucharist does its sacramentalizing. The meal serves as a symbolic way of remembering Christ in his death and resurrection. It can do so because of what the Christian story tells about the meals Jesus shared with his disciples, after his resurrection as well as during his earthly life, and particularly about the solemn way he shared a Passover meal with them just before he went to his death. The Eucharist reproduces significant details of that Last Supper that Jesus took with his disciples. It is a meal of bread and wine. The bread and wine are prayed over, broken and distributed by the one who presides and acts as host at the meal, just as Jesus did at the Last Supper. He says the same words that Jesus said about the bread and wine: 'this is my body . . . my blood'. These words define how Jesus is being remembered in the Eucharist. He is being remembered in his body and blood. That means he is being remembered as a person of flesh and blood, real and alive, as he was at the Last Supper and as he showed himself to his disciples after the resurrection, still capable of sharing a meal with humans. It also means that he is being remembered in the events that brought him to this state. Jesus died violently. His blood flowed from his body. Giving bread as his body ('flesh') and wine ('blood of the grape') as his blood is a powerful reminder that he died on the cross. What is remembered is not just the fact that Jesus died but the meaning he himself gave to his death. This is conveyed sacramentally by the way the words of his that are repeated in the Eucharist evoke the Jewish Passover, with its sacrifice of the lamb, and the covenant, which was ratified by a blood sacrifice. Jesus is being remembered as offering himself in sacrifice on the cross for the salvation of the new covenant People. It is being recognized that it was in so offering himself in sacrifice that he became life-giving in his body and blood at the resurrection.

Thus the Eucharist sacramentalizes eternal life for humans by sacramentalizing Jesus becoming the source of eternal life in the sacrifice he made of himself to the Father in his body and blood, in his receiving of that life in his own flesh and blood at the resurrection, and as risen Lord sending that life into the world in the gift of the Spirit.

9.8.3   For the forgiveness of sins

The Eucharist sacramentalizes the taking-away of sin. The world that Jesus brought life to was a world in which death was reigning. There was death because there was sin. To give life Jesus had to take away sin. Sin was present in the behaviour of humans: in their individual lives and in the institutions in which their world pursued sinful goals. It cut people off from God and divided them from one another. Instead of accepting the common Fatherhood of God people worshipped racial, political or ideological gods which they invented to justify their own sinfulness. Instead of being able to sit down together to share God's life-giving gifts, individuals isolated themselves, or grouped together in selfishness, building up hostilities to others that were always, in one way or another, death-dealing. People set about becoming rich in ways that inevitably made others poor; they provided food for themselves in ways that left others hungry; they embarked on forms of self-indulgence that required others to be abused in body and spirit . . . . Only God could take away the sin of the world, by forgiving and healing it. In his merciful design, revealed throughout the Old Testament, the taking-away of sin was to be realized and manifested in the life of a representative of humanity who would proclaim the truth about God in the face of human sinfulness, and suffer the consequences. Jesus was put to death by a sinful world because he made the ultimate challenge to its sinfulness. He accepted his death, giving in it the supreme proof of love that allowed God to forgive human sinfulness. God raised him from the dead, showing that in him sin and its consequences had been forgiven and overcome. People who unite around Jesus receive the forgiveness of their sins; they are given life and become life-giving for one another. Baptism is the sacrament of the initial and radical taking-away of sin. But the struggle against sin and its consequences is life-long. The reality of it and the victory gained in it are sacramentalized again and again in the Eucharist. What people are initiated to once for all in Baptism is worked out day by day in the eucharistic celebration of the reconciliation brought about by Jesus. People who forgive and are forgiven in him sit down together at a common table, at which they receive life from God and become life-giving for one another and for the world. They represent a new order of things in which there is no longer place for selfishness and self-indulgence, for divisions, oppressions and the feeding of some through making others hungry. The eucharistic table offers hospitality to everyone who is open to the life that comes from the death and resurrection of Jesus. It is a meal of reconciliation, as were the meals Jesus shared with publicans and sinners. It is a meal where the poor and hungry of the world are remembered, and where those who eat together are pledged to take away the hunger of the world and all the sinful forces that cause it. It is the sacrament of the taking-away of sin that Jesus did once for all in his death and resurrection, and that is being worked out day by day in the lives of those who are remembering him.

9.8.4   Presence of Christ in the sacrament

To say that the Eucharist sacramentalizes Christ in his dying and rising is already to state that he is present in it. A sacrament by definition makes the action of God in Christ present in a rite. The fact that the Eucharist realizes a unique presence of Christ (in the consecrated species) is no reason for forgetting the general presence that is realized in every sacrament. The Eucharist is, indeed, the prototype of sacramental presence. The ideas of memorial and mystery, which are the biblical and patristic antecedents of the technical concept of sacrament, were introduced pre-eminently to deal with it. All that the word 'sacrament' has come to say about presence must be fully realized in the Eucharist. Systematic theology devoted a good deal of attention to the analysis of sacramental presence, or 'mystery-presence' in connection with the theology of mystery proposed by Odo Casel. The effort needs to be continually made. To say that the presence is 'in mystery' is not to say that it is unintelligible. If it is real it must be subject to some kind of thoughtful verification. It must be seen to be consonant with what is known otherwise about reality, and to make sense in real terms. Presence is very clearly affirmed by the notion of 'memorial'. In biblical terms to say that the Eucharist is a memorial of the death and resurrection of Jesus is to say that the divine saving act that was present in the death and resurrection of Jesus is present and effective when the Eucharist is celebrated. But that too needs verification. It is a claim of faith that is attested in the Bible. A biblical scholar justifies the realistic interpretation of memorial on the basis of what he knows about Semitic mentality and the general use of the term in the Bible. But the fact that the people who wrote the Bible believed that God was present in his saving acts when a memorial was made of them does not of itself establish the truth of that belief. People have believed things that turned out to be fantasies or confidence tricks. Systematic theology, by critically examining the possibility and the positive credibility of the claim on the basis of a metaphysics of reality and presence, offers that verification to the assent of faith.

The theology of sacramental presence has been done in different ways in recent years. Thomist and neo-Scholastic theologians generally made strenuous efforts to provide a metaphysically tenable theology that would sustain and give some clarity to the affirmation about the mystery-presence that Casel recovered from the Fathers (for an account see Filthaut, Gaillard; for examples see Schillebeeckx, *Christ the Sacrament*, pp. 64–109, O'Neill, *Meeting Christ*, pp. 63–95). Theologians working from phenomenology have also made the effort (e.g. Vogel). Such theologies of presence need to be given their place in the theology of the Eucharist. They provide the context in which the particular question of the presence of Christ in the bread and wine have to be treated. They show how the community, its ministers, the word of God and the general liturgical setting enfold the presence in the species and with it manifest the personal saving action of God. Such theological clarification is important in ecumenical theology. The idea of memorial, and also that of mystery/sacrament, have proved very useful in ecumenical statements about the Eucharist. When these texts are interpreted in particular churches they are subject to the influences of different confessional traditions and of more or less conscious philosophical assumptions. Different interpretations of memorial and mystery/sacrament will arise. If there has not been some shared measure of theological understanding about the way terms like memorial and mystery/sacrament have been used in agreed statements, the different interpretations they receive may show that the agreement did not go much beyond the verbal.

The question about presence in memorial and mystery is fundamentally one about how God is present and acts in and on the created world, and about how that presence/action occurs in Christ. Thomas Aquinas asks these sort of questions in Part Ia of the *Summa* (e.g. in q. 8 on the existence of God in things; in q. 105, on how things (and people) are changed by God). He uses the principles worked out in these metaphysical discussions to understand God's presence and action in the history of salvation, and specifically how Christ in his humanness is present as the instrument of God in the grace of the New Testament. Even if one finds the answers of Thomas unsatisfactory one has to face in some form the questions that he asks. Otherwise one cannot claim to be thinking theologically (i.e. on the level of the divine) about Christian belief that the saving act of God realized in the death and resurrection of Christ is present when that act is ritually remembered in the Eucharist. On the Christological level one has to understand how the incarnation gives a divine dimension to all Christ's human actions. One also needs to have some reasoned explanation of how the moral choice of Christ to offer himself in sacrifice for his Father, which found expression in his body and blood on the cross, is still present and finding expression in the ritual remembering of the cross that is multiplied through time and space in the Eucharist (see above, 3.1). It was in that choice that Christ realized his vocation of being a priest forever according to the order of Melchizedek, and entered into the heavenly sanctuary where he is 'ever living to make intercession for us'. If the theory that Christ enjoyed the beatific vision during his life is discounted as an explanation of how he could be involved by some kind of human choice in the multiplicity of eucharistic memorials of his death, one has to look for some other explanation. One could, perhaps, find it in the comprehensiveness of the final option that Christ made in death and in the way that final option was given a timeless permanence in his passage into glory. It could be argued that his final option, already made at the Last Supper, bore not alone on the giving of his body and blood in historical death but on the ritual remembering of the giving of his body and blood that his disciples would do in the future while they waited for him to come again. In that case his human intentions, fixed forever at the moment of his death, would be as really present and expressed in the bread and wine that is made his body and blood in the Eucharist as they were in his body and blood on the cross. His presence thus understood would be a real presence of the priestly action of Christ, through which the divine action of giving eternal life is mediated.

9.8.5   Presence of the body and blood of Christ

The Eucharist sacramentalizes the giving and receiving of eternal life through the priestly mediation of Christ by making his body and blood be really and abidingly present as the food of immortality. The bread and wine that are prayed over and shared in the rite of the Church are proclaimed to be the body and blood of Christ. The specific sacramentality of the Eucharist requires that this statement be taken in its literal truth. What is sacramentalized in other rites of the Church are different moments of passage in the journey of members of the Christian community towards eternal life. What is sacramentalized in the Eucharist is the permanent hold they have on life during that journey — the state of being alive, of staying alive, of enjoying the growth which is inseparable from living, of being part of a community in which life can be lived to the full. What gives people a permanent hold on eternal life can only be the body and blood of Christ. Because they are the direct and permanent object of his priestly offering (he offered himself in offering his body and blood), only in them can the priestly act of sacrifice and intercession of Christ that gives eternal life be contacted. This is the body and blood that became life-filled and life-giving at the resurrection. Wherever the body and blood of Christ are, there, and only there, is eternal life being offered as a permanent possession to those who are open to receive it. To have eternal life is to be joined to the living body of Christ and to continue drawing life from it until one is transformed into its likeness at the resurrection. The Eucharist, then, is a sacrament only when the bread and wine have become the body and blood of Christ. The 'matter' of the sacrament is, indeed, bread and wine. These together are the sign of everything that is realized in the Eucharist. But they do their symbolizing and are a sacrament precisely in becoming the body and blood of Christ. The 'form' that determines their symbolism in a specific way is a divine word proclaiming in the Church that they are the body and blood of Christ, and doing what it says. This is the sacramental context in which the question of the real presence has to be discussed.

Before there were heresies about the real presence the theology of the Eucharist did not give extended treatment to the question. The controversies that eventually came to a head in the condemnation of Berengarius earned the question quite a lot of attention in Western theology. At the Reformation it became one of the two major areas of debate. One hopes that the ecumenical direction of contemporary theology is making it possible to scale down the treatment somewhat within a more broadly-based understanding of the Eucharist. Nevertheless, the question of the real presence of the body and blood of Christ in the eucharistic bread and wine has to be dealt with thoroughly. Theologically the issue is not just a matter of fact: it is also a matter of understanding the fact affirmed by faith. Accepting the affirmation of faith already requires a measure of understanding of what is being affirmed. It also requires a readiness to think about any reasonable questions that the fact raises for an enquiring mind. One cannot discount the questions simply by saying that they would never have occurred to the writers of the New Testament — because of their Semitic mentality or whatever. Nor can one discount all questions simply by pointing to a number of silly questions that have been asked about the real presence, for example in mediaeval theology. It is wishful thinking to claim that Christians will find it easier to agree about the Eucharist if they rely on simple formulas and do not ask too many questions about what they mean. Formulas, no matter how simple, are inevitably interpreted. If the interpretation of one person differs in some significant way from that of others, what seemed to be agreement may turn out to have been based on a misunderstanding. A theology of the real presence would want to clarify what is meant by the affirmation of faith at least to the point of eliminating basic misunderstandings.

Among the critical questions that clarify what one means by real presence the one about change must be the most urgent. The affirmation of faith in the real presence is about something that, before it is prayed over eucharistically, is clearly bread and wine and nothing else. After the prayer it is, in the judgement of faith, something else. Something in, or about, the bread and wine has changed. The patristic tradition was never afraid to affirm the real presence by affirming change in the bread and wine. When the hesitations came at the Reformation they were more about the kind of change than about the fact of change. The kind of change that is postulated must be in keeping with what the tradition of faith says about the kind of presence of the body and blood of Christ that is brought about in the change. What the tradition says is that the presence is both real and sacramental. Because it is real it is not merely symbolical, as Christ might be said to be present in a crucifix being used to bless people, or in an actor who plays the part of Christ in a Passion play. Because it is sacramental it is not realistic, as was the presence of Christ in Peter's boat or with Mary when she embraced him after the resurrection; it is somehow a presence in bread and wine.

The best way to go about understanding the kind of change that reconciles realism with sacramentality would seem to be to distinguish between what changes and what does not change in the Eucharist. Something of what is there must remain bread and wine because it has to serve as the symbol in which the sacramental presence is realized; something of what is there must no longer be bread and wine on a level of reality that is sufficiently profound to allow the body and blood of Christ to be really and truly what is there. This is the kind of affirmation and explanation of change that one finds in the teaching of the Council of Trent about transubstantiation. Trent affirms the faith of the Church that the body and blood of Christ are really and sacramentally present in the consecrated bread and wine; it teaches that this requires a real change in the bread and wine, so that after the consecration what is present is no longer the reality of bread and wine but only their appearances; it uses the word 'substance' to describe the level of being on which the change occurs and teaches that the substance of bread is changed into the substance of Christ's body and that of wine into his blood; it says that this change is fittingly called 'transubstantiation'; and all of this is said in order to confess in faith that what is eaten and drunk sacramentally under the appearances of bread and wine is truly, really and substantially the body and blood of Christ.

9.8.6 Theologies of the real presence

A Catholic theology of the Eucharist that wants to obey the dogmatic teaching of Trent might turn spontaneously to a theology of transubstantiation such as was worked out by Scholastic masters and developed by their disciples. That was the kind of theology that was on the mind of most of the Fathers and theologians of Trent. However, a critical hermeneutic of Trent can establish that what is affirmed there as being of faith does not require the acceptance of any particular Scholastic theology of transubstantiation, nor of the Aristotelian or other philosophical categories that might be used by it. Since Trent the faith of the Catholic Church in the real presence cannot be stated without reference to the dogma of transubstantiation. But it is possible to do a Catholic explanation of the real presence that would not use transubstantiation as a theological category. It may even be necessary to do so. There are philosophical difficulties about the way the categories of substance and accident are used in the theory, and about the meaning of change on the level of substance. Some would argue that substance cannot cover and relate two such disparate realities as material bread and the personal reality of Christ: to say Christ is present as the substance of bread was present would be to give that carnal, local meaning to his presence that was rejected so decisively in the patristic tradition, especially by Augustine. Others point out that the postulate of the accidents of bread and wine subsisting without a substance in which to inhere is something of a *deus ex machina* solution that is metaphysically untenable. Others still wonder how one substance can change into another already existing substance, and whether transubstantiation does not eventually come to something like the changing of water into wine, which obviously does not yield an adequate explanation of the sacramental presence of Christ in the Eucharist. If a theology of transubstantiation has these weaknesses it could, paradoxically, have the effect of obscuring the very truths that Trent affirmed by the dogma of transubstantiation. In any case, even if the philosophical and theological difficulties are overcome, there could still be an ecumenical reason for avoiding the concept substance in a theology of the eucharistic presence. The rejection of the term in the theology of the Eucharist is so deeply lodged in the traditions of the Protestant churches that to claim one cannot explain the mystery of the real presence theologically without it would be to put a major block in the way of a common understanding of the Eucharist.

Theories of transignification and transfinalization (see above, 9.5) avoid many of the difficulties of transubstantiation. Perhaps nowadays they offer the best way to begin thinking about the kind of change that brings about the real presence. They give a good account of the sacramentality of the presence, and of how it is experienced and responded to by humans. They draw attention to the personal quality of Christ's presence in his body and blood, and to the personal significance for humans of eating his body and drinking his blood. They affirm a real change in the bread and wine, and a real presence of the body and blood on a level corresponding to the change. The theological difficulty that arises at that point, however, is whether or not the level of reality at which the change and presence are postulated is the deep, ontological level at which the tradition of faith affirms the presence. Does transignification affirm unambiguously that what is eaten and drunk in the Eucharist is really the body and blood of Christ? A convinced phenomenologist will say that it does, because the theory is talking about the ultimate level of being: existentially there is nothing more profound in bread than the meaning it has in the world of humans. The debate then becomes philosophical. What is at stake is not just the ontological issue but how things depend in their being on God. In the tradition of faith it is the word of God, not just the word of man that changes the bread and wine in the Eucharist. The word of God is creative: it makes things be what they are said to be; it gives them their ultimate reality. From the theological point of view things are significant in human life because of what they are by God's making, not the other way around. Theologies of transignification recognize this and make much of it. However, it is questionable whether the philosophy they employ gives an adequate basis for distinguishing the ontological effect of the creative word of God from the effect of merely human changes of meaning. Like Christologies 'from below' (with which they have many affinities) in relation to the incarnation, they leave one wondering if they have said the last word about what God is doing in the mystery of the Eucharist.

Scholastic theories of transubstantiation certainly give priority to the action of God and its effects over human giving of meaning — often to the point of ignoring entirely the human mediation of meaning. It is worth looking at such a theory again to see if it cannot give a better account than transignification of the level at which the change to the body and blood of Christ occurs; to ask if it can do so without sacrificing the valuable explanations of the sacramentality of the presence that are offered by transignification; and to speculate if it can do it without running into insuperable philosophical contradictions. Even in the modest presentation of Thomas's theory of transubstantiation given above (9.3.2) one can see that the change being postulated as bringing about the eucharistic presence is the work of God, who alone can reach things on the level of substance. 'Substance' is being used here as a philosophical term. Its meaning is not conveyed by the images or concepts that the term evokes in physics and chemistry. The term 'substance' is not hopelessly tied to and compromised by these images. A glance at the variety of meanings it is given in any comprehensive dictionary of the English language is enough to confirm that it is often used in ways that have nothing whatever to do with analyses of physical reality, and still less with Aristotelian forms of it. In a theology of transubstantiation the 'substance of bread' means the ultimate level of its reality, at which it exists independently as a piece of bread and as nothing else. 'Accidents' mean its shape and size and taste and other characteristics of it, which can be changed without the thing of which they are shape, size, taste . . . ceasing to be bread. Transubstantiation as a theological theory postulates that God acts on bread in a way that leaves the characteristics of bread unchanged (because they are needed for sacramentality) but changes the substance of bread into the substance of the body of Christ in such a way that what used to exist as bread, and was recognized as such by its accidents, now exists as body of Christ. What exists is recognized as body of Christ only by faith in the words that have been spoken about it by the priest; it is accepted as life-giving in an act of eating made possible by the accidents of bread, to which it has become sacramentally related by the act of change. The substance of what is there and eaten is no longer bread but the body of Christ. The ontological assumption of transubstantiation is that if Christ is not there in his substance he is not really there at all. He is there as substance because the bread yields to him by being changed in its substance into him.

Christ becomes present in the Eucharist according to the theory of transubstantiation, not because anything happens to him but because of what happens to the bread and wine. Christ in his substance becomes the term of a metaphysical movement of the bread and wine towards him. The term of the change of bread is his body, that of wine is his blood. Metaphysically Christ is one living substance, so that where his body is substantially there also is his blood, with his soul and divinity, and everything else that makes him be who he is. His substantiality, however, can be predicated separately of those two life-principles that are body and blood. Different aspects of his substantial existence were expressed in them during his life. They need to be expressed sacramentally in the Eucharist if it is to make him present as life-giving. Hence the sacramental act of transubstantiation changes the substance of bread into his body as substantial, and the substance of wine into his blood as substantial. Sacramentally (*ex vi sacramenti*, as the Scholastics and the Council of Trent said) the bread is his body and the wine his blood. But because of the substantial unity of Christ, where the substance of his body is there also is his blood and all the other components of his substantial existence. This is the presence of the *totus Christus, ex reali concomitantia*, which the Scholastics and the Council of Trent affirmed as the correlative of the presence *ex vi sacramenti*.

If the term of the change postulated is the substance of Christ, his presence in the Eucharist must be of the kind proper to substance. This would explain how everything that makes him be this individual person (including his shape, appearance, sound of voice etc.) is present in the Eucharist, but not in the natural mode of existence that these have in heaven. This concept of presence by way of substance (*per modum substantiae*) is the feature of the theory that would eliminate any suggestion of the presence being carnal or spatial or the result of some local movement of Christ towards where the Eucharist is being celebrated. Substance is the object of mind, not directly of sense. One only knows what something is on the level of its independent existence by thinking about it and judging what it is. Furthermore, the substance of the body and blood of Christ that is made present in the Eucharist can only be known by a mind whose thoughts and judgements are enlightened by the word of God. The presence of Christ in the Eucharist *per modum substantiae* is the object of a judgement of faith. Contact with the physical, tangible aspects of Christ's bodiliness is on the level of mind not of sense. What (i.e. the substance that) one eats and drinks is truly Christ who is a person of flesh and blood. But one does not have sense-contact with his flesh and blood as such. The sense-contact is with the accidents of bread and the accidents of wine in eating and drinking. As that sense-contact formerly put one's mind in touch with the substances of bread and wine (and made one judge: 'I am eating bread and drinking wine and being nourished by them'), so now that same sense-contact puts one's mind in touch with Christ and what he is in his body (known in the eating of bread) and blood (known in the drinking of wine): as one eats and drinks one is judging in faith: 'I am drawing from Christ the life that he gained for me and now offers me in this body and blood of his'. The objective basis of the judgement is that the substance of bread and wine have been changed into the substance of Christ's body and blood. By the change the accidents of bread and wine are related now to Christ present as substance. They do not become his accidents but they do become his sacrament. They allow him to offer humans a fully human contact, of sense and spirit, with himself. Christ exists in flesh and blood in heaven. Persons who are not in heaven can contact him really and in a way that makes him known as a person of flesh and blood in a sacrament of bread and wine. The act of faith in which this contact occurs is not just general faith in Jesus. It includes a very concrete judgement that the bread and wine which one is eating and drinking in faith are Christ really giving himself in his body and blood in a celebration of his Church at this particular point of place and time.

The philosophical difficulties about transubstantiation have to be answered philosophically. If it were demonstrated that the doctrine involves some metaphysical contradiction it would become untenable. But because the doctrine was developed, and is currently sustained or opposed, in discussions about a reality that is experienced only in faith, it is more likely that the difficulties come from a sort of philosophical awkwardness about what is being postulated theologically rather than from what are seen to be outright contradictions that are demonstrated on purely philosophical grounds. The theologian would want to meet the philosopher as far as possible on the philosopher's own ground. But he would also want to remind the philosopher that the reality being analysed in the theory of transubstantiation is something unique and not verifiable by reason alone. It is hardly surprising that it stretches the categories of rationality. The theory is also appealing to the creative action of God, who alone can act on creatures on the level of substance. The act of creation is something about which philosophy is notoriously tentative. Transubstantiation is also assuming that the frontiers of being are stretched in that new creation that has been begun by the pouring-out of the Spirit in the world. The theologian could argue that it is not unreasonable to expect some philosophical surprises when the things of this world, like bread and wine, are already caught up, by the power of the Spirit, in that transformation which makes the world of things become more and more the world of persons, and makes material things become more and more means of contact between persons rather than barriers between them. Philosophy might be interested also in exploring the suggestions that come out of the debate on transubstantiation about the connection between the ontological and the phenomenological. The theology of transubstantiation expounded here would claim to be a complement and deepening of theologies of transignification. It would claim to be so because it pushes a phenomenological analysis of the Eucharist that accounts well for the sacramentality of Christ's presence towards an ontological analysis that accounts better for its realism.

One would hope that the ecumenical difficulties of the term substance would be softened and eventually overcome by the kind of theological analysis of it that has been presented here. In ecumenical dialogue Catholic theologians will always need to explain what this word, that is so much part of their own tradition, really means in eucharistic theology. And all theologians must eventually face the fact that the word has been in the language of faith since the Lord's Prayer was formulated in the gospel of Matthew (see 9.3.1 above). It was well established in theology before Aristotelian philosophy began to leave its mark on the way it was used in the theology of the Eucharist. Over many centuries it has put minds in touch with a level of reality that Christian faith has constantly to bring to the attention of humanity: that is, the level on which the creative, formative and sustaining action of God occurs, and on which the ultimate transformation of reality in the new creation is being worked out. A well-defined concept of substance might manage to earn a degree of ecumenical toleration in the theology of the real presence, and eventually might even be found useful for equipping theology to deal with the ultimate level of reality on which the mystery occurs.

9.8.7   Sacrament of the Church

As a community meal at which the body of Christ is given for eating and his blood for drinking, the Eucharist sacramentalizes the Church, which is the mystical body of Christ that draws its life from his personal body and makes that life available in the world. The Church is the fruit of the Eucharist. It is also the maker of the Eucharist. The Eucharist is, indeed, the supreme instance of the ecclesiological principle that the Church 'is both community of the redeemed and redeeming institution'. God builds up the Church through the Eucharist; at the same time he uses the Church as his instrument to make the Eucharist be the body and blood of Christ. In gathering people together for a community meal the Church is setting up a sign of the way that God gives life to humans by uniting them with one another in the body of Christ. In human terms the fellowship of a meal gives the participants access to the company and gifts of others, the stimulus of their conversation, the enjoyment of their friendship; it raises individuals to higher planes of life; it gives a sense of belonging that promises security and a future. It is in such a community meal that eternal life coming from the body and blood of Christ is given. The Church gathers and is gathered by the Holy Spirit. The Spirit joins those who believe in Christ in a community of love, which is equipped with all the spiritual gifts needed to make it alive and life-giving. These are the gifts that make them be a prophetic and priestly people. Some are gifts that allow them to hear and proclaim the word of God. Others are 'anointings with the Spirit', or sacramental characters and other relationships with Christ which allow them as his members to represent him and do things that he will recognize as his own. These gifts contribute in various ways to the celebration of the Eucharist. Some of them are indispensable for it. There can be no Eucharist without people who can proclaim and receive God's word authentically: the Eucharist requires prophets. Neither can there be a Eucharist without the baptized and the ordained: the Eucharist requires priests. The Church employs all its resources in the celebration of the Eucharist. Conversely all these resources are given ecclesial status through the Eucharist. Although the Eucharist is a family celebration of the Church, restricted to those who have been properly initiated and live in accordance with the Gospel, it is also a sacrament of the mission of the Church in the world. The word that is proclaimed in it is the prophetic word that is for the salvation of all. The poor and hungry are reached out to in charity. Prayers are said for the salvation of the whole world. The Church is sent forth from it to bring the reconciling message of the Gospel to all. The Eucharist is an open table awaiting all who receive the word and are baptized.

9.8.8   Through the ministry of priests

To constitute a eucharistic community the prophetic and priestly people must be gathered under the presidency of a bishop or presbyter who is ordained to the ministry of priesthood. The fundamental reason is sacramental. To be the Eucharist a meal must sacramentalize not just the body and blood of Christ but Christ himself as priest, giving life to those gathered at table by giving his body and blood for them and to them as food. Christ the Priest is the real host of the eucharistic meal. While all those present have a share in his priesthood which allows them to receive his sacrifice as their own, they do not represent him in his priestly action of giving himself to and for others by giving them his body and blood. The representation of Christ as he who gives to others is done by the one who presides at the Eucharist, acting as head of the community and host of the meal in the rôle of Christ (*ex persona Christi*). This person is a priest in a distinctive sacramental sense because he is appointed by God to take the initiative and signify the giving in sacrifice without which the Eucharist can never be made. (The use of masculine pronouns to speak about ordained priests here and subsequently reflects the actual discipline of the Catholic Church.) The faithful receive the gift from him that activates their own priesthood. The special sacramental relationship of the ordained priest with Christ is manifested liturgically in the fact that it is he who proclaims the narrative of the institution: he does so in a way that allows the words of Christ about the bread and wine being his body and blood to be heard again by the community as Christ spoke them at the Last Supper. He also says the sacramental prayer for the coming of the Holy Spirit on the bread and wine. He does these two things within the Eucharistic Prayer, in which he leads the thanksgiving of the community for the bread and wine that Christ makes to be the sacrifice of his body and blood.

There is also an ecclesiological reason why the Eucharist is presided over by an ordained priest. To be the body of Christ each particular community of Christians must be in communion with the whole Church, both in the present time and in that historical continuity that goes back to the Church of the apostles. While continuity and communion are ensured by all the members of a Christian community, it is signified and made effective in the continuity of ministry. The ordained ministers of the Church continue that part of the ministry of the apostles which ensures the internal unity of Christian communities and their bond with other communities by giving them faith and sacraments that are guaranteed as coming from Christ, the ultimate centre of unity.

9.8.9   Sacrifice of the Church

As sacrament of all that the Church is, the Eucharist sacramentalizes the Church's participation in the sacrifice of Christ. The sacrifice of Christ is present in the Eucharist because he is offering his body and blood in it. His body and blood are the permanent expressions of his self-offering to the Father for the salvation of sinful humanity: they became so on the cross and remain so in the resurrection. When they are made sacramentally present in bread and wine in the Eucharist, in an act of the Church that has within it the action of an ordained priest, they bring with them Christ's priestly act of oblation. This is the unique sacrifice which brings the forgiveness of all human sin, ratifies the new covenant and assembles the Church as the new People of God. It is now the only sacrifice that is pleasing to God. It is made sacramentally present in the Eucharist so that its effects can be applied to those whom God gathers into the Church throughout the course of time and across the reaches of space. The theological question — which is inevitably marked by the disagreements of the Reformation — is about the sense in which the laying-hold of those effects by the Church might itself be an act of sacrifice. The forgiveness of sin and a growing hold on life in the body of Christ that are the effects of the Eucharist are pure grace. The receiving of them, in human freedom, is also the effect of grace. The question is whether this grace of God moves those who receive the effect of Christ's sacrifice to an act that can itself be called sacrifice and, as such, play some part in bringing about the fruits of salvation. The answer depends on how one sees the relationship between God's action and human freedom in the working out of grace. A radically Protestant theology of grace would deny all value to human action in relation to the gift of justification. Applied to the Eucharist this would mean that the sacrifice of Christ produces its effects in it without any morally valuable action that might be a form of identification with Christ's sacrifice on the part of those receiving grace: the Lord's Supper, as Holy Communion, would be seen as proclaiming the descending mediation of Christ that is the application of the fruits of his sacrifice on the cross, but not in any way as a sacramentalizing of his upward mediation in the actions of those who receive grace. Radical Protestantism would allow that there is an upward movement of praise and thanksgiving for gifts received in the Eucharist, which could be called a sacrifice of praise, but would not allow that this enters into the sacramental giving of grace. The Catholic tradition is that, under the grace of God, humans make free acts of acceptance that are meritorious in relation to the gift of grace and satisfactory (propitiatory) in relation to the taking away of sin. It can, therefore, see a God-ward movement in the Eucharist in which Christians unite themselves with the upward mediation of Christ, and specifically with his sacrifice of himself to the Father. It sees the sacramentality of these actions ensured by the characters of Baptism, Confirmation and Ordination which are, in different ways, sharings in Christ's priesthood. By such priestly actions Christ's sacrifice is offered sacramentally in and by the Church. The gifts of grace received from the sacrifice of the cross in the Eucharist are seen to be simultaneously, and without any derogation from the uniqueness and all-sufficiency of Christ's sacrifice, fruits of the Eucharist itself. The liturgical form in which the Eucharist was universally celebrated up to the time of the Reformation, as well as the sacrificial language widely used by the Fathers about the Eucharist, are believed to require this Catholic doctrine.

A theological penetration of the Catholic confession of faith about the Eucharist as sacrifice requires one to explain the meaning that the term 'sacrifice' has when applied to the Eucharist. It will not do to simply take an ethical or anthropological definition of sacrifice from studies of religious behaviour, and show that it is verified in the Eucharist. The Eucharist must be a sacrifice in the sense that the cross is a sacrifice. When the epistle to the Hebrews uses the category of sacrifice to explain the saving value of the death of Christ it gives more attention to the way it differs from other sacrifices than to what it has in common with them: it is God himself who takes the initiative in it, rather than human pleading, sending his Son as definitive covenant word and eternal High Priest; it is valuable for all humans, and not just for those of one people or epoch, because of the solidarity which the High Priest has in flesh and blood with the whole human family that needs to be saved from sin; it is offered by Christ the High Priest in loving self-dedication to the will of the Father and accomplished in the shedding of his own blood, rather than in any formal ritual action; it is seen to be accepted once and for all, to the absolute discounting of any other sacrifice, by Christ's entry into the heavenly sanctuary where he lives forever pleading efficaciously for the salvation of those who believe that God's promise is fulfilled in him. The conclusion must be that technical elements that form part of anthropological definitions of sacrifice can be used in Christian theology only if they reflect the uniqueness of Christ's sacrifice. The idea of oblation can express the inner heart of sacrifice, provided it is seen as the total dedication of self to God the Father in an obedience that is better than sacrifice. Immolation can be used to describe the consecration, or setting-apart for God of something in sacrifice, provided what is set apart is the only victim that is now pleasing to God, which is the body and blood of Christ. Propitiation can be used to talk about the way sacrifice takes away sin, provided it is understood that the only thing that takes away sin is the death and resurrection of Christ. Priesthood can be attributed to those who make and offer sacrifice, provided it is understood that the only priesthood now operative is that of Christ. Once these technical terms, and any definition of sacrifice constructed from them, are used in the meaning they have been given by the cross of Christ, they can be applied to the Eucharist without the risk of making it seem a sacrifice that would be somehow independent of the cross.

Before applying the idea of sacrifice to the Eucharist, one has to see how it was verified in the Last Supper. What Jesus did at the Last Supper was a ritual anticipation of what he did on the cross. The sense of self-oblation to the Father that marked his whole life was fixed, on that night before he suffered, on the end that would be made of his life on the cross by people who were already preparing his death. He knew at the Last Supper what giving his life to the Father was going to cost him. The thought of death was a thought about his body and blood: what happened to them on the cross and afterwards was to be the ultimate test of his dedication to the Father and of the Father's acceptance of him. The food that was being eaten at the Last Supper was already a reminder of the Passover sacrifice that brought liberation to the People of the Mosaic covenant and of the sealing of that covenant in blood. When Jesus took bread and wine, gave it to his disciples and said it was his body and blood given for the remission of sin and the ratifying of the new covenant, he was anticipating the immolation of his body and blood on the cross for the forgiveness of sin and the sealing of the new covenant. What he did with the bread and wine was an act of symbolic immolation that expressed his oblation. In giving his body and blood as food to his disciples he was proclaiming that his sacrifice was life-giving for them. When he told them to go on doing the same thing in memory of him, he was assuring them that it would go on being life-giving. It would be life-giving in being a memorial of his sacrifice.

The traditions about the Last Supper were written down by Paul and the evangelists to help Christians understand what Christ meant their 'breaking of bread' to be. What they wrote surely tells the Church that Christ offers himself sacrificially in the Eucharist, as he offered himself at the Last Supper. He does so through the whole complex of persons, actions and words that make up the Eucharist. The people who form the Christian community are people whose whole life is meant to be a sacrifice (Rom 12:1: ' . . . present your bodies as a living sacrifice, holy and acceptable to God, which is your spiritual worship'). Their daily sacrifice is modelled on the sacrifice which Christ made in his body; it is made in the strength of the grace drawn from his sacrifice. It is worked out in the relations they have with one another in the Church: as members of Christ they give themselves to one another, sharing their life and their goods to the extent that this is necessary for the life of the community; out of that Christian solidarity they are also ready to give themselves for the life of the world, even if that means being made to suffer by the world. When they come together for the Eucharist the sacrificial sense of their life is heightened and focused. They are assembled as the People of the new covenant called together to hear again the covenant word proclaimed in Christ and to renew the ratification of it that he made in his blood. The symbolism of the meal lends itself to the expression of covenant sacrifice. The people are sharing their food and drink, giving what they have to one another as they give themselves. They are recognizing that their food, like their fellowship, is a gift of God and want to say so in an act of worship, which takes the form of a prayer of thanks said over bread and wine. The prayer of the community is said by the one who presides over the meal. He can represent all and signify their unity by reason of a special rôle he has been given to represent Christ as head and spokesman of those who form his body. The sacramental likeness of the ordained minister to Christ also consists in the way he represents Christ as host of the meal, who gives his very self as food. Without this representation of Christ the giver, the food taken and shared could not be recognized as bearing eternal life. In being said by one who is consecrated in this special representational likeness of Christ by ordination and in being assented to by the Amen of the whole community, the Eucharistic Prayer is an act of the Church formally constituted as Body of Christ. It fully sacramentalizes his priestly worship.

The Eucharistic Prayer is made in that attitude of offering and readiness to give oneself in sacrifice that pervades Christian life to the extent that it is lived in imitation of Christ. It thanks God for his gifts and in doing so recognizes that anything it has to offer is already his gift. It makes a petition about the bread and wine that the community has set aside for sharing as the symbol of the spirit of giving and receiving in which it is gathered. It asks that they should become, through the power of God's Spirit, the body and blood of Christ, and it grounds the petition on the promise of Christ's own words at the Last Supper. This is a petition for consecration, that is, for the setting-aside of a gift of God and all it symbolizes, so that he can take it to himself again and use it exclusively for uniting people to himself in holiness. The consecration that is asked for — bread and wine becoming the body and blood of Christ — is the identification of what is being prayed over with something that already belongs totally to God, because given to him in sacrifice on the cross, and that exists totally for the uniting of humanity with God in holiness. What the Church asks is that the sacrifice of Christ become its own sacrifice, so that the expression of its own self-offering to God would be none other than that body and blood in which Christ offers himself eternally to the Father. The Eucharistic Prayer becomes an act of faith that the worship being offered by the Church is the sacrifice of Christ, having as victim Christ himself, whose real immolation on Calvary is made present sacramentally in the consecrated bread and wine. The worship of the Church is sacrifice because it is the sacrifice of Christ. The Eucharistic Prayer passes from the consecrated bread and wine to a remembering (*anamnēsis*) of the death and glorification of Christ and it is from this Passover mystery of his that it expects the grace of the Holy Spirit to be given for the building up of the Body of Christ. In its act of sacrifice, which

1 ~~4616~~ 3:40 yest.
2 Z.
3 11:30 today, Matt Cam. → first Mass
4 May 20
5 ~~And~~ Book! Aurora

630-338
5015

Score

Al le lu ia! Al le

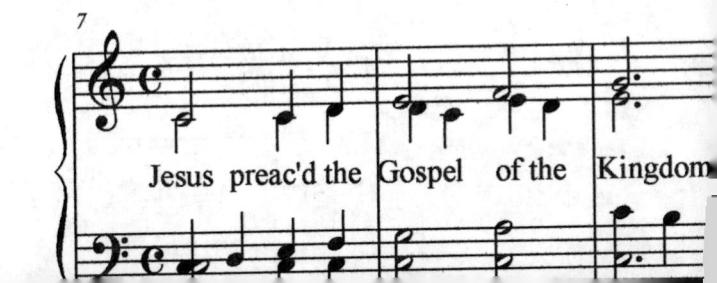

Jesus preac'd the Gospel of the Kingdom

is already the fruit of Christ's sacrifice, the Church is opening itself further to the life that comes from the sacrifice of Christ. The Eucharist has, then, the double movement, of sanctification and worship, that is found in every Christian sacrament: grace is received from God in an act of worship of God which is itself his grace. The Eucharist differs from the other sacraments in that the act of worship made in it is an act of sacrifice.

9.8.10   *Effects of the Eucharist*

Like every sacrament, the Eucharist effects what it signifies. The reality signified in it is God's giving of eternal life as a stable, growing possession, to those who are being gathered together in the Church by the death and resurrection of Christ and the sending of the Spirit, and in that Church being sent to bring God's life to the world while it waits for the coming of the Lord. Participation in this reality is the special grace effect, or sacramental grace of the Eucharist. It is the grace of the Holy Spirit. Its specifically eucharistic quality is defined by the tradition in categories drawn from the general theology of grace. It is analysed (a) as charity, (b) as ecclesial charity, or communion in the Body of Christ, (c) as eschatological charity that anticipates and prepares the world for the coming of the Lord.

Before examining the grace of the Eucharist according to those three dimensions of charity, there are some general observations that need to be made about it. Firstly, the grace of the Eucharist is absolutely necessary (*necessitate medii*) for salvation. There is no salvation without charity, without membership of the Body of Christ, and without being in the world in a way that reflects the 'already' and 'not yet' of the Kingdom. Corresponding to this ontological necessity of the grace of the Eucharist there are ecclesiastical precepts binding people to take part in the Eucharist regularly enough to receive its grace (normally every Sunday and with full sacramental participation at least during the Easter season). The fulfilment of the precepts is subject to all the normal qualifications. If one cannot do what is required in fact, one must do it in desire. The desire of the Eucharist is, indeed, already included in Baptism and Confirmation and its grace is operative in them (cf. above, 7.5.5; 7.6). Even in the Baptism of desire that is postulated in the salvation of those who are saved by a moral choice of goodness that is not specifically Christian or perhaps even religious, there must be a desire for the Eucharist. People who choose salvation choose the kind of things that the Eucharist stands for — the celebration of life and fellowship and joy, and the transformation of the world by good people. It is easier to find the desire requisite for salvation in choices of that sort than it is to find it in the choice of more abstract values like goodness or even God. Most ethical or religious systems within which people work out their salvation outside historical Christianity have some rites or images which express these human values. They can serve as secular or religious pointers towards the Eucharist, and help one to understand how all salvific grace is eucharistic.

The grace of salvation that, as far as the receiving subject is concerned, might seem to be given outside the Eucharist is made explicitly eucharistic in the celebration of the giving Church. This is a second general observation that needs to be made about the effects of the Eucharist. Every Eucharist sacramentalizes the giving of all saving grace. Other sacraments ask for and give grace only to those who are actually present and participating in the celebration. The Eucharist asks for and gives grace to a limitless range of persons. It can do this because it embodies the sacrifice of Christ and the Church's universal mediation of his grace. The Eucharistic Prayer expresses this universal intention and effectiveness of the Eucharist. It asks that the sacrifice of Christ which it makes sacramentally present may have its effect on an ever-widening circle of people. It gives pride of place to those who are present and taking part by sacramentally eating the body of Christ and drinking his blood. It also asks for and gives grace to those who are present but not communicating. It does likewise for others who are not present but are being prayed for (in that the Mass is being offered for them), to all those who are remembered as being joined to the Church through the bonds of ecclesial communion, to the faithful departed who are still in need of some purification before they are ready to enter the heavenly liturgy, and eventually to all people 'of good will' who are open to the grace of salvation. There is a theological tradition that describes the grace given to those who do not communicate as an effect of the Eucharist as sacrifice, and contradistinguishes it to the grace given to communicants, which is described as the effect of the Eucharist as sacrament (see above, 9.3.2; 9.4.2). The distinction is valuable for explaining an aspect of the Eucharist that makes it different from the other sacraments of the Church. But it is one of those distinctions that should be used, almost before it is made, to unite what it divides. Failure to do so has had unfortunate consequences for Catholic theology in the past. Because the Eucharist is a sacrament, the grace that it gives as a sacrifice is already sacramental. It is sacramentalized by the 'matter' of the Eucharist within which the sacrifice is realized, because the table of bread and wine is open to all and the body and blood are given for all. It is sacramentalized in the Eucharistic Prayer, which as 'form' of the Eucharist makes the sacrifice and directs the grace that comes from it towards its recipients.

Among the petitions that are expressed in the Eucharistic Prayer are those of the celebrating priest. Because of his ministry his intentions in offering the Eucharist are wide-ranging. He can be expected to remember in a special way those who by their alms and offerings support him and his ministry. He will want to make his own any petitions they may commend to him. He can make those petitions be the petitions of the whole eucharistic assembly by including them, at least by intention, in the Eucharistic Prayer. This is the theological ground for what are called Mass intentions, and for the custom of linking such special intentions of the priest with the acceptance of a gift, called a 'stipend', from a benefactor. It is a practice that has a long tradition behind it in the Catholic Church. It is, without doubt, open to misunderstanding and abuse. The Church has regulated it by law and practical moral teaching. Sometimes this discipline has been accompanied by a theology which suggests that the giving of a stipend is some kind of legal transaction based on the give-and-take of justice. Mass intentions and stipends must, however, be seen and judged above all as an exercise of eucharistic charity. A Christian community is grateful to any of its members who support its ministers and make it possible for them to live in the service of the Church. Its thankfulness is felt in a special way in the celebration of the Eucharist. The priest is particularly sensitive to the needs and wishes of those who contribute to his support and to the well-being of the Church. If he should choose to single out and pray for the intentions of one or more of those benefactors at a particular Eucharist, and to commend their intentions to the Church, his choice is adopted by the community, so that the intention of priest and benefactor is taken up into the Church's eucharistic sacrifice. The benefactor has the comfort of knowing that his or her gift and intention, in becoming the intention of the Church, is offered to God with the unique love and thanksgiving that the Eucharist realizes. The effect of that offering will occur according to the normal process of eucharistic grace: it will be received by those who open themselves to grace and let themselves be caught up in the charity that flows from the Eucharist. If the gift sought is of a material sort (rain, a good harvest, peace etc.) it can only be considered an effect of the Eucharist to the extent that it draws people in grace to thankfulness and love. There is no way of measuring the grace or the gift against the stipend offered. The issue is not one of justice. Questions of justice may arise because of the discipline of the Church regarding Mass stipends, which, obviously, has to be conscientiously obeyed. But they do not prevail over the fundamental reality of gift-giving and gift-receiving, measured only by the bonds and responsibilities of love, which is the give and take that belongs intrinsically to the Eucharist. People can have the full benefit of the Eucharist, and a priest can direct it to whomsoever he wishes, quite independently of the practice of giving and receiving stipends.

The grace that is given as fruit of the eucharistic sacrifice is not just generic grace; it is specifically eucharistic. Its eucharistic quality is obvious for those who actually eat and drink the body and blood. But it is also there in the grace given to those who do not communicate. What is offered to them as fruit of the sacrifice is a reaching-out of the charity of the Church drawing them into its communion. If they are Christians the grace offered will meet and correspond to the desire for eucharistic communion which they must have, and will be confirmed and increased when they actually do receive communion at another Eucharist. The effects of the Eucharist as sacrifice, or fruits of the Mass as they have often been called in the Catholic tradition, are eucharistic for the faithful departed: they draw them into the ultimate communion of saints in the heavenly banquet. They are eucharistic for all those who, as a result of prayers offered for them in the Eucharist, are saved without becoming Christian, because they draw them into various expressions of fellowship and peace and service of the world that reflect the Eucharist. Conversely, it must be recognized that what has been called the grace of the Eucharist as sacrament is always the fruit of the sacrifice. It is obviously so for those who receive the body and blood of Christ in the course of a full eucharistic celebration. It is so for the sick to whom the sacrament is brought when they are unable to be present at the Eucharist, or for people who receive it 'outside Mass' for any other reason. The attitudes that the grace of the Eucharist provokes in them are precisely those expressed in the sacrificial movement formulated in the Eucharistic Prayer. The Lord's Prayer expresses these same attitudes, and is well used as a preparation for receiving the sacramental body and blood of Christ.

A third preliminary general remark about the grace of the Eucharist has to do with the measure in which it is given. The reality signified by the Eucharist is of limitless saving worth and power. Because of the limited capacity of the human heart, however, it is received in limited measures. And yet, because it can be repeated again and again there is no end to the receiving of it. The multiplication of it is not done mathematically. To say that nine Masses are better than one is really to say nothing: if one is talking about the objective worth of the Mass, nine times infinity is not any more than infinity; if one is talking about the subjective laying-hold of the grace that comes from the Mass one has to qualify the statement with reference to the capacity of those for whom the Eucharist is being celebrated before it makes any sense. The Eucharist is a sacrament for human life. As there are rhythms for taking food that suit human life and nourish health and growth, so there are rhythms for taking part in the Eucharist that suit the life of grace. They suit the celebrating community and the individuals who belong to it. They can vary at different stages of the life of grace and from one community to another. To upset them, either by excess or defect, is to do a certain violence to life. The rhythm set by the main liturgical traditions is of weekly celebration, on the Lord's Day, for the living of a full Christian life; more frequent, even daily, for a more intense level of waiting for the coming of the Lord; and an annual celebration of special solemnity at Easter for all. There may be virtue in a certain modest abstinence from the Eucharist (there are examples of renunciation of daily Eucharist in the liturgical tradition, and it has been used with effect in some forms of spirituality) and in an occasional 'over-indulgence' (like the three Masses on Christmas Day and All Souls' Day) but the criterion is never mathematical. One does not deprive others of grace by measuring the celebration of the Eucharist according to the rhythms of the life of the celebrating community and its members. A Eucharist well and truly celebrated according to the rhythms set by the liturgical tradition reaches out to others more realistically, and is therefore more grace-bearing, than a numerically multiplied Eucharist that does a kind of violence to the body of Christ because it does not respect the rhythm of its life.

It was proposed at the beginning of this section to use the theological categories of (a) charity, (b) ecclesial charity or communion, (c) eschatological anticipation, to analyse the specific grace of the Eucharist.

(a) Life is realized to the full in love. In giving eternal life the Eucharist gives that special kind of love that Christians call charity. Everything about the Eucharist promotes charity. It is the supreme expression of God's love, which Christ made his own: the only response to that love is love. It breaks down the barriers to love by taking away sin. People are reconciled to one another in being reconciled to God by Christ. They can sit down at table together because they are being brought together by the body of Christ. The joy of love is promoted by the joy of a common festive celebration. Gifts are shared because they are being recognized with thanks as being from God and are being consecrated to him. The charity that is the effect of the Eucharist is experienced first and foremost within the celebrating community. But it is no inward-looking cosiness. Because it is the charity of God it reaches out to the whole world. It reaches out in the prayer that is offered but also in a readiness to act. It is concerned with the needs of the poor in a realistic way, and especially with the divisions and lack of care that they reflect within the human family. A practical readiness to help the needy is part of the sacramentality of the Eucharist. One can document it from the tradition, although there have been periods when little enough was made of it in the Church. The courage to take the social and political action that the real care of the poor always requires is present in the charity given by the Eucharist. So is the firmness of love and even the anger of love towards those who deprive the poor of the gifts of God and so contradict the Eucharist. But eucharistic charity has the passion to reconcile rather than to further divide. It is always an invitation to people to sit down together at the Eucharist itself and become life-giving rather than death-dealing for one another in the body of Christ. The prayer for peace that is made in the Eucharist is not only a prayer that Christians will be left in peace by the world but that the whole world will be given the fruit of Christ's sacrifice in the form of a just and reconciling love that brings peace.

(b) The charity caused by the Eucharist is ecclesial. The relationships that it forms and in which its fidelity is proved are those of the Body of Christ. The Body is the community of those who accept the word of God in faith and are baptized, who live in accordance with the Gospel, who accept the ministry of those who have been ordained in the apostolic succession, and who accept the canonical discipline of communion. The Eucharist supposes these visible and institutional bonds of unity, reinforces them and fills them with the life of love. It is in giving charity within this community that the Eucharist ultimately brings about the unity of the Body of Christ, and gives it the power to change the world by the witness and practice of love.

In making the Church grow in unity charity has to overcome sin. All sin is a failure to love God and a breach of unity with those who are together in his love. No Christian community or any member of it is perfect in love or fully faithful to the bonds of communion that express it. Eucharistic charity brings growth in unity by overcoming the daily sins of Christians and reconciling them in love. The rite itself signifies ecclesial reconciliation in many ways, and most of all by letting those who are reconciled eat and drink together the body and blood of Christ. There are, however, some sins that the Church attempts to overcome by a discipline of temporary exclusion from full participation in the Eucharist. They are especially the sins that break the unity of the Church. Those who are judged to have broken the unity of faith by heresy or the union of love by schism, those who are judged to have seriously transgressed the law of Christ that Christians are agreed to live by, those whose Baptism has made them members of a church which is judged to be outside Catholic communion — all those are excluded in various degrees from the Eucharist. Initially the exclusion is self-imposed. Those who culpably refuse the love of God and the bonds of Christian communion cannot mean what the Eucharist signifies or be open to its grace. Their sin is incompatible with full sacramental participation in the Eucharist. Subsequently the exclusion becomes a matter of discipline, administered by the pastoral authorities of the Church, who can determine some of its modalities and conditions. It is not a punitive process, as if the Eucharist were a reward for good behaviour that could be taken away as a punishment. The discipline of exclusion is for the reconciliation of sinners. It takes as its model Jesus, who went to eat with sinners because 'it is those who are sick who need the physician'. The purpose of exclusion is eventually to draw sinners back into full eucharistic communion. The charity of the Eucharist is endlessly forgiving. The judgement of the Church is that in excluding someone from the Eucharist for a specific reason it is proclaiming to them and to the whole Church the importance of the bond which they are transgressing for their relationship with God, for the internal unity of the Church and for the credibility of its mission to the world. It is saying that the sin they are committing is incompatible with the Eucharist. It is challenging them to recognize this, to repent, and offering them a joyful welcome back into full eucharistic communion. That proclamation is believed to strengthen all the members of the Church in their own fidelity to the bonds of love. Christians generally recognize the value of this discipline of exclusion. Those who have sinned seriously will not take full sacramental part in the Eucharist until the grace of God has moved them to repentance and they have been reconciled with the Church in accordance with its penitential discipline. Christians who are cut off from communion with a church will not normally want to take part in its Eucharist until the situation which is responsible for their exclusion has been resolved. They may draw grace from the Eucharist by being prayed for in it and by feeling the charity of the Church that reaches out to them in reconciling love, but not by sacramental communion.

Because the discipline of exclusion is itself an exercise of eucharistic charity it has to be done with great delicacy. Very special care is needed when those who are being excluded are, in fact, living in a faith and charity that already unites them in a deep way to the eucharistic community. This is the situation of repentant sinners who have not yet fulfilled the canonical requirements of sacramental confession, penance and absolution. The discipline of exclusion is not absolute in this case. It allows that repentant sinners can take full part in the Eucharist before fulfilling the requirements of reconciliation, if they are prevented from doing so for a reasonable cause. They are, however, required to make confession and receive absolution as soon as possible afterwards. The thinking would seem to be that the power of the Eucharist to strengthen charity and take away sin by uniting a repentant sinner to the body of Christ and in it to his members (who are, all of them, also repentant sinners) is too valuable at that moment to be denied by a strict enforcement of the discipline of exclusion. The obligation of subsequent confession shows that what brought about the original exclusion has not been treated lightly. A similar care is called for when the

exclusion is due to the absence of communion between churches. There are
Christians who share the faith of the Catholic Church and live in a charity which
unites them deeply to its members, but are excluded from its Eucharist because
they belong to a church which is not in communion with it. The discipline is not
absolute here either, because Christians from other churches are, in fact, admitted
to the Eucharist in certain circumstances. The charity that the Eucharist causes
will always strive to use the discipline of exclusion in a way that will contribute
to the unity of all Christians in the Church. It will find itself torn between two
lines of reasoning about what is best for Christian unity, and trying to find a
practical solution to the dilemma generated by the contrasting conclusions they
often reach. It can be argued, on the one hand, that Christians who, although they
do not belong to the Catholic Church, are already united with its members in
faith and love and are actively committed to Christian unity have, in fact, already
overcome the fundamental barrier to eucharistic communion; their participation
in a Catholic Eucharist can be a precious uniting grace for them as well as for the
Catholic community. It will be argued along this line that because such Christians
are actively working for full institutional communion between the churches, their
present lack of full communion cannot be culpable and will be repaired as soon
as possible. The charity that flows from the Eucharist will want to argue that to
waive the discipline of exclusion in particular cases of this sort, for the sake of
letting the uniting grace of the Eucharist be fully availed of, both by those
received to eucharistic communion and by the Catholic community that receives
them, is to be faithful to the reconciling grace of the Eucharist. It will want to
argue that Catholics are well enough informed about ecumenical issues nowadays
to be protected from unnecessary scandal by such a practice. The same charity,
however, and the sense of responsibility that goes with it, especially in those
whose ministry makes them responsible for the unity of the Church, will argue
along another line and reach a different conclusion. The principle will be that a
Eucharist that is readily open to those who are not in full communion with the
celebrating Church contradicts itself, because it professes a unity which does not
in fact exist. It will be pointed out that many Christians do not appreciate the
importance of full ecclesial communion and will see in the practice of intercom-
munion an encouragement to believe that it does not matter very much what
church one belongs to, or whether churches are in communion with one another
or not. It will be argued that a strict enforcement of the discipline of exclusion
is more honest and ultimately does more for promoting real Christian unity.
Those who exercise pastoral authority in the churches have to decide between the
conflicting claims of these two lines of arguments in the way they regulate the
discipline of exclusion in ecumenical relations between the churches (see Vatican
II, Decree on Ecumenism, n. 8, and the Declaration of the Secretariat for
Promoting Christian Unity, 7 January 1970; Flannery, pp. 461, 502). The
discipline is an essential feature of the respect the Church owes to the truth of the
Eucharist. At the same time it will never be an absolute norm. The Eucharist that
it is serving, while being a sign and anticipation of the perfect communion of
heaven, is also the food of a pilgrim people, giving them the kind of love that

must survive and even grow amidst the strains and accommodations forced on those who travel.

(c) The charity which is the effect of the Eucharist, and which builds the Church as communion in the body of Christ, is eschatological. It is already a possession of eternal life and an anticipation of heaven. It looks to the resurrection and to being with Christ beyond the veil of sacramentality. The Eucharist is the food of immortality for body and spirit. Those who are nourished by it live forever. In the Eucharistic Prayer they make their own the 'Holy, Holy, Holy' that is sung eternally before the transcendent majesty of God. They touch there the high-point of contemplation. They celebrate communion with Mary and all the saints in the heavenly liturgy. At the same time, because those who celebrate the Eucharist are not yet in full possession of eternal life their access to the transcendent mystery of the All-Holy God is an act of contemplation of the earthly kind, needing to be nourished by and nourishing dedication to the practice of contemplative prayer. Communion with Mary and the saints includes an appeal to their intercession and a desire to follow their example. The Eucharistic Prayer, and the prayers and songs that are used on the feasts of Christ and the saints, are the words of people who are at home with the Lord and yet still on the way to their heavenly home. Because those who take part in it are still in the body, the Eucharist gives a charity that is appropriate to the present age of the world and to what has to be done there by those who are waiting for the coming of the Lord. Every Eucharist is a viaticum, that nourishes the body in nourishing the spirit. It gives Christians the grace to live in love in their bodies in view of the resurrection. Both Christian marriage and Christian celibacy are caught up in eucharistic charity. So is people's management of property and their exercise of social responsibility. So are other experiences of bodiliness, such as health-care and healing, asceticism, and all the arts in which the body becomes joy and celebration. The eschatological charity of the Eucharist transfuses bodiliness with faith and hope in the resurrection.

The eschatological quality of the effects of the Eucharist would seem to be particularly valuable for understanding the practice of reserving some of the consecrated bread after the celebration, and also the various forms of devotion to the reserved host that are practised in the Western Catholic tradition. If the Eucharist is the sacrament of life for those who are waiting for the Lord, there are advantages in having it always available: it gives perfect readiness for meeting the Lord. A full celebration of the Eucharist cannot be arranged for every Christian who is ill or dying; but they can be given communion from hosts reserved for this purpose. This is the historical and theological reason for reservation. That the reserved sacrament should be adored is a natural consequence of belief in the real abiding presence of Christ in it. That Christians should use that adoration to prolong their sense of the mystery celebrated in the Eucharist, to revive the grace of the sacrament, and to practise the kind of contemplation that the Eucharist offers to those who long for the vision of the All-Holy God is quite in keeping with its nature as sacrament for those who are meant to be at all times waiting for the coming of the Lord. It is, no doubt, possible that those who practise such devotions are using them as a substitute for or distraction from the primary act of eucharistic devotion, which is the liturgical celebration of the sacrament itself with sacramental eating and drinking of the body and blood of the Lord. But it does not have to be so. One can quite well find the essential effect of the Eucharist in its liturgical celebration and then find a prolongation of it in other exercises of eucharistic devotion. On the other hand, it cannot be said that those who do not practise such additional forms of eucharistic devotion are, by that very fact, rejecting the essential values of the sacrament or neglecting its grace.

As a grace of the time of waiting for the coming of the Lord the grace of the Eucharist is a sending on mission. It equips Christians for the task of preparing the whole world for its final destiny, which will be revealed when Christ comes to judge. In building itself up as Body of Christ through the Eucharist the Church is becoming the instrument that proclaims the Lordship of Christ to all people. The Eucharist makes it do so with the love that Christ himself showed, and also with a readiness to suffer for the sake of love which made the cross the supreme expression of his love. The Church's word to humanity is always a call to the kind of unity that it itself experiences in the Eucharist. It calls people unashamedly to faith in Christ and Baptism. In doing so it also calls them to the Eucharist. It dares to hope that, even if they do not join with the Church in the sacrament that is celebrated in this time of waiting, they will so live as to join it in the reality of the Eucharist that is celebrated in heaven.

STUDY QUESTIONS

1 Do an exegetical study of one of the Synoptic accounts of the Last Supper, with a view to setting the narrative of institution in its full context of biblical theology.
2 Study how the different senses Paul gives to the term 'body of Christ' are interconnected in his thinking about the Eucharist.
3 Detail the influences which the Christology of John has on his teaching about the Eucharist.
4 What can be gathered from the New Testament about a ministry of presiding at the Eucharist?
5 Trace the application of the prophecy of Malachi 1:10–11 to the Eucharist in the Fathers of the first four centuries.
6 Examine how the theology of the incarnation is used during the first four centuries to illustrate how the bread and wine of the Eucharist is the body and blood of Christ.
7 Study the relationship between the Eucharist and the Church in St Augustine.
8 Read and analyse a text from one of the Latin theologians who wrote on the Eucharist between AD 800 and 1100; evaluate the text in the light of the profession of faith required of Berengarius.
9 Explain what the phrase *per modum substantiae* means in St Thomas's theology of the presence of Christ in the Eucharist.
10 Read and evaluate, both historically and theologically, Luther's discussion on the Eucharist in *The Pagan Servitude of the Church*.
11 Study one of the canons of the Council of Trent on the Eucharist in the light of the teaching of the Reformers and of the debate that led to the formulation of that canon at the Council.

12   Study a writer who puts forward a theory of transignification or transfinalization to explain Catholic faith in the real presence of Christ in the Eucharist; evaluate the theory in the light of the Encyclical *Mysterium Fidei* of Paul VI.
13   Study reactions from theologians of different churches to any one of the statements on the Eucharist that have issued from a major ecumenical dialogue.
14   Write a theological commentary on the antiphon from the liturgy of the feast of Corpus Christi: 'O sacred feast in which we partake of Christ, his sufferings are remembered, our minds are filled with his grace and we receive a pledge of the glory that is to be ours'.

FURTHER READING

New Testament material on the Eucharist from articles on 'Breaking of bread', 'Lord's Supper', 'Eucharist' in biblical dictionaries, and from commentaries on eucharistic passages in the Synoptics, Paul and John; also:

J. Delorme and others, *The Eucharist in the New Testament* (London, 1964).
J. Jeremias, *The Eucharistic Words of Jesus* (trans. from 3rd German ed.; London, 1966).
M. Thurian, *The Eucharistic Memorial*, I: *The Old Testament*, II: *The New Testament* (London, 1960).
J.-M. R. Tillard, OP, *The Eucharist: Pasch of God's People* (New York, 1976).

Patristic texts on the Eucharist in:

P. Palmer, SJ, *Sacraments and Worship* (London, 1957).
J. J. Sheerin, *The Eucharist* (Message of the Fathers of the Church 7; Wilmington, 1986).

On the eucharistic theology of the Fathers:

E. J. Kilmartin, SJ, *The Eucharist in the Primitive Church* (Englewood Cliffs, 1965).
W. Rordorf and others, *The Eucharist of the Early Christians* (New York, 1978).
R. J. Halliburton, 'The Patristic Theology of the Eucharist' in *The Study of Liturgy*, ed. C. Jones, G. Wainwright and E. Yarnold (New York, 1978), pp. 201–208.
F. van der Meer, *Augustine the Bishop* (London, 1961).
A. F. Donegan, *St Augustine and the Real Presence* (Washington, 1972).

On mediaeval theology of the Eucharist:

J. de Ghellinck, 'Eucharistie au XIIe siècle en occident' in *DTC* 5, 1233–1302 (Paris, 1924).
H. de Lubac, SJ, *Corpus Mysticum: l'eucharistie et l'église au Moyen Age* (2nd revised ed.; Paris, 1949).
H. Jorissen, *Die Entfaltung der Transubstantiationslehre bis zum Beginn der Hochscholastik* (Münster, 1965).
J. F. McCue, 'The Doctrine of Transubstantiation from Berengar through the Council of Trent' in *Lutherans and Catholics in Dialogue*, III: *The Eucharist* (Washington/New York, 1967).
E. Schillebeeckx, *The Eucharist* (London, 1968).
J. Pelikan, *The Growth of Mediaeval Theology (600–1300)*, vol. III of *The Christian Tradition* (Chicago/London, 1978).
G. Macy, *The Theologies of the Eucharist in the Early Scholastic Period. A Study of the Salvific Function of the Sacrament according to the Theologians c. 1080–1220* (Oxford, 1984).
Thomas Aquinas, *Summa Theologiae*, Pars IIIa, qq. 73–83; ed. and English trans. W. Barden, OP (qq. 73–78; Blackfriars ed., vol. 58; London/New York, 1965) and T. Gilby, OP (qq. 79–83; Blackfriars ed., vol. 59; London/New York, 1975).

On late mediaeval theology and the teaching of the Reformers:

F. Clark, SJ, *Eucharistic Sacrifice and the Reformation* (2nd ed.; Chulmleigh, Devon, 1981).
Y. Brilioth, *Eucharistic Faith and Practice, Evangelical and Catholic* (trans. from Swedish; London, 1930).
G. Dix, *The Shape of the Liturgy* (London, 1945).
B. Thompson, *Liturgies of the Western Church* (Cleveland/New York, 1962).

On the teaching of the Council of Trent:

M. Lepin, *L'Idée du Sacrifice de la Messe* (Paris, 1926).
K. Rahner, SJ, 'The Presence of Christ in the Sacrament of the Lord's Supper' in *Theological Investigations* 4 (Baltimore/London, 1966), pp. 287–311.
E. Schillebeeckx, OP, *The Eucharist*.
D. N. Power, OMI, *The Sacrifice We Offer. The Tridentine Dogma and its Reinterpretation* (Edinburgh, 1987).

Modern works on the Eucharist are mentioned in the text. On theories of transignification/transfinalization:

J. M. Powers, SJ, *Eucharistic Theology* (New York, 1967).
C. O'Neill, OP, *New Approaches to the Eucharist* (Dublin, 1967).

Eucharistic theology inspired by Vatican II in:

P. McGoldrick (ed.), *Understanding the Eucharist* (Dublin, 1969).
N. Lash, *His Presence in the World. A Study of Eucharistic Worship and Theology* (London, 1968).

For contemporary ecumenical discussion:

Modern Eucharistic Agreement (with Foreword by Bishop Alan C. Clark and Introduction by Bishop H. R. McAdoo; London, 1973).
M. Thurian, 'The Eucharistic Memorial, Sacrifice of Praise and Supplication' in *Ecumenical Pespectives on Baptism, Eucharist and Ministry* (Geneva, 1983), pp. 90–103.
J.-M. R. Tillard, OP, 'The Eucharist, Gift of God', *ibid.*, pp. 104–118.
E. J. Kilmartin, SJ, 'The Lima Text on Eucharist' in *Catholic Perspectives on Baptism, Eucharist and Ministry: A Study Commissioned by the Catholic Theological Society of America*, ed. M. Fahey (Lanham, MD/New York/London, 1986), pp. 135–160.

10

Epilogue

10.1 THE THEOLOGIAN AND THE CATECHIST

Every Christian initiation is a unique, unrepeatable event. So is every celebration of the Eucharist. Persons who are initiated are addressed by name; and there is warrant in the tradition for naming the person who is being given the body and blood of Christ in communion. The rite is personalized by the word; and the word is for this person alone. If they are to be life-giving, rite and word must touch and transform the individual life of a person in all its particularity. Humans have only one life which, although it can be analysed on different levels, is all of a piece. This is what Scholastic theologians were saying when they talked about grace building on nature. If the grace-life given in a sacrament is not in continuity with the full range of life-forces that are at work within the participant it will be rootless and die like the gospel seed thrown on stony ground. Obviously there is a sameness about the word and rite that are used in every sacramental celebration. There are certain things that the Church, as bearer of God's grace, must always do in Baptism, Confirmation and Eucharist. But what is done for individuals in their Baptism, Confirmation and Eucharist is always more than can be written in rituals or theologized about in books. It is an event of the Church, individualized and personalized by the participants and by the care which ministers of the Church give to each one of them, in preparation, celebration and pastoral follow-up, to ensure that the sacrament will be life-giving for them. Individual celebration is the province of pastoral ministry rather than of theological programming. It is a work of art rather than a construct of science. People who write books about the theology of sacraments need to be constantly reminded that the reality of sacraments goes beyond what can be written in a book. The last word does not lie with the theologian. The people who are described generically by the theologian as participants and ministers are named individuals, each with a personal life-story and with personal gifts and skills, in the actual making of a sacrament. A theology which does not remain very sensitive to this pastoral reality, and open to being translated into a realistic, life-connected word in an actual celebration, will be a poor theology of sacrament.

The theologian can look with wonder and respect on the gifts of those who make good sacraments: on their skills with words and their skills with rites; on their ability to make the sacrament be so much part of the life of the participants that its life-giving, life-transforming potential can be released in them. These are the teachers and catechists, the liturgists and ministers, and the presiding pastors, who together make sacraments happen for people. They are the prophets and the priests who have always been present in the community of God's People, to make the word relevant to life and to keep the rites real and God-centred. The theologian is something of a prophet, but he or she also has the rôle of a scribe. If the prophets and priests do not know the tradition of God's People they may invent stories and manipulate rites in a way that seems to correspond well with the life-situation of their People but may be empty of the life that comes from God. In telling the story of sacraments, of how they have been done and what has been believed and thought about them in the Church, and in making some systematic sense of them in terms of a contemporary human wisdom, the theologian is offering the catechist and the liturgist an invitation. It is an invitation to hear the whole story about sacraments: to develop a feel for the tradition of words and rites that lies behind present-day teaching and liturgical forms; to evaluate them critically and systematically; to have reliable intellectual criteria for judging how well any given insertion of a sacrament in an individual life-situation is being true to the divinely given reality of the sacrament.

A theology of sacraments can be heard as an invitation by catechists and liturgists only if it is open to real contemporary life-situations. The theologian must have verified his or her thinking by some experience in actual sacramental practice, or at least have a proven ability to listen to and learn from those who do. A theology can be recognized as having this relevance to life while being fully technical and scientific. Some such theologies remain on a quite general level, developing those universal aspects of the tradition of faith that are shared by all Christians and unite them in a common level of human experience in the Body of Christ. Others already begin to direct the reading of the tradition towards the life-situations of people within a particular culture or within a particular historical moment of cultural change. They can be technical and scientific theologies. They can develop a sociological, psychological and philosophical analysis of the life-situation of a particular group of people and, on the basis of it, do a hermeneutic-ally sound interpretation of what the Christian tradition about sacraments means for that group of people. The result can be a distinctive set of words and ideas to explain and accompany sacraments, with proposals for distinctive ways of celebrating them. Latin American theologians, for example, have been doing such a theology of sacraments in recent years, and they have been followed by theologians from other areas of the Church where a life-situation distinct from that in which classical Western theologies of sacraments were formed is being recognized. A theology of this sort must distance itself from certain features of an established European sacramental theology. Indeed, so too must a contempor-ary contextual theology of Europe itself and of North America: the life-situations they address are as dramatically new in many ways as are those of Latin America. At the same time, classical European theology of the sacraments cannot be ignored, or listened to selectively. The fact is that the biblical and patristic tradition of faith about sacraments has been transmitted through the traditions of Eastern and Western Europe. There is no serious sacramental theology that does not listen to them carefully. The re-reading has always to be of the complete tradition, not merely of the parts of it that are found to be congenial.

Christian communities draw on the sacramental theologies that are available to them under the influence of the life-situation which they share with those who are being initiated into membership and brought to participate in actual sacramental celebrations. Sacramental theology and the rituals of today's Church want the whole community to be active in this pedagogy of life. There is a range of liturgical ministries provided for in every celebration of initiation: bishop, presbyters, deacons, readers, sponsors, parents, choir each have their rôles. There is also a range of catechetical responsibilities. The bishop is the first catechist of his church: presbyters, deacons, parents, school-teachers and those who are formally recognized as catechists by the community each play a part. The re-appearance of catechists, the status given to them and the training they receive, is undoubtedly one of the graces given to the Church of Vatican II. That there are fully-trained and full-time catechists is a grace. That there are part-time catechists — lay-people in every sense of the word — who, with training from those qualified, give their service to the community in the work of preparing candidates for initiation is an added grace. If sacramental initiation and practice is from life to the fullness of life it cannot but gain from having as wide a range as possible of life-experience introduced into its catechesis.

10.2   THE UNITY OF INITIATION IN THEOLOGY AND CATECHESIS

It takes three sacraments to initiate a person into full Christian life. If a catechesis is to help human life to grow into the fullness of life through these sacraments, it must keep the unity of the process of initiation clearly before it. To confront human life with one of the sacraments of initiation in isolation is to run the risk of giving a misleading view of the gift of life that God offers. It is easier for theology to maintain a sense of the unity of initiation than it is for catechesis. Theology can choose, as has been done in this book, to do its primary study of the sacraments of initiation on the form they take when celebrated in a continuous rite for the benefit of adults. It can then add the necessary qualifications that have to be made for understanding the sacraments as celebrated for children, or any one of them when it is celebrated apart from the others. The catechist, however, rarely has that ideal candidate for initiation that the theologian can set up as the subject of his reflection. The life-situation that the catechist has to take into account includes the age of the candidate and the sequence and time-lapse between the different sacraments. The catechist also has to allow for the fact that his or her work has sometimes to be preparation for a sacrament yet to be received, and at other times, or perhaps at the same time, retrospective reflection on a sacrament already received. The complexities of the task call for a keen sense of the relationship between the three sacraments of initiation.

Meeting the concerns of theology about the unity of initiation should come easiest to the catechist who is dealing with the preparation of adults for full initiation. It should also come easily in the retrospective catechesis that is the required follow-up to initiation (*RCIA*, nn. 234–241 [235–239]. That catechesis will want to centre in a special way on the Eucharist, not only because it is the fullness of initiation but because the newly-initiated are taking part in it regularly as the stable consequence of their initiation. But it will be a catechesis that draws explicit attention to the dependence of the Eucharist on Baptism and Confirmation.

When children who have reached the age of discretion are being fully initiated (*RCIA*, Part II, nn. 242–306 [306–369]) the catechetical requirements for maintaining the unity of initiation will be the same as for adults, although there will be obvious pedagogical adjustments. When children have already been baptized in infancy the catechesis will be directed to Confirmation. The theological concern would be that this catechesis should also be a retrospective catechesis of Baptism. It is the point at which the promises made on behalf of the child at Baptism have to be put to it clearly and a personal acceptance of Baptism included in the acceptance of Confirmation. The catechesis will also need to make it clear how the Eucharist completes initiation and prepare the one being confirmed to enter fully into the mystery of the Eucharist. In the practice of the Latin Church the first catechesis of those baptized in infancy will not, however, be preparing them for Confirmation but for their first eucharistic communion. The anomaly of communion before Confirmation remains, but the catechesis for First Communion must at least be a retrospective catechesis of Baptism.

At whatever age people are initiated they require a continuous retrospective catechesis of the sacraments of initiation. The framework for it is provided in the liturgical year, which offers a catechumenate experience for the whole Church during Lent and a baptismal re-enactment during the Easter Vigil, and which recalls Confirmation by prolonging the Easter giving of the Spirit into the celebration of Pentecost. The Easter Eucharist, with its dramatic elaboration on Holy Thursday and Good Friday, invites a catechesis of how the Eucharist completes Baptism and Confirmation and becomes the constantly repeated sacramental centre of Christian life. Perhaps the most important skill that a theologian, concerned to affirm the unity of Christian initiation, would want a catechist to have is an ability to make the Eucharist the centre of all sacramental catechesis. The Eucharist, indeed, needs to be understood in the light of Baptism and Confirmation. But that understanding will be communicated effectively if everything that is taught about Baptism and Confirmation reaches forward to the Eucharist. The life-experiences and situations on which the catechesis of these sacraments draws must be of the sort that are open to the gift of eternal life that the Eucharist sacramentalizes.

10.3   FROM LIFE TO FULLNESS OF LIFE

The pedagogical skill of the catechist takes on a special character when dealing with sacraments. It is providing a 'mystagogical catechesis', which is a teaching that shows how the rites of Baptism, Confirmation and Eucharist can draw a candidate for initiation from familiar life-situations and experiences into the mystery of eternal life. The theologian will hope that the life-situations on which the catechist may want to build are already implicit in the theology that is being provided, so that the link between teaching and life can be comfortably made. At the same time he or she will want to ensure that the life-situations that are employed are of the kind that are open to the full mystery of eternal life that is being realized in the sacraments. There are human life-experiences that offer intimations of eternal life. These are moments when human limitations and the passage of time are felt to be overcome. They are moments of self-transcendence and of unqualified happiness. They may be moments of discovery in the intimacy of love, moments of vision in the search for truth, moments of delight in the perception of beauty, moments of success in some treasured project, moments of power being exercised decisively for the well-being of some group. But they also may be moments of emptiness and defeat, of social helplessness and the failure of dreams, in which self-transcendence is experienced in yielding oneself in trust to another. Anything less than such moments of depth can hardly serve in a pedagogy of introduction to the fullness of life that is being offered in Christian initiation. A catechesis that settles for trivial life-experiences could reduce initiation to the banal level of some social graces.

The movement from life to the fullness of life is presented in the catechesis of initiation with full theological explicitness as a movement towards God, who is the goal as well as the giver of eternal life. People can have widely differing experiences of God, not all of them life-giving. One cannot assume that people who come out of an explicitly religious culture, even a Christian one, understand the word 'God' in a way that corresponds to the reality of the one who is revealed and named Father by Jesus. Nor can one be sure that in the personal experience of every candidate the word 'Father' stands for someone who is loving and life-giving. And one has to recognize the profound truth being uncovered by those who want God to be also experienced as and named Mother. The trinitarian theology which permeates the rites of initiation is not always ready-made for catechesis. Furthermore, one has to face the possibility that a candidate for initiation might be so bereft of life-giving personal relationships that the whole idea of receiving life from another, be it a divine or a human person, or one who is both divine and human, has to be put very carefully to him or her. When people are locked into self-centredness — whether from fear or selfishness — their relationships with others are fraught with myth and fantasy. There is in everyone something of this tendency to see others, not as they really are, but as they might fulfil one's own felt needs. Catechesis has the task of helping people to break out of self-centredness and to accept the mysterious other, the God of our Lord Jesus Christ, who gives life in the Christian sacraments. To present Christian initiation merely as human self-fulfilment carries the risk of reducing the trinitarian theology, that alone can account for the mystery that is in the rites, to what is at best a healing, satisfying myth and at worst an escapist fantasy.

Everything that happens in Christian initiation is said to happen in and through Christ. The theological word about sacraments is also a Christological word. The catechist realizes that what a candidate for initiation thinks about Christ is affected by what he or she thinks about what it is to be divine and what it is to be human; and then, by how they conceive someone being both divine and human. People can be brought to a sense of the divine in Christ in a way that leaves them with problems about his being human. It takes great intellectual daring and tenacity to affirm full humanness in one who is fully divine. It takes great pedagogical skill to communicate this truth, not just as an intellectual judgement but as a fact of life, on which those who are being initiated are staking their future. How that humanness is appreciated must be related to how the candidate perceives what it is to be human; for if Jesus is not thought to be human in the same sense that the candidate is human he cannot be really accepted as Saviour. And yet he has to be presented as perfect in his humanness, with a perfection befitting one who is Son of God. It seems easier to attribute perfect goodness and saving power to Jesus in his divinity than to make the laborious and risky effort to understand how he was perfectly good and grace-filled in his humanity, with the same kind of holiness by which other humans are made holy; and that he is active as our Saviour in the sacraments of initiation precisely as a good man. Even when Jesus is recognized as perfectly human, and as uniquely perfect in his way of being human, there is still the pedagogical problem of dealing with the different images people have of the 'perfect man'. These may be derived from stories about Jesus himself heard in childhood, or from the way he is presented in Christian art. They may be derived from ancient myths about heroes or modern myths about superstars. Or they may be derived from scientific anthropologies which give their own profile of human perfection. Catechists will have to use the images that speak to a candidate for initiation in order to convey the humanness and human saving power of Jesus. But they will always measure the images they use against the theological teaching of Christian faith. Otherwise the call to life that is contained in the sacraments of initiation may not be heard as a call to the fullness of life that is in Christ, but to some scaled-down version of it.

Initiation into eternal life in Christ is initiation into the Church which is his Body gathered together and animated by his Spirit. As Body of Christ, gifted by the Spirit and structured in a variety of ministries, the Church is a sociological as well as a theologist reality. It shares the fortunes of human society and becomes part of its history. As temple of the Spirit it is an eschatological and missionary reality in the last times of the world. This mystery of the Church has to be presented to those being initiated as it is realized in a particular local community. It is in such a local community that they are being given access to the universal Church. To be initiated into the Church is also a sociological experience and requires sociological options. They cannot be neglected by catechesis on the pretext that initiation is entry into the mystery of Christ and his Spirit. The mystery is certainly more than a sociological reality, but it is realized in sociological and historical choices, as it was in Christ's own life. The theology of Christian initiation deals in general terms with the worldly implications of the gift of eternal life. Catechesis has to help candidates to discover what those implications are in their own particular situation. It has to take account of how they experience the reality of the society to which they belong: how they are living its successes and its failures, its tensions and divisions; how they relate to the poor and what responsibility they are prepared to take for social structures. In particular it will help candidates to discover the social significance which the Church they are entering has in their own local world. They will have to identify with the rôle that the local church has and take some responsibility for it. They will have to be given confidence in the prophetic and priestly gifts that initiation brings them, and some assurance that these gifts will strengthen and when necessary can change the rôle of the local church in the world it touches. On the basis of that assurance they can have the confidence to take on the mission which members of the Church have for the salvation of the world.

It is on the issue of giftedness that the catechesis of initiation will take the understanding of initiation beyond the sociological into the distinctive realm of the Spirit. The tradition of faith suggests that it is in the experience of being gifted, and in the interiority that necessarily accompanies it, that the Holy Spirit is recognized and accepted by believers. To explain convincingly to people that the Holy Spirit is given to them in Christian initiation one needs to be able to call on some real demonstration that the Church they are entering encourages the spiritual gifts of its members and builds itself up from their complementarity. The task of the catechist is made difficult when the local church to which people are being initiated does not reflect these great truths about the manifold gifts of the Holy Spirit and the way their interaction builds up the Church as the Body of Christ. At the same time the experience of giftedness that is used to communicate a sense of what the Holy Spirit means in initiations is of the sort that is in keeping with the Gospel of Christ and with the faith of the apostles. It is of the sort that respects the ministerial structures of the Church and obeys those in authority. Life-experiences of the Spirit that are divisive and insensitive to the bonds of communion within the Church are not good material for a catechesis of initiation.

A catechesis of initiation has to help candidates for initiation to make the signs and symbolic actions used in the sacraments, and explained in sacramental theology, become real signs of life. The symbolism is not always immediately evident. Some story-telling has to be done to let it come through. Other uses of the same symbol, or analogous symbols, can be appealed to. One can do a certain amount of this in general theology but a catechist will be able to do it on the basis of the known life-experience of those being initiated. The theologian will want to warn against letting this use of analogy turn into a hankering after imitation. To reduce any part of the rite of Christian initiation to an imitation of the rites of human growth and human fellowship would be to compromise its sacramentality. A rite in which the God of salvation is acting through Christ in the Church can have real similarities with rites that evolve in human culture. One can be invited to live it with the same imagination that one puts into the familiar rites of one's spontaneous culture. But the sacramental rite has imperatives that arise from the mystery it holds within it. It is not merely a creation and projection of human life; it is also a projection and an offer of the divine life that fills it. If a true sense of God and of eternal life is being communicated in catechesis, if the mystery of Christ and of the gift of his Spirit in the Church is being recognized, the demands that sacramentality makes in the rites of initiation will be more readily appreciated.

10.4   LIFE CHOICES

It is in helping candidates to discover the personal decision that the grace of the sacraments of initiation calls forth that the catechist enters most deeply into their life-situation. Moral choices have to be made within and about real life-situations if the grace of the sacrament is to be life-giving. The kinds of choice that are presented in catechesis must be of sufficiently profound and even dramatic seriousness to match the mystery of life and death that is being played out in the sacramental rites. Baptism is the giving of new life through dying to an old life. It calls for a life-and-death decision. What have to be looked for in catechesis are situations that candidates would experience as matters of life and death. Nothing else will convince them about the seriousness of Baptism and stir them to the kind of moral decision it requires. Confirmation sacramentalizes the eschatological gift of the Spirit and the effect which it has on human relations with God and on human responsibility for the salvation of the world. Candidates for initiation will have experiences of taking responsibility for their own lives, of doing so under hostile pressure from others, of having to take responsibility for others. They will have some special experiences of being 'the last resort', of situations in which they have a feeling that 'the end of the world has come'; they will know what it is to 'stand firm' in such situations, because of confidence in their own inner resources. The theology of Confirmation suggests that it is out of reflection on such situations that the moral challenge of the sacrament will be given realism and continuity with real life. The Eucharist calls people to choose solidarity with and in the Body of Christ in the belief that this is what gives eternal life now and forever. The choices in favour of human solidarity that can be used in a catechesis of the Eucharist must be those that are life-giving, that are reconciling, that want to be a force for unity within the whole human family rather than a sectarian going apart from others, that commit one to work and suffer and sacrifice for the sake of joy, that can live with the disappointment of not having everything all at once and be prepared to wait in hope. Anything less will not convey the mystery that is being entered into in the decision to accept eucharistic fellowship.

   The catechetical process of presenting the grace of the sacraments of initiation in continuity with the choices of real life makes it possible for that grace really to transform the life of those who are initiated, and to build up the Church as a community that can transform the real world. The grace of initiation will be ready to be prolonged in the other four sacraments that mark the critical moments of human life in the Church and the world. It will affect decisions that the initiated make singly and together about the whole range of human concerns. It will touch the secular with the sacred, but with a sacredness that is not an escape from the secular, because it is embodied in the secular. It will be an incarnational grace. As the incarnation filled the human reality of Jesus with the life of God, the sacraments will take the reality of human lives and fill them with the life of God, making them in the process not less but more fully human.

10.5   THE STORY OF SALVATION

The concerns outlined in this Epilogue about the theological quality of the catechesis of initiation are drawn from dogmatic, moral and sacramental teaching. Careful doctrine about faith and morals is indispensable for the life of God's People, and the Creed is at the heart of every catechesis. It must, however, be recognized that it is not doctrinal formulations that ultimately make people live. As was suggested in the Introduction to this book, peoples and communities live by stories, and it is their stories that they act out in their rites. No one knows this better than a good catechist. A catechist will share the theologian's concern about the true meaning of eternal life, of the word 'God', of the incarnation, of the trinitarian mystery of Father, Son and Spirit, of the Church . . . . But he or she will find these great truths as they emerge and are remembered in the story of God's People: as they are written in its Scriptures and woven into life in its traditions about saints and sinners, in its pilgrimages to holy places, in the monuments left behind by the growth and decline of local churches, in the tragic residue of doctrinal disputes and heresies, in the firm judgements of Councils, in the variety of liturgical families and schools of spirituality. These — but especially those of the origins that are written in Scripture — are the stories that a catechist will tell and re-tell in a way that makes them stories for today. Theological sensitivity will ensure that they are told in depth, with accuracy and consistency; good pedagogy will help candidates to identify with the stories and make them their own; a feeling for ritual will communicate a sense of how the rites of initiation can make the story life-giving for people of today.

10.6   THE LAST WORD

If the tone of this Epilogue is becoming somewhat oratorical it is perhaps a hint that the last word about the sacraments of initiation might belong, not to the theologian nor to the catechist, but to the preacher. The theologian does the thinking and the catechist the teaching, but it is the preacher who does the talking at an actual celebration of the sacraments. His is the prophetic word that points to the Lord's anointed summoned to the sacramental celebration and says to him or to her 'you are the one'. The story of salvation is coming true here and now for an individual person in the sacramental rite. The story of the newly-initiated is, from now on, being written into the story of salvation and its unfolding in their lives will be celebrated in every Eucharist which they join. The preacher needs to know both the story of salvation and the story of the people who are being initiated and celebrating, if he is to tell how the two stories are being brought together in the sacramental rite. He needs to be a theologian and he needs to have some of the skills of the catechist. But his own gift is different from theirs, and he does best when he builds on their gifts and does not duplicate them. He tells what is happening here and now, and why it is happening, and what is needed to make it happen to the full.

The time comes, however, for the preacher too to be silent. The final word is not about the sacrament or about the story of salvation: it is the sacramental word itself. It is said by the minister(s), who perform the priestly task of making the rite. It is the climax of all the talk that surrounds and builds up the sacrament and points it towards the participant. It is the personal word of Christ in which his present intentions towards this person are revealed. It is received in faith by the whole Church as embodying the presence and the power of Christ. It is the word that finally demands belief, and the here and now consequences of belief, from those who are taking part in the sacrament. It is the word spoken within the rite that finally gives life.

Bibliography

The Scriptures are quoted from the Revised Standard Version of the Bible: Old Testament, copyright 1952; New Testament, 1st edition copyright 1946; 2nd edition copyright 1971; the Apocrypha, copyright 1957; Third and Fourth Book of Maccabees and Psalm 151, copyright 1977. All above copyrights held by the Division of Christian Education of the National Council of the Churches of Christ in the United States of America.

The rites are referred to in the ICEL English translation, available in official editions, but also in *The Rites of the Catholic Church* (Pueblo, New York, 1976); new translation of the introductions in *Documents on the Liturgy 1963–1979* (Liturgical Press, Collegeville, MN, 1982).

The Fathers are quoted in translations, which are acknowledged in the text by the name of the translator and described in detail in this Bibliography.

Texts from the *magisterium* are quoted in the translation of J. Neuner, SJ, and J. Dupuis, SJ, detailed below, apart from those of Vatican II, which are from the edition of A. Flannery, OP.

The following works are referred to in the text:

Anglican-Roman Catholic International Commission (ARCIC I), *An Agreed Statement on Eucharistic Doctrine* (Windsor, 1971): text in *Modern Eucharistic Agreement* and in Meyer and Vischer.

C. Argenti, 'Chrismation' in *Ecumenical Perspectives on Baptism, Eucharist and Ministry* (Geneva, 1983), pp. 46–67.

J. P. Audet, 'Esquisse historique du genre littéraire de la "bénédiction" juive et de l'"eucharistie" chrétienne', *Revue Biblique* 65 (1958), 370–399; trans. as 'Literary Form and Contents of a Normal *Eucharistia* in the First Century' in *The Gospels Reconsidered* (Oxford, 1960).

G. Austin, OP, *Anointing with the Spirit. The Rite of Confirmation. The Use of Oil and Chrism* (New York, 1985).

W. Barden, OP, *The Eucharistic Presence*, vol. 58 of Thomas Aquinas, *Summa Theologiae* (IIIa, qq. 73–78) (Blackfriars ed.; London/New York, 1965).

C. K. Barrett, *A Commentary on the First Epistle to the Corinthians* (London, 1968).

K. Barth, *The Teaching of the Church Regarding Baptism* (trans. from German of 1943; London, 1948).

G. R. Beasley-Murray, *Baptism in the New Testament* (London, 1963).

W. M. Bedard, *Symbolism of the Baptismal Font* (Washington, 1951).

W. H. Beekenkamp (ed.), Berengarius of Tours, *De sacra coena adversus Lanfrancum* (The Hague, 1941).

P. Benoit, OP: *see* Delorme and others.

Berengarius: *see* Beekenkamp.

L. Billot, SJ, *De Ecclesiae Sacramentis* (7th ed.; 2 vols, Rome, 1929–31).

R. Bocock, *Ritual in Industrial Society* (London, 1973).

M. Bohen, *The Mystery of Confirmation* (New York, 1963).

M. E. Boismard, OP: *see* George and others; Delorme and others.

D. Bourke, *The Sacraments*, vol. 56 of Thomas Aquinas, *Summa Theologiae* (IIIa, qq. 60–65) (Blackfriars ed.; London/New York, 1975).

L. Bouyer, *Liturgical Piety* (Notre Dame, 1956)/*Life and Liturgy* (London, 1956).

  Rite and Man (trans. from French; Notre Dame, 1963).

  Eucharist. Theology and Spirituality of the Eucharistic Prayer (trans. from French; Notre Dame, 1968).

Y. Brilioth, *Eucharistic Faith and Practice, Evangelical and Catholic* (trans. from Swedish; London, 1930).

R. E. Brown, *The Gospel According to John* (Anchor Bible 29, 29a; 2 vols, Garden City, NY, 1966–70/London, 1971).

  The Community of the Beloved Disciple (New York/London, 1979).

C. G. Browne and J. E. Swallow (trans.), *Select Orations of Saint Gregory Nazianzen* (in LNPF ser. 2, vol. 7; Buffalo, NY, 1900; repr. Grand Rapids, 1952).

J. Calvin, *A Short Treatise on the Lord's Supper*, trans. from French J. K. S. Reid (Library of Christian Classics XXII; Philadelphia, 1954).

P.-T. Camelot, OP, 'Réalisme et symbolisme dans la doctrine eucharistique de S. Augustin', *Revue des Sciences Philosophiques et Théologiques* 31 (1947), 394–410.

H. Carey (trans.), *The Epistles of St Cyprian, Bishop of Carthage and Martyr. The Council of Carthage on the Baptism of Heretics* (Library of Fathers of the Holy Catholic Church 17; Oxford/London, 1844).

O. Casel, OSB, *The Mystery of Christian Worship* (trans. from German; London, 1962).

H. Cazelles, 'L'Anaphore et l'Ancien Testament' in B. Botte and others, *Eucharisties d'Orient et d'Occident* (Paris, 1970), pp. 11–21.

  'Eucharistie, bénédiction et sacrifice dans l'Ancien Testament', *La Maison Dieu* 123 (1975), 7–28.

F. Clark, SJ, *Eucharistic Sacrifice and the Reformation* (2nd ed.: Chulmleigh, Devon, 1981).

Y. M.-J. Congar, OP, *The Mystery of the Church* (trans. from French; London, 1960).

  Un peuple messianique (Paris, 1975).

  I Believe in the Holy Spirit (trans. from French; 3 vols, London/New York, 1983).

J. D. Crichton, *Christian Celebration: The Mass; The Sacraments; The Prayer of the Church* (London, 1971; 1973, 2nd ed. 1980; 1976; 1-vol. ed., London, 1981).

O. Cullmann, 'The Meaning of the Lord's Supper in Primitive Christianity' in *Essays on the Lord's Supper* (London, 1958); trans. of art. in *Revue d'Histoire et de Philosophie Religieuses* (1936).

  Baptism in the New Testament (trans. from German; London, 1950).

  Le foi et le culte dans l'église primitive (Neuchâtel, 1963); pub. in part in *Early Christian Worship* (London, 1953).

J. J. Cunningham, OP, *Baptism and Confirmation*, vol. 57 of Thomas Aquinas, *Summa Theologiae* (IIIa, qq. 66–72) (Blackfriars ed.; London/New York, 1975).

Cyprian: *see* Carey.

J. Daniélou, SJ, *The Bible and the Liturgy* (trans. from French; Notre Dame, 1965).

J. G. Davies, *The Architectural Setting of Baptism* (London, 1962).

J. de Ghellinck, *Pour l'histoire du mot 'Sacramentum'* (Louvain, 1924).

  'Eucharistie au XIIe siècle en Occident' in *Dictionnaire de Théologie Catholique* 5, 1233–1302 (Paris, 1924).

L. Deiss, *Early Sources of the Liturgy* (New York, 1967).

M. de la Taille, SJ, *Mysterium Fidei* (Paris, 1921).

  Esquisse du Mystère de la foi (Paris, 1925).

J. Delorme: *see* George and others.

J. Delorme, P. Benoit, OP, J. Dupont, OSB, M. E. Boismard, OP, D. Mollat, SJ, *The Eucharist in the New Testament* (trans. from French; London, 1964).

H. de Lubac, SJ, *Corpus Mysticum: l'eucharistie et l'église au Moyen Age* (2nd rev. ed.; Paris, 1949).

R. de Vaux, OP, *Ancient Israel. Its Life and Institutions* (trans. from French; London, 1961). *Didachē: see* Kleist.

J. C. Didier, *Faut-il baptiser les enfants?* (Paris, 1967).

F. W. Dillistone, *Christianity and Symbolism* (London, 1955).

G. Dix, *The Apostolic Tradition of St Hippolytus of Rome* (2nd ed., intro. H. Chadwick; London, 1968).

> *The Shape of the Liturgy* (London, 1945).

A. F. Donegan, *St Augustine and the Real Presence* (Washington, 1972).

J. D. G. Dunn, *Baptism in the Holy Spirit* (London, 1970).

J. Duplacy: *see* George and others.

J. Dupont, OSB: *see* Delorme and others.

F. X. Durrwell, CSsR, *Holy Spirit of God* (trans. from French; London, 1986).

M. Eliade, *Patterns in Comparative Religion* (New York/London, 1958).

> *Birth and Rebirth* (New York, 1958).
>
> *The Sacred and the Profane* (London, 1959).

J. Emminghaus, *The Eucharist: Essence, Form, Celebration* (trans. from German; Collegeville, MN, 1978).

M. Fahey (ed.), *Catholic Perspectives on Baptism, Eucharist and Ministry: A Study Commissioned by the Catholic Theological Society of America* (Lanham, MD/New York/ London, 1986).

T. Filthaut, *La théologie des mystères. Exposé de la controverse* (Paris, 1954).

J. D. C. Fisher, *Christian Initiation in the Mediaeval West* (London, 1965).

> *Christian Initiation, the Reformation Period* (London, 1970).
>
> *Confirmation Then and Now* (London, 1978).

A. Flannery, OP (ed.), *Vatican Council II. The Conciliar and Post-Conciliar Documents* (2nd ed.; Dublin, 1980).

G. Fourez, SJ, *Sacraments and Passages* (Notre Dame, 1983).

J. Gaillard, OSB, 'Chronique de liturgie', *Revue Thomiste* 57 (1957), 510–550.

J. Gallagher, *Significando Causant. A Study of Sacramental Causality* (Fribourg, 1965).

J. Galot, SJ, *La nature du caractère sacramental* (Brussels, 1956).

P. Garland, *The Definition of Sacrament according to St Thomas Aquinas* (Ottawa, 1959).

F. Gavin, *The Jewish Antecedents of the Christian Sacraments* (London, 1928).

A. George, SM, J. Delorme, D. Mollat, SJ, J. Guillet, SJ, M. E. Boismard, OP, J. Duplacy, J. Giblet, Y. B. Tremel, OP, *Baptism in the New Testament. A Symposium* (trans. from French of 1956; London, 1964).

J. Giblet: *see* George and others.

J. Gietl (ed.), Roland Bandinelli, *Sententiae* (Fribourg, 1891).

T. Gilby, OP, *Holy Communion*, vol. 59 of Thomas Aquinas, *Summa Theologiae* (IIIa, qq. 79–83) (Blackfriars ed.; London/New York, 1975).

C. Gore, *The Body of Christ* (London, 1901).

Gregory of Nazianzus: *see* Browne and Swallow.

J. Guillet, SJ: *see* George and others.

P. Gumpel, 'Unbaptized Infants: Can They Be Saved?', *Downside Review* 72 (1954), 342–358; and bibliography, *Downside Review* 73 (1955), 313–346.

T. Guzie, *Jesus and the Eucharist* (New York, 1974).

M. Gwinnell, 'Confirmation: Sacrament of Initiation', *The Clergy Review* 69 (1984), 126–135.

R. J. Halliburton, 'The Patristic Theology of the Eucharist' in C. Jones and others (eds), *The Study of Liturgy* (New York, 1978), pp. 201–208.

M. Hellwig, *The Eucharist and the Hunger of the World* (New York, 1976),

Hippolytus: *see* Dix.

D. R. Holeton, 'Confirmation in the 1980s' in *Ecumenical Perspectives on Baptism, Eucharist and Ministry* (Geneva, 1983), pp. 68–89.

M. Hurley, SJ, 'Baptism in Ecumenical Perspective', *One in Christ* 14 (1978), 106–123.

Irenaeus: *see* Keble.

F. Isambert, *Rite et efficacité symbolique. Essai d'anthropologie symbolique* (Paris, 1979).

E. O. James, *Sacrifice and Sacrament* (London, 1962).

R. C. D. Jaspers and G. J. Cuming, *Prayers of the Eucharist: Early and Reformed* (London, 1975).

J. Jeremias, *Infant Baptism in the First Four Centuries* (trans. from German; London, 1960).
      The Origins of Infant Baptism (trans. from German; London, 1963).
      The Eucharistic Words of Jesus (trans. from 3rd German ed.; London, 1966).

C. Jones, G. Wainwright and E. Yarnold, SJ (eds), *The Study of Liturgy* (New York, 1978).

H. Jorissen, *Die Entfaltung der Transubstantiationslehre bis zum Beginn der Hochscholastik* (Münster, 1965).

C. Journet, *La Messe. Présence du Sacrifice de la Croix* (Paris, 1957).

J. A. Jungmann, SJ, *Missarum Sollemnia. The Mass of the Roman Rite* (trans. from German; 2 vols, New York, 1951–55; abridged 1-vol. ed., London/New York, 1959).

A. Kavanagh, OSB, *The Shape of Baptism: The Rite of Christian Initiation* (New York, 1978).

J. Keble (trans.), *Five Books of St Ireneus, Bishop of Lyons, Against Heresies* (Library of Fathers of the Holy Catholic Church 42; Oxford, 1872).

J. N. D. Kelly, *Early Christian Doctrines* (4th ed.; London, 1968).

E. J. Kilmartin, SJ, *The Eucharist in the Primitive Church* (Englewood Cliffs, NJ, 1965).
      'The Lima Text on Eucharist' in M. Fahey (ed.), *Catholic Perspectives on Baptism, Eucharist and Ministry* (Lanham, MD/New York/London, 1986).

J. A. Kleist, SJ (trans.), *The Epistles of St Clement of Rome and St Ignatius of Antioch* (Ancient Christian Writers 1; Westminster, MD/London, 1961).
      The Didaché, The Epistle of Barnabas, The Epistles and the Martyrdom of St Polycarp, The Fragment of Papias, The Epistle to Diognetus (Ancient Christian Writers 6; Westminster, MD/London, 1948).

G. M. H. Lampe, *The Seal of the Spirit* (2nd ed.; London, 1967).

H. Lang, *Aurelii Augustini. Textus eucharistici selecti* (Florilegium Patristicum fasc. 35; Bonn, 1933).

N. Lash, *His Presence in the World. A Study of Eucharistic Worship and Theology* (London, 1968).

H. Leclercq, OSB, 'Baptistère' in *Dictionnaire d'Archéologie Chrétienne et de Liturgie* 2, I, cols 382–469 (Paris, 1910).

B. Leeming, SJ, *Principles of Sacramental Theology* (London, 1956).

F. J. Leenhardt, 'This Is My Body' in *Essays on the Lord's Supper* (London, 1958); trans. from *Cahiers Théologiques* 37 (Neuchâtel/Paris, 1955).

M. Lepin, *L'Idée du Sacrifice de la Messe* (Paris, 1926).

H. Lietzmann, *Mass and the Lord's Supper* (trans. of *Messe und Herrenmahl*, 1926; fascs 1–11, Leiden, 1953–76).

L. Ligier, 'From The Last Supper to the Eucharist' in L. Sheppard (ed.), *The New Liturgy* (London, 1970), pp. 113–150.
      La Confirmation (Paris, 1973).

Martin Luther, *The Pagan Servitude of the Church*, trans. and ed. B. L. Woolf in *The*

Reformation Writings of Martin Luther 1 (London, 1953); repr. in J. Dillenberger, *Martin Luther* (New York, 1961).

J. F. McCue, 'The Doctrine of Transubstantiation from Berengar through the Council of Trent' in *Lutherans and Catholics in Dialogue* III: *The Eucharist* (Washington/New York, 1967).

P. McGoldrick (ed.), *Understanding the Eucharist* (Dublin, 1969).

G. Macy, *The Theologies of the Eucharist in the Early Scholastic Period. A Study of the Salvific Function of the Sacrament According to the Theologians c. 1080–1220* (Oxford, 1984).

T.A. Marsh, 'The sacramental Character' in D. O'Callaghan (ed.), *Sacraments* (Dublin, 1964).

       'A Study of Confirmation', *Irish Theological Quarterly* 39 (1972), 149–163 and 40 (1973), 125–147.

       Gift of Community. Baptism and Confirmation (Wilmington, DE), 1984).

A. G. Martimort, *The Signs of the New Covenant* (trans. from French; Collegeville, MN, 1959).

A. G. Martimort and others, *The Church at Prayer* (trans. from French; rev. ed., 4 vols, Collegeville, MN/London, 1986–88), esp. II: *The Eucharist* (1986/87) and III: *The Sacraments* (1988).

J. Martos, *Doors to the Sacred. A Historical Introduction to Sacraments in the Christian Church* (London, 1981).

E. L. Mascall, *Corpus Christi* (London, 1953).

H. Meyer and L. Vischer (eds), *Growth in Agreement. Reports and Agreed Statements of Ecumenical Conversations on a World Level* (New York/Geneva, 1984).

A. Milner, OP, *The Theology of Confirmation* (Cork, 1971).

L. Mitchell, *The Meaning of Ritual* (New York, 1977).

Modern Eucharistic Agreement (Foreword by Bishop Alan C. Clark, Introduction by Bishop H. R. McAdoo; London, 1973).

C. Mohrmann, *Latin vulgaire, latin des chrétiens* (Paris, 1952).

D. Mollat, SJ: *see* Delorme and others; George and others.

R. Moloney, SJ, 'The Early Eucharist: the Jewish Background', *Irish Theological Quarterly* 47 (1980), 34–42.

       Our Eucharistic Prayers (Wilmington, DE, 1986).

J. C. Navickas, *The Doctrine of St Cyprian on the Sacraments* (Würzburg, 1924).

J. Navone, SJ, *Gospel Love. A Narrative Theology* (Wilmington, DE, 1985).

J. Neuner, SJ, and J. Dupuis, SJ (eds), *The Christian Faith in the Doctrinal Documents of the Catholic Church* (rev. ed.; Bangalore, 1982/London, 1983).

B. Neunheuser, OSB, *Baptism and Confirmation* (trans. from German; New York, 1964).

M.-J. Nicolas, OP, *L'Eucharistie* (Paris, 1959).

J. M. Nielen, *The Earliest Christian Liturgy* (trans. from German; St Louis/London, 1941).

D. O'Callaghan (ed.), *Sacraments* (Dublin, 1964).

C. E. O'Neill, OP, *Meeting Christ in the Sacraments* (New York/Cork, 1964).

       New Approaches to the Eucharist (Dublin, 1967).

       Sacramental Realism (Dublin, 1983).

P. Palmer, SJ, *Sacraments and Worship. Liturgy and Doctrinal Development of Baptism, Confirmation, and the Eucharist* (London, 1957).

J. Patout Burns, SJ, and G. M. Fagin, SJ (eds), *The Holy Spirit* (Message of the Fathers of the Church 3; Wilmington, DE, 1984).

J. Pelikan, *The Growth of Mediaeval Theology (600–1300) (The Christian Tradition* III; Chicago/London, 1978).

D. N. Power, OMI, *The Sacrifice We Offer. The Tridentine Dogma and Its Reinterpretation* (Edinburgh, 1987).

J. M. Powers, SJ, *Eucharistic Theology* (New York, 1967).

J. Quasten, *Patrology* (3 vols, Utrecht/Antwerp and Westminster, MD, 1950, 1953, 1960).

H. Rahner, SJ, *Greek Myth and Christian Mystery* (trans. from German; London, 1963).

K. Rahner, SJ, *The Church and the Sacraments* (trans. from German; Freiburg/New York/London, 1963).

      'The Word and the Eucharist' in *Theological Investigations* 4 (Baltimore/London, 1966), pp. 253–286.

      'The Presence of Christ in the Sacrament of the Lord's Supper', *ibid.*, pp. 287–311.

      'Introductory Observations on Thomas Aquinas' Theology of the Sacraments in General' in *Theological Investigations* 14 (Baltimore/London, 1980), pp. 149–160.

L. Renwart, 'Le baptême des enfants et les limbes. A propos d'un document pontifical récent', *Nouvelle Revue Théologique* 80 (1958), 449–467.

J. Roberto (ed.), *Confirmation in the American Catholic Church* (Washington, 1978).

A. M. Roguet, OP, *Christ Acts Through the Sacraments* (trans. from French; Collegeville, MN, 1954).

W. Rordorf and others, *The Eucharist of the Early Christians* (trans. from French; New York, 1978).

J. B. Ryan, *The Eucharistic Prayer* (New York, 1974).

E. Schillebeeckx, OP, *Christ the Sacrament of Encounter with God* (trans. from Dutch; London, 1963).

      The Eucharist (trans. from Dutch; London, 1968).

M. Schmaus, *Dogma* 5: *The Church as Sacrament* (trans. from German; London, 1975).

R. Schnackenburg, *Baptism in the Thought of St Paul* (trans. from German; New York/Oxford, 1964).

E. Schweizer and others, '*Pneuma*' in G. Friedrich (ed.), *Theological Dictionary of the New Testament* VI (Grand Rapids, 1964), pp. 332–452.

Secretariat for Promoting Christian Unity, *Catholic Response to 'Baptism, Eucharist, Ministry' (BEM)* in SPCU Information Service, no. 65 (1987), 121–139.

J. L. Segundo, SJ, *The Sacraments Today* (trans. from Spanish; New York, 1973).

J. Shea, *Stories of God: An Unauthorized Biography* (Chicago, 1978).

      Stories of Faith (Chicago, 1980).

J. Sheerin (ed.), *The Eucharist* (Message of the Fathers of the Church 7; Wilmington, DE, 1986).

A. Shorter, WF, *Revelation and Its Interpretation* (London, 1983).

A. Souter (trans.), *Tertullian's Treatises Concerning Prayer, Concerning Baptism* (London, 1919).

Tertullian: *see* Souter.

Thomas Aquinas: *see* Barden; Bourke; Cunningham; Gilby.

B. Thompson, *Liturgies of the Western Church* (Cleveland/New York, 1962).

K. C. Thompson, 'I Cor. 15, 29 and Baptism for the Dead' in *Studia Evangelica* II (Berlin, 1964), pp. 647–659.

L. S. Thornton, *Confirmation, Its Place in the Baptismal Mystery* (Westminster, London, 1954).

M. Thurian, *The Eucharistic Memorial* I: *The Old Testament*, II: *The New Testament* (trans. from French; London, 1960).

      'The Eucharistic Memorial, Sacrifice of Praise and Supplication' in *Ecumenical Perspectives on Baptism, Eucharist and Ministry* (Geneva, 1983), pp. 90–103.

      (ed.), *Churches Respond to BEM: Official Responses to the 'Baptism, Eucharist and Ministry' Text* I, II (Faith and Order Papers 129, 132; Geneva, 1986), III (Faith and Order Paper 135; Geneva, 1987).

J.-M. R. Tillard, OP, *The Eucharist: Pasch of God's People* (trans. from French; New York, 1976).

        'The Eucharist, Gift of God' in *Ecumenical Perspectives on Baptism, Eucharist and Ministry* (Geneva, 1983), pp. 104–118.

T. Tilley, *Story Theology* (Wilmington, DE, 1985).

D. Tracy, *The Analogical Imagination* (London, 1981).

B. Tremel, OP: *see* George and others.

V. W. Turner, *The Ritual Process* (London, 1969).

C. Vagaggini, OSB, *Theological Dimensions of the Liturgy* (trans. from Italian; Collegeville, MN, 1959).

        The Canon of the Mass and Liturgical Reform (trans. from Italian; Staten Island, NY/London, 1967).

F. J. van Beeck, *Grounded in Love: Sacramental Theology in an Ecumenical Perspective* (Washington, 1981).

L. A. van Buchem, *L'Homélie Pseudo-Eusébienne de Pentecôte* (Nijmegen, 1967).

G. van der Leeuw, *Religion in Essence and Manifestation* (trans. from Dutch; London, 1938).

F. van der Meer, *Augustine the Bishop* (trans. from Dutch; London, 1961).

A. van Gennep, *The Rites of Passage* (1908; repub. Chicago, 1960).

W. A. van Roo, SJ, 'Infants Dying Without Baptism', *Gregorianum* 35 (1954), 405–456.

A. Vogel, *God's Presence in Man's World* (London, 1975).

A. Vonier, OSB, *A Key to the Doctrine of the Eucharist* (1925); rev. ed. in *The Collected Works of Abbot Vonier* 2 (London, 1952).

G. Wainwright, *Christian Initiation* (Richmond, VA/London, 1969).

        'Christian Initiation in the Liturgical Movement', *Studia Liturgica* 12 (1977), 67–86.

        see also Jones and others.

L. Walsh, OP, 'Liturgy in the Theology of St Thomas', *The Thomist* 38 (1974), 557–583.

T. Ware, *The Orthodox Church* (Harmondsworth, Middx, 1963).

E. C. Whitaker (ed.), *Documents of the Baptismal Liturgy* (2nd ed.; London, 1970).

V. Wilkin, SJ, *From Limbo to Heaven. An Essay on the Economy of Redemption* (London, 1961).

World Council of Churches, *Baptism, Eucharist and Ministry* (Faith and Order Paper 111; Geneva, 1982).

E. Yarnold, SJ (ed.), *The Awe-Inspiring Rites of Christian Initiation. Baptismal Homilies of the Fourth Century* (Slough, 1972).

        see also Jones and others.

R. C. Zaehner, *At Sundry Times* (London, 1958).

Index